Lecture Notes in Computer Science 4187

Commenced Publication in 1973
Founding and Former Series Editors:
Gerhard Goos, Juris Hartmanis, and Jan van Leeuwen

José Júlio Alferes   James Bailey
Wolfgang May   Uta Schwertel (Eds.)

Principles and Practice of Semantic Web Reasoning

4th International Workshop, PPSWR 2006
Budva, Montenegro, June 10-11, 2006
Revised Selected Papers

 Springer

Volume Editors

José Júlio Alferes
Universidade Nova de Lisboa
Faculdade de Ciências e Tecnologia
Department of Computer Science, 2829-516 Caparica, Portugal
E-mail: jja@di.fct.unl.pt

James Bailey
University of Melbourne
Department of Computer Science and Software Engineering
Vic. 3010, Australia
E-mail: jbailey@csse.unimelb.edu.au

Wolfgang May
Universität Göttingen
Institut für Informatik
Lotzestrasse 16-18, 37083 Göttingen, Germany
E-mail: may@informatik.uni-goettingen.de

Uta Schwertel
Universität München
Institut für Informatik
Oettingenstr. 67, 80538 München, Germany
E-mail: uta.schwertel@ifi.lmu.de

Library of Congress Control Number: Applied for

CR Subject Classification (1998): H.4, H.3, I.2, F.4.1, D.2

LNCS Sublibrary: SL 3 – Information Systems and Application, incl. Internet/Web and HCI

ISSN   0302-9743
ISBN-10   3-540-39586-5 Springer Berlin Heidelberg New York
ISBN-13   978-3-540-39586-7 Springer Berlin Heidelberg New York

Springer is a part of Springer Science+Business Media

springer.com

© Springer-Verlag Berlin Heidelberg 2006
Printed in Germany

Typesetting: Camera-ready by author, data conversion by Scientific Publishing Services, Chennai, India
Printed on acid-free paper   SPIN: 11853107   06/3142   5 4 3 2 1 0

Preface

The papers in this volume represent the technical program of the *4th Workshop on Principles and Practice of Semantic Web Reasoning*, PPSWR 2006, held on June 10-11, 2006 in Budva, Montenegro, co-located with the 3rd European Semantic Web Conference, in the young country of Montenegro after its independence on June 3, 2006.

The Semantic Web is a major endeavor aiming at enriching the existing Web with meta-data and processing methods so as to provide web-based systems with advanced, so-called "intelligent", capabilities. These advanced capabilities, striven for in most Semantic Web application scenarios, primarily call for reasoning.

Specialized reasoning capabilities are already offered by Semantic Web languages currently being developed such as the OWL family together with Triple, SPARQL, or ontology-based application-specific languages and tools like BPEL. These languages, however, are developed mostly from functionality-centered (e.g. ontology reasoning or access validation) or application-centered (e.g. Web service retrieval and composition) perspectives. A perspective centered on the reasoning techniques complementing the above-mentioned activities appears desirable for Semantic Web systems and applications. Moreover, there is the general reasoning underlying the Semantic Web technologies, such as Description Logics, Hybrid Logics, and others like F-Logic and Logic Programming semantics.

The workshop series on *"Principles and Practice of Semantic Web Reasoning – PPSWR"* began in 2003 (cf. Springer LNCS 3208) in response to the need for a forum for the discussion of emerging work on various forms of reasoning that are or can be used on the Semantic Web, with a strong interest in rule-based languages and methods. The workshop addresses both reasoning methods for the Semantic Web, and Semantic Web applications relying upon various forms of reasoning. Since 2003, when the conference was held in Mumbai, India, co-located with ICLP, ASIAN, and FSTTCS, the workshop has been organized yearly: the second workshop (LNCS 3208) took place in 2004 in St. Malo, France, in conjunction with ICLP 2004; the third workshop took place in the Dagstuhl Conference Center in Germany, within a one week Dagstuhl Seminar (LNCS 3703).

The technical program of PPSWR 2006 comprised an invited talk by Harold Boley on *"The RuleML Family of Web Rule Languages"*, and the presentation of 14 refereed technical articles selected by the Program Committee among the 25 submitted. These 14 articles discuss various aspects of reasoning on the Semantic Web ranging from more theoretical work on reasoning methods that can be applied to the Semantic Web, concrete reasoning methods and query languages for the Semantic Web, to practical applications.

Besides the presentation of the technical articles, one session was devoted to the presentation and demonstration of 6 systems, all of them related to reasoning on the Semantic Web. A description of each of these systems is also part of this volume.

During the workshop, informal on-site proceedings were distributed. The papers in this volume have been revised by the authors based on the comments from the refereeing stage and ensuing discussions during the workshop and have been subject to a final acceptance by the Program Committee.

The workshop has partly been supported by the 6th Framework Programme (FP6), Information Society Technologies (IST) project REWERSE (cf. `http://rewerse.net`), project reference number 506779, funded by the European Commission and by the Swiss State Secretariat for Education and Research.

We would also like to thank the developers of the EasyChair conference management system (`http://www.easychair.org/`). EasyChair assisted us in the whole process of collecting and reviewing papers, in interacting with authors and Program Committee members, and also in assembling this volume.

Last, but not least, we would like to thank the authors of all papers and system descriptions that were submitted to PPSWR 2006, the members of the Program Committee, and the additional experts who helped with the reviewing process, for contributing and ensuring the high scientific quality of PPSWR 2006.

July 2006

José Júlio Alferes
James Bailey
Wolfgang May
Uta Schwertel

Organization

Workshop Coordination

Program Committee Chairs:
José Júlio Alferes, Universidade Nova de Lisboa, Portugal
James Bailey, University of Melbourne, Australia
Proceedings Chair:
Wolfgang May, Georg-August-Universität Göttingen, Germany
Local Organization:
Uta Schwertel, Ludwig-Maximilians-Universität München, Germany

Program Committee

José Júlio Alferes
Grigoris Antoniou
Matteo Baldoni
Robert Baumgartner
James Bailey
Sara Comai
Włodek Drabent
Guido Governatori
Nicola Henze
Michael Kifer

Georg Lausen
Francesca Alessandra Lisi
Jan Małuszyński
Wolfgang May
Paula-Lavinia Pătrânjan
Michael Schröder
Uta Schwertel
Dietmar Seipel
Carlos Viegas Damásio
Gerd Wagner

Additional Reviewers

Sacha Berger
Sebastian Brandt
Gihan Dawelbait
Norbert Eisinger
Benedikt Linse
Sergey Lukichev
Hans Jürgen Ohlbach

Daniel Olmedilla
Vineet Padmanabhan
Riccardo Rosati
Loic Royer
Claudio Schifanella
Umberto Straccia

Table of Contents

The RuleML Family
of Web Rule Languages*

Harold Boley

Institute for Information Technology – e-Business,
National Research Council of Canada,
Fredericton, NB, E3B 9W4, Canada
harold.boley AT nrc DOT gc DOT ca

Abstract. The RuleML family of Web rule languages contains derivation (deduction) rule languages, which themselves have a webized Datalog language as their inner core. Datalog RuleML's atomic formulas can
be (un)keyed and (un)ordered. Inheriting the Datalog features, Hornlog
RuleML adds functional expressions as terms. In Hornlog with equality,
such uninterpreted (constructor-like) functions are complemented by interpreted (equation-defined) functions. These are described by further orthogonal dimensions "single- vs. set-valued" and "first- vs. higher-order".
Combined modal logics apply special relations as operators to atoms with
an uninterpreted relation, complementing the usual interpreted ones.

1 Introduction

Efforts in Web rules have steadily increased since they were brought
into focus by the RuleML Initiative [http://ruleml.org] in 2000, including DARPA's DAML Rules [http://www.daml.org/rules], IST's REWERSE
[http://rewerse.net], ISO's Common Logic [http://cl.tamu.edu], OMG's Production Rule Representation (PRR) [http://www.omg.org/docs/bmi/06-02-08.pdf]
as well as Semantics of Business Vocabulary and Business Rules (SBVR)
[http://www.businessrulesgroup.org/sbvr.shtml], and W3C's Rule Interchange Format (RIF) [http://www.w3.org/2005/rules]. RuleML has co-evolved with some of
these other efforts as well as with the Semantic Web Rule Language (SWRL)
[http://www.w3.org/Submission/SWRL], the Semantic Web Services Language
(SWSL) [http://www.w3.org/Submission/SWSF-SWSL], and the Web Rule Language (WRL) [http://www.w3.org/Submission/WRL]. This has been supported
by, and influenced, RuleML's modular design.

The specification of RuleML constitutes a modular **family** of Web sublanguages, whose root accesses the language as a whole and whose members identify
customized, combinable subsets of the language. Each of the family's sublanguages
has an XML Schema definition, Web-addressed by a URI, which permits inheritance between sublanguage schemas and precise reference to the required expressiveness. The family structure provides an expressive inclusion hierarchy for the

---

* Thanks to David Hirtle for creating the family's XML Schemas, and the RuleML
  Steering Committee for guidance. This research was partially supported by NSERC.

J.J. Alferes et al. (Eds.): PPSWR 2006, LNCS 4187, pp. 1–17, 2006.

sublanguages, and their URIs are the subjects of (model-theoretic) semantic characterization. The modular system of XML Schema definitions [BBH+05] is currently in version 0.9 [http://www.ruleml.org/modularization].

The RuleML family's top-level distinctions are derivation rules, queries, and integrity constraints as well as production and reaction rules. The most developed branch groups derivation (deduction) rule languages, which themselves have a webized Datalog language as their inner core. Hornlog RuleML adds functional expressions as terms. In Hornlog with equality, such uninterpreted (constructor-like) functions are complemented by interpreted (equation-defined) functions. This derivation rule branch is extended upward towards First Order Logic, has subbranches for negation-as-failure, strong-negation, or combined languages, and languages with 'pluggable' built-ins.

This paper takes a fresh look at the family from the perspectives of three orthogonally combinable branches: the generalized Object-Oriented RuleML (section 2) as well as the new Functional RuleML (section 3) and the preliminary Modal RuleML (section 4).

2   Rules in the Key-Order Matrix

This section will propose extensions to OO RuleML [Bol03]. RuleML's global markup conventions provide common principles for the family. XML elements are used for representing trees while XML attributes are used for distinguishing variations of a given element and, as in RDF, for webizing. Variation can thus be achieved by different attribute values rather than requiring different elements. Since the same attribute can occur in different elements, a two-dimensional classification accrues, which has the potential of quadratic tag reduction.

The data model of RuleML accommodates XML's arc-ordered, node-labeled trees and RDF's arc-labeled ('keyed'), node-labeled graphs [http://www.dfki.uni-kl.de/~boley/xmlrdf.html]. For this, RuleML complements XML-like elements – upper-cased *type* tags, as in Java classes – by RDF-like properties – lower-cased *role* tags, as in Java methods. Both kinds of tag are again serialized as XML elements, but case information makes the difference. This model with unkeyed, ordered child elements (subsection 2.1) and keyed, unordered children (subsection 2.2) has recently been generalized to a 'key-order' matrix also permitting keyed, ordered as well as unkeyed, unordered children (subsection 2.3).

As a running example, we will consider RuleML versions of the business rule "A customer is premium if their spending has been min 5000 euro in the previous year." This can be serialized using various equivalent concrete syntaxes, all corresponding to the same abstract syntax that reflects the data model.

2.1   Arguments in Order

In RuleML's most RDF-like, fully 'striped' syntax (with alternating type and role tags), the example can, e.g., be serialized interchangeably as follows:

```
<Implies>                          <Implies>
  <head>                             <body>
    <Atom>                             <Atom>
      <op><Rel>premium</Rel></op>        <op><Rel>spending</Rel></op>
      <arg index="1">                    <arg index="1">
        <Var>customer</Var>                <Var>customer</Var>
      </arg>                             </arg>
    </Atom>                            <arg index="2">
  </head>                                <Ind>min 5000 euro</Ind>
  <body>                               </arg>
    <Atom>                             <arg index="3">
      <arg index="1">                    <Ind>previous year</Ind>
        <Var>customer</Var>              </arg>
      </arg>                           </Atom>
      <arg index="3">                  </body>
        <Ind>previous year</Ind>       <head>
      </arg>                             <Atom>
      <arg index="2">                      <op><Rel>premium</Rel></op>
        <Ind>min 5000 euro</Ind>           <arg index="1">
      </arg>                               <Var>customer</Var>
      <op><Rel>spending</Rel></op>       </arg>
    </Atom>                            </Atom>
  </body>                            </head>
</Implies>                         </Implies>
```

The right-hand serialization is in <Implies> **normal form**, with the <body>
role tag before the <head> role tag, the <op> role before all <arg> roles, and the
<arg> roles ordered according to increasing <index> attribute values.

Once in <Implies> normal form, all <op> and <arg> roles can be omitted
(left), and the <body> and <head> roles, too (right):

```
<Implies>                          <Implies>
  <body>
    <Atom>                             <Atom>
      <Rel>spending</Rel>                <Rel>spending</Rel>
      <Var>customer</Var>                <Var>customer</Var>
      <Ind>min 5000 euro</Ind>           <Ind>min 5000 euro</Ind>
      <Ind>previous year</Ind>           <Ind>previous year</Ind>
    </Atom>                            </Atom>
  </body>
  <head>
    <Atom>                             <Atom>
      <Rel>premium</Rel>                 <Rel>premium</Rel>
      <Var>customer</Var>                <Var>customer</Var>
    </Atom>                            </Atom>
  </head>
</Implies>                         </Implies>
```

The right-hand serialization shows RuleML's most XML-like, fully 'stripe-
skipped' syntax [http://esw.w3.org/topic/StripeSkipping]. Notice that in all of
these syntaxes the three argument positions of the ternary **spending** relation

carry information that must be known, e.g. via a signature declaration, for correct interpretation.

2.2 Slots are Key

There is an alternative to signature declarations for determining the roles of children in atomic formulas. In Object-Oriented RuleML [Bol03], the earlier *positional* representation style is complemented by a *slotted* style: the 'system-level' data model with type and role tags is also made available on the 'user-level', permitting F-logic-like role→filler pairs.

For this, a single (system-level) metarole <slot> with two children is employed, the first naming different (user-level) roles, and the second containing their fillers.

For example, the fully stripe-skipped positional <Implies> rule above can be made slotted with user-level roles <spender> etc.:

```
<Implies>
  <Atom>
    <Rel>spending</Rel>
    <slot><Ind>spender</Ind><Var>customer</Var></slot>
    <slot><Ind>amount</Ind><Ind>min 5000 euro</Ind></slot>
    <slot><Ind>period</Ind><Ind>previous year</Ind></slot>
  </Atom>
  <Atom>
    <Rel>premium</Rel>
    <slot><Ind>client</Ind><Var>customer</Var></slot>
  </Atom>
</Implies>
```

The correct interpretation of the three spending arguments is no longer position-dependent and additional arguments such as region can be added without affecting any existing interpretation. A child element, rather than an attribute, was decided upon for naming the role to provide an extension path towards (e.g., F-logic's) schema-querying options. Although problematic in general [http://www.daml.org/listarchive/joint-committee/1376.html], we did not want to exclude the possibility in RuleML to query a role constant like <Ind>period</Ind> above through a role variable like <Var>time</Var>.

2.3 Making Independent Distinctions

Recent work on the Positional-Slotted Language [http://www.ruleml.org/#POSL] led to orthogonal dimensions extending the RuleML 0.9 roles <arg . . .> and <slot>. So far, the *unkeyed* <arg index="..."> was always *ordered*, as indicated by the mandatory index attribute, and the *keyed* <slot> was always *unordered*, as indicated by the lack of an index attribute. This can be generalized by allowing an optional index attribute for both roles, as shown by the independent distinctions in the following **key-order matrix**:

	ordered	*unordered*
keyed	`<slot index="...">`	`<slot>`
unkeyed	`<arg index="...">`	`<arg>`

Two extra orthogonal combinations are obtained from this system.
First, *keyed, ordered* children permit positionalized slots, as in this `cost` fact:

```
<Atom>
  <Rel>cost</Rel>
  <slot index="1"><Ind>item</Ind><Ind>jewel</Ind></slot>
  <slot index="2"><Ind>price</Ind><Data>6000</Data></slot>
  <slot index="3"><Ind>taxes</Ind><Data>2000</Data></slot>
</Atom>
```

Here, slot names `item`, `price`, and `taxes` are provided, e.g. for readability, as well as index positions 1-3, e.g. for efficiency.

Second, *unkeyed, unordered* children permit elements acting like those in a bag (finite multiset), as in this `transport` fact:

```
<Atom>
  <Rel>transport</Rel>
  <arg><Ind>chair</Ind></arg>
  <arg><Ind>chair</Ind></arg>
  <arg><Ind>table</Ind></arg>
</Atom>
```

Here, the arguments are specified to be commutative and 'non-idempotent' (duplicates are kept). Ground bags can be normalized using some canonical (e.g., lexicographic) order, and then linearly compared for equality. Results in (non-ground) bag unification are also available (e.g., [DV99]).

The RuleML 0.9 rest terms (normally variables) can be correspondingly generalized by allowing a role `<ordertail>` to unify with `index`-attributed rest elements, `<arg index="...">` and `<slot index="...">`, as well as a role `<commutail>` to unify with `index`-less rest elements, `<arg>` and `<slot>`.

The unkeyed RuleML case can be compared with Xcerpt [SB04] in that both distinguish ordered/unordered and total/partial term specifications, where the latter in RuleML is notated as the absence/presence of an `<orderest>` role with a fresh (e.g., anonymous) variable. However, following our XML-RDF-unifying data model [http://www.dfki.uni-kl.de/~boley/xmlrdf.html], in RuleML these distinctions are made for term normalization and unification; in Xcerpt, for matching query terms to data terms.

3   Equality for Functions

While section 2 dealt with RuleML for logic programming (LP) on the Semantic Web, functional programming (FP) [BKPS03] is also playing an increasing Web role, with XSLT and XQuery [FRSV05] being prominent examples. We present here the design of Functional RuleML, developed via orthogonal notions and freely combinable with the previous Relational RuleML, including OO RuleML [Bol03], discussed in section 2. This branch of the family will also allow for FP/LP-integrated programming (FLP), including OO FLP, on the Semantic Web. Some background on FLP markup languages was given in [Bol00a].

Since its beginning in 2000, with RFML [http://www.relfun.org/rfml] as one of its inputs, RuleML has permitted the markup of oriented (or directed) equations for defining the value(s) of a function applied to arguments, optionally conditional on a body as in Horn rules. Later, this was extended to logics with symmetric (or undirected) equality for the various sublanguages of RuleML, but the Equal element has still often exploited the left-to-right orientation of its (abridged) textual syntax.

It has been a RuleML issue that the constructor (Ctor) of a complex term (Cterm) is disjoined, as an XML element, from the user-defined function (Fun) of a call expression (Nano), although these can be unified by proceeding to a logic with equality. For example, while currently call patterns can contain Cterms but not Nanos, obeying the "constructor discipline" [O'D85], the latter should also be permitted to legalize 'optimization' rules like reverse(reverse(?L)) = ?L.

This section thus conceives both Cterms and Nanos as expression (<Expr>) elements and distinguishes 'uninterpreted' (constructor) vs. 'interpreted' (user-defined) functions just via an XML attribute; another attribute likewise distinguishes the (single- vs. set-)valuedness of functions (subsection 3.1). We then proceed to the nesting of all of these (subsection 3.2). Next, for defining (interpreted) functions, unconditional (oriented) equations are introduced (subsection 3.3). These are then extended to conditional equations, i.e. Horn logic implications with an equation as the head and possible equations in the body (subsection 3.4). Higher-order functions are finally added, both named ones such as Compose and λ-defined ones (subsection 3.5).

3.1 Interpretedness and Valuedness

The different notions of 'function' in LP and FP have been a continuing design issue:

LP: *Uninterpreted functions* **denote** unspecified values when applied to arguments, not using function definitions.

FP: *Interpreted functions* **compute** specified returned values when applied to arguments, using function definitions.

Uninterpreted function are also called 'constructors' since the values denoted by their application to arguments will be regarded as the syntactic data structure of these applications themselves.

For example, the function first-born: $Man \times Woman \rightarrow Human$ can be uninterpreted, so that first-born(John, Mary) just denotes the first-born child; or, interpreted, e.g. using definition first-born(John, Mary) = Jory, so the application returns Jory.

The distinction of uninterpreted vs. interpreted functions in RuleML 0.9 is marked up using different elements, <Ctor> vs. <Fun>. Proceeding to the increased generality of logic with equality (cf. introductory discussion), this should be changed to a single element name, `<Fun>`, with different attribute values, `<Fun in="no">` vs. `<Fun in="yes">`, respectively: The use of a Function's interpreted attribute with values "no" vs. "yes" directly reflects uninterpreted vs. interpreted functions (those for which, in the rulebase, no definitions are expected vs. those for which they are). Functions' respective RuleML 0.9 [http://www.ruleml.org/0.9] applications with Cterm vs. Nano can then uniformly become Expressions for either interpretedness.

The two versions of the example can thus be marked up as follows (where "u" stands for "no" or "yes"):

```
<Expr>
  <Fun in="u">first-born</Fun>
  <Ind>John</Ind>
  <Ind>Mary</Ind>
</Expr>
```

In RuleML 0.9 as well as in RFML and its human-oriented Relfun syntax [Bol99] this distinction is made on the level of expressions, the latter using square brackets vs. round parentheses for applications. Making the distinction through an attribute in the `<Fun>` rather than `<Expr>` element will permit higher-order functions (cf. subsection 3.5) to return, and use as arguments, functions that include interpretedness markup.

A third value, "semi", is proposed for the interpreted attribute: *Semi-interpreted functions* **compute** an application if a definition exists and **denote** unspecified values else (via the syntactic data structure of the application, which we now write with Relfun-like square brackets). For example, when "u" stands here for "semi", the above application returns Jory if definition `first-born(John, Mary) = Jory` exists and denotes `first-born[John, Mary]` itself if no definition exists for it. Because of its neutrality, `in="semi"` is proposed as the default value.

In both XML and UML processing, functions (like relations in LP) are often *set-valued* (*non-deterministic*). This is accommodated by introducing a **val**ued attribute with values including "1" (deterministic: exactly one) and "0.." (set-valued: zero or more). Our **val** specifications can be viewed as transferring to functions, and generalizing, the cardinality restrictions for (binary) properties (i.e., unary functions) in description logic and the determinism declarations for (moded) relations in Mercury [SHC96].

For example, the set-valued function children: $Man \times Woman \rightarrow 2^{Human}$ can be interpreted and set-valued, using definition `children(John, Mary) =` $\{$Jory, Mahn$\}$, so that the application `children(John, Mary)` returns $\{$Jory, Mahn$\}$.

The example is then marked up thus (other legal **val** values here would be "0..3", "1..2", and "2"):

```
<Expr>
  <Fun in="yes"
       val="0..">children</Fun>
  <Ind>John</Ind>
  <Ind>Mary</Ind>
</Expr>
```

Because of its highest generality, `val="0.."` is proposed as the default.

While uninterpreted functions usually correspond to `<Fun in="no" val="1">`, attribute combinations of `in="no"` with a `val` unequal to `"1"` will be useful when uninterpreted functions are later to be refined into interpreted set-valued functions (which along the way can lead to semi-interpreted ones).

Interpretedness and valuedness constitute orthogonal dimensions in our design space, and are also orthogonal to the dimensions of the subsequent subsections, although space limitations prevent the discussion of all of their combinations in this section.

3.2   Nestings

One of the advantages of interpreted functions as compared to relations is that the returned values of their applications permit nestings, avoiding flat relational conjunctions with shared logic variables.

For example, the function `age` can be defined for Jory as `age(Jory) = 12`, so the nesting `age(first-born(John, Mary))`, using the `first-born` definition of subsection 3.1, gives `age(Jory)`, then returns 12.

Alternatively, the function `age` can be defined for the uninterpreted `first-born` application as `age(first-born[John, Mary]) = 12`, so the nesting `age(first-born[John, Mary])` immediately returns 12.

Conversely, the function `age` can be left uninterpreted over the returned value of the `first-born` application, so the nesting `age[first-born(John, Mary)]` denotes `age[Jory]`.

Finally, both the functions `age` and `first-born` can be left uninterpreted, so the nesting `age[first-born[John, Mary]]` just denotes itself.

The four versions of the example can now be marked up thus (where "u" and "v" can independently assume "no" or "yes"):

```
<Expr>
  <Fun in="u">age</Fun>
  <Expr>
    <Fun in="v">first-born</Fun>
    <Ind>John</Ind>
    <Ind>Mary</Ind>
  </Expr>
</Expr>
```

Nestings are permitted for set-valued functions, where an (interpreted or uninterpreted) outer function is automatically mapped over all elements of a set returned by an inner (interpreted) function.

For example, the element-valued function `age` can be extended for `Mahn` with `age(Mahn) = 9`, and nested, interpreted, over the set-valued interpreted function `children` of subsection 3.1: `age(children(John, Mary))` via `age({Jory, Mahn})` returns `{12, 9}`.

Similarly, `age` can be nested uninterpreted over the interpreted `children`: `age[children(John, Mary)]` via `age[{Jory, Mahn}]` returns `{age[Jory], age[Mahn]}`.

The examples can be marked up thus (only `"u"` is left open for `"no"` or `"yes"`):

```
<Expr>
  <Fun in="u">age</Fun>
  <Expr>
    <Fun in="yes"
         val="0..">children</Fun>
    <Ind>John</Ind>
    <Ind>Mary</Ind>
  </Expr>
</Expr>
```

3.3   Unconditional Equations

In subsections 3.1 and 3.2 we have employed expression-defining equations without giving their actual markup. Let us consider these in more detail here, starting with *unconditional equations*.

For this, we introduce a modified RuleML 0.9 `<Equal>` element, permitting both symmetric (or undirected) and oriented (or directed) equations via an `oriented` attribute with respective `"no"` and `"yes"` values. Since it is more general, `oriented="no"` is proposed as the default.

Because of the potential orientedness of equations, the RuleML 0.9 `<side>` role tag within the `<Equal>` type tag will be refined into `<lhs>` and `<rhs>` for an equation's left-hand side and right-hand side, respectively.

For example, the subsection 3.1 equation `first-born(John, Mary) = Jory` can now be marked up thus:

```
<Equal oriented="yes">
  <lhs>
    <Expr>
      <Fun in="yes">first-born</Fun>
      <Ind>John</Ind>
      <Ind>Mary</Ind>
    </Expr>
  </lhs>
  <rhs>
    <Ind>Jory</Ind>
  </rhs>
</Equal>
```

While the explicit `<lhs>` and `<rhs>` role tags emphasize the orientation, and are used as RDF properties when mapping this markup to RDF graphs, they can be omitted via stripe-skipping [http://esw.w3.org/topic/StripeSkipping]: the `<lhs>` and `<rhs>` roles of `<Equal>`'s respective first and second subelements can still be uniquely recognized.

This, then, is the stripe-skipped example:

```
<Equal oriented="yes">
  <Expr>
    <Fun in="yes">first-born</Fun>
    <Ind>John</Ind>
    <Ind>Mary</Ind>
  </Expr>
  <Ind>Jory</Ind>
</Equal>
```

Equations can also have nested left-hand sides, where often the following restrictions apply: The `<Expr>` directly in the left-hand side must use an interpreted function. Any `<Expr>` nested into it must use an uninterpreted function to fulfill the so-called "constructor discipline" [O'D85]; same for deeper nesting levels. If we want to obey it, we use `in="no"` within these nestings. An equation's right-hand side `<Expr>` can use uninterpreted or interpreted functions on any level of nesting, anyway.

For example, employing binary `subtract` and nullary `this-year` functions, the equation `age(first-born[John, Mary]) = subtract(this-year(),1993)` leads to this stripe-skipped 'disciplined' markup:

```
<Equal oriented="yes">
  <Expr>
    <Fun in="yes">age</Fun>
    <Expr>
      <Fun in="no">first-born</Fun>
      <Ind>John</Ind>
      <Ind>Mary</Ind>
    </Expr>
  </Expr>
  <Expr>
    <Fun in="yes">subtract</Fun>
    <Expr>
      <Fun in="yes">this-year</Fun>
    </Expr>
    <Data>1993</Data>
  </Expr>
</Equal>
```

3.4   Conditional Equations

Let us now proceed to oriented *conditional equations*, which use a (defining, oriented) <Equal> element as the conclusion of an <Implies> element, whose condition may employ other (testing, symmetric) equations. An equational condition may also bind auxiliary variables. While condition and conclusion can be marked up with explicit <body> and <head> roles, respectively, also allowing the conclusion as the first subelement, we will use a stripe-skipped markup where the condition must be the first subelement.

For example, using a unary `birth-year` function in the condition, and two ("?"-prefixed) variables, the conditional equation (written with a top-level "$\Rightarrow$") ?B = birth-year(?P) $\Rightarrow$ age(?P) = subtract(this-year(),?B) employs an equational condition to test whether the `birth-year` of a person ?P is known, assigning it to ?B for use within the conclusion. This leads to the following stripe-skipped markup:

```
<Implies>
  <Equal oriented="no">
    <Var>B</Var>
    <Expr>
      <Fun in="yes">birth-year</Fun>
      <Var>P</Var>
    </Expr>
  </Equal>
  <Equal oriented="yes">
    <Expr>
      <Fun in="yes">age</Fun>
      <Var>P</Var>
    </Expr>
    <Expr>
      <Fun in="yes">subtract</Fun>
      <Expr>
        <Fun in="yes">this-year</Fun>
      </Expr>
      <Var>B</Var>
    </Expr>
  </Equal>
</Implies>
```

Within conditional equations, relational conditions can be used besides equational ones.

Thus, using a binary `lessThanOrEqual` relation in the condition, the conditional equation lessThanOrEqual(age(?P),15) $\Rightarrow$ discount(?P,?F) = 30 with a free variable ?F (flight) and a data constant 30 (percent), gives this markup:

```
<Implies>
  <Atom>
    <Rel>lessThanOrEqual</Rel>
    <Expr>
      <Fun in="yes">age</Fun>
      <Var>P</Var>
    </Expr>
    <Data>15</Data>
  </Atom>
  <Equal oriented="yes">
    <Expr>
      <Fun in="yes">discount</Fun>
      <Var>P</Var>
      <Var>F</Var>
    </Expr>
    <Data>30</Data>
  </Equal>
</Implies>
```

Notice the following interleaving of FP and LP (as characteristic for FLP): The function `discount` is defined using the relation `lessThanOrEqual` in the condition. The `<Atom>` element for the `lessThanOrEqual` relation itself contains a nested `<Expr>` element for the `age` function.

For conditional equations of Horn logic with equality in general [Pad88], the condition is a conjunction of `<Atom>` and `<Equal>` elements.

3.5   Higher-Order Functions

Higher-order functions are characteristic for FP and thus should be supported by Functional RuleML. A *higher-order function* permits functions to be passed to it as (actual) parameters and to be returned from it as values.

Perhaps the most well-known higher-order function is `Compose`, taking two functions as parameters and returning as its value a function performing their sequential composition.

For example, the composition of the `age` and `first-born` functions of subsection 3.1 is performed by `Compose(age,first-born)`. Here is the markup for the interpreted and uninterpreted use of both of the parameter functions (where we use the default `in="semi"` for the higher-order function and let `"u"` and `"v"` independently assume `"no"` or `"yes"` for the first-order functions):

```
<Expr>
  <Fun>Compose</Fun>
  <Fun in="u">age</Fun>
  <Fun in="v">first-born</Fun>
</Expr>
```

The application of a parameterized `Compose` expression to arguments is equivalent to the nested application of its parameter functions.

For example, when interpreted with the definitions of subsection 3.1, Compose(age,first-born)(John, Mary) via age(first-born(John, Mary)) returns 12.

All four versions of this sample application can be marked up thus (with the usual "u" and "v"):

```
<Expr>
  <Expr>
    <Fun>Compose</Fun>
    <Fun in="u">age</Fun>
    <Fun in="v">first-born</Fun>
  </Expr>
  <Ind>John</Ind>
  <Ind>Mary</Ind>
</Expr>
```

Besides being applied in this way, a Compose expression can also be used as a parameter or returned value of another higher-order function.

To allow the general construction of anonymous functions, Lambda formulas from λ-calculus [Bar97] are introduced. A λ-*formula* quantifies variables that occur free in a functional expression much like a ∀-*formula* does for a relational atom. So we can extend principles developed for explicit-quantifier markup in FOL RuleML [http://www.w3.org/Submission/FOL-RuleML], where quantifiers are allowed on all levels of rulebase elements.

For example, the function returned by Compose(age,first-born) can now be explicitly given as λ(?X, ?Y)age(first-born(?X, ?Y)). Here is the markup for its interpreted and uninterpreted use (with the usual "u" and "v"):

```
<Lambda>
  <Var>X</Var>
  <Var>Y</Var>
  <Expr>
    <Fun in="u">age</Fun>
    <Expr>
      <Fun in="v">first-born</Fun>
      <Var>X</Var>
      <Var>Y</Var>
    </Expr>
  </Expr>
</Lambda>
```

This Lambda formula can be applied as the Compose expression was above. The advantage of Lambda formulas is that they allow the direct λ-*abstraction* of arbitrary expressions, not just for (sequential or parallel) composition etc. An example is λ(?X, ?Y)plex(age(?X), xy, age(?Y), fxy, age(first-born(?X, ?Y))), whose markup should be obvious if we note that `plex` is the interpreted analog to RuleML's uninterpreted built-in function for n-ary com`plex`-term (e.g., tuple) construction.

By also abstracting the parameter functions, `age` and `first-born`, `Compose` can be defined generally via a `Lambda` formula as `Compose(?F, ?G) =` λ`(?X, ?Y) ?F(?G(?X, ?Y))`. Its markup can distinguish object (first-order) **Var**iables like `?X` vs. function (higher-order) ones like `?F` via attribute values `ord="1"` vs. `ord="h"`.

4   Combining Modal Logics

This section introduces a preliminary extension of RuleML for modal logics, whose relevance to the Semantic Web has been known for quite some time [Bol00b]. Modal operators can be represented *generically* as special relations at least one of whose arguments is a proposition represented as an embedded atom that has an uninterpreted relation (including another modal operator), complementing the usual main atoms that have interpreted relations:

- **Alethic** operators: The relations `necessary` (□) and `possible` (◇) represent the operators of modal logic in the narrow sense.
- **Deontic** operators: The relations `must` and `may` are used to express obligations and permissions (e.g., in business rules).
- Further modal operators can be introduced as relations for temporal (e.g., to plan/diagnose reactive rules), epistemic (e.g., in authentication rules), and other modalities.

These logics are based on Kripke-style possible worlds semantics, usually focusing one pair of operators at a time. However, recently logicians have begun to develop *many-dimensional modal* [GKWZ03] and *multi-modal* [Hen06] systems in which, e.g., alethic, epistemic, and temporal operators can be combined in unified formal frameworks. Motivated by the co-occurrence of several modalities in RuleML application (e.g., business) domains and enabled by the combination principle of sublanguages in the RuleML family, such combined modal logics are proposed for the Modal RuleML extension.

Modal **Rel**ations are indicated by a `modal="yes"` attribute setting, where the default value, for non-modal **Rel**ations, is `modal="no"`. Furthermore, we regard the **Atom**s in the contexts created by modal relations as counterparts to the **Expr**essions with an `in="no"` function used by relations beyond Datalog: the `in`terpretedness attribute for **Fun**ctions is also allowed for **Rel**ations. While `in="semi"` is the proposed default value for functions, `in="yes"` is proposed as the default value for relations to keep their interpretation for non-modal sublanguages unchanged when no `in` attribute is given. The use of **Atom**s with an un`in`terpreted **Rel**ation for embedded propositions can be regarded as a customized form of the universally usable **Reify** element introduced for RuleML's SWSL-Rules sublanguage [http://www.w3.org/Submission/SWSF-SWSL/#ruleml-reification]. These modal-logic characteristics will be further explored through the examples below.

The unary alethic fact $\Box prime(1)$ is serialized thus (the main `Rel` by default obtains `in="yes"`; the embedded `Rel` gets `modal="no"`):

```
<Atom>
  <Rel modal="yes">necessary</Rel>
  <Atom>
    <Rel in="no">prime</Rel>
    <Data>1</Data>
  </Atom>
</Atom>
```

The binary epistemic fact $knows(Mary, material(moon, rock))$ likewise becomes this serialization:

```
<Atom>
  <Rel modal="yes">knows</Rel>
  <Ind>Mary</Ind>
  <Atom>
    <Rel in="no">material</Rel>
    <Ind>moon</Ind>
    <Ind>rock</Ind>
  </Atom>
</Atom>
```

With the *veridicality* axiom $Knows_{Agent} proposition \rightarrow proposition$, here in a unary notation, the non-modal fact $material(moon, rock)$ can be derived, which is serialized thus (using defaults `<Rel modal="no" in="yes">`):

```
<Atom>
  <Rel>material</Rel>
  <Ind>moon</Ind>
  <Ind>rock</Ind>
</Atom>
```

The nested epistemic-alethic fact $knows(Mary, \Box prime(1))$ of a combined modal logic can then be serialized as follows:

```
<Atom>
  <Rel modal="yes">knows</Rel>
  <Ind>Mary</Ind>
  <Atom>
    <Rel modal="yes" in="no">necessary</Rel>
    <Atom>
      <Rel in="no">prime</Rel>
      <Data>1</Data>
    </Atom>
  </Atom>
</Atom>
```

Here, the `knows` and `necessary` `Rel`ations are modal, hence are attributed with `modal="yes"`. However, the `necessary` relation is furthermore attributed as uninterpreted, since it occurs in the context of the `knows` relation, which itself, by default, is interpreted.

5 Conclusions

The key-order matrix of the generalized Object-Oriented RuleML presented in this paper – when used for expressions with uninterpreted functions rather than for atoms – makes four data containers available in a systematic manner: (keyed) positionalized records and ordinary records as well as (unkeyed) tuples and bags.

The *unordered* column of the matrix could be extended by a column for 'idempotent' slots and arguments (duplicates are merged), leading to data containers for unique-key records and sets. Unification algorithms could be based on earlier work (e.g., [DV99]).

The design of Functional RuleML as presented here also benefits other sublanguages of RuleML, e.g. because of the more 'logical' complex terms. Functional RuleML, as a development of FOL RuleML, could furthermore benefit all of SWRL FOL [http://www.w3.org/Submission/2005/01]. However, there are some open issues, two of which will be discussed below.

Certain constraints on the values of our attributes cannot be enforced with DTDs and are hard to enforce with XSDs, e.g. `in="no"` on functions in call patterns in case we wanted to always enforce the constructor discipline (cf. subsection 3.3). However, a semantics-oriented validation tool will be required for future attributes anyway, e.g. for testing whether a rulebase is stratified. Thus we propose that such a static-analysis tool should be developed to make fine-grained distinctions for all 'semantic' attributes.

The proposed defaults for some of our attributes may require a future revision. It might be argued that the default `in="semi"` for functions is a problem since equations could be invoked inadvertently for functions that are applied without an explicit `in` attribute. However, notice that, intuitively speaking, the default `oriented="no"` for equations permits to 'revert' any function call, using the same equation in the other direction. Together, those defaults thus constitute a kind of 'vanilla' logic with equality, which can (only) be changed via our explicit attribute values.

While our logical design does not specify any evaluation strategy for nested Expressions with interpreted Functions, we have preferred 'call-by-value' in implementations [Bol00a]. A reference interpreter for Functional RuleML is planned as an extension of OO jDREW [BBH+05]; an initial step has been taken by implementing oriented ground equality via an `EqualTable` data structure for equivalence classes [http://www.w3.org/2004/12/rules-ws/paper/49].

The preliminary design of a Modal RuleML with combined modalities addresses modeling needs of the business rules community. As Hornlog RuleML uses relations over embedded expressions with an uninterpreted function, modal operators are special relations applied to embedded atoms with an uninterpreted relation. Efficiently implementing combined modal logics is a current challenge.

References

[Bar97]   Henk Barendregt. The Impact of the Lambda Calculus in Logic and Computer Science. *The Bulletin of Symbolic Logic*, 3(2):181–215, 1997.

[BBH$^+$05] Marcel Ball, Harold Boley, David Hirtle, Jing Mei, and Bruce Spencer. The OO jDREW Reference Implementation of RuleML. In *Proc. Rules and Rule Markup Languages for the Semantic Web (RuleML-2005)*. LNCS 3791, Springer-Verlag, November 2005.

[BKPS03]   Paul A. Bailes, Colin J. M. Kemp, Ian Peake, and Sean Seefried. Why Functional Programming Really Matters. In *Applied Informatics*, pages 919–926, 2003.

[Bol99]   Harold Boley. Functional-Logic Integration via Minimal Reciprocal Extensions. *Theoretical Computer Science*, 212:77–99, 1999.

[Bol00a]   Harold Boley. Markup Languages for Functional-Logic Programming. In *9th International Workshop on Functional and Logic Programming, Benicassim, Spain*, pages 391–403. UPV University Press, Valencia, publication 2000/2039, September 2000.

[Bol00b]   Harold Boley. Relationships Between Logic Programming and RDF. In *Proc. 1st Pacific Rim International Workshop on Intelligent Information Agents (PRIIA 2000)*. University of Melbourne, Australia; LNCS 2112, August 2000.

[Bol03]   Harold Boley. Object-Oriented RuleML: User-Level Roles, URI-Grounded Clauses, and Order-Sorted Terms. In *Proc. Rules and Rule Markup Languages for the Semantic Web (RuleML-2003)*. LNCS 2876, Springer-Verlag, October 2003.

[DV99]   E. Dantsin and A. Voronkov. A Nondeterministic Polynomial-Time Unification Algorithm for Bags, Sets and Trees. *Lecture Notes in Computer Science*, 1578:180–196, 1999.

[FRSV05]   Achille Fokoue, Kristoffer Rose, Jérôme Siméon, and Lionel Villard. Compiling XSLT 2.0 into XQuery 1.0. In *Proceedings of the Fourteenth International World Wide Web Conference*, pages 682–691, Chiba, Japan, May 2005. ACM Press.

[GKWZ03]   Dov M. Gabbay, Ágnes Kurucz, Frank Wolter, and Michael Zakharyaschev. *Many-Dimensional Modal Logics: Theory and Applications*. Elsevier, Amsterdam, 2003.

[Hen06]   Vincent F. Hendricks. *Mainstream and Formal Epistemology*. Cambridge University Press, New York, 2006.

[O'D85]   M. J. O'Donnell. *Equational Logic as a Programming Language*. MIT Press, Cambridge, Mass., 1985.

[Pad88]   P. Padawitz. *Computing in Horn Clause Theories*. EATCS Monographs on Theoretical Computer Science, Vol. 16. Springer, 1988.

[SB04]   Sebastian Schaffert and François Bry. Querying the Web Reconsidered: A Practical Introduction to Xcerpt. In *Proceedings of Extreme Markup Languages 2004, Montreal, Quebec, Canada (2nd–6th August 2004)*, 2004.

[SHC96]   Z. Somogy, F. Henderson, and T. Conway. The Execution Algorithm of Mercury, An Efficient Purely Declarative Logic Programming Language. *Journal of Logic Programming*, 29(1-3):17–64, 1996.

Automated Reasoning Support for First-Order Ontologies

Peter Baumgartner[1] and Fabian M. Suchanek[2]

[1] National ICT Australia (NICTA)
Peter.Baumgartner@nicta.com.au
[2] Max-Planck Institute for Computer Science, Germany
suchanek@mpi-sb.mpg.de

Abstract. Formal ontologies play an increasingly important role in demanding knowledge representation applications like the Semantic Web. Regarding automated reasoning support, the mainstream of research focusses on ontology languages that are also Description Logics, such as OWL-DL. However, many existing ontologies go beyond Description Logics and use full first-order logic. We propose a novel transformation technique that allows to apply existing model computation systems in such situations. We describe the transformation and some variants, its properties and intended applications to ontological reasoning.

1 Introduction

1.1 Motivation

Recent years have seen an increasing interest in formal knowledge bases (KBs). Demanding application areas – notably the *Semantic Web* – will have to remain a vision without powerful automated reasoning support.

The mainstream of research on automated reasoning focuses on ontology languages that are also Description Logics (DLs), such as OWL-DL. Yet, there are good reasons to also consider larger fragments of first-order logic as ontology languages. One reason is the ability to add "rules" to the ontology, as in languages like SWRL [HB+04]. An example for a rule is the statement [GHVD03]: individuals who live and work at the same location are home workers. This can be expressed as a Horn rule (clause) homeWorker$(x) \leftarrow$ work$(x, y) \land$ live$(x, z) \land$ loc$(y, w) \land$ loc(z, w), but is not expressible in current DL systems.

Another reason for considering even full first-order logic is the existence of numerous KBs that go beyond Description Logics. One example is the largest formal public ontology available today, the Suggested Upper Merged Ontology SUMO [NP01]. SUMO is written in KIF, the Knowledge Interchange Format [KIF], which is basically first-order logic with equality and some higher-order features. Together with its domain-specific extensions, SUMO contains more than 20'000 terms and 60'000 axioms. Unfortunately, only limited automated reasoning is available today for first-order KBs. For instance, to our knowledge, the only theorem prover applied to SUMO so far is Vampire [RV01].

This situation seems somewhat surprising, given the demonstrated usefulness of description logic systems for KBs written in $\mathcal{ALC}$-like languages [BCM+02]. Why has

J.J. Alferes et al. (Eds.): PPSWR 2006, LNCS 4187, pp. 18–32, 2006.

this success story not been repeated for KBs in first-order logic? The answer from a technical point of view might be that DL systems are so successful because they usually *decide* the satisfiability problem of their input language. This is an important feature, as it allows, for instance, to prove that a speculated subsumption relation between concepts does *not* hold. Furthermore, it allows the "debugging" of KBs.

Although such decision procedures cannot exist for first-order KBs, reasoning support by automated theorem provers may be attempted nevertheless. Indeed, within the Semantic Web framework a number of off-the-shelf first-order theorem provers have been tested on various KBs, unsatisfiable ones and satisfiable ones[1]. The provers generally performed well in solving the unsatisfiable test cases. However, they often could not solve the satisfiable ones, i.e., they did not terminate.

1.2   Contribution

To address the problem of non-termination of the prover, we propose a novel transformation technique on first-order logic KBs that allows to compute models more often. Our transformation is rather general regarding the underlying system to be used. We target at model computation systems as developed within the logic programming community or at bottom-up clausal theorem provers as long as they support a (weak) default negation principle. The rationale is to capitalize on these well-investigated techniques and lift them to a more general language, viz., first-order logic, and strengthen the model-building capabilities of such systems. Among the systems that are suitable are dlv [CEF$^+$97], smodels [NS96] and KRHyper [Wer03]. In our experiments we have chosen KRHyper, simply because we know it best.

Our transformation is applicable to any first-order logic KB, but it is geared towards application to first-order logic ontologies. It differs from the textbook transformation to clause logic in several ways:

1. It transforms away equality, so that model generation systems can be used, even though they usually do not include built-in equality handling.
2. Optionally, it respects a certain form of the Unique Name Assumption (UNA). This is useful in the context of ontologies, when different constants are best considered to denote different objects.
3. It allows to avoid unnecessary Skolem terms, if an existentially quantified role is already filled. This keeps the resulting models slim and meaningful.
4. It allows for a non-standard reading of existentially quantified formulas, namely as *integrity constraints*. That is, the model building process can be instructed to fail if an existentially quantified formula is not already fulfilled by the KB.
5. Finally, it allows for a "loop check", by which infinite models can be avoided in some cases by detecting finite ones.

1.3   Related Work

From a methodological point of view, we were helped to achieve our results by considering insights and combining results and techniques from automated theorem proving,

---

[1] http://www.w3.org/2003/08/owl-systems/test-results-out

description logic and logic programming. For instance, we employ default negation, as available in logic programming systems, as a tool to realize the mentioned "loop check", which is modeled after the "blocking" technique commonly found in Description Logic systems.

Because of the use of default negation, we cannot use a theorem prover for classical (first-order) logic. Since the ontology may contain "disjunctive" formulas like $\forall x \ (\text{man}(x) \lor \text{woman}(x) \leftarrow \text{person}(x))$, Horn-logic is not expressive enough and we need a system that accepts *disjunctive* programs. Thus, we cannot use, e.g., the widely available Prolog-like logic programming systems based on SLDNF-resolution (see e.g. [Llo87]), which support default negation but do no not support disjunctive programs.

An approach closely related to ours in methodology is the translation approach in [GHVD03]. It allows to translate certain DL fragments to a certain class of logic programs. However, this approach is restricted to definite programs, i.e. it cannot treat disjunctions as in the example above. This limitation could easily be overcome by translating to positive disjunctive logic programs (DLPs) instead. Yet, the method has a more severe limitation, which essentially forbids existential quantification to introduce new individuals. For example, consider the expression "every person has a father", expressed as a DL axiom

person $\sqsubseteq \exists$father . $\top$

or as a first-order logic formula

$\forall x \exists y \ (\text{father}(x,y) \leftarrow \text{person}(x))$.

Such formulas cannot be treated by the method in [GHVD03] and thus are not part of their input language. The technical difficulty with formulas of this kind is that they introduce Skolem terms (e.g. $f(x)$, intended to denote the "father" of an object x), which in general lead to non-termination of model computation systems. From that point of view, the purpose of our approach is to address this very problem: to achieve termination even in presence of existential quantifiers.

Our approach is somewhat related to model construction by hyper resolution e.g. [FL93, GHS02, GHS03]. One difference is our use of default negation, which is not available in hyper resolution systems. The perhaps closest related work is the translation scheme in [BB04]. However, that work is concerned with one specific ontology, FrameNet, and it is shown how to translate it to a logic program. The approach in this paper is thus much more general.

The rest of this paper is structured as follows. Section 2 contains preliminaries. Section 3 is the main part, it contains the transformations. In Section 4 we turn to the treatment of equality. In Section 5 we report on first experiments carried out on the SUMO ontology. Finally, in Section 6 we draw some conclusions.

2   Preliminaries

We use standard terminology from first-order logic and automated reasoning (see e.g. [Llo87]). Our formulas, and specifically clauses, are built over a signature Σ, usually left implicit in the following. We assume that Σ contains a distinguished nullary predicate symbol false and a 2-ary predicate symbol $\approx$, equality, used infix. We deviate from the standard definitions by distinguishing between constants and nullary function symbols. This allows us to take the Unique Name Assumption (UNA) into account: constants are subject to the UNA, i.e. no model shall assign true to $c_1 \approx c_2$ for any two different constants c_1 and c_2. Nullary function symbols, by contrast, are not affected by the UNA, so that our definitions are compatible with the standard semantics.

A *(program) rule* is an expression of the form $H_1 \vee \cdots \vee H_m \leftarrow B_1, \ldots, B_k,$ not $B_{k+1}, \ldots,$ not B_n, where $m \geq 1$, $n \geq k \geq 0$ and H_i, for $i = 1, \ldots m$, and B_j, for $j = 1, \ldots, n$ are (possibly non-ground) atoms (over Σ). Each H_i is called a *head literal*, and each B_j is called a *body literal*. The *negative* body literals are those that include the default negation operator not, the other body literals are the *positive* ones. We write $H \vee \mathcal{H} \leftarrow B, \mathcal{B},$ not $B', \mathcal{B}_{\text{not}}$ to mean a program rule containing the head literal H, the positive body literal B and the negative body literal not B'. In a *positive* rule it holds $k = n$. We treat the terms "positive rule" and "clause" as synonyms.

A *disjunctive logic program (DLP)*, also just *program*, is a finite set of rules. A *positive DLP* consists of positive rules only; it is thus the same as a *clause set*. In a *normal* program each rule has exactly one head literal. We consider only *domain restricted* programs, where every variable occurring in a rule must also occur in some positive body atom $B_1, \ldots, B_k$. This is a common assumption and is present in systems like KRHyper [Wer03] and smodels [NS96]. As an example, consider the following (propositional) program:

$$\text{whiskey} \vee \text{water} \leftarrow \text{thirsty}, \text{not hungry} \tag{1}$$

$$\text{water} \leftarrow \text{whiskey} \tag{2}$$

$$\text{thirsty} \leftarrow \tag{3}$$

Program rules can be read operationally in a top-down or in a bottom-up fashion. The top-down paradigm (of normal programs) became popular with Prolog and its underlying SLDNF Resolution (see [Llo87]). The bottom-up paradigm became popular with the observation that it often better realizes the idea of purely *declarative* programming. The purely declarative nature renders these approaches suitable in particular for knowledge representation applications, which is our interest here.

A bottom-up evaluation of the above sample program assigns *true* to thirsty, because the (empty) body of rule (3) is (trivially) satisfied, and so its head thirsty must be satisfied. But then, as hungry is *false* (by default), the body of rule (1) is satisfied, and so must be its head. For that, there is a choice of satisfying whiskey or water (or both). Notice, in the first case rule (2) becomes applicable and water must become *true*, too. In sum, we have the two models, {thirsty, whiskey, water} and {thirsty, water}. Indeed, the literature discusses various alternatives to assign semantics to DLPs. For instance, the *stable model semantics* would reject the first model, because it is not a minimal one. The *possible model semantics* admits both. None of them admits the classical model that assigns *true* to hungry and thirsty but nothing else (the intuition is that there is no rule to justify the truth of hungry). Either semantics is usable in our case.

Furthermore, the programs constructed below will be *stratified*,[2] which guarantees that they will have a stable/possible model if and only if the original ontology has a classical first-order model (which is its intended semantics.) Without going into details, we only note that the KRHyper system [Wer03], which we used for our experiments, computes possible models of domain-restricted stratified DLPs, and thus is suitable in the sense just mentioned. We further note that the above notions concerning semantics of logic programs lift to first-order logic by letting a rule stand for the set of all its ground instances, i.e. by the set of variable-free rules obtainable by replacing each variable in the rule by some variable-free term, in all possible ways. A good overview on DLPs can be found in [Nie99] (although on normal programs only). A more comprehensive textbook is [Bar03].

For space reasons, we omit here various technical details. The interested reader is referred to the long version of this paper, which can be obtained from `http://rsise.anu.edu.au/~baumgart/publications/`.

3   Translating First-Order Formulae to DLPs

We assume as given some ontology, e.g. an OWL ontology. The ontology may contain facts as well as non-taxonomic axioms and it could contain "rules" (cf. the introduction). We assume it to be written as a sentence in first-order logic. This section describes how to transform the first-order sentence to a DLP. The first steps of the transformation are concerned with flattening the possibly deeply structured sentence towards the flat form of DLP rules. An important, non-standard aspect hereby is to isolate and name subformulas containing existentially quantified variables. Once we described how to isolate these subformulas, Section 3.1 proposes four different ways of translating them to a DLP.

We first fix some notation. If x is a sequence of variables $x_1, \ldots, x_k$, for some $k \geq 0$, then $\forall x$ denotes the sequence $\forall x_1 \cdots \forall x_k$. The expression $\exists x$ is defined analogously, and Qx stands for any sequence $Q_1 x_1 \cdots Q_k x_k$, where $Q_i \in \{\forall, \exists\}$, for all $i = 1, \ldots, k$, $k \geq 0$. When ψ is a formula, the notation $\psi(x)$ means that ψ contains no more free variables than those in the sequence of variables x. We assume, without loss of generality, that the first-order logic sentence ϕ is given in prenex negation normal form. Thus, it is of the form $\phi = Qz\ \psi(z)$, where Qz is the quantifier prefix and $\psi(z)$ is a quantifier-free formula, built with logical operators $\wedge$, $\vee$ and $\neg$, where $\neg$ occurs only in front of atoms.

We define our transformation $\tau(\phi)$ as follows. The quantifier prefix Qz may contain an existential quantifier, or not. If it does not, set $\tau(\phi) = \{\phi\}$. Otherwise ϕ can be written as

$$\phi = Qz\ \psi(z) = \forall x \exists y Q'z'\ (\Delta(x) \vee \psi'(xyz')) \ , \tag{1}$$

where Q' is either empty or starts with a universal quantifier. The intention is to separate Ψ into two parts, the part Δ containing universally quantified variables only, and the remainder Ψ' containing at least one existentially quantified variable. We may assume

---

[2] Stratification means that the call-graph of a program does not contain circles containing negative body atoms.

that $\psi'(xyz')$ is not a disjunction such that one of its immediate subformulas contains at most the variables x, because then this subformula could be part of Δ. Notice that by replacing $\psi(z)$ in ϕ by false $\vee \psi(z)$, the form (1) is indeed a general form ($\Delta(x)$ could be the atom false).

Suppose ϕ is of the form (1) and consider the following sentences derived from ϕ:

$$\phi_1 = \forall x \exists y (\Delta(x) \vee def_{\psi'}(x,y))$$
$$\phi_2 = \forall x \forall y \mathbf{Q}'z'(\neg def_{\psi'}(x,y) \vee \psi'(xyz'))$$
$$\phi_3 = \forall x \forall y \overline{\mathbf{Q}'z'}(\mathrm{NNF}(sat_{\psi'}(x,y) \vee \neg \psi'(xyz'))) \ ,$$

where $def_{\psi'}$ and $sat_{\psi'}$ are fresh predicate symbols of appropriate arity. The intention is to introduce in ϕ_2 a name $def_{\psi'}$ for the subformula Ψ', which allows to replace Ψ' in ϕ by $def_{\psi'}$. Regarding the formula ϕ_3, $\overline{\mathbf{Q}'z'}$ denotes the quantifier prefix obtained from $\mathbf{Q}'z'$ by replacing every universal quantifier by an existential one and vice versa, and NNF converts its argument to negation normal form. The formula ϕ_3 will play a role only later, in Section 3.1. Roughly, the purpose of the new name $sat_{\psi'}$ is to iden-tify situations when Ψ' holds true. One can prove that these transformations preserve satisfiability. More precisely, ϕ is satisfiable if and only if $\phi_1 \wedge \phi_2 \wedge \phi_3$ is satisfiable.

For illustration, consider the formula

$$\forall x(p(x) \rightarrow \exists y\, q(x,y) \vee r(x)) \ . \tag{1}$$

We rewrite it as

$$\phi = \forall x \exists y(\neg p(x) \vee r(x) \vee q(x,y))$$

so that it is of the form (1) with $\Delta(x) = \neg p(x) \vee r(x)$ and $\psi'(x,y) = q(x,y)$. We derive the following sentences:

$$\phi_1 = \forall x \exists y(\neg p(x) \vee r(x) \vee def_{\psi}(x,y))$$
$$\phi_2 = \forall x \forall y(\neg def_{\psi}(x,y) \vee q(x,y))$$
$$\phi_3 = \forall x \forall y(sat_{\psi}(x,y) \vee \neg q(x,y))$$

It is not too difficult to see that already ϕ_1 and ϕ_2 together are equisatisfiable with ϕ. Regarding ϕ_3, suppose that, say, $q(a,b)$ holds true in some interpretation. By ϕ_3, $sat_{\psi}(a,b)$ must be true as well, which can be exploited to conclude that the formula $\exists y\, q(a,y)$ holds true. (As said, ϕ_3 can be ignored for now, but it will be crucial for the improvement in Section 3.1 below.)

Recall that Δ is a part of ϕ that contains universally quantified variables only. Now, Δ can be written as[3]

$$\Delta = \neg B_1(x) \vee \cdots \vee \neg B_m(x) \vee \Delta'(x),$$

for some formula Δ', negative literals $\neg B_i$, for all $i = 1, \ldots, m$, $m \geq 0$, where m is chosen as large as possible. Notice we allow $m = 0$. Hence Δ can indeed be written this way.

---

[3] Similarly to above, we allow $\Delta'(x)$ to be false.

We write Δ this way with the intention to turn it into a flat formula, basically an implication between atoms. While its literals $\neg B_1(\boldsymbol{x}), \ldots, \neg B_m(\boldsymbol{x})$ pose no problems, its subformula $\Delta'(\boldsymbol{x})$ need not be a disjunction of atoms. To overcome this problem, we introduce a fresh name for $\Delta'(\boldsymbol{x})$. More precisely, from Δ derive the formulas

$$\Delta_1 = \neg B_1(\boldsymbol{x}) \vee \cdots \vee \neg B_m(\boldsymbol{x}) \vee def_{\Delta'}(\boldsymbol{x})$$
$$\Delta_2 = \forall \boldsymbol{x}(\neg def_{\Delta'}(\boldsymbol{x}) \vee \Delta'(\boldsymbol{x})) \;,$$

where again $def_{\Delta'}$ is a fresh predicate symbol of appropriate arity. In the example, this yields:

$$\Delta_1 = \neg p(x) \vee def_\Delta(x)$$
$$\Delta_2 = \forall x \, (\neg def_\Delta(x) \vee r(x))$$

The next step is to replace Δ in ϕ_1 by Δ_1, which yields

$$\phi_1^{\Delta_1} = \forall \boldsymbol{x} \exists \boldsymbol{y}(\neg B_1(\boldsymbol{x}) \vee \cdots \vee \neg B_m(\boldsymbol{x}) \vee def_{\Delta'}(\boldsymbol{x}) \vee def_{\psi'}(\boldsymbol{x}, \boldsymbol{y})) \;.$$

In our example,

$$\phi_1^{\Delta_1} = \forall x \exists y \, (\neg p(x) \vee def_\Delta(x) \vee def_\psi(x, y)) \;.$$

Above we already defined $\tau(\phi) = \{\phi\}$ for the case that $\mathbf{Q}z$ does not contain an existential quantifier. We are now ready to define $\tau(\phi)$ if $\mathbf{Q}z$ does contain an existential quantifier:

$$\tau(\phi) = \{\phi_1^{\Delta_1}, \Delta_2\} \cup \tau(\phi_2) \cup \tau(\phi_3) \;.$$

In our example, this boils down to

$$\tau(\phi) = \{\forall x \exists y \, (\neg p(x) \vee def_\Delta(x) \vee def_\psi(x, y)),$$
$$\forall x \, (\neg def_\Delta(x) \vee r(x)),$$
$$\forall x \forall y \, (\neg def_\psi(x, y) \vee q(x, y)),$$
$$\forall x \forall y \, (sat_\psi(x, y) \vee \neg q(x, y))\} \;.$$

It might be instructive to compare this result, in particular the first formula, to the formula (1) we started with.

To see the termination of the transformation τ, observe that both ϕ_2 and ϕ_3 are strictly smaller than ϕ in the (well-founded) ordering on formulas with quantifier prefixes of same length induced by the lexicographic ordering on quantifier sequences, where $\exists$ is greater than $\forall$.

Introducing names (like $def_{\psi'}(\boldsymbol{x}, \boldsymbol{y})$ above) for subformulas and adding definitions for them, like our transformation does, is a standard technique used in clause normal form transformations. It is well-know that such transformations preserve satisfiability[4].

---

[4] Because existential quantifiers are not eliminated, τ even preserves models, in both ways (in the sense of conservative extensions for the newly introduced symbols).

Notice that *all* sentences in $\tau(\phi)$ containing an existential quantifier are of the (simple) syntactic form as obtained in $\phi_1^{\Delta_1}$. These are "almost" rules, except for the circumstance that the variables y are existentially quantified (in a rule all variables are implicitly universally quantified). All other sentences in $\tau(\phi)$ are of the form $\forall x \, \Delta(x)$ and can be converted to clausal form (i.e. a positive DLP) easily by means of well-known techniques.

3.1 Treating Existentially Quantified Subformulas

At this point, we assume that all universally quantified formulas in $\tau(\phi)$ have been transformed to clausal form. The remaining formulas contain existential quantifiers, which are all of the form as denoted by $\phi_1^{\Delta_1}$ above. Let Φ be a formula of this kind. We propose four different options to translate Φ to a DLP, each designed for a specific purpose: The *Skolemization Option* translates Φ by the use of Skolem terms, resulting in a traditional Skolemized DLP. The *Recycling Option* allows to introduce Skolem terms only if they are necessary, resulting in slimmer and more meaningful models. The *Model Checking Option* treats the existential quantification as an *integrity constraint*. With this option, the model building process is instructed to fail if there is no role filler in the model for the existential role. Last, the *Loop Check Option* allows to re-use existing Skolem terms in such a way that preference is given to a finite model.

Skolemization Option. With this option, a Skolem term is chosen as a default value to satisfy – in Description Logic terminology – an existentially quantified role. Technically, the formula Φ is translated to the following (domain-restricted) DLP:

$$def_{\Delta'}(x) \vee def_{\psi'}(x, sk_{\Phi}(x)) \leftarrow B_1(x), \ldots, B_m(x) \tag{2}$$

Here, $sk_{\Phi}(x)$ is a list of Skolem terms made from the variables x. Intuitively speaking, the premise of Φ implies that either the universally quantified part of Φ or the existentially quantified part of Φ must be satisfied. The existentially quantified part is given a Skolem filler for the existential variable. Thereby, our transformation includes the usual Skolemization as its simplest option.

Recycling Option. This option allows to avoid the introduction of a Skolem term if there is already a role filler present in the model. This can be achieved by translating Φ as follows:

$$def_{\Delta'}(x) \vee \mathsf{check\_sat}_{\psi'}(x) \vee def_{\psi'}(x, sk_{\Phi}(x)) \leftarrow B_1(x), \ldots, B_m(x) \tag{3}$$

$$\mathsf{false} \leftarrow def_{\Delta'}(x), \mathsf{check\_sat}_{\psi'}(x) \tag{4}$$

$$\mathsf{false} \leftarrow \mathsf{check\_sat}_{\psi'}(x), def_{\psi'}(x, y) \tag{5}$$

$$\mathsf{false} \leftarrow \mathsf{check\_sat}_{\psi'}(x), \mathsf{not}\ sat1_{\psi'}(x) \tag{6}$$

$$sat1_{\psi'}(x) \leftarrow sat_{\psi'}(x, y) \tag{7}$$

$$\mathsf{false} \leftarrow def_{\psi'}(x, y), sat_{\psi'}(x, z), \mathsf{not}\ \mathsf{equal}_{|y|}(y, z) \tag{8}$$

$$\mathsf{equal}_{|y|}(x_1, \ldots, x_n, y_1, \ldots, y_n) \leftarrow x_1 \approx y_1, \ldots, x_n \approx y_n \tag{9}$$

Rule (3) contains one more head literal than (2), which is $check\_sat_{\psi'}(x)$. This literal signals that there *exists* already a role-filler in the model for the existentially quantified role. The other rules realize certain exclusivity tests among the alternatives.

For illustration, consider again the formula

$$\phi = \forall x(p(x) \rightarrow \exists y\, q(x,y) \vee r(x))\ .$$

The translation τ with the recycling option applied to ϕ yields for the rule scheme (3) the DLP

$$def_r(x) \vee check\_sat_q(x) \vee def_q(x,sk(x)) \leftarrow p(x)\ .$$

Suppose additionally the fact $p(a)$ as given. Then, the model must satisfy the formula $\exists y\, q(a,y) \vee r(a)$. This can be achieved in three different ways:

1. The atom $r(a)$ is added to the model, i.e. the part of ϕ that is outside the scope of the $\exists$-quantifier is assigned true. This is achieved by the first alternative in rule (3), which, together with the rule $r(x) \leftarrow def_r(x)$ in $\tau(\phi)$, derives $r(a)$.
2. The model already contains an atom $q(a,t)$, for some term t. This is tested by the alternative $check\_sat_q(x)$. If the model does not already contain some such atom $q(a,t)$, *false* is derived and the third alternative is chosen.
3. The atom $q(a,sk(a))$ with the Skolem term $sk(a)$ is added to the model. This is achieved by the third alternative in rule (3), which, together with the rule $q(x,y) \leftarrow def_q(x,y)$ in $\tau(\phi)$, derives $q(a,sk(a))$. In this case, rule (8) makes sure that no other filler will or has been inserted that is equal to $sk(a)$. The test for (non-)equality is necessary, because later, $sk(a)$ could be equated to some other term. For instance, if $q(a,b)$ is also present and $sk(a) \approx b$ is not present, this model candidate will be rejected and the alternative $check\_sat_q(a)$ will be chosen.

The formula $\exists y\, q(a,y)$ will thus be satisfied in one way or the other, with a preference to a filler different from the Skolem term[5].

Model Checking Option. Sometimes, it is useful to regard existential formulae as integrity constraints for a KB – for instance, to check if the objects mentioned in a given database suffice to extend it to a model for a given KB. Instead of creating fillers by means of Skolem terms, the model construction process must check that fillers are already present. This can be achieved by translating Φ according to the "recycling option", where (3) is replaced by the following scheme:

$$def_{\Delta'}(x) \vee check\_sat_{\psi'}(x) \leftarrow B_1(x),\ldots,B_m(x) \tag{10}$$

This transformation ensures that no Skolem terms can be inserted by the model computation. The only way to satisfy the existentially quantified part then is by proving that it is already satisfied.

---

[5] Assuming that the model generation system processes the alternatives in the order given by (3)

Loop Check Option. The introduction of Skolem terms leads easily to nontermination of model-generation systems. Instead of creating new Skolem terms, we propose to "re-use" existing Skolem terms, if they qualify as role fillers – similarly to the blocking techniques found in description logic systems (although more general). This can be achieved by translating Φ according to the "recycling option", where the rule (3) is replaced by the following rules:

$$def_{\Delta'}(x) \vee \text{check\_sat}_{\psi'}(x) \vee choose\_default\_filler_{\Phi}(x) \vee$$
$$def_{\psi'}(x, sk_{\Phi}(x)) \leftarrow B_1(x), \dots, B_m(x) \tag{11}$$

$$other\_filler_{\Phi}(x, sk_{\Phi}(y)) \vee def_{\psi'}(x, sk_{\Phi}(y)) \leftarrow$$
$$choose\_default\_filler_{\Phi}(x), sat_{\psi'}(x_1, sk_{\Phi}(y)) \tag{12}$$

$$\text{false} \leftarrow def_{\psi'}(x,y), other\_filler_{\Phi}(x,z) \tag{13}$$

$$\text{false} \leftarrow def_{\psi'}(x,y), def_{\psi'}(x,z), \text{not equal}_{|y|}(y,z) \tag{14}$$

$$\text{false} \leftarrow choose\_default\_filler_{\Phi}(x), \text{not } some\_default\_filler_{\Phi}(x) \tag{15}$$

$$some\_default\_filler_{\Phi}(x) \leftarrow def_{\psi'}(x,y) \tag{16}$$

Compared to rule (3), rule (11) contains again an additional head literal, which is *choose_default_filler*$_{\Phi}(x)$. Together with rule (12) this has the effect of nondeterministically selecting a default filler among all Skolem terms previously introduced to satisfy the existential quantification of (another instance of) the formula. The nondeterministic selection process is realized by the *other_filler*$_{\Phi}$-alternative in the head, which allows to choose a default filler – or not. The remaining rules achieve that exactly one default filler will be generated.

For illustration, consider the following example from the Tambis Ontology [SPB+04]:

$$\forall x \, (\text{chapter}(x) \rightarrow \exists y \, (\text{in\_book}(x,y) \wedge \text{book}(y))) \tag{17}$$

$$\forall x \, (\text{book}(x) \rightarrow \exists y \, (\text{has\_chapter}(x,y) \wedge \text{chapter}(y))) \tag{18}$$

$$\forall x \, \neg(\text{book}(x) \wedge \text{chapter}(x)) \tag{19}$$

Notice the terminological cycle. To get the model computation started, suppose an additional fact chapter(a). Leaving away many uninteresting facts, the model generation process will first satisfy (17) by deriving

$$\text{book}(f_1(a)) \tag{20}$$

$$\text{in\_book}(a, f_1(a)) \ . \tag{21}$$

Next, it will satisfy (18) by deriving

$$\text{chapter}(f_2(f_1(a))) \tag{22}$$

$$\text{has\_chapter}(f_1(a), f_2(f_1(a))) \ . \tag{23}$$

Now, (17) requires the existence of a book for the newly created chapter $f_2(f_1(a))$. Instead of creating a new Skolem term, rule (12) will find that $f_1(a)$ can be used as a default filler. Thus, the model generation process terminates by deriving

$$\text{in\_book}(f_2(f_1(a)), f_1(a)) \ . \tag{24}$$

In summary, the natural infinite model will be avoided by the loop check option. Thus, the loop check option can allow for a finite model in cases where a naive translation to clauses may only have an infinite model.

3.2   The Loop Check Option in Practice

Up to now, the loop check option has been introduced in a purely declarative way. More considerations are necessary to make it effective in practice. First of all, the loop check is not designed to prove the *unsatisfiability* of a set of formulae. Unsatisfiability can be proven more easily without the loop check option, because the search space is much smaller without the additional rules. Instead, the loop check aims at the more difficult problem of proving the *satisfiability* of a set of formulae.

If the loop check-transformation of a set of formulae has a finite model, then the original set of formulae also has a finite model. Unfortunately, model generation systems may have difficulties in finding this finite model, even if it exists.

The issue is to realize a *fair* search for a model. This is not trivial, as, in general, the Herband universe of the programs obtained by the translation is infinite. For instance, the search strategy of KRHyper is fair in the sense that it guarantees *refutational* completeness (in particular when the Herbrand universe is infinite). In contrast, even for very simple satisfiable programs obtained with the loop check option of Section 3.1, KRHyper will not terminate – the search strategy is just not fair for (finite) model building. The iterative deepening scheme KRHyper uses may lead into an infinite branch in the search tree and may thereby miss an alternative branch leading to a model. Other systems, like smodels, require full grounding-out of their input clause set, which is obviously, in general, not possible in presence of function symbols.

A solution to these problems is to generate (finite) interpretations as candidates, check them explicitly for being a model of the program and stop this search as soon as a model has been found. A systematic way to do so is to run the systems with a bound on the resources allowed, checking if a model has been found and increasing these resources in a fair way on failure (iterative deepening). For KRHyper, for instance, this can be achieved by running it with a limit on the term depth on the generated terms. Regarding smodels, one could work with growing approximations of the infinite set of all ground instances.

For the check for modelship the following rules are added to the loop check translation of a formula Φ:

$$unsatisfied_\Phi(x) \leftarrow B_1(x), \ldots, B_m(x), \text{not } sat1_{\Psi'}(x) \tag{25}$$

$$unsatisfied\_some \leftarrow unsatisfied_\Phi(x) \tag{26}$$

Last, one adds the rule

$$satisfiable \leftarrow \text{not } unsatisfied\_some . \tag{27}$$

Now, the idea is to conclude if a model contains the atom satisfiable then the set of formula is indeed satisfiable (in a finite model) and no further deepening is necessary.

However, this conclusion is not true if the given formula, and hence the obtained translated program, contains function symbols other than Skolem functions and constants. The test not $sat1_{\psi'}(x)$ in the body of the first clause is too weak then.

In practice, the situation is perhaps not as bad as it might seem. Many interesting ontologies can be formulated without function symbols at all (as is witnessed already by the existence of numerous interesting DL ontologies, which do not contain function symbols). We conjecture that our transformation will find a finite model whenever one exists, provided function symbols as mentioned are not present. For future work we intend to improve the transformation to cope better with function symbols.

4   Equality

Ontologies typically make use of equality. For example, equality is used in function definitions or in *integrity constraints* to state that certain objects are different. Another common use of equality is to state that two objects must be equal under certain circumstances. For example, the "age" of twins must be "equal".

At this point of the paper, we may assume that the ontology has been converted to a DLP. As a running example, consider the following DLP, which contains one equation:[6]

$$p(c, h()) \leftarrow \tag{28}$$
$$x \approx f(g(d)) \leftarrow p(x, h()) \tag{29}$$

The model of this DLP will contain the fact $p(c, h())$. Rule (29) will derive $c \approx f(g(d))$. However, equational consequences like $f(g(d)) \approx c$ (by symmetry of $\approx$) are not derived. Hence, the $\approx$-predicate requires special treatment. The most advanced techniques to *efficiently* treat equality have been developed in the field of *automated theorem proving* for refutational theorem provers (see [BG98]). Unfortunately, none of these techniques has been implemented in the model computation systems we target at.

One generic option to treat equality is by means of adding the equality axioms. However, the search space induced by the resulting clause set is prohibitively high and achieving termination is practically impossible. The most problematic axioms in this regard are substitution axioms, like $f(x) \approx f(y) \leftarrow x \approx y$. As soon as the model contains one equation, say $a \approx b$, and one unary function symbol f, the substitution axioms generate infinitely many facts of the form $f(f(f(a))) \approx f(f(f(b)))$. An alternative option is to "compile away" equality. The probably most well-known method in this direction is the "modification method" in [Bra75], which was later improved in [BGV97]. We follow this direction and propose an *equality transformation for DLPs*.

We say that a rule is *flat* if (1) the only proper subterms of terms in equations are either variables or constants, and (2) all arguments to predicate symbols are either variables or constants. Every rule can be turned into a flat one by recursively replacing an offending subterm t by a fresh variable x and adding the equation $t \approx x$ to the rule body(see again [BGV97]). For example, a flat version of the above DLP is

---

[6] Remember that we distinguish constants (like c, subject to the UNA) and nullary functions (like h(), not subject to the UNA).

$$p(c, v_1) \leftarrow v_1 \approx h()$$
$$x \approx f(v_1) \leftarrow p(x, v_2), v_2 \approx h(), v_1 \approx g(d) .$$

The purpose of flattening is to achieve the effect of the substitution axioms. To axiomatize the Unique Name Assumption (wrt. constants), one adds the rules false $\leftarrow c \approx d$, for each pair c, d of different constants. Next, $\approx$ has to be confined to an equivalence relation by means of the rules[7]

$$x \approx x \leftarrow$$
$$x \approx y \leftarrow y \approx x$$
$$x \approx z \leftarrow x \approx y, y \approx z .$$

The addition of these axioms completes the equality transformation.

For the simple example above, any reasonable bottom-up model computation system will terminate on its equality transformation and report as the result $\{c \approx f(g(d)), f(g(d)) \approx c, p(c, h()), x \approx x\}$, which describes the expected model of the original program. Note that any such system would not have terminated on the original program when equipped with the equality axioms. Our transformation is correct, i.e., the transformed clause set is satisfiable if and only if the given one is satisfiable wrt. interpretations where $\approx$ is interpreted as the equality relation. See the long version of this paper for a proof (http://rsise.anu.edu.au/~baumgart/publications/).

5 Preliminary Experiments

We applied our transformation to the core of the Suggested Upper Merged Ontology SUMO [NP01]. SUMO contains *meta-predicates*, i.e. predicates that define the properties of other predicates. We translated these predicates appropriately to first-order logic. For example, we translated the (higher-order) sentence disjoint_classes(Man, Woman) to the rule

$$\text{false} \leftarrow \text{instance}(x, \text{Man}), \text{instance}(x, \text{Woman}) . \tag{30}$$

SUMO occasionally uses other higher order formulae, which we had to filter out. The resulting first-order KB contains about 1800 formulae.

Running KRHyper on the DLP transformation revealed numerous inconsistencies in SUMO. These included misspelled and hence unbound variables as well as semantic inconsistencies in connection with the Mid-level-ontology extensions. For example, one can derive that planetEarth is a geographicArea. Since each geographicArea is a geographicSubregion of planetEarth, it follows that planetEarth is a geographicSubregion of itself. This contradicts the irreflexivity of geographicSubregion. We reported the errors to the developers of SUMO and removed them. Then, KRHyper can calculate a model for our DLP translation within a few seconds. The model consists of roughly 2000 facts.

---

[7] Strictly speaking, the reflexivity rule $x \approx x \leftarrow$ is not domain-restricted. But this case is harmless and usually poses no problems.

To test the equality transformation, we added the following facts to SUMO: France lies west of Germany and Germany's biggest trading partner lies east of Germany.

    orientation(germany, france, west)

    orientation(germany, biggestTradingPartner(germany), east) .

By help of the axioms in SUMO, KRHyper deduces (among others) the following facts:

    orientation(france, germany, east)

    orientation(biggestTradingPartner(germany), germany, west)

    between(germany, france, biggestTradingPartner(germany))

Now, we add the fact biggestTradingPartner(germany) $\approx$ france. As a result, KRHyper derives a contradiction, as expected, because France cannot lie both east and west of Germany. To test our default value transformation, we added the following facts to SUMO:

    instance(p, judicialProcess)

    agent(p, a)

In SUMO, each judicial process is a political process. Furthermore, each political process requires an agent. Hence the model generation produces the fact agent(p, f(p)). However, if the recycling option is chosen, a qualifies as a default filler for the agent role. Consequently, the above fact is *not* derived with the recycling option.

SUMO contains numerous axioms that lead to infinite models. Unfortunately, in many cases they cannot be detected (finitely) by the current version of our loop check option. In these cases, the prover does not terminate.

6   Conclusions

We presented a transformation from first-order logic formulae to disjunctive logic programs. The programs resulting from the transformation can be fed into many existing logic programming model generation systems. As special features, our transformation allows the efficient treatment of equality, and it includes a certain form of the unique name assumption. Using Description Logic terminology, it allows a flexible handling of existentially quantified roles, including the avoidance of unnecessary Skolem terms, or the re-use of existing Skolem terms. By re-using existing Skolem terms, our transformation allows to generate finite models in certain cases, so that termination of the theorem prover can be achieved more often. (Of course, the general problem is undecidable, which puts natural limits on what can be achieved.)

Our main results are of a theoretical nature, namely soundness and completeness results. We carried out preliminary experiments with the SUMO ontology. Unfortunately our transformation did not prove strong enough to compute a finite model for the whole SUMO. The equality treatment and the flexible handling of existential roles, however, proved already applicable and useful, e.g. to subsets of SUMO. For future work, we intend to strengthen the transformation, so that finite models can be detected more often.

Acknowledgements. We wish to thank the reviewers for their helpful suggestions.

References

[Bar03]   C. Baral. *Knowledge representation, reasoning and declarative problem solving.* Cambridge University Press, 2003.

[BB04]   P. Baumgartner and A. Burchardt. Logic Programming Infrastructure for Inferences on FrameNet. In J. Alferes and J. Leite, eds., *JELIA'04*, LNAI 3229, Springer, 2004.

[BCM+02]   F. Baader, D. Calvanese, D.L. McGuinness, D. Nardi, and P.F. Patel-Schneider, eds. *Description Logic Handbook.* Cambridge University Press, 2002.

[BG98]   L. Bachmair and H. Ganzinger. Chapter 11: Equational Reasoning in Saturation-Based Theorem Proving. In W. Bibel and P. H. Schmitt, eds., *Automated Deduction. A Basis for Applications*, Volume I. Kluwer, 1998.

[BGV97]   L. Bachmair, H. Ganzinger, and A. Voronkov. Elimination of Equality via Transformation with Ordering Constraints. In Proc. CADE 15, LNAI 1421, Springer 1998.

[Bra75]   D. Brand. Proving theorems with the modification method. *SIAM Journal on Computing*, 4:412–430, 1975.

[CEF+97]   S. Citrigno, Th. Eiter, W. Faber, G. Gottlob, Chr. Koch, N. Leone, C. Mateis, G. Pfeifer, and F. Scarcello. The dlv system: Model generator and advanced frontends (system description). In *Workshop Logische Programmierung*, 1997.

[FL93]   C. Fermüller and A. Leitsch. Model Building by Resolution. In *Computer Science Logic: CSL'92, LNCS 702*, Springer, 1993.

[GHS02]   L. Georgieva, U. Hustadt, and R. A. Schmidt. A new Clausal Class Decidable by Hyperresolution. In *CADE-18, LNAI* 2392. Springer, 2002.

[GHS03]   L. Georgieva, U. Hustadt, and R. A. Schmidt. Hyperresolution for Guarded Formulae. *J. Symbolic Computat.*, 36(1–2):163–192, 2003.

[GHVD03]   B. N. Grosof, I. Horrocks, R. Volz, and S. Decker. Description Logic Programs: Combining Logic Programs with Description Logic. In *WWW 2003*, ACM, 2003.

[HB+04]   I. Horrocks, H. Boley, and M. Dean. SWRL: A Semantic Web Rule Language Combining OWL and RulMl. http://www.w3.org/Submission/SWRL/, May 2004.

[KIF]   Kif - knowledge interchange format. http://www.csee.umbc.edu/kse/kif/.

[Llo87]   J. Lloyd. *Foundations of Logic Programming.* Springer, 1987.

[Nie99]   I. Niemelä. Logic Programs with Stable Model Semantics as a Constraint Programming Paradigm. *Annals of Mathematics and AI*, 25(3-4):241–273, 1999.

[NP01]   I. Niles and A. Pease. Towards a standard upper ontology. In C. Welty and B. Smith, eds., *In Proceedings of the 2nd International Conference on Formal Ontology in Information Systems (FOIS-2001)*, 2001.

[NS96]   I. Niemelä and P. Simons. Efficient Implementation of the Well-Founded and Stable Model Semantics. In *Proceedings of JICSLP*, The MIT Press, 1996.

[RV01]   A. Riazonov and A. Voronkov. Vampire 1.1 (system description). In *Proc. IJCAR*, LNCS 2083. Springer, 2001.

[SPB+04]   R. D. Stevens, N. W. Paton, S. K. Bechhofer, G. K. Ng, M. Peim, P. G. Baker, C. A. Goble, and A. M. Brass. Tambis: Transparent Access to Multiple Bioinformatics Services. *Genetics, Genomics, Proteomics, and Bioinformatics*, January 2004.

[Wer03]   Christoph Wernhard. System Description: KRHyper. Fachberichte Informatik 14–2003, Universität Koblenz-Landau, Universität Koblenz-Landau, Institut für Informatik, Rheinau 1, D-56075 Koblenz, 2003.

Combining Safe Rules and Ontologies
by Interfacing of Reasoners

Uwe Aßmann[1], Jakob Henriksson[1], and Jan Małuszyński[2]

[1] Technical University of Dresden, Fakultät Informatik, D-01062 Dresden, Germany
uwe.assmann@tu-dresden.de,
jakob.henriksson@tu-dresden.de
[2] Linköping University, Department of Computer and Information Science, 581 83
Linköping, Sweden
janma@ida.liu.se

Abstract. The paper presents a framework for hybrid combination of
rule languages with constraint languages including but not restricted to
Description-Logic-based ontology languages. It shows how reasoning in
a combined language can be done by interfacing reasoners of the component languages. A prototype system based on the presented principle
integrates Datalog with OWL by interfacing XSB Prolog [2] with a DIG-
compliant [1] DL reasoner (e.g. Racer [17]).

1 Introduction

This paper addresses the issue of building the rule level on top of the ontology
level of the Semantic Web tower [7]. As argued, e.g. in [26], applications need
rules, which cannot be expressed in DL languages, such as OWL-DL. On the
other hand, the rule languages should make it possible to integrate the structural knowledge provided by ontologies. There have already been several proposals in that direction, defining different specific languages integrating rules and
ontologies (see e.g. [18,14,11,15,3,21,22,24,25]). The diversity of the languages
seems to be unavoidable since different kind of applications will call for different
languages integrating rules and ontologies. In contrast to the proposals mentioned above, our main objective is not to define a specific language integrating
rules and ontologies, but a generic scheme for *hybrid* integration. A reasoner of
an integrated language is then obtained by applying the scheme by interfacing
existing reasoners of the component languages.

The idea of *hybrid* reasoning appeared already in [12], and was adopted, among
others, in the well-known $\mathcal{AL}$-log work [10] on integrating Datalog and DL. It is
also present in the CARIN work [23], even if this aspect is not explicitly stressed
therein. In the context of the Semantic Web it is used in [11] for combining
answer set reasoning with DL reasoning, and in [25] where theoretical issues of
integration of disjunctive Datalog with OWL-DL are discussed.

This paper addresses the problem of hybrid integration of rules and ontologies
in a more general framework of integrating rules with constraints expressed in
a language of an external theory. The proposed framework applies to a class of

J.J. Alfieres et al. (Eds.): PPSWR 2006, LNCS 4187, pp. 33–47, 2006.
© Springer-Verlag Berlin Heidelberg 2006

rule languages with fixpoint semantics. We define a generic scheme for extending such rule languages by adding constraints in rule bodies. A fixpoint semantics of an extended language obtained in this way is formally defined by referring to the semantics of the components. The paper shows how to reason in the extended language by interfacing of existing reasoners of the components instead of fully integrating them into a new dedicated system. We illustrate the scheme by a reasoner for the integration of Datalog with OWL obtained by interfacing XSB Prolog [2] with any DIG [1] compliant DL reasoner (e.g. Racer [17]).

Another instance of the scheme, mentioned but not developed in this paper, is an integration of the rule-based XML query and transformation language Xcerpt [8] with OWL, which make possible semantic filtering of the XML documents obtained by Xcerpt queries.

When the rule language considered is Datalog and the constraint theory is expressed in a DL, our framework provides integrated languages that coincide with previous approaches (see Section 5 for more discussion). The main contributions of this paper is however a more general framework for integrating rule languages, not restricted to logical languages, with constraint theories (not necessarily a DL theory). The paper shows how the queries to an integrated KB can be answered by re-using existing reasoners of the component languages, specifically illustrated by a prototype system integrating Datalog with OWL using XSB Prolog [2] and a DL reasoner.

2   Preliminaries

The question addressed in this paper is how to combine a rule language with an ontology language so that reasoning in the integrated language can be done by interfacing reasoners of the component languages. This section formulates general requirements for the component languages and refers to the languages satisfying them.

2.1   Rules

We consider rules of the form

$$H \leftarrow B_1, \ldots, B_n$$

where, $n \geq 0$ and $H, B_1, \ldots, B_n$ are some primitive/atomic syntactic constructs (*atoms*) over a certain alphabet, including variables. As usual, we will call H the *head* of the rule and $B_1, \ldots, B_n$ its *body*. Instances of a rule are created by *substitutions*, which map variables of the rule to terms. A rule with empty body (i.e. with $n = 0$) is sometimes called a *fact*. A rule will be called *safe* if all variables of the head appear in the body; thus safe facts are ground (i.e. variable-free). In this paper we only consider safe rules. To define the syntax of a specific rule language we thus have to define the syntax of the primitive rule constructs and the syntax of the terms. By a *rule program* we mean a finite set of rules.

The rules we consider can be used to derive new atoms from given ground atoms. For this a matching relation has to be defined between (possibly nonground) body atoms and ground atoms. As a result of successful matching of body atoms and some given ground atoms the variables of the body atoms become bound to ground terms. Due to the safeness assumption the resulting binding(s) applied to the head determines its ground instance(s) derived from the ground atoms matched by the body atoms. For every specific rule language a formally defined concept of matching makes it possible to associate an operator T_P on sets of ground atoms with every rule program P:

$$T_P(S) = \{H\theta \mid (H \leftarrow B_1, \ldots, B_n) \in P \text{ and}$$
$$(B_1, \ldots, B_n) \text{ matches some } A_1, \ldots, A_n \text{ in } S \text{ with result } \theta\}$$

The operator is monotone, since the atoms which match a given pattern in a set S will also match it in any superset S' of S. Thus $T_P(S) \subseteq T_P(S')$ for any $S \subseteq S'$. The semantics of P can now be defined as the least fixpoint of T_P. We will call it the *standard model*[1] of P. Intuitively, the operator T_P reflects the mechanism for deriving ground atoms with rules of P.

Examples of rule languages in the discussed category are:

- Datalog (without negation), which is a decidable subset of FOL. The terms of Datalog are variables and constants. The atoms are built in a usual way from predicate symbols and terms. The semantics is based on syntactic matching (syntactic unification with ground terms). It is well-known that for a Datalog program P the least fixpoint of T_P is the least Herbrand model of P, which is the set of all ground atomic logical consequences of the rules of P considered as the formulae of FOL.
- A negation-free subset of the XML query and transformation language Xcerpt[2] [8]. Ground atoms of Xcerpt are called *data terms* and can be seen as abstraction of XML documents. A data term is either a constant or it is of the form $p[t_1, \ldots, t_n]$ or of the form $p\{t_1, \ldots, t_n\}$, $n \geq 0$ where p is a *label* and $t_1, \ldots, t_n$ are data terms. Intuitively, Xcerpt labels model XML tags. Thus, in contrast to predicate letters they do not have fixed arity and the number n of direct sub-terms t_i of a data term with label p may vary. The direct sub-terms of a data term may be ordered (which is indicated by square brackets) or unordered (which is indicated by braces). Body atoms of Xcerpt rules are called *query terms*. They are patterns matched against data terms and usually include variables, for which bindings to data terms are produced by successful matchings. The heads of Xcerpt rules are data terms with variables. The rule produces data terms by applying the bindings, obtained by matching of its body, to the head. The concept of matching is quite elaborate. A data term matched against a query term may produce more than one binding. There is no logical counterpart of the fixpoint semantics.

---

[1] This terminology is justified by the fact that in the special case of Datalog, the least fixpoint of T_P is indeed a model in the sense of logic.

[2] The following presentation is oversimplified, neglecting many details. The objective is to give a minimal information needed to discuss integration of Xcerpt with OWL.

A common task to be solved by a rule reasoner is querying of the standard model of a given rule program. An atomic query is an atom A with variables. The answer is any substitution θ such that $A\theta$ is an element of the model.

As Datalog is a subset of Prolog, queries may be answered by Prolog systems based on SLD-resolution. The work presented in this paper uses XSB Prolog. Reasoning in the Xcerpt prototype[3], which is implemented in Haskell, is based on backward chaining and uses a special kind of unification.

2.2   Ontologies

In this paper, we consider ontologies formalized in Description Logics (DLs) [6], which are decidable subsets of first-order logic (FOL). The syntax of a DL is built over the distinct alphabets of *class names* $\mathcal{C}$ (also known as *concepts*), *property names* $\mathcal{R}$ (also known as *roles*) and individual names $\mathcal{O}$. Depending on the kind of DL, different constructors are provided to build class expressions (or briefly *classes*) and property expressions (or briefly *properties*). Intuitively, classes are used to represent sets of individuals of a domain and property expressions are used to represent binary relations over individuals. The names of the individuals are used to represent them and can be seen as logical constants. In Description Logics, it is often assumed that different names represent different individuals of the domain (*unique name* assumption).

By an *ontology* we mean a finite set of DL axioms of the form: $A \equiv C$ (*concept definition*), $C \sqsubseteq D$ (*concept inclusion*), $R \equiv S$ (*role definition*), $R \sqsubseteq S$ (*role inclusion*), $C(a)$ (*concept assertion*) and $R(a, b)$ (*role assertion*), where A is an atomic concept, C, D arbitrary concepts, R, S roles and a, b individuals. The axioms are thus of two different kinds and can accordingly be divided into two parts:

- a *T-Box* (terminology) consisting of concept (resp. role) definitions and inclusions;
- an *A-Box* (assertions) describing concept (resp. role) assertions relating to individuals.

Class expressions, property expressions and assertions can be seen as an alternative representation of FOL formulae. For example, class expression C where C is a class name corresponds to the FOL formula $C(x)$, and property expression R where R is a property name corresponds to the FOL formula $R(x, y)$, where x and y are free variables. Similarly, expressions built with constructors can also be seen as FOL formulae. The inclusion axioms are equivalent to the universally quantified implications, e.g. $R \sqsubseteq S$, where R and S are property names corresponds to the formula $\forall x, y R(x, y) \rightarrow S(x, y)$. The assertions correspond to atomic formulae. Thus, the semantics of DLs is defined by referring to the usual notions of interpretation and model.

Due to the restricted syntax, Description Logics are decidable and are supported by dedicated reasoners.

---

[3] http://www.xcerpt.org

Given an ontology Σ the reasoner is used to answer *queries*. The query languages supported by different reasoners may vary. For the work presented in this paper we are mostly interested in reasoning related to the A-Box of the underlying DL KB. Traditionally DL reasoners provide limited forms of querying on the A-Box, the most important service being the *instance check*, checking whether an individual is a member of some class. In our work we will need DL queries obtained by disjunction and/or by conjunction of *basic conjunctive queries* defined as follows:

Definition 1. *A basic conjunctive query is the existential closure of a formula of the form $C(t)$ and $R(t_1, t_2)$ where C is a concept, R is a role and t, t_1, t_2 are constants or variables, or the existential closure of the conjunction of such formulae.*

These are boolean queries: a query Q is to check if Q is a logical consequence of Σ. Only a few existing reasoners (see Section 4.1) answer conjunctive queries with additional syntactic restrictions. Disjunctive queries are usually not allowed.

There have been several proposals for ontology specification languages. A recent W3C standard OWL comes in three versions, where OWL-DL is based on a highly expressive Description Logic and is supported by several reasoners.

3   Hybrid Integration of Safe Rules and External Theories

This section presents our framework for hybrid combination of rules and ontologies. Existing proposals are often restricted to rules with logical semantics. This makes it possible to provide logical semantics of the combined language and to prove that the proposed reasoning algorithm is sound and complete. The rule languages considered in this paper are assumed to have a fixpoint semantics. This does not exclude the cases of logical rule languages, like Datalog, but opens for languages for which a logical semantics may not be defined. Even for such rules there may be a practical motivation to integrate them with ontologies. For example consider an XML database including culinary recipes. Each recipe lists ingredients using terminology of a food ontology. The ontology defines classes of products, e.g. a class of gluten-free products. We may use Xcerpt rules to query the database for recipes, but to filter-out dishes containing gluten we have to extend Xcerpt with ontology queries. This section outlines a systematic way for defining such extensions.

Let R be a rule program in a rule language and let Σ be a set of axioms in a first-order language L, to be called an *external theory*. In this paper we focus on external theories given by DL axioms encoded in OWL, but the discussion in this section is not restricted to this case. We assume that the languages share constants and variables while the predicate letters of the external theory are not in the alphabet of the rule language.

We define the language of extended rules by allowing formulae of L to be (optionally) added in the bodies of the rules of R. If a formula of L added to the body of a rule has free variables, they must also appear in the original rule. Thus an extended rule p has the form

$$H \leftarrow B_1, \ldots, B_m, C$$

where $H \leftarrow B_1, \ldots, B_m$ is a rule in R (called the *core rule* of p and denoted $p \downarrow$) and C, if present, is a formula of L called the *constraint*, whose free variables do not appear in the core.

A finite set P of extended rules will be called an *extended rule program*. By $P \downarrow$ we denote the set $\{p \downarrow | p \in P\}$. An extended rule p is said to be *safe* iff $p \downarrow$ is safe. We only consider safe rules. We assume that C is (implicitly) existentially quantified on all its free variables that do not appear in the core of the rule. Such a variable will be called *internal*. Notice, that due to the safety condition every free variable of a constraint that appears in the head must also appear in the body of the core rule.

Intuitively the constraints restrict the standard model of $P \downarrow$ by referring to the external theory Σ. Formally, we will consider *constrained* atoms of the form $A; C$ where A is a ground atom in R and C is a formula in L without free variables. A ground atom A is considered to be a constrained atom of the form $A; true$. By the *core atom* of a constrained atom $A; C$ to be denoted $(A; C) \downarrow$ we mean the atom A. The notation is extended to sets of constrained atoms: $S \downarrow = \{A \mid (A; C) \in S\}$.

We will first extend the definition of T_P to sets of constrained atoms:

$$T_P(S) = \{H\theta; (C\theta \wedge C_1 \wedge \ldots \wedge C_n) \mid (H \leftarrow B_1, \ldots, B_n, C) \in P \text{ and}$$
$$\text{for some } A_1; C_1, \ldots, A_n; C_n \text{ in } S$$
$$(B_1, \ldots, B_n) \text{ matches } A_1, \ldots, A_n \text{ with result } \theta\}$$

It follows by this definition that $lfp(T_{P\downarrow}) = \{A \mid (A; C) \in lfp(T_P)\}$ since the extended operator does not use constraints for derivation of core atoms, but simply takes the conjunction of constraints as the associated constraints of the derived core atom. Thus the extended operator derives the same core atoms as the $T_{P\downarrow}$ operator but associates them with constraints. The semantics of the extended rule program P can now be defined as a subset of the standard model of $P \downarrow$ by referring to the associated constraints of the core atoms. Denote by C_A the disjunction of all constraints C such that the constrained atom $A; C$ is in the least fixpoint of T_P.

Definition 2. The *standard model of an extended rule program P over an external theory Σ* is defined as the set

$$\mathcal{M}(P) = \{A \mid A \in lfp(T_{P\downarrow}) \text{ and } \Sigma \models C_A\}$$

Thus we restrict the standard model of $P \downarrow$ to those elements A for which the disjunction of all constraints associated with A by T_P is true in all models of the external theory Σ. In this way the semantics of the extended language is defined as a combination of the fixpoint semantics of the rule language with the logical semantics of the external theory. This applies to any particular rule language in the considered class and to any particular external theory. Obviously the membership problem for $\mathcal{M}(P)$ may be undecidable.

Consider the special case when the rule language component is Datalog (without negation). In this case extended rules are formulae of FOL. It can be proved that the standard model of an extended rule program P over Σ consists of atomic formulae that are logical consequences of the knowledge base $P \cup \Sigma$.

The least fixpoint of T_P can be computed by iterating T_P starting from the empty set. Due to the safety condition the core of any constrained atom produced by an iteration of T_P is ground and in the associated constraint all free variables are instantiated to some constants that appear in the program. Thus there is only a finite number of different constraint atoms that can be produced. An atom A is in $\mathcal{M}(P)$ iff it appears as a core of some constraint atoms in the least fixpoint of T_P and if the disjunctive constraint C_A is a logical consequence of the axioms of the external theory. Thus, if the theory is decidable so is the membership problem for the standard model of any extended rule program over this theory. This applies in particular to combinations of Datalog with Description Logics, such as CARIN [23], restricted to safe extended rules. Note that our notion of a safe extended rule is different from the notion of a *role-safe* rule introduced in CARIN. Role-safe rules were introduced as a sufficient condition for decidability of the problem of whether or not a ground atom is a logical consequence of a given CARIN knowledge base.

In practice we want to query extended programs, e.g. by checking if a given ground atom A is in the standard model of P over Σ. This can be done by (1) constructing derivations of A and collecting the disjunction of the associated constructs (constructing C_A) (2) checking if C_A is a logical consequence of Σ. The reasoner of the rule language is able to query $P \downarrow$ with A. This is usually done by backward or forward rule chaining. However, it is not clear how to re-use the reasoner for P so that all associated constraints of A can be constructed. Problem (2) limits the approach to theories supported by sufficiently powerful reasoners.

In the rest of this paper we show how the above mentioned problems can be solved for the special case of integrating Datalog with OWL, by interfacing XSB Prolog with a DL reasoner.

As discussed above, the query answering problem for an extended rule language may be undecidable. Even though the outlined approach may be used for answering (some) queries. Well known examples of extended rule languages are:

- $\mathcal{AL}$-log [10] where the external axioms are in the language of the Description Logic $\mathcal{ALC}$ and Datalog rules are extended with constraints of the form $C(x)$ where C is a concept and x is a variable or a constant. Query answering in $\mathcal{AL}$-log is decidable. For every query the number of associated constraints is finite. The algorithm discussed in [10] uses SLD-resolution to construct them and a DL reasoner for checking validity of their disjunction wrt to a given theory.
- CARIN-$\mathcal{ALCNR}$ where the external axioms are in the language of the Description Logic $\mathcal{ALCNR}$ and Datalog rules are extended with constraints of the form $C(x)$ or $R(x, y)$ where C is a concept expression, R is a role expression and x, y are variables or constants. It should be noticed that CARIN rules may not be safe in our sense. It is only required that the variables of

the head appear in the body, but their occurrence in non-constraint atoms is not assumed. Query answering in recursive CARIN is undecidable.

4   Interfacing Existing Systems

This section describes applications of the proposed approach to interface existing systems. In Section 4.1 we survey existing DL reasoners and specifically the query languages they support. In Section 4.2 we describe a prototype system which interfaces XSB Prolog with a DL reasoner.

4.1   Ontology Reasoners

In the rest of this paper, the only kind of constraints that we consider to appear in rules, are ontological. When we want to re-use existing reasoning engines for solving these constraints it is important to know what kind of constraints can be handled by these systems. Here we provide a short overview of existing reasoners and query interfaces to reasoners.

DQL Server. This is an implementation of DQL[4] OWL documents. By using a rolling-up technique (see e.g. [19]) DQL Server is able to answer conjunctive queries by transforming the query into one which can be answered by any existing DIG [1] compliant reasoner. The query language supports both distinguished and non-distinguished variables, i.e. variables that must be bound to known individuals and variables that does not, respectively. Both concepts and roles are allowed to appear in the query, but only acyclic queries are allowed.

KAON2. KAON2[5] implements a reasoner directly in Java based on transforming a DL KB into a disjunctive Datalog program. KAON2 supports conjunctive queries. However, it does not fully support non-distinguished variables, i.e. all variables must be bound to known individuals in the KB.

Pellet OWL Reasoner. Pellet[6] implements a traditional tableaux based reasoning algorithm in Java. It supports conjunctive queries by using a rolling-up technique [19]. The queries uses an SQL style syntax.

DL-Lite. DL-Lite [9] was designed with data complexity in mind and the possibility to deal with a large number of individuals while still being efficient. The conceptual language supported in DL-Lite is limited but still serves as a basic ontology language. The main reasoning service provided is that of the conjunctive query supporting both distinguished and non-distinguished variables.

Racer and nRQL. The query language nRQL [16] for Racer [17] supports conjunctive queries but require that all variables be bound to known individuals in the KB.

Systems supporting conjunctive queries are thus available with some limitations on what kind of variables are used (distinguished or non-distinguished) and

---

[4] http://www.daml.org/dql/
[5] http://kaon2.semanticweb.org/
[6] http://www.mindswap.org/2003/pellet/index.shtml

how they may appear in the query. However, the constraints that we are required to solve, according to the description in Section 3, are disjunctive and may include non-distinguished variables. The existence of non-distinguished variables is due to our safety restriction. Thus, none of the above query languages are sufficient for our purposes. Instead, we implement support for disjunctive queries (limited to concepts) which makes use of existing DL reasoners that are able to check satisfiability of the underlying KB (see Section 4.2).

4.2 Combining Datalog with OWL Using XSB Prolog and a DL Reasoner

As mentioned in Section 3 we need a way to collect the constraints associated with a query A in order to interface a rule reasoner and a solver for the external theory. This collecting of constraints must be specific for every existing rule reasoner that is to be re-used in this hybrid context. In this section we show how this can be achieved using a standard Prolog system (XSB Prolog) and also how we verify if the disjunction of the collected constraints is indeed a logical consequence of the associated theory. The external theory in this setting is a set of DL axioms represented as an OWL ontology.

We make use of the list-construct available in XSB Prolog to collect the constraints, i.e. atoms that are not to be solved by the rule reasoner. An extended rule program P is transformed into a corresponding program P' in the following manner. Every predicate is extended with a new parameter to represent the constraint associated with that atom. A rule fact has an empty body and is therefore associated with an empty list of constraints. E.g. a fact $p(a, b)$ is transformed into $p(a, b, [])$. The constraint atoms appearing in the body of a rule are moved into an additional head parameter and constructed as a list. E.g. the rule $p(X, Y) \leftarrow q(X, Y), R(X, Y), C(X)$, where R and C are ontological constraints, is transformed into $p(X, Y, [R(X, Y), C(X)|A]) \leftarrow q(X, Y, A)$. If there are more rule predicates in the body, the constraints of all of them are joined together into a single list using the list-construct *append* provided by Prolog. We also show this transformation on an example below.

The transformed program P' thus hides the external constraints in Prolog lists making sure that they are not evaluated by the rule engine. At the same time, the variables appearing in the constraints are properly grounded as expected when the rule is being evaluated. The program P' is executable in a Prolog system. Each derivation for a query A results in a conjunction of constraints. As already argued, we need to collect the constraints from all derivations of a query A and construct their disjunction. This is also how we treat the collected constraint list constructed by querying a transformed program P' (see example below).

The brief DL query language survey in Section 4.1 informed us that the support for disjunctive queries is not well supported by existing DL systems. However, the theoretical solution of how to handle disjunctive queries (restricted to class expressions) is documented in literature (see e.g. [5],[19]). Most DL solvers implement satisfiability verification of a KB as the main reasoning service. All other services provided are reduced to the problem of checking satisfiability of

Σ T-Box: $European \sqcap American$ $\sqsubseteq \bot$
              $EuropeanAssociate$ $:= \exists Associate.European$
              $AmericanAssociate$ $:= \exists Associate.American$
              $NoFellowCompany$ $:= \forall Associate.\neg American$
              $InternationalCompany$ $:= EuropeanAssociate \sqcup AmericanAssociate$

A-Box: $\top(a), \top(high), InternationalCompany(b)$

Fig. 1. Company ontology described as DL axioms

the KB [6]. For example, to verify if the individual a is a member of the class C (*instance check*) the KB would be extended with the following axiom $\{a : \neg C\}$ whereupon satisfiability of the KB would be checked. The query $C(a)$ is a logical consequence of the KB if the extended KB is not satisfiable. A disjunctive query $C(a) \vee D(b)$ is solved by extending the KB with $\{a : \neg C, b : \neg D\}$ and again resolving to verifying (un)satisfiability [5]. Our safety condition does not enforce groundness of collected constraints but assures that no variable in a collected constraint is free. In particular, the internal variables of rules that appear in the collected constraints may be handled by the ontology reasoners discussed in Section 4.1 as *non-distinguished* variables. We might have a constraint involving a non-distinguished variable like $C(X)$ where C is a concept and X a variable. In this case the KB is augmented with the axiom $\top \sqsubseteq \neg C$ whereupon (un)satisfiability of the extended KB is verified. A disjunctive query $Q_1 \vee \ldots \vee Q_n$ where the disjuncts are conjuncts of class expressions (what would be the result of evaluating a query wrt. a transformed Prolog program P' as described above) can be solved in the following manner [19]. The query is transformed into its conjunctive normal form (CNF). Each conjunct is a disjunction of class expressions which can be solved as described above. If all the conjuncts are held to be logical consequences of the underlying theory, then so is the original query.

We will look at an example (taken from [23] but slightly modified) where we show the steps performed by our prototype system to solve a query wrt. a hybrid knowledge base consisting of an extended Datalog rule-set and an OWL document.

Π r_1: price-in-usa(X,high) :- made-by(X,Y), NoFellowCompany(Y).
     r_2: price-in-usa(X,high) :- made-by(X,Y), AmericanAssociate(Y),
                        monopoly-in-usa(Y,X).
     r_3: made-by(a,b).
     r_4: monopoly-in-usa(b,a).

Fig. 2. Price rules

Given the query *price-in-usa(a,high)* wrt. the KB $\Sigma \cup \Pi$ (Figure 1 and 2), the following steps are executed by our prototype system to solve the query.

1. The rule-base Π is transformed into Π' (Figure 3).
2. The query *price-in-usa(a,high,A)* is run by XSB Prolog wrt. the rule program Π'. The result as returned by XSB is:

$$A = [[c\_\_NoFellowCompany(c\_b)], [c\_\_AmericanAssociate(c\_b)]]$$

where the prefix $c\_\_$ is simply used for convenience to refer to the specific underlying ontology.

3. Each sublist of the answer A correspond to a conjunction of class expressions. This disjunctive normal form (DNF) is turned into its CNF (one conjunct):

$$NoFellowCompany(b) \lor AmericanAssociate(b)$$

4. The underlying ontology is extended with the following two axioms:

$$b : \neg NoFellowCompany, b : \neg AmericanAssociate$$

and then a check is performed to see if the newly extended KB is satisfiable. If the extended KB is not satisfiable we conclude that the original query holds wrt. $\Sigma \cup \Pi$.

As explained in [23], the query *price-in-usa(a,high)* is true because b is either a member of the class *NoFellowCompany* or the class *AmericanAssociate* in all models of Σ (i.e. the constraint is a logical consequence of the KB).

This examples also gives a motivation as to why we need to collect the constraints from all derivations and construct a disjunctive constraint which then has to be verified wrt. the underlying KB. This can be seen since neither *NoFellowCompany(b)* nor *AmericanAssociate(b)* are logical consequences of Σ, but their disjunction is.

Π' r_1: price-in-usa(X,high,[NoFellowCompany(Y)|A]) :- made-by(X,Y,A).
        r_2: price-in-usa(X,high,[AmericanAssociate(Y)|A]) :- made-by(X,Y,A1),
               monopoly-in-usa(Y,X,A2), append(A1,A2,A).
        r_3: made-by(a,b,[]).
        r_4: monopoly-in-usa(b,a,[]).

Fig. 3. Transformed price rules

The prototypical system interfaces XSB Prolog with any DIG [1] compliant DL reasoner. DIG is a language for dealing with statements of DL. The Java library Jena[7] is used to handle the underlying ontology referenced by the rules. When solving the disjunctive DL queries, Jena is used to augment the KB with the additional axioms. Checking for satisfiability of the extended KB is also done via Jena to which a DIG compliant DL reasoner is connected. A well known DIG compliant reasoners used today is RACER [17].

5   Related Work

Our work extends the ideas of $\mathcal{AL}$-log [10] to a more general framework for hybrid integration of rules and constraint theories. An instance of the proposed

---

[7] http://jena.sourceforge.net/

framework is the prototype system of Section 4.2, an $\mathcal{AL}$-log style integration of Datalog and OWL-DL, based on re-use of existing reasoners.

In the language of extended rules supported by our prototype the constraint predicates are restricted to OWL concepts. Also in $\mathcal{AL}$-log constraints are restricted to concepts. This restriction is lifted in CARIN [23], where both concepts and roles are allowed as constraints in rules. The logic obtained in that way is undecidable in general. In contrast to CARIN our rules are safe, in which case allowing roles in constraints does not introduce undecidability.[8] Further extension of our prototype to such a subset of CARIN is possible, but would require a reasoner supporting disjunctive DL queries, where roles are allowed to appear.

Our approach is restricted to rules without negation and does not support non-monotonic reasoning. This facilitates definition of the semantics of an extended rule program as a restriction of the semantics of the underlying core rules. The core rules are assumed to have fixpoint semantics, and are not restricted to logical formulae. The approach can be easily extended to *stratified* rule programs with negation (for the notion of stratified logic program see e.g. [4]). This kind of negation is used, among others in Xcerpt. More advanced forms of negation and non-monotonic reasoning can only be handled by specific restrictions imposed on the considered rule languages. For example, some recent work on hybrid inegration of rules and ontologies is based on *stable model* semantics or *answer set* semantics [13] for Datalog rules with negation. In the approach of [11,22] the bodies of the extended rules may include ontology queries possibly locally modifying the A-Box of the ontology. The reasoning in the extended language can be done by re-using a rule reasoner supporting the stable model semantics and a DL-reasoner answering the DL queries. An extension and refinement of [11] is described in [22] which makes it possible to handle several DL KBs. Both [11] and [22] however do not take into account the issues discussed in [10,23] with regards to completeness of the integration, whereas we do. *Safe hybrid knowledge bases* discussed in [25] provide a general formal framework for integrating DL ontologies and rules, where the rule languages considered include various subsets of disjunctive Datalog with stable model semantics. This approach allows DL predicates in the heads of rules, so that the interaction between DL and rules is more advanced than in our approach. The paper focuses on the semantic issues but sketches also a two-step algorithm for deciding satisfiability of a given hybrid KB, where one of the steps relies on standard DL reasoning and the other on standard search of stable model of Datalog rules.

Another approach to combining rules and ontologies does not stress hybrid reasoning but instead aims at defining a logical language extending DLs with rules. In such an approach there is no distinction between rule predicates and DL predicates, so that both the heads and the bodies of rules are built from concepts and roles. Examples of this approach include a decidable logic: the Description Logic Programs of [14] and an undecidable logic whose XML encoding is known as the Semantic Web Rule Language (SWRL) [18]. A closely related approach

---

[8] Notice that our safety condition is different from that known as role-safeness, defining a decidable subset of CARIN.

to [18] is a recent extension of OWL-DL with rules [24]. The integrated language is similar to the language in our prototype but we do not allow DL-predicates to appear in the heads of rules. Our safety condition is different from DL-safety of [24]. The latter requires that each variable of an integrated rule appears in a non-DL-atom in the rule body, while we only require that each variable in the head appears in a non-DL-atom of the body. The main distinction is that the query answering in [24] is done by using a compilation of the integrated program to disjunctive Datalog, while our prototype is a hybrid reasoner interfacing existing reasoners of the component languages.

The objectives of our work, aiming at re-using existing reasoners are not compatible with the language extension approach where a new reasoner has to be constructed for every new defined extension.

6   Conclusions and Future Work

We presented a general scheme for combining various kinds of safe rules with various kinds of constraints. For a particular rule language with a fixpoint semantics and for a particular constraint language the scheme defines the syntax and the semantics of their composition. The language obtained in that way allows for specification of knowledge bases, consisting of extended rules and FOL axioms. Our scheme shows how reasoners of the underlying languages should be interfaced for querying the knowledge bases. The idea is to use the original rule reasoner on the cores of the extended rules while the constraints are to be checked by the original constraint reasoner. For this the rule reasoner has to be able to collect and instantiate the constraints associated with the core rules involved in reasoning. This feature is not supported by the existing rule reasoners but, as illustrated by our prototype, can sometimes be implemented by transformation of the source of the extended rules. To make existing rule reasoners applicable in our framework one should develop techniques for collecting constraints during their operation and for scheduling cooperation between the rule reasoner and the constraint solver. Waiting for construction of a complete disjunctive query before handing it out to the constraint solver might not be the best approach in practice.

We have in this paper considered a layered approach where a rule layer is put on top of an ontology layer. One can also consider several layers interleaving components of rules and ontologies. In the special case, when constraints are formulated in a DL, the A-Box can be specified by extended rules. To achieve such a multi-layering of rules and ontology components, one needs to define a component model describing how the components are interfaced with one another. From a software engineering perspective, this component model opens up the way of interoperability between various combinations of logical languages, for which type mappings between types in interfaces can be given. It would enable us to encapsulate the reasoners for the languages and to connect them via proxies, mapping the different data formats to each other. This would define a CORBA-like mechanism for logical languages, which is an inevitable interoperability mechanism for the future Semantic Web.

The prototype described in Section 4.2 now only allows ontological constraints as *concepts*. It would be desirable to also support usage of *roles* in constraints as done in e.g. CARIN [23]. This is doable by plugging in already developed techniques for rolling-up of queries involving roles into queries which only contain concepts. Once this process is done, the constraint is rid of any roles and the techniques in Section 4.2 can be used as described.

Another relevant topic is how to organize interaction of different constraint solvers when different kinds of constraints are used.

As the underlying rules of any extended rule program P are safe, the constraints in our approach are only used to restrict the finite model of $P \downarrow$. Admission of unsafe rules would enhance the expressive power of the extended rule languages. The family of extended rule languages obtained in that way would have a close relation to the CLP(X) family of constraint logic programming languages [20]. Clarification of this relation would allow for re-use of existing expertise of CLP in the Semantic Web.

Acknowledgement

The authors are very grateful to Boris Motik, Michael Wessel and Birte Glimm for their helpful comments on the state of query languages of existing DL reasoners, to Wlodek Drabent for stimulating discussions and to the anonymous reviewers for their constructive criticism and pointing to related work.

This research has been co-funded by the European Commission and by the Swiss Federal Office for Education and Science within the 6th Framework Programme project REWERSE number 506779 (cf. http://rewerse.net).

References

1. DIG Interface. WWW Page, 14 March 2006. Available at http://dig.sourceforge.net/.
2. XSB. WWW Page, 14 March 2006. Available at http://xsb.sourceforge.net/.
3. G. Antoniou. Nonmonotonic rule systems using ontologies. In *Proc. Intl. Workshop on Rule Markup Languages for Business Rules on the Semantic Web*, 2002.
4. K. Apt and R. Bol. Logic programming and negation: A survey. *J. of Logic Programming*, 19/20:9–71, 1994.
5. F. Baader, H.-J. Bürckert, B. Hollunder, W. Nutt, and J. H. Siekmann. Concept logics. Technical Report RR-90-10, 1990.
6. F. Baader, D. Calvanese, and D. McGuiness(et.al.), editors. *The Description Logic Handbook*. Cambridge University Press, 2003.
7. T. Berners-Lee. Semantic web tower. WWW Page. Available at http://www.w3.org/2001/09/06-ecdl/slide17-0.html
8. F. Bry and S. Schaffert. The XML query language Xcerpt: Design principles, examples, and semantics. In *Web and Databases, Proc of the 2nd Int. Workshop*, LNCS2593. Springer Verlag, 2002.
9. Diego Calvanese and De Giacomo, Giuseppe and Domenico Lembo and Maurizio Lenzerini and Riccardo Rosati and Guido Vetere. DL-lite: Practical Reasoning for Rich DLs. In *Proceedings of the 2004 Description Logic Workshop (DL 2004)*. CEUR Electronic Workshop Proceedings, http://ceur-ws.org/Vol-104, 2004.

10. F. Donini, M. Lenzerini, D. Nardi, and A. Schaerf. AL-Log: Integrating datalog and description logics. *Intelligent Information Systems*, 10(3):227–252, 1998.
11. T. Eiter, T. Lukasiewicz, R. Schindlauer, and H. Tompits. Combining answer set programming with description logics for the semantic web. In *Proc. of the International Conference of Knowledge Representation and Reasoning (KR'04)*, 2004.
12. A. Frisch and A. Cohn. Thoughts and afterthoughts on the 1988 workshop on principles of hybrid reasoning. *AI Mag.*, 11(5):77–83, 1991.
13. M. Gelfond and V. Lifschitz. The stable model semantics for logic programming. In R. A. Kowalski and K. Bowen, editors, *Proceedings of the Fifth International Conference on Logic Programming*, pages 1070–1080, Cambridge, Massachusetts, 1988. The MIT Press.
14. B. Grosof, I. Horrocks, R. Volz, and S. Decker. Description logic programs: Combining logic programs with description logic. In *Proceedings of 12th International Conference on the World Wide Web*, 2003.
15. Guido Governatori. Defeasible Description Logics. In *RuleML*, pages 98–112, 2004.
16. V. Haarslev. The New Racer Query Language - nRQL. PDF document. Available at www.cs.concordia.ca/~haarslev/racer/racer-queries.pdf.
17. V. Haarslev and R. Möller. Description of the RACER system and its applications. In *DL2001 Workshop on Description Logics, Stanford, CA*, 2001.
18. I. Horrocks and P. F. Patel-Schneider. A proposal for an OWL rules language. In *Proc. of the Thirteenth International World Wide Web Conference (WWW 2004)*, pages 723–731. ACM, 2004.
19. I. Horrocks and S. Tessaris. A conjunctive query language for description logic aboxes. In *Proceedings of the Seventeenth National Conference on Artificial Intelligence and Twelfth Conference on Innovative Applications of Artificial Intelligence*, pages 399–404. AAAI Press / The MIT Press, 2000.
20. Joxan Jaffar and Michael J. Maher. Constraint Logic Programming: A Survey. *Journal of Logic Programming*, 19/20:503–581, 1994.
21. Kewen Wang, David Billington, Jeff Blee and Grigoris Antoniou. Combining Description Logic and Defeasible Logic for the Semantic Web. In *RuleML*, pages 170–181, 2004.
22. Kewen Wang, Grigoris Antoniou, Rodney W. Topor and Abdul Sattar. Merging and Aligning Ontologies in dl-Programs. In *RuleML*, pages 160–171, 2005.
23. A. Levy and M. Rousset. CARIN: A representation language combining horn rules and description logics. *Artificial Intelligence 104(1 2):165 209*, 1998.
24. B. Motik, U. Sattler, and R. Studer. Query Answering for OWL-DL with Rules. *J. of Web Semantics*, 3:41–60, 2005.
25. R. Rosati. Semantic and computational advantages of the safe integration of ontologies and rules. In F. Fages and S. Soliman, editors, *Principles and Practice of Semantic Web Reasoning*, LNCS3703, pages 50–64. Springer Verlag, 2005.
26. S. Staab(ed.). Where are the rules. *IEEE Intelligent Systems*, pages 76–83, September/October 2003.

Realizing Business Processes with ECA Rules: Benefits, Challenges, Limits

François Bry, Michael Eckert, Paula-Lavinia Pătrânjan, and Inna Romanenko

Institute for Informatics, University of Munich
Oettingenstr. 67, D-80538 Munich
{bry, eckert, patranjan}@pms.ifi.lmu.de, romanenk@cip.ifi.lmu.de
http://www.pms.ifi.lmu.de

Abstract. Event-Condition-Action (ECA) rules offer a flexible, adaptive, and modular approach to realizing business processes. This article discusses the use of ECA rules for describing business processes in an executable manner. It investigates the benefits one hopes to derive from using ECA rules and presents the challenges in realizing business processes. These constitute a list of requirements for an (executable) business process description language, and we take them as a basis to investigate suitability of the concrete ECA rule language XChange in realizing a business process from the EU-Rent Case Study.

1 Introduction

Success in an increasingly global and competitive market requires companies to adjust internal activities and resources in an adequate and timely manner. Without suitable enterprise computing systems, this is infeasible. Managing and automating business processes is a key factor for successful enterprise computing systems.

A business process can be described as "a structured, measured set of activities designed to produce a specified output for a particular customer or market" [1]. Different methods and tools have been developed to describe business processes both for modeling purposes and for automatic execution. Such a description is also often called *workflow* or business *protocol*, and its automatic execution often called (workflow) *enactment*. The focus of this paper is on executable business process descriptions.

Recently, interest in rules is growing in different communities: companies manage and specify their business logic in the form of business rules [2], efforts are made for standardizing formats for rule interchange [3] as required for example in policy-based trust negotiations [4], and rule languages are becoming popular for reasoning with Web and Semantic Web data [5]. Like rules in general, Event-Condition-Action rules offer a flexible, adaptive, and modular approach to realizing business processes.

In this article we analyze realizing business processes (i.e., describing business processes in an executable manner) based on ECA rules. The focus is on control

J.J. Alferes et al. (Eds.): PPSWR 2006, LNCS 4187, pp. 48–62, 2006.

flow, because this is the aspect one is most concerned about during specification; other issues are shortly discussed.

We investigate the benefits one hopes to derive from using ECA rules (Section 2) and present the challenges in realizing business processes (Section 3). These constitute a list of requirements for an (executable) business process description language, and we take them as a basis to investigate suitability of the concrete ECA rule language XChange in realizing a business process from the EU-Rent Case Study (Section 4). We close with a discussion of the practical limits of ECA rules for business processes (Section 5) and conclusions (Section 6).

2   ECA Rules for Business Processes: Benefits

Managing and automating a business process requires a machine-readable description of the business process. The most widely used language for describing business process today is the Business Process Execution Language (BPEL) [6].

Simplified, BPEL describes a process as activities (typically provided as Web Services) with control flow (e.g., sequential execution) in an imperative fashion. Additionally, handlers to catch errors or other exceptional situations in the process can be specified.

In this article we argue for a different approach to describing business processes based on ECA rules. ECA rules have the form "on *event* if *condition* do *action*" and specify to execute the action automatically when the event happens, provided the condition holds. Whereas traditional business process description languages center around activities, ECA rules put emphasis on events. An ECA-rule-based approach for specifying business processes can have the following advantages:

- Requirements are frequently specified in the form of rules expressed in either a natural or formal language, in particular business rules, legislative rules, or contractual rules. In requirements on business processes, we often find ECA rules such as "a credit card application *(event)* will be granted *(action)* if the applicant has a monthly income of more than EUR 1.500 and no outstanding debts *(condition)*." Ideally, a one-to-one mapping between rules used for requirements specifications and (executable) rules used for workflow enactment can be achieved.
- Reactive rules, especially ECA rules, easily integrate with other kinds of rules commonly used in business applications such as deductive rules (rules expressing views over data or rules used for reasoning with data) and normative rules (rules expressing conditions that data must fulfill; also called integrity constraints). Methods for automatic verification and validation of rule sets have been well-studied in the past and can be applied.
- ECA rules have a flexible nature: they are easy to adapt, alter, and maintain as requirements change, which is quite frequently the case for business processes. Even more, many rule engines allow rules to be added, modified, or deleted "on-the-fly," i.e., without interrupting running processes.

- An important part of business process descriptions is handling of errors and exceptional situations; in fact, it is often the longest and most labor-intensive part. Since errors and exceptional situations can be conveniently expressed as (special) events, ECA rules allow to treat them just like "normal" situations, thus making their handling quite easy.
- Rules can be managed in a single rule base as well as distributed in several rule bases. The latter is advantageous for cross-enterprise processes, where there is no central instance (such as a workflow management system) executing and monitoring processes.
- In an activity-centered control flow, activities are started as reaction to the (successful or unsuccessful) completion of another activity; reaction to intermediate states of activities are typically not supported [7]. ECA rules with their emphasis on events offer more flexible means to specify control flow, if appropriate events are generated by the activities.

Whether an activity-centered or an event-centered approach for describing business processes is better suited depends, of course, always on the individual process and its environment. In situations where modeling and specifying a process is better done with an activity-centered view, it is usually possible to automatically or semi-automatically derive ECA rules realizing the execution of the process.

3   Challenges for Realizing Business Processes

Every business process execution language should answer certain requirements for effective and efficient support of business processes, primarily the ability to realize separate activities (tasks or steps) and to control their cooperation (or interworking). In this section we present the essential challenges for realizing business processes.

3.1   Control Flow

Control structures are the core elements of every business process modeling (or execution) language. They describe temporal and logical dependencies between activities such as: sequential execution of activities, parallel execution, synchronization, alternative execution. Van der Aalst et al. [8] have identified 21 patterns of control flow ranging from the simple patterns just named to more complex, process specific patterns. The technical ability of a business process description language to express these patterns can be viewed as an essential indicator of the language usability to design and implement business processes.

Consider the business process for handling a rental reservation (RR) depicted in Figure 1 in Business Process Modeling Notation (BPMN) [9]. A customer invokes the business process by sending a rental reservation request to a rental company.

If the customer is already registered, the customer blacklist is checked (*check blacklist*); in case the customer is on the blacklist, the rental request is rejected

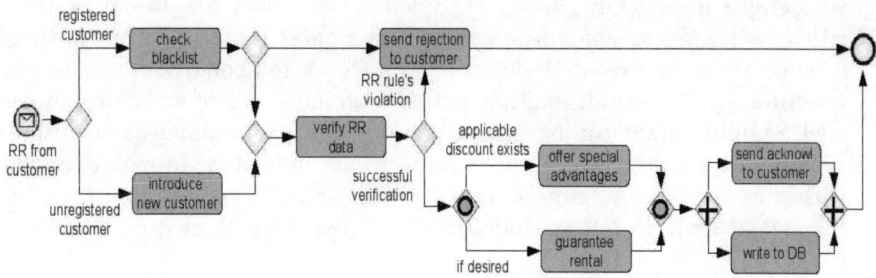

Fig. 1. Reservation business process represented in BPMN

(*send rejection to customer*) and the process ends. If the customer is not registered yet, her data are recorded (*introduce new customer*).

In the next step the reservation data is checked (*verify RR data*); e.g., that there are no overlaps with other reservations of the customer and that a car in the specified group is available. In case of a violation, the process ends again with a rental rejection.

Next, a number of activities are performed, which depend on certain conditions (possibly no activity, if none of the conditions holds). If an applicable discount exists, it is offered to the customer (*offer special advantages*). If the customer's rental request indicates that a guaranteed rental (car can be picked up within 24 hours after the scheduled pick-up time) is desired, corresponding arrangements are made (*guarantee rental*).

Finally, the customer is notified that her rental request has been accepted (*send acknowl. to customer*) and, in parallel, the rental reservation is recorded (*write to DB*). With this the process ends.

We will now analyze the control flow patterns in this example:

- **Sequence** is the most basic control pattern; it runs two (or more) activities one after the other. In the example, *introduce new customer* and *verify RR data* are in a sequence. Sequencing of activities is drawn as a solid arrow in BPMN.
- **Exclusive Choice** allows execution of exactly one alternative path chosen at the runtime based on the evaluation of a condition. In the example, one of *check blacklist* and *introduce new customer* is chosen exclusively, based on whether the customer is registered. The alternative execution paths can be brought together again with a **Simple Merge**; when the chosen activity of the Exclusive Choice finishes, execution continues with the activity after the corresponding Simple Merge. Both patterns are represented in the BPMN with simple diamonds (so-called XOR gateways).
- **Multi-Choice** is similar to Exclusive Choice, but allows *more than one* alternative paths to be chosen and executed in parallel, or even to execute no path at all. The counterpart to join the parallel execution paths (or continue execution if no path has been chosen) is the **Synchronizing Merge**, which waits for all chosen paths to finish before continuing. BPMN uses diamonds

with circles inside (OR gateways) to depict these patterns. In our example, either both *offer special advantages* and *guarantee rental*, only one of them, or none are to be executed, depending on the stated conditions.

- **Parallel Split** executes multiple paths (with independent activities) in parallel. **Synchronization** joins them again by waiting for all paths to finish. In the graphical representation both patterns are indicated through diamonds with plus symbol (AND gateways). In the example, *send acknowl. to customer* and *write to DB* are independent activities performed in parallel.

There are more control flow patterns, but the above are the most common and are supported by virtually all business process modeling or execution languages. The realization of the above patterns with ECA rules will be investigated in the next section.

3.2   Process Instances

Another challenge for a business process language is the ability to support performing of different activities within a *process instance*. A process instance is the execution representation of a process. Considering the example of handling a rental request: a process instance is created each time when a rental request from a customer is received. Several process instances corresponding to different rental requests (possibly from the same customer) run in parallel.

When a cancellation request from a customer arrives, this is specific to one of the customer's previous rental requests. It should cancel only the one corresponding process instance, not all processes. A business process language hence must provide a mechanism that assigns events that happen as well as running activities to their corresponding process instances.

3.3   Integration with Business Rules

Business rules are used for defining or constraining aspects of business, such as inserting business structure or controlling or influencing the behavior of business. They represent the business logic of a company and exist in every enterprise. Often the logic of workflow-based systems is given or influenced by business rules. Frequently the rules are embedded within the business process itself which makes changing and maintaining business rules difficult and costly. Recently business rules management, i.e., separating business processes and business rules, and formally specifying, enforcing, integrating, and maintaining business rule sets, has gained much attention.

Business rules can be classified according to their effect. A common classification [10] distinguishes three types:[1]

- structural rules (also called normative rules or constraints) define restrictions on business concepts and facts,

---

[1] Other classifications for business rules [11] or rules in general [12] exist; the presented classification is well-accepted, clear, and suitable in the framework of this article.

- derivation rules (also called deductive or constructive rules) are statements of knowledge derived from other knowledge using inference or mathematical calculations,
- dynamic rules (also called active, reactive, or reaction rules) concern dynamic aspects of the business; they constrain or control the actions of business.

In business processes, business rules play an important role at decision points, where processes change their behavior based on certain criteria or rules. The most common approaches for integrating business rules and business processes are (1) checking the rules explicitly as activities, e.g., calling a rule engine Web Service, and (2) checking the rules implicitly at decision making points. A business process language should support the integration of business rules.

3.4 Exception Handling

The ability to specify exceptional conditions and their consequences, including recovery measures, are as important for realizing business processes as the ability to define "normal behavior." An exceptional situation in the process of Figure 1 could, for example, occur during the *verify RR data* activity if the credit card of a customer has expired. Possible means for recovery include asking the customer for updated information or canceling the whole rental request.

Because of the multitude and diversity of exceptional situations, the effort for specifying exception handling often surpasses the effort for specifying normal behavior. Hence, every business process language should provide a systematic and elegant mechanism to specify, handle, and recover from exceptions.

3.5 Abstractions for Reusability and Maintainability

Business process specifications should exhibit modular structure to ease reusing and maintaining parts of the specifications such as sub-workflows. An important step towards reusability and maintainability is the integration of business rules into process specifications (see above). However, further means are required: for example, use of a sub-workflow in several other workflows requires support from the business process language and cannot be realized through the integration of business rules.

Modularity is best explored in object-oriented and procedural languages; for rule-based languages, however, modularity is still a research challenge.

4   Realization in XChange

In this section we demonstrate the capabilities of the rule-based language XChange in realizing business processes. The concrete processes go along the lines of the EU-Rent Case Study [13], a specification of business requirements for a fictive car rental company, promoted by the European Business Rules Conference [14] and the Business Rules Group [15]. Our focus is on control flow, but we also discuss the integration of business rules and other issues touched on in Section 3.

```
<xchange:event>                                 xchange:event [
  <reservation-request>                           reservation-request {
    <customer>John Q Public</customer>              customer { "John Q Public" },
    <email>john@public.com</email>                  email { "john@public.com" },
    <car>                                           car {
      <group> A </group>                              group { "A" }
    </car>                                          },
    <period>                                        period {
      <from>2006-06-10</from>                         from { "2006-06-10" },
      <duration> 2 </duration>                        duration { "2" }
    </period>                                        }
    <location>Budva</location>                      location { Budva }
  </reservation-request>                          }
</xchange:event>                                ]
```

Fig. 2. Reservation Request (RR) event in XML and term representation

```
ON      xchange:event {{
            reservation-request [[
                var Customer -> customer {{ }} ]]   }}
FROM in { resource {"http://rent.eu/customers.xml" },
        customers {{
            without var Customer }} }
DO     in { resource {"http://rent.eu/customers.xml" },
        customers {{
            insert var Customer }} }
END
```

Fig. 3. XChange ECA rule for introducing a new customer

4.1   XChange in a Nutshell

XChange is a reactive language based on ECA rules and is tailored to the Web and XML data, which makes it an interesting candidate for realizing and composing Web Services. An XChange program is located at one Web node and consists of one or more (re)active rules of the form *event query — condition query — action*. Events are represented and communicated between different Web nodes as XML messages (e.g., with SOAP [16]). Every incoming event is queried using the event query (introduced by keyword ON). If an answer is found and the condition query (introduced by keyword FROM), which can query arbitrary Web resources, has also an answer, then the specified action (introduced by keyword DO) is executed.

Event queries, condition queries and actions follow the same approach of specifying patterns for the data that is queried, updated, or constructed. XChange embeds the XML query language Xcerpt [17] and extends it with update facilities and reactivity.

The parts of an XChange ECA rule communicate through variable substitutions. Substitutions obtained by evaluating the event query can be used in the condition query and the action part, those obtained by evaluating the condition query can be used in the action part.

Example. Figure 2 depicts an incoming rental request event. On the left it is in XML syntax, on the right it is in XChange's term syntax, which is used for conciseness in data, queries, and updates. Figure 3 depicts an XChange ECA rule which reacts to this event (ON-part), checks that the customer is not yet registered (FROM-part), and inserts him into the customer database (DO-part).

In the term syntax, square brackets [ ] denote that the order of the children of an XML element is relevant, curly braces { } denote that the order is not relevant.

In event queries and condition queries, both partial (i.e., incomplete) or total (i.e., complete) query patterns can be specified. A query term t using a partial specification (denoted by double brackets or braces) for its subterms matches with all such terms that (1) contain matching subterms for all subterms of t and that (2) might contain further subterms without corresponding subterms in t. In contrast, a query term t using a total specification (denoted by single brackets or braces) does not match with terms that contain additional subterms without corresponding subterms in t. Query terms contain variables for selecting subterms of data terms that are bound to the variables. Using "->" (read "as"), a restriction can be made on the bindings of the variable left of "->"; every binding has to match the (sub-)query to the right. The results of a query are bindings for the free variables in that query. In the example, Customer is bound to customer { "John Q Public" }.

Updates in the action part are queries to Web resources, augmented with the desired update operations (insert, delete, replace-by). Another form of action supported by XChange is the raising of a new event.

XChange is a rich language and we will discuss further constructs relevant in the scope of this article as we go along. For a short introduction to XChange see [18], for a complete introduction accompanied by the specification of declarative and operational semantics see [19].

4.2   Control Flow

We start off by implementing the control flow for the process from Figure 1 by refining the rule from Figure 3. The first control flow pattern in the process is the Exclusive Choice: the next action depends on the condition of being a registered customer. Such a choice is conveniently implemented by means of an extended form of ECA rules, called ECAA rule [20]: the event is the *reservation request* (message in Figure 2), the condition *customer unregistered* (a query to a database), the action to be executed is either *introduce new customer* (in case the condition holds) or *check blacklist* (otherwise).

ECAA rules are only syntactic sugar that significantly increases readability of rule sets; every such ECAA rule can be translated into two ECA rules with one condition being the negation of the other.

Figure 4 shows an XChange ECAA rule implementing the Exclusive Choice. The action in case the customer is unregistered (DO-branch) is the update to the customer database already discussed. To continue in the process after this action, an event is raised. This event will trigger further rules implementing part of the whole process. This style of implementing the sequence pattern by passing along events is common for ECA rules [20].

```
ON    xchange:event {{
            var Rental -> reservation-request {{
                var Customer -> customer {{ }}   }}   }}
FROM in { resource {"http://rent.eu/customers.xml"},
            customers {{ without var Customer }} }
DO    and [
            in { resource {"http://rent.eu/customers.xml" },
                customers {{ insert var Customer }}
            },
            xchange:event {
                new-customer { var Rental }    }    ]
ELSE xchange:event {
            check-blacklist { var Rental } }
END
```

Fig. 4. Exclusive choice on the customer's registration status

```
ON xchange:event {{
        blacklisted { var Rental }   }}
DO reply-customer [ var Rental, "Failure", "You are blacklisted." ]
END
```

Fig. 5. Send rejection to customer if blacklisted

For the ELSE-branch, the action for *check blacklist* is simply sending a message to a Web Service implementing it. The answer from the service is another message that will (just as the event raised in the DO-branch) trigger further rules.

The rule in Figure 5 implements the reaction to a positive answer from the *check blacklist* service. The action *send rejection to customer* is implemented as a procedure and will be discussed later.

Next, the process merges a negative answer from *check blacklist* and an answer from *introduce new customer*, and continues with the *verify RR data* action. The corresponding rule in Figure 6 uses a disjunction of events to implement the Simple Merge and raises an event that is sent to a service taking care of testing compliance of the rental request with the company's business rules.

In case the rental request satisfies the rental rules, *verify RR data* replies with an event RR-ok; otherwise with RR-not-ok (which contains a reason for rejection). The rule in Figure 7 reacts to this RR-not-ok event and sends a rejection message to the customer (in analogy to the rule for blacklisted customers in Figure 5).

The rules in Figure 8 implement the Multi-Choice in the process following successful verification of the rental rules (event RR-ok). The corresponding Synchronizing Merge is implemented in the event part of the rule in Figure 9; it uses a conjunction of events to merge. Note that the events guarantee-done and

```
ON or {
        xchange:event {{ not-blacklisted { var Rental } }},
        xchange:event {{ new-customer { var Rental } }}      }
DO xchange:event { verify-RR-rules { var Rental } }
END
```

Fig. 6. Simple Merge of the *check blacklist* and *introduce new customer* branches

```
ON    xchange:event {{
          RR-not-ok { var Rental -> reservation-request {{ }},
                      var Message -> message {{ }} } }}
DO    reply-customer [ var Rental, "Failure", var Message ]
END
```

Fig. 7. Send rejection to customer if RR rules are violated

```
ON    xchange:event {{
          RR-ok { var Rental -> reservation-request {{ guarantee {"yes"} }},
                  var Price -> price {{ }} }  }}
DO    xchange:event {
          guarantee-rental [ var Rental, var Price ] }
END

ON    xchange:event {{
          RR-ok { var Rental -> reservation-request {{ guarantee {"no"} }},
                  var Price -> price {{ }} }  }}
DO    xchange:event {
          guarantee-done [ var Rental, var Price ] }
END

ON    xchange:event {{
          RR-ok { var Rental -> reservation-request {{
                    period { from { var From }, duration { var Duration } },
                    car {{ group { var Group } }}  }},
                  var Price -> price {{ }} }  }}
FROM  exist-discounts [ var From, var Duration, var Discount ]
DO    xchange:event {
          apply-discounts [ var Rental, all var Discount, var Price ] }
ELSE  xchange:event {
          discounts-done [ var Rental, var Price ] }
END
```

Fig. 8. Multi-Choice for *offer special advantages* and *guarantee rental*

`discounts-done` are generated whether the corresponding actions are executed or not. This is necessary for the merge.

The upcoming Parallel Split is also implemented in the rule in Figure 9, namely in the action part. With the actions *send acknowl. to customer* and *write to DB* the process ends. For simplicity, we skipped the Synchronization of the action before the end of the process. It could be implemented in the same manner as the Synchronizing Merge.

4.3   Abstractions and Business Rules Integration

Reusability and maintainability of business processes can be greatly increased by convenient abstraction mechanisms and the integration of business rules.

An important abstraction mechanism is the capability to bundle actions that are complex or used frequently into procedures [21]. An action used frequently in our process is the reply to a customer. Figure 10 demonstrates defining such a procedure in XChange. It is called in the rules of Figures 5, 7, and 9.

Concerning the integration of business rules, the *verify RR rules* action illustrates checking business rules explicitly as activities by calling some service. This service can actually be implemented in XChange, see Figure 11. The implementation consists of one ECA rule reacting to the incoming event `verify-RR-rules`, a

```
ON and {
     xchange:event {{
          guarantee—done {{
               var Rental —> reservation—request {{ var Var }} }} }},
     xchange:event {{
          discounts—done [
               var Rental, var Price ]  }}  }
DO and {
     in { resource {"http://rent.eu/rentals.xml" },
          rentals {{ insert rental { all var Var, var Price } }} },
     reply—customer { var Rental, "Finished", "Reservation successful." }
END
```

Fig. 9. Synchronizing Merge of the above Multi-Choice and Parallel Split for *send acknowl. to customer* and *write to DB*

```
PROCEDURE reply—customer [
               reservation—request {{ email { var Email } }},
               var Status, var Message ]
DO          xchange:event {
               xchange:recipient { var Email },
               eu—rent—reply [ var Status, var Message ]  }
END
```

Fig. 10. Procedure for sending a reply to the customer

deductive rule for `get-price` (the result of which is queried in the condition part of the ECA rule), and two procedures `car-unavailable` and `rental-overlaps` for checking their corresponding business rules. (For space reasons, the figure only shows the procedure `car-unavailable`; the other procedure is similar.) The procedures generate appropriate replies in case of violations; if no violation is detected, the `RR-ok` event is raised by the ECA rule.

4.4   Process Instances

To deal with process instances in ECA rules different approaches are conceivable:

- `Rule tied to process instances`: In this approach, rules are executed as part of a process instance; their event queries only see events that are part of this process. Special constructs are required to start and end processes, and fork and join sub-processes.
- `Rule outside process instances`: In this approach, rules run separated from process instances; events have to carry some identifier for the process they belong to. This identifier has to be explicitly queried in the event part of rules and passed on by the actions and used services.

In the presented rules the second approach has been used, using as identifier of the process instance the `rental-request`-information, which is passed along through all events.

The disadvantage of the approach with rules outside process instances is that it puts more burden on the programmer's shoulders: the rules have to query the

```
ON    verify-RR-rules {
           var Rental -> reservation-request {{
              car {{ group { var Group} }},
              period { from { var From }, duration { var Duration } } }
}} }
FROM get-price [ var Group, var From, var Duration, var Price ]
DO   or [
           car-unavailable { var Rental },
           rental-overlaps { var Rental },
           xchange:event { RR-ok [ var Rental, var Price ] } ]
END

CONSTRUCT get-price [ var Group, var From, var Duration, var Price ]
FROM       in { resource {"http://rent.eu/prices.xml" },
               desc car-group {{
                  name { var Group },
                  prices {{
                     rental {
                        duration { var Duration },
                        price { var Price } } }} }} }
END

PROCEDURE car-unavailable {
               var Rental -> reservation-request {{
                  car {{ group { var Group } }} }} }
FROM       in { resource {"http://rent.eu/rentals.xml" },
               without desc car {{
                  model { var Group },
                  car-status { "available" } }} }
DO         xchange:event {
               RR-not-ok {
                  var Rental,
                  message {"Selected car group unavailable"} } }
END
```

Fig. 11. Implementation of the *verify RR data* activity in XChange

identifier in the event part (e.g., to ensure that for a conjunction of events only events of the same process instance are used) and passed along in every event that is raised. Approaches where rules are tied to process instances are hence more convenient.

However, tying rules to process instances is sometimes not possible for distributed workflows, in particular cross-enterprise workflows or workflows depending on events from other, parallel workflows.

4.5   Exception Handling

Since exceptions can be conveniently expressed as (special) events, ECA rules are a convenient mechanism for handling exceptions. They allow to treat exceptions like any other event.

The process we presented did not contain any exceptions as such, though one could argue that a customer being blacklisted or a violation of the rental rules could be perceived as an exception.

Exception handling is not a focus in this paper; however, ECA rules have quite successfully been employed for exception handling in the past [22].

5   ECA Rules for Business Processes: Limits

While using ECA rules in realizing business processes has the benefits outlined in Section 2, the approach has also some practical limits, just like any other approach. In the following we present the limits we have identified from the concrete study of using the ECA rule language XChange for specifying executable business processes presented in Section 4.

A general limit of ECA rules is that they do not always reflect the procedural, imperative way of thinking familiar to many people from imperative or object-oriented programming. This is particularly obvious when looking at the realization of the sequence pattern with ECA rules: for sequencing of activities A and B, B is triggered by a separate rule which reacts on a finish event of A. (XChange alleviates this to some degree through the and[...] when the activities are updates, though this is only a special case.) However, for distributed workflows without a central coordinator (e.g., cross-enterprise workflows) this style of programming is not unnatural and hard to avoid.

Closely related to this is that ECA rules usually do not have a local state that is specific and internal to the current process instance. ECA rules have to explicitly maintain this state in events and databases. For example, an incoming rental request could contain information such as the customer's e-mail address. This information is not needed immediately in the process of Figure 1, but only late in the process for sending rejection or acknowledgment back. In the first rule, this information has to be either saved in a database or passed along through all rules as part of event data.

Monitoring of business processes specified with ECA rules is not as straightforward as for other approaches, which are based on some activity-centered, automata-like model (e.g., BPMN or BPEL). In activity-centered process specifications, a process's state is obvious from the finished and running activities. In contrast, in event-centered process specifications, the process's state is given through the history of events, which is less easy to comprehend.

Because of this "hidden" process state in ECA rule-based specifications, there is no clear notion of which events are expected next. (Enabled) ECA rules are triggered by every incoming event matching the event query, regardless of whether this event is expected or not. This might entail unexpected behavior, especially if events are generated "out-of-order" by faulty or malicious behavior of systems. Possible solutions to this depend on the ECA rule language's capabilities. Dynamic enabling and disabling of rules provides an approach on a meta-level; however an activity-centered solution is much simpler.

Current rule languages have only limited support for structuring rule sets. In practice, however, structuring is very much needed to reduce the complexity and expenses in the production of business process specifications. It can be expected that this issue will be overcome through further research and practical experiences, in particular by adding support for modules.

Last not least, development and maintenance of business processes is greatly supported by visual tools. For event-centered approaches, visualizing single ECA rules alone does not suffice: it is important to visualize whole rule sets with the associated control flow. Again, this issue might be overcome through further development.

Of these limits, the first four stem from the rule-based, as opposed to an imperative, programming style. How strongly this limits the applicability of ECA rules to business processes hence also depends largely on the experience with rule-based programming. The latter two limits are more a limitation of *current* rule languages and expected to be solved in the near future.

6 Conclusion and Outlook

In this article we have analyzed the realization of business processes by means of ECA rules. With a focus on control flow, we have presented an implementation of a concrete business process scenario in XChange. This work has greatly influenced and advanced the development of XChange as a reactive language. In particular, it has led to the introduction of a procedure notion, which is absent in most other rule languages. Constructs for structuring rule sets in XChange are an issue of ongoing development deserving refinement and further research.

Issues also deserving attention for future work regard exception handling in connection with transactions and compensating actions, as well as issues relating to process instances.

As this paper has shown, there is still a lot to be done for using ECA rules in business processes. The first results of this paper are promising and give requirements and guidelines for future work, in particular on language design.

Acknowledgments

This research has been funded by the European Commission and by the Swiss Federal Office for Education and Science within the 6th Framework Programme project REWERSE number 506779 (http://rewerse.net).

References

1. Davenport, T.H.: Process Innovation: Reengineering Work through Information Technology. Havard Business School Press (1993)
2. The Business Rules Group: Defining business rules – what are they really? Available at www.businessrulesgroup.org (2000)
3. World Wide Web Consortium: Rule interchange format working group charter. See www.w3.org/2005/rules/wg/charter (2005)
4. Bonatti, P.A., Olmedilla, D.: Driving and monitoring provisional trust negotiation with metapolicies. In: IEEE Int. Workshop on Policies for Distributed Systems and Networks, IEEE Comp. Soc. (2005)
5. Bry, F., Schwertel, U.: REWERSE – reasoning on the Web. AgentLink News (15) (2004)
6. Andrews, T., et al.: Business process execution language for web services version 1.1. Available at www.ibm.com/developerworks/library/ws-bpel (2003)

7. Carter, B.M., Lin, J.Y.C., Orlowska, M.E.: Customizing internal activity behaviour for flexible process enforcement. In: Proc. Australasian Database Conference, Australian Computer Society (2004)
8. van der Aalst, W.M.P., ter Hofstede, A.H.M., Kiepuszewski, B., Barros, A.P.: Workflow patterns. Distributed and Parallel Databases **14**(1) (2003)
9. White, S.A.: Introduction to BPMN. Technical report, Object Management Group (OMG) (2004) Available at www.bpmn.org.
10. Hall, J.: Business rules boot camp. Tutorial at the European Business Rules Conference (2005)
11. Wagner, G.: How to design a general rule markup language? In: Proc. Workshop on XML Technologien für das Semantic Web - XSW. Volume 14 of LNI, GI (2002)
12. Bry, F., Marchiori, M.: Ten theses on logic languages for the Semantic Web. In: Proc. Int. Workshop on Principles and Practice of Semantic Web Reasoning. Volume 3703 of LNCS, Springer (2005)
13. EU-Rent Case Study. www.eurobizrules.org/ebrc2005/eurentcs/eurent.htm (2005)
14. European Business Rules Conference. www.eurobizrules.org (2005)
15. Business Rules Group. www.businessrulesgroup.org (2005)
16. Gudgin, M., et al.: SOAP version 1.2. W3C recommendation, World Wide Web Consortium (2003)
17. Schaffert, S., Bry, F.: Querying the Web reconsidered: A practical introduction to Xcerpt. In: Proc. Extreme Markup Languages. (2004)
18. Bailey, J., Bry, F., Eckert, M., Pătrânjan, P.L.: Flavours of XChange, a rule-based reactive language for the (Semantic) Web. In: Proc. Int. Conf. on Rules and Rule Markup Languages for the Semantic Web. Volume 3791 of LNCS, Springer (2005)
19. Bry, F., Eckert, M., Pătrânjan, P.L.: Reactivity on the Web: Paradigms and applications of the language XChange. J. of Web Engineering **5**(1) (2006) 3–24
20. Knolmayer, G., Endl, R., Pfahrer, M.: Modeling processes and workflows by business rules. In: Business Process Management. Volume 1806 of LNCS, Springer (2000)
21. Bry, F., Eckert, M.: Twelve theses on reactive rules for the Web. In: Proc. Workshop Reactivity on the Web at Int. Conf. on Extending Database Technology. Volume 3268 of LNCS, Springer (2006)
22. Brambilla, M., Ceri, S., Comai, S., Tziviskou, C.: Exception handling in workflow-driven web applications. In: Proc. Int. Conference on World Wide Web, ACM (2005)

Interaction Protocols and Capabilities: A Preliminary Report*

Matteo Baldoni, Cristina Baroglio, Alberto Martelli,
Viviana Patti, and Claudio Schifanella

Dipartimento di Informatica — Università degli Studi di Torino
C.so Svizzera, 185 — I-10149 Torino, Italy
{baldoni, baroglio, mrt, patti, schi}@di.unito.it

Abstract. A typical problem of the research area on Service-Oriented
Architectures is the composition of a set of existing services with the
aim of executing a complex task. The selection and composition of the
services are based on a description of the services themselves and can exploit an abstract description of their interactions. Interaction protocols
(or choreographies) capture the interaction as a whole, defining the rules
that entities should respect in order to guarantee the interoperability;
they do not refer to specific services but they specify the roles and the
communication among the roles. Policies (behavioral interfaces in web
service terminology), instead, focus on communication from the point
of view of the individual services. In this paper we present a preliminary study aimed to allow the use of public choreography specifications
for generating executable interaction policies for peers that would like
to take part in an interaction. Usually the specifications capture only
the interactive behavior of the system as a whole. We propose to enrich
the choreography by a set of *requirements* of capabilities that the parties
should exhibit, where by the term "capability" we mean the skill of doing
something or of making some condition become true. Such capabilities
have the twofold aim of connecting the interactive behavior to be shown
by the role-player to its internal state and of making the policy executable. A possible extension of WS-CDL with capability requirements
is proposed.

1 Introduction

In various application contexts there is a growing need of being able to compose
a set of heterogeneous and independent entities with the general aim of executing
a task, which cannot be executed by a single component alone. In an application
framework in which components are developed individually and can be based on

* This research has partially been funded by the European Commission and by the
Swiss Federal Office for Education and Science within the 6th Framework Programme
project REWERSE number 506779 (cf. http://rewerse.net), and it has also been
supported by MIUR PRIN 2005 "Specification and verification of agent interaction
protocols" national project.

J.J. Alferes et al. (Eds.): PPSWR 2006, LNCS 4187, pp. 63–77, 2006.
© Springer-Verlag Berlin Heidelberg 2006

various technologies, it is mandatory to find a flexible way for glueing components. The solution explored in some in some research areas, like web services (WS) and multi-agent systems (MAS), is to compose entities based on dialogue. In web services the language WS-BPEL [20] has become the *de facto* standard for building executable composite services on top of already existing services by describing the flow of information in terms of exchanged messages. On the other hand, the problem of aggregating communicating agents into (open) societies is well-known in the research area about MASs, where a lot of attention has been devoted to the issues of defining interaction policies, verifying the interoperability of agents based on dialogue, and checking the conformance of policies w.r.t. global communication protocols [28,17,11].

As observed in [27,5], the MAS and WS research areas show convergences in the approach by which systems of agents, on a side, and composite services, on the other, are designed, implemented and verified. In both cases it is in fact possible to distinguish two levels. On the one hand we have a global view of the system as a whole, which is independent from the specific agents/services which will take part to the interaction (the design of the system). In the case of MASs [14] the design level often corresponds to a shared *interaction protocol* (e.g. represented in AUML [21]). In the case of web services this level corresponds to a *choreography* of the system (e.g. expressed in WS-CDL). In general, at this level a set of *roles*, which will be played by some peers, are defined. On the other hand we have the level concerning the implementation of the policies of the entities that will play the roles. These interactive behaviors must be given in some executable language, e.g. WS-BPEL in the case of web services.

In this proposal, we consider choreographies as *shared knowledge* among the parties. We will, then, refer to them as to *public* and non-executable specifications. The same assumption cannot be made about the interactive behavior of specific parties (be they services or agents). The behavior of a peer will be considered as being private, i.e. non-transparent from outside. Nevertheless, if we are interested in coordinating the interaction of a set of parties as specified by a given choreography, we need to *associate* parties to roles. Suppose that a service publishes the fact that it acts according to the role "seller" of a public choreography. In order to interact with that service it will be necessary to play another role, e.g. "customer", of the specified choreography, but for playing it, the service interactive behavior must *conform* to the specification given by the role [1,13,3]. *Checking* the *conformance* is a way for guaranteeing that the service can interact with services playing the other roles in the choreography [3].

Let us, now, suppose that a peer does not have a conformant policy for playing a certain role, but that is needs to take part to the interaction ruled by the choreography anyway. A possible solution is to define a method for generating, in an automatic way, a conformant policy from the role specification. The role specification, in fact, contains all the necessary information about what sending/receiving to/from which peer at which moment. As a first approximation, we can, then, think of translating the role as expressed in the specification language in a policy (at least into a policy *skeleton*) given in an executable language.

This is, however, not sufficient. In fact, it is necessary to bind the interactive (observable) behavior that is encoded by the role specification with the internal (unobservable) behavior that the peer must anyway have and with its internal state. For instance, the peer must have some means for retrieving or building the information that it sends. This might be done in several ways, e.g. by querying a local data base or by querying another service. The way in which this operation is performed is not relevant, the important point is to be sure that in principle the peer can execute it. For completing the construction of the policy, it is necessary to have a means for checking whether the peer can actually play the policy, in other words, if it has the *required capabilities*. This can only be done if we have a specification of which capabilities are required in the choreography itself. The capability verification can be accomplished role by role by the specific party willing to take part to the interaction.

This paper presents a work aimed to introduce the concept of capability in the global/local system/entity specifications, in such a way that capabilities can be accounted for during the processes that are applied for dynamically building and possibly customizing policies. Section 2 defines the setting of the work. Moreover, a first example of protocol (the well-known FIPA Contract Net protocol), that is enriched with capabilities, is reported. Section 3 introduces our notion of *capability test*, making a comparison with systems in which this notion is implicit. The use of reasoning techniques that can be associated with the capability test for performing a customization of the policy being constructed is also discussed. In Section 4 a possible extension of WS-CDL [29] with capability capability requirements is sketched. Conclusions follow.

2   Interaction Protocols and Capabilities

The concept of "interaction protocol" derives from the area of MASs. MASs often comprise heterogeneous agents, that differ in the way they represent knowledge about the world and about other agents, as well as in the mechanisms used for reasoning about it. In general, every agent in a MAS is characterized by a set of actions and/or a set of behaviors that it uses to achieve a specific goal. In order to interact with the others, an agent specification must describe also the communicative behavior.

When a peer needs to play a role in some interaction ruled by a protocol but it does not own a conformant policy, it is necessary that it *adopts* a new interaction policy. In an agent-framework, one might think of enriching the set of behaviors of the agent, which failed the conformance test, by asking other agents to supply a correct interaction policy. This solution has been proposed from time to time in the literature; recently it was adopted in Coo-BDI architectures [2]. CooBDI extends the BDI (*Belief, Desire, Intention*) model so that agents are enabled to cooperate through a mechanism of plan exchange. Such a mechanism is used whenever it is not possible to find a plan for pursuing a goal of interest by just exploiting the current agent's knowledge. The ideas behind the CooBDI theory have been implemented by means of WS technologies, leading to CooWS agents

[8]. Another recent work in this line of research is [26]: in the setting of the DALI language, agents can cooperate by exchanging sets of rule that either define a procedure, or constitute a module for coping with some situation, or are just a segment of a knowledge base. Moreover, agents have reasoning techniques that enable them to evaluate how useful the new information is. These techniques, however, cannot be directly imported in the context of Service-oriented Computing. The reason is that, while in agent systems it is not a problem to find out *during* the interaction that an agent does not own all the necessary actions, when we compose web services it is fundamental that the analogous knowledge is available before the interaction takes place.

A viable alternative is to use the protocol definition for supplying the service with a new policy that is obtained directly from the definition of the role, that the peer would like to play. A policy skeleton could be directly synthesized in a semi-automatic way from the protocol description. A similar approach has been adopted, in the past, for synthesizing agent behaviors from UML specifications in [18]. However, a problem arises: protocols only concern communication patterns, i.e. the interactions of a peer with others, abstracting from all references to the internal state of the player and from all actions/instructions that do not concern observable communication. Nevertheless, in our framework we are interested in a policy that the peer will *execute* and, for permitting the execution, it is necessary to express to some extent also this kind of information. The conclusion is that if we wish to use protocols for synthesizing policy skeletons, we need to specify some more information, i.e. actions that allow us the access to the peer's internal state. Throughout this work we will refer to such actions as *capability requirements*.

The term "capability" has recently been used by Padgham et al. [22] (the work is inspired by JACK [9] and it is extended in [23]), in the BDI framework, for identifying the "ability to react rationally towards achieving a particular goal". More specifically, an agent has the capability to achieve a goal if its plan library contains at least one plan for reaching the goal. The authors incorporate this notion in the BDI framework so as to constrain an agent's goals and intentions to be compatible with its capabilities. This notion of capability is orthogonal w.r.t. what is proposed in our work. In fact, we propose to associate to a choreography (or protocol) specification, aimed at representing an interaction schema among a set of yet unspecified peers, a set of *requirements* of capabilities. Such requirements specify "actions" that peers, willing to play specific roles in the interaction schema, should exhibit. In order for a peer to play a role, some verification must be performed for deciding if it matches the requirements.

In this perspective, our notion of capability resembles more closely (sometimes unnamed) concepts, that emerge in a more or less explicit way in various frameworks/languages, in which there is a need for defining interfaces. One example is Jade [15], the well-known platform for developing multi-agent systems. In this framework policies are supplied as partial implementations with "holes" that the programmer must fill with code when creating agents. Such holes are represented by methods whose body is not defined. The task of the programmer is to implement the specified methods, whose name and signature is, however, fixed in the partial policy. Another example is powerJava [6,7], an extension of the Java language that accounts for roles and institutions. Without getting into the depths of the language, a role in powerJava represents an interlocutor in the interaction schema. A role definition contains only the implementation of the interaction schema and leaves to the role-player the task of implementing the internal actions. Such calls to the player's internal actions are named "requirements" and are represented as method prototypes.

Checking whether a peer has the capability corresponding to a requirement is, in a way, a complementary test w.r.t. checking conformance. With a rough approximation, when I check conformance I abstract away from the behavior that does not concern the communication described by the protocol of interest, focussing on the interaction with a set of other peers that are involved, whereas checking capabilities means to check whether it is possible to tie the description of a policy to the execution environment defined by the peer.

2.1   An Example: The Contract Net Protocol

For better explaining our ideas, in this section we consider as a choreography the well-known FIPA ContractNet Protocol [12], pinpointing the capabilities that are required to a peer which would like to play the role of *Participant*. ContractNet is used in electronic commerce and in robotics for allowing entities, which are unable to do some task, to have it done. The protocol captures a pattern of interaction, in which the initiator sends a *call-for-proposal* to a set of participants. Each participant can either accept (and send a proposal) or refuse. The initiator collects all the proposals and selects one of them. Figure 1 describes the interactions between the *Initiator* and one of the *Participants* in a UML notation, that is enriched with dotted rectangles representing *capability requirements*. The capability requirements act as connecting points between the external, communicative behavior of the candidate role player and its internal behavior. In the example, three different capabilities can be detected, one for the role of *Initiator* and two for the *Participant*. Starting from an instance of the concept Task, the *Participant* must be able to evaluate it by performing the *evaluateTask* capability, returning an instance of the concept Proposal. Moreover, if its proposal is accepted by the *Initiator*, it must be able to execute the task by using the capability *executeTask*, returning an instance of concept Result. On the other side, the *Initiator* must have the capability *evaluateProposal* that chooses a proposal among those received from the participants.

In order to play the role of *Participant* a peer will, then, need to have the capabilities *evaluateTask* and *executeTask*, whereas it needs to have the capability *evaluateProposal* if it means to play the role of *Initiator*. As it emerges from the example, a capability identifies an action (in a broad sense) that might require some inputs and might return a result. This is analogous to defining a method or a function or a web service. So, for us, a capability will be specified by its name, a description of its inputs and a description of its outputs. This is not the only possible representation, for instance if we interpret them as actions, it would make sense to represent also their preconditions and effects.

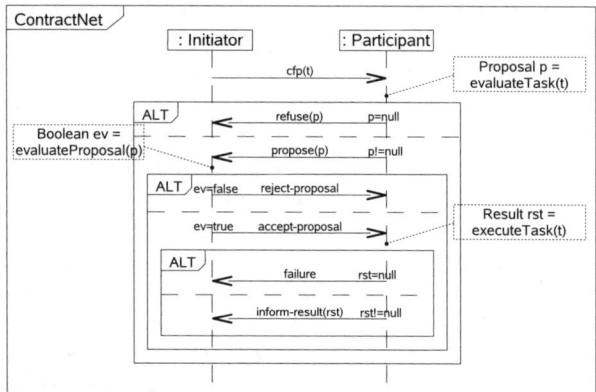

Fig. 1. The FIPA ContractNet Protocol, represented by means of UML sequence diagrams, and enriched with capability specifications

3   Checking Capabilities

In this section we discuss about possible implementations of the capability test, intended as the verification that a service satisfies the capability requirements given by a role. The capability test obviously depends on the way in which the policy is developed and therefore it depends on the adopted language. In Jade [15] there is no real capability test because policies already supply empty methods corresponding to the capabilities, the programmer can just redefine them. In powerJava the check is performed by the compiler, which verifies the implementation of a given interface representing the requirements. For further details see [6], in which the same example concerning the ContractNet protocol is described. In the scenario outlined in the previous section, the capability test is done *a priori w.r.t. all the capabilities required by the role specification* but the way in which the test is implemented is not predefined and can be executed by means of different matching techniques. We could use a simple *signature matching*, like in classical programming languages and in powerJava, as well more flexible forms of matching.

We consider particularly promising to adopt *semantic matchmaking* techniques proposed for matching web service descriptions with queries, based on *ontologies* of concepts. In fact semantic matchmaking supports the matching of capabilities with different names, though connected by an ontology, and with different numbers (and descriptions) of input/output parameters. For instance, let us consider the *evaluateProposal* capability associated to the role *Initiator* of the ContractNet protocol (see Figure 1). This capability has an input parameter (a proposal) and is supposed to return a boolean value, stating whether the proposal has been accepted or refused. A first example of flexible, semantics-based matchmaking consists in allowing a service to play the part of *Initiator* even though it does not have a capability of name *evaluateProposal*. Let us suppose that *evaluateProposal* is a concept in a shared ontology. Then, if the service has a capability *evaluate*, with same signature of *evaluateProposal*, and *evaluate* is a concept in the shared ontology, that is more general than *evaluateProposal*, we might be eager to consider the capability as matching with the description associated to the role specification.

Semantic matchmaking has been thoroughly studied and formalized also in the Semantic Web community, in particular in the context of the DAML-S [24] and WSMO initiatives [16]. In [24] a form of semantic matchmaking concerning the input and output parameters is proposed. The ontological reasoning is applied to the parameters of a semantic web service, which are compared to a query. The limit of this technique is that it is not possible to perform the search on the basis of a goal to achieve. A different approach is taken in the WSMO initiative [16], where services are described based on their preconditions, assumptions, effects and postconditions. Preconditions concern the structure of the request, assumptions are properties that must hold in the current state, as well as effects will hold in the final state, while postconditions concern the structure of the answer. These four sets of elements are part of the "capability" construct used in WSMO for representing a web service. Moreover, each service has its own choreography and orchestration, although these terms are used in a different way w.r.t. our work. In fact, both refer to subjective views, the former recalls a state chart while the latter is a sequence of if-then rules specifying the interaction with other services. On the other hand, users can express goals as desired postconditions. Various matching techniques are formalized, which enable the search for a service that can satisfy a given goal; all of them presuppose that the goal and the service descriptions are ontology-based and that such ontologies, if different, can be aligned by an ontology mediator. Going back to our focus concerning capability matching, in the WSMO framework it would be possible to represent a "capability requirement", associated with a choreography, as a WSMO goal, to implement the "capabilities" of the specific services as WSMO capabilities, and then apply the existing matching techniques for deciding whether a requirement is satisfied by at least one of the capabilities of a service.

In order to ground our proposal to the reality of web services, in Section 4, we will discuss a first possible extension of WS-CDL with capability requirements expressed as input and output parameters. For performing the capability test on this extension, it will be possible to exploit some technique for the semantic matchmaking based on input and output parameters, e.g. the one in [24].

3.1   Reasoning on Capabilities

In the previous sections we discussed the simple case when the capability test is performed w.r.t *all* the capabilities required by the role specification. In this case, based on some description of the required capabilities for a playing the role, we perform the matching among all required and actual service capabilities, thus we can say that the test allows to implement policies that perfectly fit the role, by envisioning all the execution paths foreseen by the role. This is, however, just a starting point. Further customization of the capability test w.r.t. some characteristic or goal of the service that intend to play a given role can be achieved by combining the test with a reasoning phase on capabilities. For instance, by reasoning on capabilities from the point of view of the service candidate for playing the role, it would be possible to find out policies that implement the role but do not envision all the execution paths and thus do not require the entire list of capabilities associated to the role to be implemented.

Let us take the abstraction of a policy implementing a role w.r.t. all the capabilities required as a procedure with different *execution traces*. Each execution trace corresponds to a branch in the policy. It is likely that only a subset of the capabilities associated to a role will be used along a given branch. As an example, Figure 2 shows three alternative execution traces for a given policy, which contain references to different capabilities: one trace exploits capabilities *C1* and *C3*, the second one exploits *C1* and *C4*, the third one contains only *C2*.

We can think of a variant of the capability test in which only the execution traces concerning the specific call, that the service would like to enact, are considered. This set will tell us which capabilities are actually necessary in our execution context (i.e. given the specified input parameter values). In this perspective, it is not compulsory that the service has all the capabilities associated to the role but it will be sufficient that it has those used in this set of execution traces. Consider Figure 2 and suppose that for some given input values, only the first execution trace (starting from left) might become actually executable. This trace relies on capabilities *C1* and *C3* only: it will be sufficient that the service owns such capabilities for making the *policy call* executable.

Such kind of reasoning could be done by describing the ideal complete policy for a service aiming at implementing a given role in a declarative language that supports a-priori reasoning on the policy executions. In fact, if a *declarative representation* of the complete policy were given, e.g. see [4], it would be possible to perform a rational inspection of the policy, in which the execution is simulated. By reasoning we could select the execution traces that allow the service to complete the interaction for the inputs of the given call. Finally we could collect the capabilities used in these traces only (*C1*, *C3*, and *C4* but not *C2*) and restrict the capability test to that subset of capabilities.

Another possible customization task consists on reasoning about those execution traces that, after the execution, make a certain condition become true in

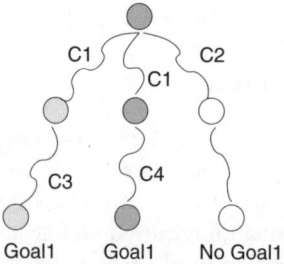

Fig. 2. Execution traces for a policy: two traces allow to reach a final state in which *goal1* is true but exploiting different capabilities

the service internal state. For instance, with reference to Figure 2, two out of the three possible executions lead to a final situation in which *goal1* holds. As a simple example of this case, let us suppose that a peer that wishes to play the role of "customer" with the general goal of purchasing an item of interest from a seller of interest, has a second goal, i.e. to avoid the use of credit cards. This goal can actually be seen as a constraint on the possible interactions. If the policy implementing the complete role allows three alternatives forms of payment (by credit card, by bank transfer and by check), the candidate customer is likely to desire to continue the interaction because some of the alternatives allow reaching the goal of purchasing the item of interest without using credit cards. It can, then, customize the policy by deleting the undesired path. If some of the capabilities are to be used *only* along the discarded execution path, it is not necessary for the candidate customer to have it.

Nevertheless a natural question arises: if I remove some of the possible execution paths of a policy, will it still be conformant to the specification? To answer to this question we can rely on our conformance test. In the specific case of the example, the answer would be positive. It would not be positive if we had a candidate seller that, besides having the general goal of selling items, has the second requirement of not allowing a specific form of payment (e.g. by bank transfer) and deletes the undesired path from the policy. Indeed, a customer that conforms to the shared choreography might require this form of payment, which is foreseen by the specification, but the candidate seller would not be able to handle this case leading to a deadlock.

It is also possible to generalize this approach and selecting the set of the execution traces that can possibly be engaged by a given service by using the information about the actual capabilities of the services. In fact, having the possibility of inspecting the possible evolutions of an ideal policy implementing the complete role, one could single out those execution traces that require the subset of capabilities that the service actually can execute. In this way, the policy can be customized w.r.t. the characteristic of the service, guaranteeing the success under determined circumstances.

Last but not least, the set of capabilities of a service could be not completely predefined but depending on the context and on privacy or security policies defined by the user: I might have a capability which I do not want to use in that circumstance. Also this kind of reasoning can be integrated in the capability test. In this perspective, it would be interesting to explore the use of the notion of *opportunity* proposed by Padmanabhan et al. [23] in connection with the concept of capability (but with the meaning proposed in [22], see Section 1).

4   A Case Study: Introducing Capability Requirements in WS-CDL

The most important formalism used to represent interaction protocols is WS-CDL (Web Services Choreography Description Language) [29]: an XML-based language that describes peer-to-peer collaborations of heterogeneous entities from a global point of view. In this section, we propose a first proposal of extension of the WS-CDL definition where capability requirements are added in order to enable the automatic synthesis of policies described in the previous sections. Capability requirements are expressed as input and output parameters, then semantic matchmaking based on input and output parameters could be exploited as technique for performing the capability checking. The schema that defines this extension can be found at `http://www.di.unito.it/~ alice/WSCDL_Cap_v1/`.

```
1   <silentAction roleType="Participant">
2      <capability name="evaluateTask">
3         <input>
4            <parameter variable="cdl:getVariable('tns:t','','')"/>
5         </input>
6         <output>
7            <parameter variable="cdl:getVariable('tns:p','','')"/>
8         </output>
9      </capability>
10 </silentAction>
```

Fig. 3. Representing a capability in the extended WS-CDL. The tag *input* is used to define one of the input parameters, while *output* is used to define one of the output parameters.

In this scenario an operation executed by a peer often corresponds to an invocation of a web service, in a way that is analogous to a *procedure call*. Coherently, we can think of representing the concept of capability in the WS-CDL extension as a new tag element, the tag *capability* (see for instance Figure 3), which is characterized by its *name*, and its *input* and *output parameters*. Each parameter refers to a variable defined inside the choreography document. The notation `variable="cdl:getVariable('tns:t','','')"` used in Figure 3 is a reference to a variable, according to the definition of WS-CDL. In this manner inputs and outputs can be used in the whole WS-CDL document in standard ways (like Interaction, Workunit and Assign activities). In particular parameters can be used in guard conditions of Workunits inside a Choice activities in order to choose alternative paths (see below for an example). Notice that each variable refers also to a concept in a defined ontology.

A capability represents an operation (a call not a declaration) that must be performed by a role and which is non-observable by the other roles; this kind of activity is described in WS-CDL by *SilentAction* elements. The presence of silent actions is due to the fact that WS-CDL derives from the well-known *pi-calculus* by Milner *et al.* [19], in which silent actions represent the non-observable (or private) behavior of a process. We can, therefore, think of modifying the WS-CDL definition by adding capabilities as child elements of this kind of activity [1].

---

[1] Since in WS-CDL there is not the concept of observable action, capability requirements can describe only silent actions.

Returning to Figure 3, as an instance, it defines the capability *evaluateTask* for the role *Participant* of the Contract Net protocol. More precisely, *evaluateTask* is defined within a silent action and its definition comprises its name plus a list of inputs and outputs. The tags *capability*, *input*, and *output* are defined in our extension of WS-CDL. It is relevant to observe that each parameter refers to a variable that has been defined in the choreography.

```
1   <choice>
2     <workunit name="informResultWorkUnit"
3       guard="cdl:getVariable('tns:rst', '', '', 'tns:Participant') !=
                                                            'failure' ">
4       <interaction name="informResultInteraction">
5         ...
6       </interaction>
7     </workunit>
8     <interaction name="failureExecuteInteraction">
9       ...
10    </interaction>
11 </choice>
```

Fig. 4. Example of how output parameters can be used in a *choice* operator of a choreography

Choreographies not only list the set of capabilities that a service should have but they also identify the points of the interaction at which such capabilities are to be used. In particular, the values returned by a call to a capability (as a value of an output parameter) can be used for controlling the execution of the interaction. Figure 4 shows, for example, a piece of a choreography code for the role *Participant*, containing a *choice* operator. The *choice* operator allows two alternative executions: one leading to an inform speech act, the other leading to a failure speech act. The selection of which message will actually be sent is done on the basis of the outcome, previously associated to the variable *rst*, of the capability *executeTask*. Only when such variable has a non-null value the inform will be sent. The guard condition at line 3 in Figure 4 amounts to determine whether the task that the *Participant* has executed has failed.

To complete the example we sketch in Figure 5 a part of the ContractNet protocol as it is represented in our proposal of extension for WS-CDL. In this example we can detect three different capabilities, one for the role of *Initiator* and two for the role *Participant*. Starting from an instance of the type *Task*, the *Participant* must be able to evaluate it by performing the *evaluateTask* capability (lines 4-9), returning an instance of type *Proposal*. Moreover, it must be able to execute the received task (if its proposal is accepted by the *Initiator*) by using the capability *executeTask* (lines 26-31), returning an instance of type *Result*. On the other side, the *Initiator* must have the capability *evaluateProposal*, for choosing a proposal out of those sent by the participants (lines 15-20).

```
1  <sequence>
2    <interaction name="callForProposalInteraction"> ...
3    </interaction>
4    <silentAction roleType="Participant">
5      <capability name="evaluateTask">
6        <input> ...  </input>
7        <output> ...  </output>
8      </capability>
9    </silentAction>
10   <choice>
11     <workunit name="proposeWorkUnit" guard=...  >
12       <sequence>
13         <interaction name="proposeInteraction">
14         </interaction>
15         <silentAction roleType="Initiator">
16           <capability name="evaluateProposal">
17             <input> ...  </input>
18             <output> ...  </output>
19           </capability>
20         </silentAction>
21         <choice>
22           <workunit name="acceptProposalWorkUnit" guard=...  >
23             <sequence>
24               <interaction name="proposeInteraction">
25               </interaction>
26               <silentAction roleType="Participant">
27                   <capability name="executeTask">
28                       <input> ...  </input>
29                       <output> ...  </output>
30                   </capability>
31               </silentAction>
32               <choice>
33                 <workunit name="informResultWorkUnit"
34                   guard=...  >
35                   <interaction name="informResultInteraction">
36                   </interaction>
37                 </workunit>
38                 <interaction name="failureExecuteInteraction">
39                 </interaction>
40               </choice>
41             </sequence>
42           </workunit>
43           <interaction name="rejectProposalInteraction">
44           </interaction>
45         </choice>
46       </sequence>
47     </workunit>
48     <interaction name="evaluateTaskRefuseInteraction">
49     </interaction>
50   </choice>
51 </sequence>
```

Fig. 5. A representation of the FIPA ContractNet Protocol in the extended WS-CDL

As we have seen in the previous sections, it is possible to start from a representation of this kind for performing the capability test and check if a service can play a given role (e.g. *Initiator*). Moreover, given a similar description it is also possible to synthesize the skeleton of a policy, possibly customized w.r.t. the capabilities and the goals of the service that is going to play the role. To this aim, it is necessary to have a translation algorithm for turning the XML-based specification into an equivalent schema expressed in the execution language of interest.

5   Conclusions

This work presents a preliminary study aimed to allow the use of public choreography specifications for automatically synthesizing executable interaction policies for peers that would like to take part in an interaction but that do not own an appropriate policy themselves. To this purpose it is necessary to link the abstract, communicative behavior, expressed at the protocol level, with the internal state of the role player by means of actions that might be non-communicative in nature (capabilities). It is important, in an open framework like the web, to be able to take a decision about the possibility of taking part to a choreography before the interaction begins. This is the reason why we have proposed the introduction of the notion of capability at the level of choreography specification. A capability is the specification of an action in terms of its name, and of its input and output parameters. Given such a description it is possible to apply matching techniques in order to decide whether a service has the capabilities required for playing a role of interest. In particular, we have discussed the use of semantic matchmaking techniques, such as those developed in the WSMO and DAML-S initiatives [24], for matching web service descriptions to queries.

We have shown how, given a (possibly) declarative representation of the policy skeletons, obtained from the automatic synthesis process, it is possible to apply further reasoning techniques for customizing the implemented policy to the specific characteristic of the service that will act as a player. Reasoning techniques for accomplishing this customization task are under investigation. In particular, the techniques that we have already used in previous work concerning the personalization of the interaction with a web service [4] seem promising. In that work, in fact, we exploited a kind of reasoning known as *procedural planning*, relying on a logic framework. Procedural planning explores the space of the possible execution traces of a procedure, extracting those paths at whose end a goal condition of interest holds. It is noticeable that in presence of a sensing action, i.e. an action that queries for external input, all of the possible answers are to be kept (they must all lead to the goal) and none can be cut off. In other words, it is possible to cut only paths that correspond to some action that are under the responsibility of the agent playing the policy. The waiting for an incoming message is exactly a query for an external input, as such the case of the candidate seller that does not allow a legal form of payment cannot occur.

Our work is close in spirit to [25], where the idea of keeping separate procedural and ontological descriptions of services and to link them through semantic annotations is introduced. In fact our WS-CDL extension can be seen as procedural description of the interaction enriched with capabilities requirements, while semantic annotations of capability requirements enable the use of ontological reasoning for the capability test phase. Presently, we are working at more thorough formalization of the proposal that will be followed by the implementation of a system that turns a role represented in the proposed extension of WS-CDL into an executable composite service, for instance represented in WS-BPEL. WS-BPEL is just a possibility, actually any programming language by means of which it is possible to develop web services could be used.

References

1. M. Alberti, M. Gavanelli, E. Lamma, P. Mello, and P. Torroni. Specification and verification of agent interactions using social integrity constraints. In *Proc. of the Workshop on Logic and Communication in Multi-Agent Systems, LCMAS 2003*, volume 85(2) of *ENTCS*, 2003. Elsevier.
2. D. Ancona and V. Mascardi. Coo-BDI: Extending the BDI Model with Cooperativity. In *Proceedings of the 1st Declarative Agent Languages and Technologies Workshop (DALT'03)*, pages 109–134. Springer-Verlag, 2004. LNAI 2990.
3. M. Baldoni, C. Baroglio, A. Martelli, and Patti. Verification of protocol conformance and agent interoperability. In *Post-Proc. of CLIMA VI*, volume 3900 of *LNCS State-of-the-Art Survey*, pages 265–283. Springer, 2006.
4. M. Baldoni, C. Baroglio, A. Martelli, and V. Patti. Reasoning about interaction protocols for customizing web service selection and composition. *J. of Logic and Algebraic Programming, special issue on WS and Formal Methods*, 2006. To appear.
5. M. Baldoni, C. Baroglio, A. Martelli, V. Patti, and C. Schifanella. Verifying the conformance of web services to global interaction protocols: a first step. In *Proc. of 2nd Int. Workshop on Web Services and Formal Methods, WS-FM 2005*, volume 3670 of *LNCS*, pages 257–271. Springer, September, 2005.
6. M. Baldoni, G. Boella, and L. van der Torre. Bridging Agent Theory and Object Orientation: Importing Social Roles in Object Oriented Languages. In *Post-Proc. of the Int. Workshop on Programming Multi-Agent Systems, ProMAS 2005*, volume 3862 of *LNCS*, pages 57–75. Springer, 2006.
7. M. Baldoni, G. Boella, and L. van der Torre. powerjava: Ontologically Founded Roles in Object Oriented Programming Languages. In *Proc. of 21st SAC 2006, Special Track on Object-Oriented Programming Languages and Systems*, 2006. ACM.
8. L. Bozzo, V. Mascardi, D. Ancona, and P. Busetta. CooWS: Adaptive BDI agents meet service-oriented computing. In *Proc. of the Int. Conference on WWW/Internet*, pages 205–209, 2005.
9. P. Busetta, N. Howden, R. Ronquist, and A. Hodgson. Structuring BDI agents in functional clusters. In *Proc. of the 6th Int. Workshop on Agent Theories, Architectures, and Languages (ATAL99)*, 1999.
10. N. Busi, R. Gorrieri, C. Guidi, R. Lucchi, and G. Zavattaro. Choreography and orchestration: a synergic approach for system design. In *Proc. of 4th International Conference on Service Oriented Computing (ICSOC 2005)*, 2005.
11. F. Dignum, editor. *Advances in agent communication languages*, volume 2922 of *LNAI*. Springer-Verlag, 2004.

12. Foundation for Intelligent Physical Agents. http://www.fipa.org.
13. F. Guerin and J. Pitt. Verification and Compliance Testing. In *Communication in Multiagent Systems*, volume 2650 of *LNAI*, pages 98–112. Springer, 2003.
14. M. P. Huget and J.L. Koning. Interaction Protocol Engineering. In *Communication in Multiagent Systems*, volume 2650 of *LNAI*, pages 179–193. Springer, 2003.
15. Jade. http://jade.cselt.it/.
16. U. Keller, R. Laraand A. Polleres, I. Toma, M. Kifer, and D. Fensel. D5.1 v0.1 wsmo web service discovery. Technical report, WSML deliverable, 2004.
17. A. Mamdani and J. Pitt. Communication protocols in multi-agent systems: A development method and reference architecture. In *Issues in Agent Communication*, volume 1916 of *LNCS*, pages 160–177. Springer, 2000.
18. M. Martelli and V. Mascardi. From UML diagrams to Jess rules: Integrating OO and rule-based languages to specify, implement and execute agents. In *Proc. of the 8th APPIA-GULP-PRODE Joint Conf. on Declarative Programming (AGP'03)*, pages 275–286, 2003.
19. R. Milner. *Communicating and Mobile Systems: the Pi-Calculus*. Cambridge University Press, 1999.
20. OASIS. Business process execution language for web services.
21. J. H. Odell, H. Van Dyke Parunak, and B. Bauer. Representing agent interaction protocols in UML. In *Agent-Oriented Software Engineering*, pages 121–140. Springer, 2001. http://www.fipa.org/docs/input/f-in-00077/.
22. L. Padgham and P. Lambrix. Agent capabilities: Extending BDI theory. In *AAAI/IAAI*, pages 68–73, 2000.
23. V. Padmanabhan, G. Governatori, and A. Sattar. Actions made explicit in BDI. In *Advances in AI*, number 2256 in LNCS, pages 390–401. Springer, 2001.
24. M. Paolucci, T. Kawmura, T. Payne, and K. Sycara. Semantic matching of web services capabilities. In *First International Semantic Web Conference*, 2002.
25. M. Pistore, L. Spalazzi, and P. Traverso. A minimalist approach to semantic annotations for web processes compositions. In *ESWC*, pages 620–634, 2006.
26. Arianna Tocchio and S. Costantini. Learning by knowledge exchange in logical agents. In *Proc. of WOA 2005: Dagli oggetti agli agenti, simulazione e analisi formale di sistemi complessi*, november 2005. Pitagora Editrice Bologna.
27. W. M. P. van der Aalst, M. Dumas, A. H. M. ter Hofstede, N. Russell, H. M. W. Verbeek, and P. Wohed. Life after BPEL? In *Proc. of WS-FM'05*, volume 3670 of *LNCS*, pages 35–50. Springer, 2005. Invited speaker.
28. Michael Wooldridge and Simon Parsons. Issues in the design of negotiation protocols for logic-based agent communication languages. In *Agent-Mediated Electronic Commerce III, Current Issues in Agent-Based Electronic Commerce Systems*, volume 2003 of *LNCS*. Springer, 2001.
29. WS-CDL. http://www.w3.org/tr/ws-cdl-10/.

Semantic Web Reasoning for Analyzing Gene Expression Profiles

Liviu Badea

AI Lab, National Institute for Research and Development in Informatics
8-10 Averescu Blvd., Bucharest, Romania
badea@ici.ro

Abstract. We argue that Semantic Web reasoning is an ideal tool for analyzing gene expression profiles and the resulting sets of differentially expressed genes produced by high-throughput microarray experiments, especially since this involves combining not only very large, but also semantically and structurally complex data and knowledge sources that are inherently distributed on the Web. In this paper, we describe an initial implementation of a full-fledged system for integrated reasoning about biological data and knowledge using Sematic Web reasoning technology and apply it to the analysis of a public *pancreatic cancer dataset* produced in the Pollack lab at Stanford.

1 Introduction and Motivation

The recent breakthroughs in genomics have allowed new rational approaches to the diagnosis and treatment of complex diseases such as cancer or type 2 diabetes. The role of *bioinformatics* in this domain has become essential, not just for managing the huge amounts of diverse data available, but also for extracting biological meaning out of heterogeneous data produced by different labs using widely different experimental techniques. Although the completion of the sequencing of the genomes of a large number of organisms (including the Human Genome) has identified the (more or less) complete lists of genes of these organisms, we only have a partial view of the complexity of the interactions among these genes.

Thus, determining the molecular-level details of complex diseases is a challenging issue. Traditional genetic methods are inapplicable since, typically, there is no single gene responsible for the disease. Rather, a complex interplay of pathways is usually involved, so that many *different* genetic (possibly somatic) defects[1] may affect the same pathway. Despite the large body of existing biological knowledge, even the pathways are only partially known and, even worse, may interact in very complex ways.

The study of complex diseases has been revolutionized by the advent of whole-genome measurements of gene expression using *microarrays*. These allow the determination of gene expression levels of virtually all genes of a given organism in a variety of different samples, for example coming from normal and diseased tissues.

However, the initial enthusiasm related to such microarray data has been tempered by the difficulty in their interpretation. It has become obvious that additional available

---

[1] Such as Single Nucleotide Polymorphisms (SNP), chromosomal translocations, chromosomal segment amplifications or deletions, etc.

J.J. Alferes et al. (Eds.): PPSWR 2006, LNCS 4187, pp. 78 – 89, 2006.
© Springer-Verlag Berlin Heidelberg 2006

knowledge has to be somehow used in the data analysis process. However, the complexity of the types of knowledge involved renders any known data analysis algorithm inapplicable. Thus, we need to integrate at a deep semantic level the existing domain knowledge with the partial results from data analysis. *Semantic Web* technology, and especially the *reasoning* facilities that it will offer turn out to be indispensable in the biological domain at all levels:

- At the lower data access level, we are dealing with huge data- and knowledge bases that are virtually impossible to duplicate on a local server. A mediator-type architecture [16] would therefore be useful for integrating the various resources and for bridging their heterogeneity.
- At the level of data schemas, we frequently encounter in this domain very complex semi-structured data sources – accessing their contents at a semantic level requires precise machine-interpretable descriptions of the schemas.
- Finally, the data and knowledge refer to complex conceptual constructions, which require the use of common domain ontologies for bridging the *semantic* heterogeneities of the sources.

In this paper, we describe an initial attempt at developing a full-fledged system for integrated reasoning about biological data and knowledge using Semantic Web reasoning technology. The system is designed as an open system, able to quickly accommodate various data sources of virtually all types (semi-structured, textual, databases, etc.). At this time, we have a working system prototype that uses the state-of-the-art XML query language XQuery [9] for implementing the wrappers to the Web-based sources (either in XML or possibly non-well-formed HTML), the Flora2 [10] F-logic implementation for reasoning and a Tomcat-based implementation of the Web application server.

2   The Pancreatic Cancer Dataset

In the following we describe an application of the technology to the analysis of a public *pancreatic cancer dataset* produced in the Pollack lab at Stanford [1].

Despite the enormous recent progress in understanding cancer at a molecular level, the precise details are still elusive for many types of carcinomas. Pancreatic cancer is a particularly aggressive disease, with a very poor prognosis, requiring a more precise understanding of its molecular pathogenesis. The technological progress initiated by the introduction of gene expression microarrays about a decade ago has enabled large scale whole genome studies with the aim of identifying disease-specific genes. Although limited by the relatively low number of samples (due to the large costs of the technology), these gene expression studies have revealed a much more complex molecular-level picture than previously expected. Tens to a few hundreds genes were found to be differentially expressed in the samples analyzed, and their precise roles in the (signaling) pathways leading to cancer are only partially known. Even worse, it seems extremely difficult to discern between genetic abnormalities that play a causal role in oncogenesis and those that are merely side-effects. Obviously, the task of identifying new therapeutic targets depends essentially on being able to identify the causal details.

The results of published studies [1,2,3] have emphasized the complexity of the genetic abnormalities involved in pancreatic cancer. There seem to be few, if any, amplifications or deletions common to all patients thus leading to a more complex picture of the disease in which perturbations of distinct components of certain key pathways are triggered in various different ways, while leading to similar phenotypes.

The fact that our knowledge of the various signaling pathways involved is only partial makes the task of identifying the precise details of oncogenesis even more difficult, requiring a combination of all the available data and knowledge.

More precisely, Bashyam et al. [1] have performed simultaneous *array Comparative Genomic Hybridization* and *microarray expression* measurements on a set of 23 human pancreatic cell lines (with two additional normal-normal reference array-CGH measurements) using cDNA microarrays containing 39632 human cDNAs (representing about 26000 named human genes). Array-CGH measurements involved co-hybridizing Cy5-labeled genomic DNA from each cell line along with Cy3-labeled sex-matched normal leukocyte DNA. Expression profiling was performed with reference RNA derived from 11 different human cell lines.

We retrieved the normalized intensity ratios from the Stanford Microarray Database [5] and used the CGH-Miner software [4] as described in [1] to identify DNA copy number gains and losses. Expression ratios were called significant if they $_{EXPR-} = 0.5$.

Since for certain microarray spots expression ratios may be poorly defined (mainly due to low intensities in one of the two channels), we only retained genes whose expression ratios were well measured in at least 14 of the 23 samples. Unlike Bashyam et al. who performed mean centering of the (log-)expression ratios of the genes (to emphasize their relative levels among samples), we avoid mean-centering or variance normalization of the ratios since we are interested in identifying systematically over/under-expressed genes, the expression level being important for this purpose. Finally, we constructed two lists of "common" up- and respectively down-regulated genes *Common* and *Common*, which we use in the following.

3 The Data Sources

The architecture of the application is presented in Figure 2 in the Appendix. The application uses various data and knowledge sources, ranging from semi-structured data to databases of literature-based paper abstracts.

We initially integrated the following sources:

NCBI/Gene. The e-utilities [11] interface to the NCBI Gene database [12] returns gene-centred information in XML format. We extracted using an XQuery wrapper gene symbols, names, descriptions, protein domains (originating from Pfam or CCD), and literature references. We also extracted the Gene Ontology (GO) [13] annotations of the genes, as well as the pathways[2] and interactions[3] in which these are known to be involved.

TRED. The Transcriptional Regulatory Element Database TRED [8] contains knowledge about transcription factor binding sites in gene promoters. Such information is essential for determining potentially co-expressed genes and for linking them to signaling pathways.

---

[2] Originating from KEGG or Reactome.
[3] Taken e.g. from BIND or HPRD.

Biocarta [7] is a pathway repository containing mostly graphical representations of pathways contributed by an open community of researchers. We have developed an XQuery wrapper that currently extracts the lists of genes involved in the various pathways.

Pubmed. Literature references to genes and their interactions extracted from Pubmed abstracts [14] will also be integrated into the system.

The above sources contain complementary information about the genes, their interactions and pathways, neither of which can be exploited to their full potential in isolation. For example, the GO annotations of genes can be used to extract the main functional roles of the genes involved in the disease under study. Many such genes are receptors or their ligands, intra-cellular signal transducers, transcription factors, etc. And although many of these genes are known to be involved in cancer (as oncogenes or tumor suppressors), the GO annotations will not allow us to determine their interactions and pathway membership. These can only be extracted from explicit interaction or pathway data-sources, such as TRED, BIND, Biocarta, etc.

4   A Unified Model of the Data Sources

In order to be able to jointly query the data sources, a unified model is required. We used the prototype system described in [17] to implement a mediator over the above-mentioned data sources. The system uses *F-logic* [23] for describing the content of information sources as well as the domain ontology for several important reasons.

First, although the distinctive feature of the Semantic Web is reasoning, the various related W3C standards are not easy to use by a reasoner, especially due to their heterogeneity (XML, RDF, RuleML, etc.). A *uniform* internal level, optimized for efficiency is required for supporting inference and reasoning. The architecture of our system therefore separates a so-called *"public" level* from the *internal level.* The public level refers to the data, knowledge and models exchanged on the Web and between applications and conforms to the current and emerging Web standards such as XML, RDF(S), RuleML, etc. F-logic is used at the "internal" level.

Second, the tabling mechanism of Flora2 [4] is essentially equivalent to the Magic Sets method [24] for bottom-up evaluation in database query engines, which, combined with top-down evaluation, can take advantage of the highly optimized compilation techniques developed for Prolog, resulting in a very efficient deductive engine.

Moreover, F-logic combines the logical features of Prolog with the frame-oriented features of object-oriented languages, while offering a more powerful query language (allowing e.g. aggregation and meta-level reasoning about the schema). Last but not least, F-logic is widely used in the Semantic Web community [18,19,20]. However, we also consider the possibility of using Xcerpt [21] at this level.

4.1   Mapping Rules

Since the sources are heterogeneous, we use so-called *"mapping rules"* to describe their content in terms of a common representation or ontology. For example, we can retrieve direct interactions either from the gene-centred NCBI Gene database, or from TRED:

---

[4] Flora2 is the F-logic implementation we use.

```
di(I):direct_interaction[gene->G1, other_gene->G2, int_type->IntType, source->'ncbi_gene',
                            description->Desc, pubmed->PM] :-
    query_source('ncbi_gene_interactions', 'bashyam')@query,
    I:interaction[gene->G1, other_gene->G2, description->Desc,
                        pubs->PM]@'ncbi_gene_interactions',
    if (str_sub('promoter',Desc,_)@prolog(string))
    then IntType = 'p-d'
    else IntType = 'p-p'.

di(I):direct_interaction[gene->G1, other_gene->G2, int_type->IntType, source->'tred'] :-
    query_source('tred', 'bashyam')@query,
    I:interaction[tf->G1, gene->G2]@'tred',
    IntType = 'p-d'.
```

The common representation refers to direct interactions by the direct_interaction Flora2 object. We distinguish between two types of interactions:

- protein-to-DNA ('*p-d*'), which refers to transcription regulatory influences between a protein and a target gene, and
- protein-to-protein ('*p-p*'), which comprises all other types of interactions.

The distinction is important since the gene expression data analyzed reveals only changes in expression levels. Thus, while the protein-to-DNA interactions could in principle be checked against the expression data, the protein-to-protein interactions are complementary to the expression data[5] and could reveal the cellular functions of the associated proteins.

While certain types of knowledge are more or less explicit in the sources (for example, the interaction type is '*p-d*' if the description of the interaction contains the substring '*promoter*'), in other cases we may have to describe implicit knowledge about sources (i.e. knowledge that applies to the source but cannot be retrieved from it – for example, the TRED database contains only interactions of type '*p-d*', but this is nowhere explicitly recorded in the data).

4.2 Model Rules

Although in principle the wrappers and the mapping rules are sufficient for being able to formulate and answer any query to the sources, it is normally convenient to construct a more complex model, that is as close as possible to the conceptual model of the users (molecular biologists/geneticists in our case). This is achieved using so called "*model rules*" which refer to the common representation extracted by the mapping rules to define the conceptual view (model) of the problem.

For example, we may want to query the system about "*functional*" interactions (which are not necessarily *direct* interactions). More precisely, a functional interaction between two genes can be either due to a direct interaction, or to the membership in the same pathway, or to their co-reference in some literature abstract from Pubmed:

```
pi(I1,I2):pathway_interaction[gene->G1, other_gene->G2, int_type->IntType,
                    source->[Src1,Src2], pathway->P, role(G1)->R1, role(G2)->R2] :
    I1:pathway[name->P, gene->G1, gene_description->GN1, role(G1)->R1, source->Src1],
    I2:pathway[name->P, gene->G2, gene_description->GN2, role(G2)->R2, source->Src2],
    interaction_type(R1,R2,IntType).
```

---

[5] i.e. cannot be derived from it.

```
interaction_type(target_gene, target_gene, coexpression) :  !.
interaction_type(target_gene, Role2, transcriptional) :  Role2 \= target_gene, !.
interaction_type(Role1, target_gene, transcriptional) :  Role1 \= target_gene, !.
interaction_type(Role1, Role2, same_pathway) :  Role1 \= target_gene, Role2 \= target_gene, !.

fi(I):functional_interaction[gene->G1, other_gene->G2, int_type->IntType, source->Src] :
        I:direct_interaction[gene->G1, other_gene->G2, int_type->IntType, source->Src]
        ; I:pathway_interaction[gene->G1, other_gene->G2, int_type->IntType, source->Src]
        ; I:literature_interaction[gene->G1, other_gene->G2, int_type->IntType, source->Src].
```

We may also define classes of genes based on their GO annotations. For example, the following rules extract receptors, ligands and respectively transcription regulators:

```
r(I):gene_role[gene->G, category->C, role->receptor, source->Src] :
        I:gene_category[gene->G, category->C, source->Src],
        str_sub('receptor',C,_)@prolog(string),
        str_sub('activity',C,_)@prolog(string).

r(I):gene_role[gene->G, category->C, role->ligand, source->Src] :
        I:gene_category[gene->G, category->C, source->Src],
        str_sub('receptor',C,_)@prolog(string),
        ( str_sub('binding',C,_)@prolog(string) ;
          str_sub('ligand',C,_)@prolog(string) ).

r(I):gene_role[gene->G, category->C, role->transcription_regulator, source->Src] :
        I:gene_category[gene->G, category->C, source->Src],
        ( str_sub('DNA binding',C,_)@prolog(string) ;
          str_sub('transcription',C,_)@prolog(string) ).
```

Such classes of genes can be used to "fill in" *templates* of signaling chains, such as ligand → receptor → signal transducer →...→ transcription factor, which could in principle be reconstructed using knowledge about interactions:

```
generic_signaling_chain_interaction(ligand, receptor, 'p-p').
generic_signaling_chain_interaction(receptor, signal_transducer, 'p-p').
generic_signaling_chain_interaction(signal_transducer, signal_transducer, 'p-p').
generic_signaling_chain_interaction(signal_transducer, transcription_factor, 'p-p').
generic_signaling_chain_interaction(transcription_factor, target_gene, 'p-d').
generic_signaling_chain_interaction(modulator, receptor, 'p-p').
generic_signaling_chain_interaction(modulator, signal_transducer, 'p-p').
generic_signaling_chain_interaction(modulator, transcription_factor, 'p-p').

signaling_chain(sig_chain(G), G, Role) :

        Role = receptor,
        _:gene_role[gene->G, role->Role].
signaling_chain(S, G2, Role2) :

        signaling_chain(S, G1, Role1),
        generic_signaling_chain_interaction(Role1, Role2, IntType),
        _:direct_interaction[gene->G1, other_gene->G2, int_type->IntType],
        _:gene_role[gene->G2, role->Role2].
```

Note that the signaling chains are initialized with receptors, since these are the starting points of signaling cascades and are typically affected in most cancer samples (including our pancreatic cancer dataset).

In our cancer dataset analysis application, the transcription factors play an important role, since their gene targets' co-expression can reveal the groups of genes that are differentially co-regulated in the disease:

```
tf_binding(G1, G2, IntType) :
    _:gene_role[gene->G1, category->C1, role->transcription_regulator],
    _:direct_interaction[gene->G1, other_gene->G2, int_type->IntType, source->Src],
    _:gene_list[gene->G2, list->common].
```

Figure 1 below shows the graph generated by the system in response to the following query (Cytoscape [22] is used for visualization):

```
?- show_graph(${tf_binding(TF,G,IntType)}, [TF,G,IntType]).
```

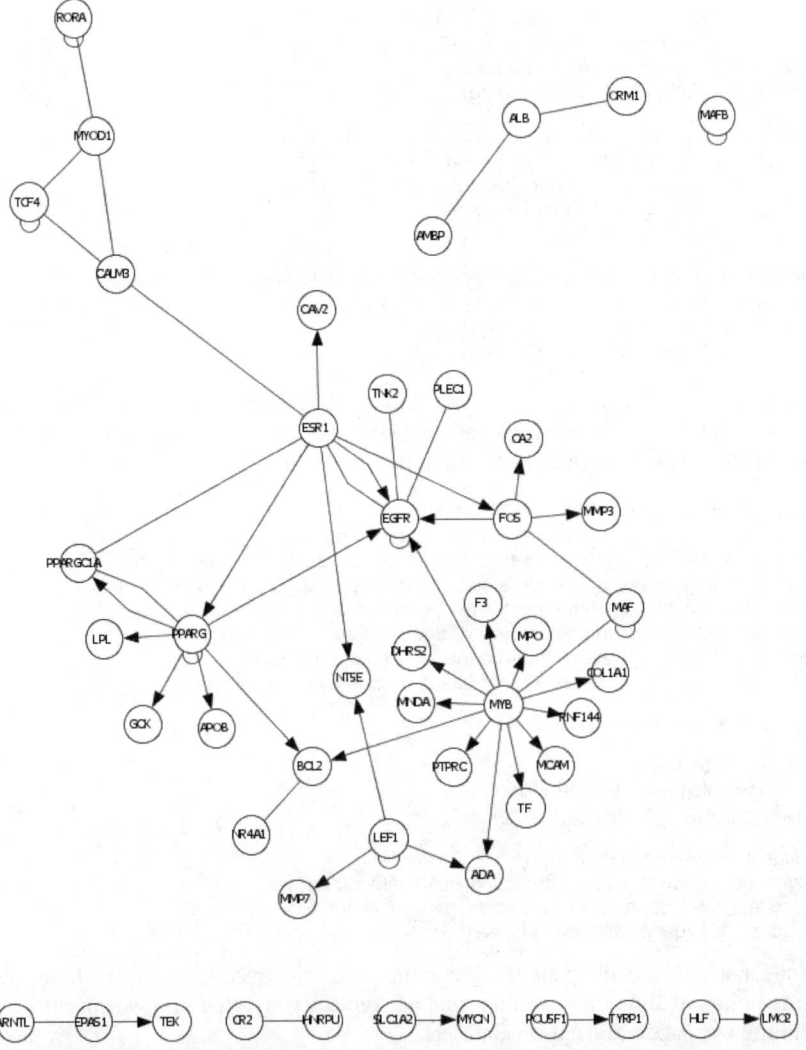

Fig. 1. Transcription regulatory relationships among "common" genes in the Bashyam et al. pancreatic cancer dataset (arrows: 'p-d', undirected edges: 'p-p' interactions)

5   Conclusions and Future Work

Our initial experiments confirmed the feasibility of our approach and lead to a number of interesting observations. Although all processing was performed in-memory, the system was able to deal with the complete data-sources mentioned above for the selection of "common" genes (359 genes):

- NCBI Gene interactions: 2239
- TRED interactions: 10717
- Biocarta gene to pathway membership relations: 5493
- NCBI gene to pathway membership relations: 622
- Other pathway membership relations: 5095
- GO annotations: 2394
- Protein domains: 614.

From a certain perspective, the approach is a combination of *remote-source mediation* and *data-warehousing*. As in a mediation approach, only the *relevant* entries of remote data sources are retrieved, but these are stored in a local warehouse by the wrappers (in XML format) to avoid repetitive remote accesses over the Web.

Such exploratory queries involving large datasets and combinatorial reasoning typically have slow response times (typically seconds to minutes if the relevant sources have been accessed previously and are therefore in the local warehouse; if not, response times depend on the size of the data to be transferred from remote sources and on the connection speed). However, as far as we know, other existing approaches are either slower[6] or cannot deal with such datasets at all.

Such exploratory queries involving large datasets and combinatorial reasoning typically have slow response times (typically seconds to minutes if the relevant sources have been accessed previously and are therefore in the local warehouse; if not, response times depend on the size of the data to be transferred from remote sources and on the connection speed). However, as far as we know, other existing approaches are either slower or cannot deal with such datasets at all.

Since reasoning in general is based on *combining* knowledge, Semantic Web reasoning will have to deal with combining knowledge *distributed* on the Web. The distributed nature of relevant knowledge in turn places significant limitations on the reasoners, due to the limited data transfer speeds of the current Web. Thus, it appears that future Semantic Web reasoning systems will be placed between two extremes, depending on the scope of the knowledge relevant to a query. At one extreme, there will be general, Google-like systems that will use local warehouses of the entire Web for answering semantic queries. At the other extreme, Web browsers will be enhanced with (semantic) reasoning capabilities, but the reasoning will be performed on a single Web page only. Our approach comes somehow in between the two extremes: the relevant and frequently used sources and Web pages are stored in a local warehouse allowing more sophisticated queries than in the "browser only" setting.

---

[6] In the case of systems based on plain Prolog (with no tabling or other similar optimizations).

We have also tried to implement fragments of the above scenario using XQuery not just for the wrappers, but also for the integrated model. (In our experiments, we have used the qizxopen [9] implementation of XQuery. The general idea consisted in implementing the reasoning rules as XQuery functions.) Although the efficiency and memory consumption are comparable to those of our F-logic-based system, using a procedural query language like XQuery posed significant problems. For example, the following XQuery function retrieves the transcription regulatory interactions involving common genes:

```
declare function local:select-NCBI_Gene-tranreg_interactions_common($NCBI_Gene_common
as node(), $common_genes as xs:string  *) as node() *
{
<RESULTS>
{
   for $int in $NCBI_Gene_common//interaction,
      $g1 in $common_genes[. = string($int/gene)],
      $g2 in $common_genes[. = string($int/other_gene)]
   let $g := $int/../..
   where contains(lower-case(string($g/Gene_Ontology/GO_category/GO_annot/GO)),
   "transcription")
   return
   <transcription_regulator_interaction_common>{$int/*}</transcription_regulator_interaction_com
mon>
}
</RESULTS>
}
```

Note the rather complex way of performing simple operations such as joins. But even if we ignore such syntactic complications, we would have to write a separate XQuery function *for each possible instantiation pattern* of a given rule head, leading to a cumbersome and hard to modify program (a modification of a rule would require synchronized modifications in all associated XQuery functions).

Finally, there are certain technical issues whose improvement would lead to a significantly better Semantic Web reasoning system:

-   Query planning
-   Streaming
-   Source capabilities
-   Support for (semi-)automated development of wrappers.

In the case of large data sources, as in the biological domain (giga- to terrabytes), it is obviously impossible to retrieve the *entire* content of such sources before starting reasoning. Also, if additional knowledge is available about the sources, some source accesses may be avoided altogether. Therefore, dealing with information sources requires a certain form of *query planning*, i.e. the ability of constructing and reasoning about alternative sequences of source accesses (plans) before actually querying these sources. Also, *streaming the query responses* may allow starting processing before the entire response is retrieved.

Since queries can involve *several* different information sources, they will have to be to be *split* into sub-queries that can be treated by the separate information sources. Since each information source may have its own (Web accessible) interface, we need to explicitly represent the *capabilities* of these interfaces. As opposed to traditional database query languages, such Web sources provide only limited query capabilities. For example, a specific Web interface may allow only certain types of selections and may also require certain parameters to be inputs (i.e. known at query time). These source capabilities would have to be taken into account during query planning.

From the biological point of view, the system has proved to be very useful for creating a global "picture" of the interactions among the genes differentially expressed in pancreatic cancer. The large number (359) of these genes [7] would have made the task extremely difficult, if not impossible for a human exploration of the data sources. For example, note the involvement of: [8]

- the Epidermal Growth Factor Receptor EGFR, known to be involved in many cancers
- BCL2, a gene involved in the apoptotic response of cells (note that the down-regulation of BCL2 in pancreatic cancer is quite unusual for an anti-apoptotic gene, since it is normally over-expressed in other tumor types [15])
- the transcription factors FOS, MYB, LEF1
- the metalloproteinases MMP3, and MMP7 (involved in tissue remodeling, invasion, tumor progression, metastasis and tumor initiation – in the case of MMP3)
- the nuclear receptor PPARG, a regulator of differentiation known to be involved in cancer and PPARGC1A, its coactivator.

The biological interpretation of the results is outside the scope of this paper and will be discussed elsewhere in a specialized paper.

Acknowledgements. I am grateful to Doina Tilivea for her contribution in implementing the F-logic system [17] and to Anca Hotaran for contributing to the development of the XQuery wrappers. This research has been partially funded by the European Commission within the 6th Framework Programme project REWERSE (506779, http://rewerse.net). I am deeply grateful to the REWERSE members for interesting discussions during the conference and for supporting this research.

References

1. Bashyam MD et al.Array-based comparative genomic hybridization identifies localized DNA amplifications and homozygous deletions in pancreatic cancer.Neoplasia. 2005 Jun;7(6):556-62
2. Heidenblad M et al. Genome-wide array-based comparative genomic hybridization reveals multiple amplification targets and novel homozygous deletions in pancreatic carcinoma cell lines. Cancer Res. 2004 64(9):3052-9.

---

[7] Amounting to 64261 potential interactions.
[8] See Figure 1.

3. Heidenblad M et al. Microarray analyses reveal strong influence of DNA copy number alterations on the transcriptional patterns in pancreatic cancer: implications for the interpretation of genomic amplifications. Oncogene. 2005 Mar 3;24(10): 1794-801.

4. Wang P, Kim Y, Pollack J, Narasimhan B, Tibshirani R. A method for calling gains and losses in array CGH data. Biostatistics. 2005 Jan;6(1):45-58.

5. Sherlock G. et al. The Stanford Microarray Database. Nucleic Acids Research, 29:152--155, 2001. http://genome-www5.stanford.edu

6. Bhattacharjee et al. Classification of human lung carcinomas by mRNA expression profiling reveals distinct adenocarcinoma subclasses. Proc. Natl. Acad. Sci. USA. 2001 Nov. 20;98(24):13790-5.

7. Biocarta. www.biocarta.com

8. Fang Zhao, Zhenyu Xuan, Lihua Liu, Michael Q. Zhang. TRED: a Transcriptional Regulatory Element Database and a platform for in silico gene regulation studies. Nucleic Acids Res. 2005 January 1; 33(Database Issue): D103–D107.

9. Qizxopen. http://www.xfra.net/qizxopen/

10. Yang G., Kifer M., Zhao C. FLORA-2: A Rule-Based Knowledge Representation and Inference Infrastructure for the Semantic Web. In Second International Conference on Ontologies, Databases and Applications of Semantics (ODBASE), Catania, Sicily, Italy, November 2003. http://flora.sourceforge.net/

11. NCBI e-utilities. http://eutils.ncbi.nlm.nih.gov/entrez/query/static/eutils_help.html

12. NCBI Gene. http://www.ncbi.nlm.nih.gov/entrez/query.fcgi?db=gene

13. Ashburner M. et al. Gene ontology: tool for the unification of biology. Nat. Genet. 2000 May;25(1):25-9. http://www.geneontology.org

14. Pubmed. http://www.ncbi.nih.gov/entrez/query.fcgi?db=PubMed

15. Westphal S, Kalthoff H.Apoptosis: targets in pancreatic cancer.Mol Cancer. 2003 Jan 7;2:6. Review.

16. Wiederhold G. Mediators in the architecture of future information systems, IEEE Comp. 25(3) 1992, 38-49.

17. Liviu Badea, Doina Tilivea, Anca Hotaran. Semantic Web Reasoning for Ontology-Based Integration of Resources. Proc. PPSWR 2004, pp. 61-75, Springer Verlag.

18. Decker S., Sintek M. 'Triple - an RDF query, inference, and transformation language', in Proc. of the 2002 International Semantic Web Conference (ISWC-2002).

19. Fensel D., Angele J., Decker S., Erdmann M., Schnurr H.P., Staab S., Studer R., Witt A., On2broker: Semantic-based Access to Information Sources at the WWW, Proceedings of WebNet, 1999, pp. 366-371.

20. Ludascher B., Himmeroder R., Lausen G., May W., Schlepphorst C. Managing Semistructured Data with FLORID: A Deductive Object-oriented Perspective. Information Systems, 23(8):589-613, 1998.

21. Berger S., Bry F., Schaffert S., Wieser C. Xcerpt and visXcerpt: From Pattern-Based to Visual Querying of XML and Semistructured Data. Proceedings VLDB03, Berlin, September 2003, http://www.xcerpt.org/.

22. Cytoscape. http://www.cytoscape.org

23. Kifer M., Lausen G., Wu J. Logical Foundations of Object-Oriented and Frame-Based Languages. Journal of the ACM, 42:741-843, 1995.

24. Bancilhon F., Maier D., Sagiv Y. and Ullman J. Magic sets and other strange ways to implement logic programs. In Proceedings PODS (1986) 1-15.

Appendix

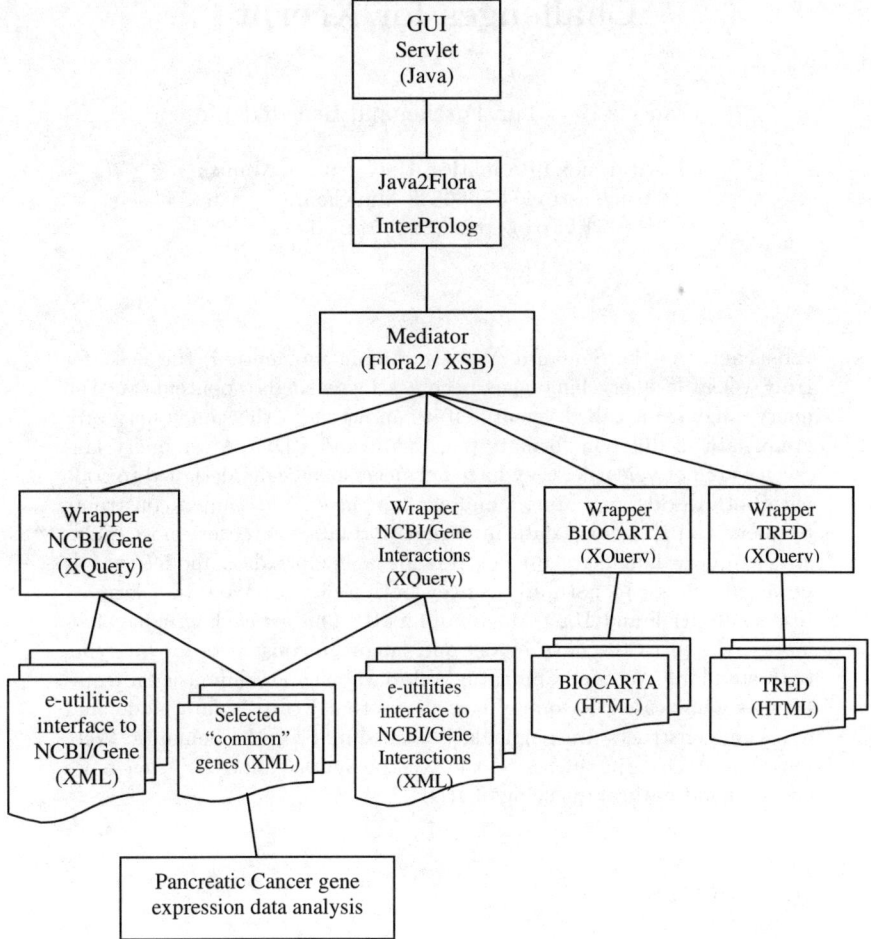

Fig. 2. The architecture of the pancreatic cancer dataset analysis application

Data Model and Query Constructs for Versatile Web Query Languages: State-of-the-Art and Challenges for Xcerpt

François Bry, Tim Furche, and Benedikt Linse

Institute for Informatics, University of Munich,
Oettingenstraße 67, 80538 München, Germany
http://pms.ifi.lmu.de/

Abstract. As the Semantic Web is gaining momentum, the need for truly versatile query languages becomes increasingly apparent. A Web query language is called versatile if it can access in the same query program data in different formats (e.g. XML and RDF). Most query languages are not versatile: they have not been specifically designed to cope with both worlds, providing a uniform language and common constructs to query and transform data in various formats. Moreover, most mainstream query languages do not provide a flexible data model that is powerful enough to naturally convey both Semantic Web data formats (especially RDF and Topic Maps) and XML. This article highlights challenges related to the data model and language constructs for querying both standard Web and Semantic Web data with an emphasis on facilitating sophisticated reasoning. It is shown that Xcerpt's data model and querying constructs are particularly well-suited for the Semantic Web, but that some adjustments of the Xcerpt syntax allow for even more effective and natural querying of RDF.

1 Introduction

Data on the web is increasingly enriched with semantic meta-data, linking it to the real world or to other information. While XML has already gained widespread acceptance, RDF is on the best way to do so. Query languages have established themselves as a valuable means for accessing both formats, and a considerable number of query languages for XML (such as XQuery[1], XPath[2], XSLT[3], Xcerpt[4–6]) and for Semantic Web data (e.g. SPARQL[7], RQL[8], Versa[9]) have been proposed and implemented, cf. [10] for a survey. XML query languages can be used to query XML serializations of RDF data. This, however, hardly yields a programmer-comfortable approach to RDF data. In fact, most of the above languages have not been specifically designed to cope with both worlds, and do not provide a uniform language and common constructs to query and transform data in the various formats. Moreover, most mainstream query languages lack a flexible data model that is powerful enough to naturally

J.J. Alferes et al. (Eds.): PPSWR 2006, LNCS 4187, pp. 90–104, 2006.

comprehend both Semantic Web data formats (especially RDF and Topic Maps) and XML.[1]

This article highlights challenges related to the data model and convenient constructs for querying both standard Web and Semantic Web data with an emphasis on facilitating sophisticated reasoning. It is shown that Xcerpt's data model and querying constructs are well-suited also for the Semantic Web, but that some adjustments of Xcerpt's syntax would allow for even more effective and natural query authoring with respect to RDF.

The rest of this article is structured according to its contributions: Section 2 examines requirements related to the data model of versatile web query languages with focus on RDF and XML. Section 3 proposes an extended edge-labeled syntax for Xcerpt terms that can be straightforwardly mapped to usual Xcerpt data terms. Section 4 illustrates that Xcerpt's constructs for handling heterogeneity are beneficial to both XML and RDF querying. Section 5 underlines the importance of grouping constructs in the scope of the Semantic Web. Finally, Section 6 concludes this article and sheds light upon further research both with respect to the language itself and its efficient evaluation.

2   Challenges Related to the Data Model

Figure 1 presents two possible representations of information about countries, their names and their border-countries in XML (on the left hand side) and RDF (on the right hand side). Nodes of the XML document tree are represented as grey rectangles containing the element name. Text nodes are distinguished by quotes and attribute-value pairs are displayed at the top right of the node they belong to. The namespace prefixes rdf, rdfs and geo are assumed to be bound to http://www.w3.org/1999/02/22-rdf-syntax-ns#, http://www.w3.org/2000/01/rdf-schema# and http://geo.org/#, respectively, in the entire article. Nodes of the RDF graph on the right are either depicted as grey rectangles containing the URI or blank node name in the case of non-literals or as oval nodes in the case of literal values.

Figure 1 naturally exemplifies that XML semi-structured data and Semantic Web data differ in various ways, complicating the conversion of the formats in either direction and impeding the use of a query language specialized on only one of the formats for accessing both. On the one hand, XML data can only be unnaturally represented as RDF, because (1) the order of outgoing edges in RDF is irrelevant, (2) nodes are uniquely identified by URIs except for literals and blank nodes, (3) RDF does not support the concept of attributes. On the other hand, XML cannot naturally comprehend RDF data, in that (1) besides nodes also the edges of RDF graphs are labeled, (2) RDF is truly graph structured, and (3) RDF graphs need not be connected and are unrooted. In this section all of these differences are discussed and it is illustrated that although Xcerpt's

---

[1] Exceptions are early query languages for semi-structured data such as XML-QL and Lorel.

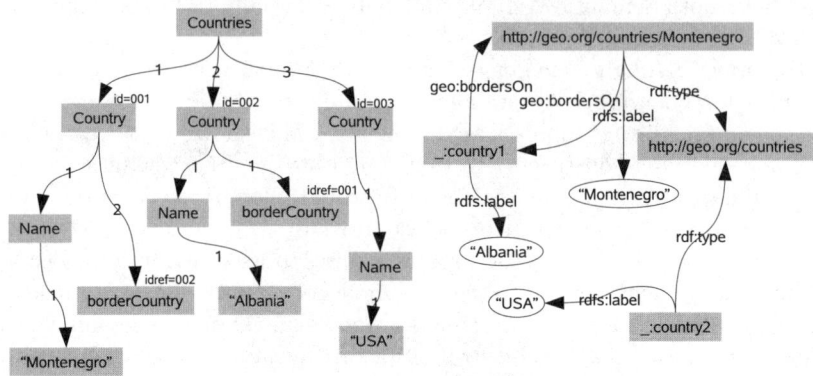

Fig. 1. XML data versus RDF data

term and graph oriented data model allows the representation also of RDF data in a very straight-forward way.

2.1   Graph Data Model and References

One of the most striking differences between Semantic Web data and XML is that XML does not allow multiple parent nodes for the same XML element and must be considered tree structured under this consideration. This is why most XML query languages such as XPath and XQuery provide a tree data model. Taking the special attributes id and idref into account, XML may also be viewed as a graph structure. When querying XML it may sometimes even be useful to consider these XML references as true parent-child relationships. In contrast, Semantic Web data is truly graph structured, in that predicates are the only way of specifying relationships amongst resources, and nodes of an RDF graph may very well have multiple incoming edges. RDF graphs are usually represented by triples without any explicit references. Nevertheless, a graph structure is implied by these triples, because RDF references are implicit in that they exploit the fact that RDF resources are uniquely identified by URIs.

Whereas for XML query languages, such as XPath, XQuery and XSLT a tree data model is a natural choice, versatile query languages that incorporate also Semantic Web data must adopt a graph data model.

From the beginning Xcerpt was designed to not only handle XML data, but also semi-structured graph data, which means that it can be adapted to natively handle Semantic Web data easier than other XML query languages.

2.2   Labeled Edges

Put simply, the XML data model is a node-labeled tree. In contrast, RDF graphs are not only node-labeled, but also edge-labeled. In XML serializations of RDF graphs such as RDF/XML, this difference is overcome by "striped" XML, which means that element nodes representing RDF nodes and edges alternate in the nested XML serialization. The *Syntactic Web Approach* suggests querying RDF serializations with XML query languages. This solution is unsatisfactory in various ways: (1) It is not coherent with the visual and intuitive representation of RDF data as graphs, and is thus more difficult to grasp. (2) It does not pay tribute to the different roles assumed by subjects, objects and predicates of the RDF graph, which complicates e.g. the determination of the set of all predicates of an RDF graph. (3) Many XML serializations (such as RDF/XML and RDF/A) offer a great amount of variability and syntactic sugar for representing RDF graphs, which makes the formulation of queries against such serializations in XML query languages cumbersome.

As a result, a truly versatile query language for the Web must offer a data model that comprehends both: node- and edge-labeled graphs as well as purely node-labeled graphs. As has been mentioned before, node- and edge-labeled graphs can be transformed into graphs without edge labels in a straightforward manner. Nevertheless, the user must be provided with a syntax (see Section 3) that clearly distinguishes between edge- and node-labels both in query constructs and in the data.

2.3   Incomplete and Unbounded Data

In the Semantic Web, resources are uniquely identifiable, and thus anybody is free to make statements about resources by simply referencing the unique URI as subject, predicate or object within one's own statements. A consequence of this ability for everyone to make statements about arbitrary resources is that one may never be sure to be aware of all statements made about a given resource (this is why RDF data can be considered inherently *incomplete*). From a graph perspective on Semantic Web data, this means that collecting all existing outgoing edges of a resource is not possible, which is a fundamental difference to XML data, where the sequence of children of an element node is fixed and can be determined simply by looking at the document containing the node in question.

A possible solution (which also yields other benefits) to this problem is to restrict one's attention to the contents of specific documents or groups of statements, which are often referred to as *Named Graphs*. "Named graphs is the idea that having multiple RDF graphs in a single document/repository and naming them with URIs provides useful additional functionality built on top of the RDF Recommendations."[2] In fact, RDF query languages such as SPARQL and TriQL provide constructs for handling and constructing named graphs.

The above observations show that the data model for a Semantic Web query language must be able to express both complete (in form of named graphs or documents) and incomplete data (information that does not belong to any graph). While conventional Xcerpt query terms may already be complete and incomplete in breadth, data terms have always been considered to be complete. As shown in

---

[2] http://www.w3.org/2004/03/trix/

section 4 data terms can be naturally extended to include incomplete data, and an extended operational semantics that takes this extension of the data model into account is being considered.

2.4 RDF Graphs as Xcerpt Data Terms

While in semi-structured data, there is always a distinguished top level term, the root, Semantic Web data does not have the concept of top level terms. Furthermore, it may not even be possible to single out a resource from which all other resources are reachable over edges in the graph, because RDF graphs may consist of disconnected subgraphs. It is, however, possible to determine a set of resources, such that each resource in the graph is reachable from at least one of them. Choosing these resources as top level nodes, RDF graphs are very conveniently represented by sets of Xcerpt data terms.

2.5 Order of Sub-terms

Another difference between RDF and XML data illustrated in Figure 1 is that RDF data usually does not impose an order on outgoing edges of a node. To be more precise, RDF data is always unordered unless otherwise specified by the use of an rdf:Seq sequence container. Hence, the data model must be able to represent both ordered and unordered information. The distinction between ordered und unordered data is especially useful in the scope of positional queries against semi-structured data as exemplified in Section 4.

Xcerpt data terms have been conceived to not only represent XML data, but also semi-structured data in general. Therefore Xcerpt already supports the concept of unordered sets of children unlike most other XML query languages and does not need to be adapted to the Semantic Web in this respect.

Summing up the particularities of XML and RDF data, the data model must support possibly cyclic and disconnected graphs with labeled and unlabeled edges, complete and incomplete data specifications, ordered and unordered child elements, implicit and explicit references, and finally multiple roots.

3   An Intuitive Syntax for Versatile Web Query Languages

In previous work [5], we have shown that due to its versatility gained from construct-query-rules and constructs for treating heterogeneous data, Xcerpt is particularly well-suited to handle XML serializations for the Semantic Web data formats RDF and Topic Maps such as RDF/A, RDF/XML and XTM. An obvious alternative to processing XML serializations of Semantic Web formats is their direct treatment. In fact, for Xcerpt's users it may be more convenient to use a syntax that better distinguishes between edges and nodes within an RDF graph. In this section, we propose a possible syntax derived from the syntax of Xcerpt data terms that represents RDF data in a very similar way to XML data.

Listing 1. The RDF Graph of Figure 1 represented as an Xcerpt data term

```
geo:countries/Montenegro{                              1
  <geo:bordersOn> _:country1{
    <geo:bordersOn> geo:countries/Montenegro,          3
    <rdfs:label> literal('Albania'),
  }                                                     5
  <rdfs:label> literal('Montenegro'),
  <rdf:type> geo:country,                               7
}

                                                        9
_:country2 {
  <rdfs:label> literal('USA'),                         11
  <rdf:type> geo:country
}                                                       13
```

In listing 1 edges (predicates) of the RDF graph in figure 1 are enclosed by an-
gle braces and appear in between the elements (subjects and objects) that stand
for the nodes of the graph. This syntax eases the authoring and understanding
of queries considerably, because subjects, predicates and objects are much more
easily distinguished.

As has been mentioned above, data with labeled edges may be transformed to
graph structured data with unlabeled edges by the introduction of an additional
node for each edge. This approach has already been used to query Semantic Web
data with Xcerpt in [11]. A graph data model with labeled edges can be offered
to the user by the internal and automatic transformation of both RDF query and
data graphs to graph data with unlabeled edges, which can already be handled
by Xcerpt. In this article it is argued that the user of a versatile query language
should be unconscious of and not be confronted with this transformation.

4   Common Query Constructs for the Web and the Semantic Web

Schema information often being unavailable, data on the Web is very heterogeneous. But even if schema information is present, it usually leaves room for
variability. In contrast to relational database query languages, Web query languages must therefore provide constructs for handling this heterogeneity.

Besides querying Semantic Web data, programmers are also interested in
transforming it. An example scenario for one such transformation is the collection of data from different sources, and its rearrangement according to a joint
schema.

Xcerpt has been designed as a declarative language rooted in logic programming. This section shows that Xcerpt's approach to querying, transforming and
reasoning is well-suited not only for ordinary semi-structured data, but also for
the Semantic Web.

4.1   Query Patterns and Answer Closedness

One of the design principles of SPARQL and Xcerpt is answer closedness. This principle dictates that all answers to queries may themselves be used as queries. By ensuring similar syntaxes for both the formulation of queries and the representation of data, answer closedness eases program understanding.

Using data terms as queries, it is just possible to check whether an RDF graph is entailed[3] by the queried data, or whether a particular XML fragment is contained within a document. In order to extract parts of the data, queries must contain logical variables. Xcerpt query terms are data terms enriched by variables and a series of constructs for handling heterogeneous data. These constructs are just as useful in the Semantic Web as for ordinary XML data. Constructs for handling heterogeneity in Xcerpt include optional term selection, double braces for incompleteness in breadth and arbitrary length traversal path expressions.

One might be interested in all resources that represent countries directly or transitively bordering on Montenegro and their names. Assuming data of a similar form as in Figure 1, the following Xcerpt query in edge-labeled notation helps out:

Listing 2. An Xcerpt query term with constructs for handling heterogeneity

```
var Country →/.*/{{                                              1
  <rdf:type> geo:country{{ }},
  desc(<geo:bordersOn> /.*/)*                                     3
    <geo:bordersOn>
      geo:countries/Montenegro{{ }},                             5
  optional <rdfs:label> var Name →literal(/.*/)
}}                                                                7
```

There are several noteworthy constructs in the above query term:

- *Variable Constraints.* In Line 1, the bindings for the variable Country is constrained to graphs matching the pattern following →.
- *Incompleteness in breadth.* The schema of data on the web is in many cases unknown. Therefore one might not know or even not care about the set of outgoing edges of an RDF node. Double curly braces are used in Xcerpt to indicate that the matched data may also contain additional siblings other than those specified by the query term.
- *Regular expressions* for labels. The logical variable Country in Listing 2 is supposed to be bound to all kinds of nodes within the queried RDF graph, no matter whether it is a blank node or a resource. The regular expression /.*/ matches arbitrary URIs and b-nodes. In order to match just blank nodes or resources, the keywords b-node and resource can be used.
- *Incompleteness in depth.* The resource r_1 matching with variable Country shall be directly or transitively connected over geo:bordersOn-predicates

---

[3] For a definition of RDF entailment see http://www.w3.org/TR/rdf-mt/ , Section 3.2.

with the resource geo:countries/Montenegro, which stands for Montenegro. The RDF nodes in between r_1 and geo:countries/Montenegro are of no interest, and therefore an *arbitrary length traversal path expression* containing a wild-card regular expression for the resources of the intermediate nodes is used in line three.

– *Optional sub-terms.* Labels for the resources r_1 are to be retrieved if present. In the absence of such a label the query is not intended to fail, but to simply restitute no binding for the variable Name. Making use of the keyword literal ensures that Name is only bound to literals, never to URIs.

Solutions to Xcerpt queries are given in the form of substitution sets, which are sets of mappings from the logical variables in the query to subgraphs of the data. The query in Listing 2 applied to the RDF graph in Figure 1 yields the following substitution set:

$$\{ \{\texttt{Country} \mapsto \texttt{\_:country1}\{ \dots \}, \texttt{ Name} \mapsto \texttt{'Albania'} \} \}$$

The fact that the variable Country is bound to the entire subgraph rooted at the resource it matches differentiates Xcerpt from other query languages such as SPARQL and RQL. Since in densely connected RDF graphs, the bindings of variables may contain large sub-graphs of the data or even the whole data graph, Xcerpt provides a second kind of variables called *label variables* which are not bound to entire subgraphs but only to the nodes they match with. The usage of a label variable in Listing 2 would be syntactically indicated by directly prefixing the double curly braces in Line 1 by the variable var Country.

Note that also SPARQL provides a way to return more information (entire subgraphs) about resources than just their URIs through the keyword describe. The exact nature of such descriptions is left unspecified by the SPARQL working draft, but the Concise Bounded Description[4] proposed by Nokia is mentioned as an example.

The semantics of the query in Listing 2 is implicitly defined by mapping the node-and-edge-labeled syntax of the query to purely node-labeled query terms.

4.2 Injectivity and Querying RDF Sequences

When specifying a query term to be matched with semi-structured data, the semantics intended by the query author is usually that sibling nodes shall *not* match with the same node of the queried graph. *Matching* a query term q and its children $q_1, \dots q_n$ with a data term d and its children $d_1, \dots, d_m$ can be formalized by a function $m : \{q_1, \dots q_n\} \to \{d_1, \dots, d_m\}$. We demand m to be *injective* to reflect the authors intention. Listing 3 shows a query selecting all pairs of countries bordering on Montenegro, and Xcerpt's semantics[5] ensures that the variables Country1 and Country2 are not bound to the same node. Note that formulating a query that allows the bindings for Country1 and Country2 to be the same can be easily expressed using Xcerpt's and connective for queries.

---

[4] http://swdev.nokia.com/uriqa/CBD.html
[5] Formally defined in [4, Chapter 8] at the aid of functions similar to m above.

Listing 3. A query selecting all pairs of countries bordering to Montenegro

```
geo:countries/Montenegro{{
  <geo:bordersOn> var Country1 →/.*/{{ }},
  <geo:bordersOn> var Country2 →/.*/{{ }}
}}
```

As has been mentioned in Section 2.5 Semantic Web data can both be ordered and unordered. Xcerpt's positional approach to querying allows to match data dependent on the order of sub-terms. Figure 2 contains a possible representation of information about spoken languages in countries using an RDF sequence container.

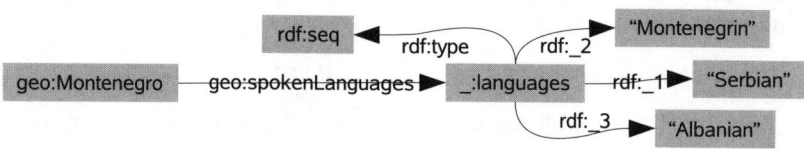

Fig. 2. An RDF sequence containing the languages in the order of their diffusion in Montenegro

The query in Listing 4 selects all countries in which Serbian is more common than Albanian assuming a schema as in Figure 2. The use of square brackets instead of curly braces indicates that the order of occurrence within the RDF sequence is relevant.

Listing 4. An Xcerpt query taking into account the order of subterms within an RDF-Container

```
var Country →/.*/{{
  <geo:spokenLanguage> /.*/[[
    </.*/> literal('Serbian'),
    </.*/> literal('Albanian')
  ]]
}}
```

4.3 Blank Node Treatment

Blank nodes (also called b-nodes) in RDF graphs are used to assert that a resource r_1 exists that is related with other resources in a certain way without associating a URI to r_1. One unresolved issue related to querying RDF data containing b-nodes concerns the redundancy of answer sets. To see this reconsider the RDF graph from Figure 1.

Listing 5. A query selecting all resources of type geo:country

```
var Country →/.*/{{<rdf:type> geo:country}}
```

Selecting all resources of the graph that are of type geo:country, the query in Listing 5 cannot determine whether _:country2 and geo:countries/ Montenegro are meant to be the same concepts. Hence, the question arises, whether both the blank node _:country2 and the resource identified by geo: countries/Montenegro should be returned or only the URI. The solution considered to be the most convincing by the authors is to exclude such query solutions that are entailed by other solutions, but to keep all others. The query in Listing 5 would therefore return both resources. In the case that the triple (_:country2, rdfs:label, 'USA') were not present, returning the blank node of the graph would be redundant.

4.4 Negation and Breadth-Complete Queries

As has been discussed in Section 2.3, Semantic Web data must be considered as inherently incomplete and unbounded in comparison to XML. Additionally taking into account that RDF statements are always positive assertions, the only sensible form of negation is scoped negation as failure, which has already been proven useful in the context of the Semantic Web[12, 13].

An approach that goes even beyond scoped negation as failure by providing explicit negative information to additionally enable strong negation is suggested in [14]. Although strong negation would certainly be helpful for Semantic Web Reasoning, it is not yet supported by Xcerpt.

While some Semantic Web query languages including the SPARQL family do not provide negation, XML query languages including Xcerpt usually do. To underline the importance of scoped negation in the Semantic Web consider the following query issued against the resource http://countries.org/country-_information.

Listing 6. Scoped negation as failure in Xcerpt query terms

```
in{ resource{ 'http://countries.org/country_information' },    1
  /.*/{{
    <rdf:type> geo:country{{ }},                                3
    <geo:bordersOn> geo:countries/Montenegro{{ }},
    <rdfs:label> var Name →literal(/.*/),                       5
    not(<geo:bordersOn> /.*/{{ <rdfs:label>
        literal('Albania') }})
  }},                                                           7
}
```

Listing 6 queries the names of all countries bordering to Montenegro but not to Albania. Matching a term with both positive and negated sub-terms with a data term is carried out as follows: At first, it is tested, whether each of the positive query sub-terms can be associated with a matching sub-term of the data respecting the injectivity requirement mentioned in Section 4.2. If this matching succeeds, it is searched for a matching sub-term of the data for the negated sub-terms. If any of the negated sub-terms can be matched, the entire matching fails. If all positive sub-terms can be matched with the data, but none of the negated ones, the entire matching succeeds. The query semantics for node- and edge-labeled query and data terms as needed for RDF data is ascribed to the semantics of purely node-labeled terms as described in [4, Section 8.2] by straight-forward normalization rules transforming edge-labeled terms to purely node-labeled terms.

Breadth-complete queries are an issue which is closely related to negated sub-terms, because they can be rewritten as breadth-incomplete queries using the without-construct. They are indicated by single curly braces or brackets instead of double ones and can only be matched with data that does not contain any additional sub-terms besides those specified in the query term. To find countries that only border to Italy (and do not appear as subject in any other statement of the RDF graph), the query in Listing 7 could be used.

Listing 7. Breadth-complete queries against RDF data

```
in{ resource{ 'http://countries.org/country_information' },
  var Country →/.*/{                                                2
    <geo:bordersOn> geo:countries/Italy{{ }},
  },                                                                4
}
```

In the same way as queries with negated sub-terms, breadth-complete queries must be scoped to a single or a set of named graphs.

4.5   Optional Sub-terms

As exemplified in Listing 2, optional constructs are of great help for Semantic Web queries in that they allow to extract certain parts of the queried data only if they are present. Closer examination of the optional construct reveals that it is only syntactic sugar for a disjunction of queries. The query in Listing 2 could also be written using the Xcerpt or construct:

Listing 8. The same query as in Listing 2 without the optional construct

```
or (                                                               1
  var Country →/.*/{{
    <rdf:type> geo:country{{ }},                                   3
    desc(<geo:bordersOn> /.*/)* <geo:bordersOn>
        geo:countries/Montenegro{{ }},
    <rdfs:label> var Name →literal(/.*/)                           5
  }},
  var Country →/.*/{{                                              7
    <rdf:type> geo:country{{ }},
    desc(<geo:bordersOn> /.*/)* <geo:bordersOn>                    9
        geo:countries/Montenegro{{ }},
    without <rdfs:label> var Name →literal(/.*/)
  }}                                                               11
)
```

As in SPARQL, multiple optional sub-terms may occur as siblings, or may even be nested. The semantics of such graph patterns seems to be straightforward at first glance: For each optional sub-term that succeeds to match, the bindings of its variables are included in the substitution set returned by the overall graph pattern. The failed matching of an optional sub-term does not prevent the overall graph pattern from returning a substitution set, which simply does not contain bindings for the variables in the unmatched optional sub-terms. Since variables may – and often do – occur multiple times in a query pattern, they may also be shared among multiple optional sub-terms, causing interdependencies among them. In particular, it may happen that only one of two optional sub-terms may be matched, but not both. While the SPARQL working draft does not define which of the sub-terms is to be picked, Xcerpt adopts the following convention: If multiple optional sub-terms impede each other from matching, all selections of these sub-terms are chosen that maximize the number of variable bindings.

5   From Queries to Transformations

While most Semantic Web query languages are limited to querying and returning sets of mappings of their variables to resources, Xcerpt – and to some extent also SPARQL – are designed to do more: by providing construct terms (in SPARQL they are called graph templates) to be filled with the variable bindings gained from the evaluation of queries, they allow the construction of results having an entirely different schema. This combination of querying and construction in so-called *construct-query-rules* (see Section 5.1 for details) gives rise to the possibility of complex transformations.

5.1   Construct-Query-Rules and User Defined Reasoning

The evaluation of Xcerpt query terms and SPARQL graph patterns against RDF data yields substitution sets. Xcerpt construct terms are Xcerpt data terms enriched by variables as place holders and grouping constructs like `all` and `some`. Substitutions are applied to construct terms by replacing the variables in the construct term by their bindings in the substitution set (for the detailed semantics see [4, Section 7.3.3]). Query and construct terms are combined by so-called *construct-query-rules*, which allow sophisticated user-defined reasoning which goes beyond the predefined rules of RDFS and OWL.

5.2   Grouping Constructs

A major difference between SPARQL graph templates and Xcerpt construct terms is that only the latter allow merging of substitution sets (called result sets in SPARQL) by using grouping constructs. Merging substitution sets is necessary because often the need arises to collect variable bindings from different matches of the query pattern with the data. In contrast, a query result form within a

SPARQL query is always filled exactly as often as the graph pattern in the WHERE clause matches with the queried RDF graph.

Reconsidering the information about countries and languages as exemplified in Figure 2, one might wish to construct an RDF graph that groups countries according to the languages which are spoken in them. To be more precise, for each language a blank node shall be constructed carrying an rdfs:label such as "Albanian", "Serbian", etc. Moreover the blank node must feature outgoing geo:spokenIn edges for each country that the language is spoken in.

Listing 9. Grouping countries according to languages

```
CONSTRUCT
  _:language{
    <rdfs:label> var Language,                                         2
    all <geo:spokenIn> var Country }
FROM                                                                    4
  var Country →/.*/{{
    <geo:spokenLanguage> /.*/{{ </.*/> var Language }} }}              6
END
                                                                       8
```

Using the grouping construct all (line 4), the query in Listing 9 collects all bindings for the variable Country that are contained within a substitution set for a fixed binding of variable Language. An important issue to note is that – just as in SPARQL – although the name _:language of the blank node in Line 2 is constant, a new blank node is constructed for each binding of the variable Language.

5.3   Versatile Access to XML and RDF

Integrated access to different data formats includes the requirement that data should be easily transformed from one format to the other, and that different formats are queried simultaneously. As an exemplary use-case imagine that information about bordering countries is available in XML format structured similarly to that in the left part of Figure 1, and that information about languages spoken in these countries is only available in RDF format as in Figure 2.

The query in Listing 10 extracts all those pairs of border-countries whose citizens understand each other, because they speak the same language. The query part of the rule is a conjunction of two query terms, the first one querying the XML resource, and the second one drawing information from an RDF file. The names of countries sharing a common border are found by comparing the values of the id and idref attributes with a value join over the variable ID (in Xcerpt, XML attributes are enclosed in parentheses; double parentheses indicate that there may be additional unspecified attributes). Similarly, pairs of countries which have the same most common language are selected by a join over the variable Language.

The query uses both constructs that are peculiar to either RDF or XML – such as variables for XML attribute values and edge-labeled query terms – and constructs that are applicable to both – such as complete and incomplete query term specifications. Notice that the variables Name1 and Name2 are shared among both conjuncts, which would be cumbersome to implement with two specialized languages for RDF and XML.

Listing 10. Versatile access to Web data Formats in Xcerpt

```
CONSTRUCT
  result[ all understanding-neighbors[ var Name1, var Name2 ] ]      2
FROM
  and (                                                               4
   in{ resource{ 'http://geo.org/countries.xml' },
     Countries {{                                                     6
       Country((var ID →id)){{ Name{ var Name1 } }},
       Country{{                                                      8
         borderCountry((var ID →idref)),
         Name{ var Name2 } }} }} },                                   10
   in{ resource{ 'http://geo.org/languages.rdf' },
     /.*/{{                                                           12
       <rdfs:label> var Name1,
       <geo:spokenLanguage> /.*/{{ <rdf:_1> var Language }} }},       14
     /.*/{{
       <rdfs:label> var Name2,                                        16
       <geo:spokenLanguage> /.*/{{ <rdf:_1> var Language }} }} }
  )                                                                   18
END
```

6   Conclusion and Outlook

Due to its graph data model, its rule-based nature and its convenient constructs for handling heterogeneity, Xcerpt turns out to be very well-suited not only for XML, but also for Semantic Web querying, transformations and reasoning. RDF data being increasingly made available as descriptive meta-data for HTML and XML documents, versatile access to both meta-data and XML in the same query program becomes ever more important for the next generation of web applications such as specialized search engines, and online booking and library systems. Developing such applications can be strongly eased by providing a query language that does not restrict itself to one of the formats, but provides integrated access to all of them, freeing the programmer from the burden of learning and combining multiple languages.

Besides laying the foundation for effective query authoring, a versatile query and reasoning language must process query programs efficiently in order to gain strong acceptance throughout the Web community. Several challenges are related to efficient query processing, demanding future work in the domain of Xcerpt.

- Efficient parsing of semi-structured data from various serializations and efficient construction of in-memory graph representations of the data. Besides parsing documents, in-memory graph representations must also be efficiently constructed from relational RDF stores.

- Efficient simulation unification of query patterns with graph data and construct terms. A large amount of research has been carried out in this direction concerning primarily tree queries, but also graph queries [6].
- Efficient backward chaining evaluation of programs. A forward chaining evaluation of Xcerpt programs is less reasonable because (a) the set of facts of an Xcerpt program can be very large, (b) the major part of derived facts may be irrelevant to the query, and (c) Xcerpt programs may have infinite fixpoints if they contain recursive rules.

Acknowledgements

This research has been funded by the European Commission and by the Swiss Federal Office for Education and Science within the 6th Framework Programme project REWERSE number 506779 (cf. http://rewerse.net).

References

1. Boag, S., Chamberlin, D., Fernandez, M., Florescu, D., Robie, J., Simeon, J.: XQuery 1.0: An XML Query Language. W3C. (2005)
2. Berglund, A., Boag, S., Chamberlin, D., Fernandez, M., Kay, M., Robie, J., Simeon, J.: XML Path Language (XPath) 2.0. W3C. (2005)
3. Clark, J.: XSL Transformations, Version 1.0. Recommendation, W3C (1999)
4. Schaffert, S.: Xcerpt: A Rule-Based Query and Transformation Language for the Web. Dissertation/Ph.D. thesis, University of Munich (2004)
5. Bry, F., Furche, T., Linse, B.: Let's Mix It: Versatile Access to Web Data in Xcerpt. Submitted for publication (2006)
6. Bry, F., Schroeder, A., Furche, T., Linse, B.: Efficient Evaluation of n-ary Queries over Trees and Graphs. Submitted for publication (2006)
7. Prud'hommeaux, E., Seaborne, A.: SPARQL Query Language for RDF. Working draft, W3C (2006)
8. Karvounarakis, G., Magkanaraki, A., Alexaki, S., Christophides, V., Plexousakis, D., Scholl, M., Tolle, K.: Querying the Semantic Web with RQL. Computer Networks and ISDN Systems Journal **42** (2003) 617–640
9. Olson, M., Ogbuji, U.: Versa Specification. Online only (2003)
10. Bailey, J., Bry, F., Furche, T., Schaffert, S.: Web and Semantic Web Query Languages: A Survey. In Maluszinsky, J., Eisinger, N., eds.: Reasoning Web Summer School 2005. Number 3564 in LNCS. Springer-Verlag (2005)
11. Bolzer, O.: Towards Data-Integration on the Semantic Web: Querying RDF with Xcerpt. Diplomarbeit/Master thesis, University of Munich (2005)
12. Donini, F.M., Nardi, D., Rosati, R.: Description Logics of Minimal Knowledge and Negation as Failure. ACM Transactions on Computational Logic (2002) 177–225
13. Wagner, G.: Web Rules need Two Kinds of Negation. Principles and Practice of Semantic Web Reasoning (2003)
14. Analyti, A., Antoniou, G., Damasio, C.V., Wagner, G.: Stable Model Theory for Extended RDF Ontologies. International Semantic Web Conference (2005) 21–36

AMAχoS—Abstract Machine for Xcerpt: Architecture and Principles

François Bry, Tim Furche, and Benedikt Linse

Institute for Informatics,University of Munich,
Oettingenstraße 67, 80538 München, Germany
http://pms.ifi.lmu.de/

Abstract. Web query languages promise convenient and efficient access to Web data such as XML, RDF, or Topic Maps. Xcerpt is one such Web query language with strong emphasis on novel high-level constructs for effective and convenient query authoring, particularly tailored to versatile access to data in different Web formats such as XML or RDF. However, so far it lacks an efficient implementation to supplement the convenient language features. AMAχoS is an abstract machine implementation for Xcerpt that aims at efficiency and ease of deployment. It strictly separates compilation and execution of queries: Queries are compiled once to abstract machine code that consists in **(1)** a code segment with instructions for evaluating each rule and **(2)** a hint segment that provides the abstract machine with optimization hints derived by the query compilation. This article summarizes the motivation and principles behind AMAχoS and discusses how its current architecture realizes these principles.

1 Introduction

Efficient evaluation of Web query languages such as XQuery, XSLT, or SPARQL has received considerable attention from both academia and industry over recent years. Xcerpt is a novel breed of Web query language that aims to overcome the split between traditional Web formats such as XML and Semantic Web data formats such as RDF and Topic Maps. Thus it avoids the impedance mismatch of using different languages to develop applications that enrich conventional Web applications with semantics and reasoning based on RDF, Topic Maps, or similar emerging formats.

However, so far Xcerpt lacks a scalable, efficient and easily deployable implementation. In this article, we propose principles and architecture of such an implementation. The proposed implementation deviates quite notably from conventional wisdom on the implementation of query languages: it is based on an abstract (or virtual[1]) machine that executes (interprets) low-level code generated from high-level query programs specified in Xcerpt.

---

[1] Little substantial difference is made in the literature between "abstract" and "virtual" machines. Some authors define virtual machines as abstract machines with *interpreters* in contrast to abstract machines such as Turing machines that are purely theoretical thought models. However this distinction is not widely adopted. In recent years, the term "virtual" machine seems to dominate outside of logic programming literature.

J.J. Alferes et al. (Eds.): PPSWR 2006, LNCS 4187, pp. 105–119, 2006.

The choice of an abstract machine for implementing a query language might at the first glance seem puzzling. And indeed proper abstract machines that separate execution and compilation have only very seldom been considered in the past for the implementation of query languages (the most notable exception being [19]). This is partially due to the perceived performance overhead introduced by the abstraction/virtualization layer. However, traditional query processors already separate between query compilation, where a high-level query is translated into a low-level physical query plan, and query execution, where the query is evaluated according to that query plan. From this the leap to an abstract machine that fully separates compilation and execution seems small and could even be considered merely a change in name. In traditional DBMS settings it has, however, never occurred due to the way query compilation is linked with query execution: cost-based optimizers consider extensively (statistical) information about the data instances, e.g., for selectivity estimates, and about actual access paths to these data instances. This information is available as the DBMS has full, central control over the data including its storage.

When implementing a Web query language such as Xcerpt, one is however faced with a quite different setting: In memory processing of queries against XML, RDF, or other Web data that may be local and persistent (e.g., an XML database or local XML documents), but just as well may have to be accessed remotely (e.g., a remote XML document) or may be volatile (e.g., in case of SOAP messages or Web Service access). In other words, it is assumed that most of the queried data is *not* under (central) control of a query execution environment like in a traditional DBMS setting, but rather that the queried data is often distributed or volatile. This, naturally, hinders the application of conventional indexing and predictive optimization techniques, that rely on local management of data and statistic knowledge about that managed data. But, it also makes separate compilation and execution possible as the query compilation is already mostly independent of data storage and instances. This is due to the fact that information about these is not available at compilation and execution time but only becomes available at query execution.

To some extent, this setting is comparable to data stream processing where also little is known about the actual data instances that are to be encountered during query evaluation. The efficient data stream systems (such as [3,1,6]) compile therefore queries into some form of (finite state or push-down) automata that is used to continuously evaluate the query against the incoming data.

AMAχoS, the abstract machine for Xcerpt on semi-structured data, can be seen as an amalgamation of techniques from these three areas: query optimization and execution from traditional databases and data stream systems, and compilation and execution of general programs based on abstract or virtual machines.

AMAχoS is designed around a small number of core principles:

1. "Compile once"—compilation and execution is separated in AMAχoS thus allowing (a) different levels of optimization for different purposes and settings and (b) the distribution of compiled query programs among query nodes making light-weight query nodes possible. For details see Section 4.2.

2. "Execute anywhere"—once compiled, AMAχoS code can be evaluated by any AMAχoS query node. It is not fixed to the compiling node. In particular, parts of a compiled program can be distributed to different query nodes. For details see Section 4.1.
3. "Optimize all the time"—not only are queries optimized predictively during query compilation, but also adaptively during execution. For details see Section 4.4.

As a corollary of these three principles AMAχoS employs a novel query evaluation framework for the unified execution of path, tree, and graph queries against both tree- and graph-shaped semi-structured data (details of this framework are discussed in Section 4.3 and [8]).

Following a brief look at the history of abstract and virtual machines for program and query execution (Section 2) and an introduction into Xcerpt (Section 3), the versatile Web query language that is implemented by the AMAχoS abstract machine, we focus in the course of this article first (Section 4) on a discussion of the *principles* of this abstract machine that also serves as a further motivation of the setting. The second part (Section 5) of the paper discusses the proposed *architecture* of AMAχoS and how this architecture realizes the principles discussed in the first part.

2   A Brief History of Abstract Machines

Abstract and virtual machines have been employed over the last few decades, aside from theoretical abstract machines as thought models for computing, in mostly three areas:

Hardware virtualization. Abstract machines in this class provide a layer of virtual hardware on top of the actual hardware of a computer. This provides the programs directly operating on the virtual hardware (mostly operating systems, device drivers, and performance intensive applications) with a seemingly uniform view of the provided computing resources. Though this has been a focus of considerable research as early as 1970, cf. [12] only recent years have seen commercially viable implementations of virtual machines as hardware virtualization layers, most recently Apple's Rosetta[2] technology that provides an adaptive, just-in-time compiled virtualization layer for PowerPC applications on Intel processors. Currently, research in this area focuses on providing scalability, fault tolerance [9] and trusted computing [11] by employing virtual machines, as well as on on-chip support for virtualization.

Operating system-level virtualization. A slightly higher level of abstraction or virtualization is provided by operating system-level virtual machines that virtualize operating system functions. Again, this technology has just recently become viable in the form of, e.g., Wine[3], a Windows virtualization layer for Unix operating systems.

---

[2] http://www.apple.com/rosetta/
[3] http://www.winehq.com/

High-level language virtual machines. From the perspective of AMAχoS the most relevant research has been on virtual machines for the implementation of high-level languages. First research dates back to the 1960s [24] and 1970s [22], but wider interest in abstract machines for high-level languages has been focused on two waves: First, in the 1980s a number of abstract machines for Pascal (p-Machine, [23]), Ada [14], Prolog [30], and functional programming languages (G-machine, [16]) have been proposed that focused on providing *platform neutrality and portability* as well as precise specifications of the *operational semantics* of the languages. Early abstract machines for imperative and object-oriented programming languages have not been highly successful, mostly due to the perceived performance penalty. However, research on abstract machines for logic and functional programming languages has continued mostly uninterrupted up to recent developments such as the tabling abstract machine [26] for XSB Prolog.

Recently, the field has seen a reinvigoration, cf. [25], triggered both by advances in hardware virtualization and a second wave of abstract machines for high-level programming languages focused this time on imperative, object-oriented programming languages like Java and $C^\sharp$. Here, *isolation and security* are added to the core arguments for the use of an abstract machine: Each instance of an abstract machine is isolated from others and from other programs on the host system. Furthermore analysis of the abstract machine byte code to ensure, e.g., safety or security properties proves easier than analysis of native machine code.

The most prominent examples of this latest wave are, of course, Sun's Java virtual machine [17] and Microsoft's common language infrastructure [15] (CLI). The latter is adding the claim of "language independence" to the arguments for the deployment of an abstract machine. And indeed quite a number of object-oriented and functional languages have been compiled to CLI code. With this second wave, design and principles of abstract machines are starting to be investigated more rigorously, e.g., in [10] and [29] that compare stack- with register-based virtual machines.

Closest in spirit and aim to the work presented in this paper and to the best knowledge of the authors' the only other work on abstract machines for Web query languages is [19] that presents a virtual machine for XSLT part of recent versions of the Oracle database. However, this virtual machine is focused on a centralized query processing scenario: a single query engine has control over all data and thus can employ knowledge about data instances and access paths for optimization and execution.

3   Xcerpt: A Versatile Web Query Language

Xcerpt is a query language designed after principles given in [7] for querying both data on the standard Web and data on the Semantic Web. More information, including a prototype implementation, is available at http://xcerpt.org.

3.1   Data as Terms

Xcerpt uses **terms** to represent semi-structured data. *Data terms* represent XML documents, RDF graphs, and other semi-structured data items. Notice that sub-terms (corresponding to, e.g., child elements) may either be "ordered" (as in an XHTML document or in RDF sequence containers), i.e., the order of occurrence is relevant, or "unordered", i.e., the order of occurrence is irrelevant and may be ignored (as in the case of RDF statements).

3.2   Queries as Enriched Terms

Following the "Query-by-Example" paradigm, queries are merely examples or *patterns* of the queried data and thus also terms, annotated with additional language constructs. Xcerpt separates querying and construction strictly.

Query terms are (possibly incomplete) patterns matched against Web resources represented by data terms. In many ways, they are like forms or examples for the queried data, but also may be *incomplete in breadth*, i.e., contain 'partial' as well as 'total' term specifications. Query terms may further be augmented by *variables* for selecting data items.

Construct terms serve to reassemble variables (the bindings of which are gained from the evaluation of query terms) so as to construct new data terms. Again, they are similar to the latter, but augmented by variables (acting as place holders for data selected in a query) and grouping constructs (which serve to collect all or some instances that result from different variable bindings).

3.3   Programs as Sets of Rules

Query and construct terms are related in **rules** which themselves are part of Xcerpt **programs**. Rules have the form:

```
CONSTRUCT construct-term
FROM and { query-term or { query-term ... } ... } END
```

Rules can be seen as "views" specifying how to obtain documents shaped in the form of the construct term by evaluating the query against Web resources (e.g. an XML document or a database).

Xcerpt rules may be *chained* like active or deductive database rules to form complex query programs, i.e., rules may query the results of other rules. More details on the Xcerpt language and its syntax can be found in [27,28].

4   Architecture: Principles

The abstract machine for Xcerpt, in the following always referred to as AMAχoS, and its architecture are organized around five guiding principles:

4.1 "Execute Anywhere"—Unified Query Execution Environment

As discussed above, possibly the strongest reason to develop virtual machines for high-level languages is the provision of a unified execution environment for programs in that high-level language. In the case of Xcerpt, AMAχoS aims to provide such a unified execution environment. In our case, a unified execution environment brings a number of unique advantages: **(1)** The *distributed execution of queries and query programs* requires that the language implementations are highly interoperable down to the level of answer representation and execution strategies. A high degree of interoperability allows, e.g., the distribution of partial queries among query nodes (see below). An abstract machine is an exceptionally well suited mechanism to ensure implementation interoperability as its operations are fairly fine granular and well-specified allowing the controlling query node fine granular control over the query execution at other ("slave") nodes. **(2)** A rigid definition of the operational semantics as provided by an abstract machine allows not only a better understanding and communication of the evaluation algorithms, it also makes *query execution more predictable*, i.e., once compiled a query should behave in a predictable behavior on all implementations. This is an increasingly important property as it eases query authoring and allows better error handling for distributed query evaluation. **(3)** Finally, a unified query execution environment makes the *transmission and distribution of compiled queries and even parts* of compiled queries among query nodes feasible, enabling easy adaptation to changes in the network of available query nodes, cf. Section 4.5.

4.2 "Compile Once"—Separation of Compilation and Execution

In the introduction, the setting for the AMAχoS abstract machine has been illustrated and motivated: In memory processing of queries against XML, RDF, or other Web data that may be local and persistent (e.g., an XML database or local XML documents), but just as well may have to be accessed remotely (e.g., a remote XML document) or may be volatile (e.g., in case of SOAP messages or Web Service access). In other words, it is assumed that most of the queried data is not under (central) control of a query execution environment like in a traditional database setting, but rather that the queried data is often distributed or volatile. This, naturally, limits the application of traditional indexing and predictive optimization techniques, that rely on local management of data and statistic knowledge about that managed data.

Nevertheless *algebraic optimization techniques* (that rely solely on knowledge about the query and possible the schema of the data, but not on knowledge about the actual instance of data to be queried) and *ad-hoc indices* that are created during execution time still have their place under this circumstances.

In particular, such a setting allows for a clean *separation of compilation and execution*: The high-level Xcerpt program is translated into AMAχoS code separately from its execution. The translation may be separated by time (at another time) and space (at another query node) from the actual execution of the query.

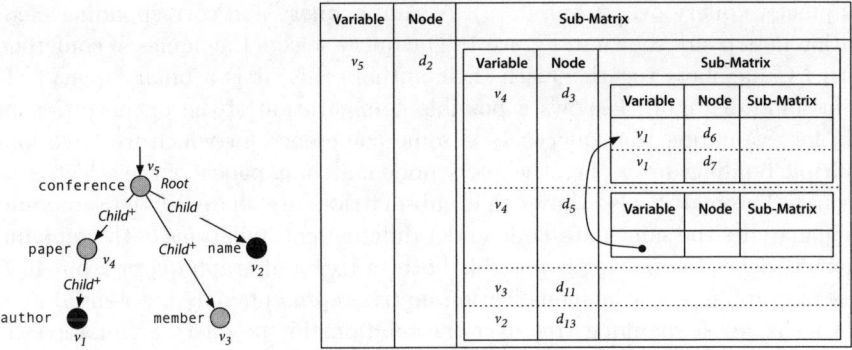

Fig. 1. Sample Query and Memoization Matrix

This is essential to enable the distribution of pre-compiled, globally optimized AMAχoS programs evaluating (parts of) queries over distributed query nodes.

Extensive Static Optimization. This separation also makes more extensive static optimization feasible than traditionally applied in an in-memory setting (e.g., in XSLT processors such as Saxon[4] or Xalan[5]). Section 5.2 and Figure 5 present a more detailed view of the query compiler and optimizer employed in the AMAχoS virtual machine. To be applicable to different scenarios, a control API for the query compilation stage allows the configuration of strategy and extent used for optimizing a query during the compilation from high-level Xcerpt programs to low-level AMAχoS code.

Aside from traditional tasks such as dead (or tautological) branch elimination, detection of unsatisfiable queries, operator order optimization and selection between different realizations for the same high-level query constructs, the AMAχoS query compiler has another essential task: the *classification of each query* in the query program by its features, e.g., whether a query is a path, tree, or graph query (cf. [20,8]) or which parts of the data are relevant for the query evaluation. This information is encoded either directly in the AMAχoS code of the corresponding construct-query rule or in a special *hint section* in the AMAχoS program. That hint section is later used by the query engine (the AMAχoS core) to tune the evaluation algorithm.

4.3 "Compile, Classify, Execute"—Unified Evaluation Algorithm

A *single evaluation algorithm* is used in AMAχoS for evaluating a large set of diverse queries and data. At the core of this algorithm stands the "memoization matrix," a data structure first proposed in [27] and refined to guarantee polynomial size in [8]), that allows an efficient representation of intermediary results during the evaluation of an Xcerpt query (or more generally an *n*-ary

---

[4] http://www.saxonica.com/
[5] http://xml.apache.org/xalan-j/

conjunctive query over graph data). A sample query and corresponding memoization matrix are shown in Figure 1: The query selects the names of conferences with PC members together with their authors (i.e., it is a binary query). The right hand of Figure 1 shows a possible configuration of the memoization matrix for evaluating that query: d_2 is some conference for which we have found multiple bindings for v_4, i.e., the query node matching **papers** of the selected conference. The matrix also shows that sub-matrices are shared if the same query node matches the same data node under different constellations of the remaining query nodes. This sharing is possible both in tree and graph queries, but in the case of graph queries the memoization matrix represents only a potential match in which only a spanning tree over the relations in the query is enforced. The remaining relations must be checked on an unfolding of the matrix. This last step induces exponential worst-case complexity (unsurprisingly as graph queries are NP-complete already if evaluated against tree data as shown in [13]), but is in many practical cases of little influence.

How to use the memoization matrix to obtain an evaluation algorithm for arbitrary n-ary conjunctive queries over graphs (that form the core of Xcerpt query evaluation), is shown in [8]. It is shown that the resulting algorithms are competitive with the best known approaches that can handle only tree data and that the introduction of graph data has little effect on complexity and practical performance.

The memoization matrix forms the core of the query evaluation in AMAχoS. As briefly outlined in [8], the method can be *parameterized with different algorithms* for populating and consuming the matrix. Thereby it is possible to adopt the algorithm both to different conditions for the query evaluation (e.g., is an efficient label or keyword index for the data available or not) and to different requirements (e.g., are just variable bindings needed or full transformation queries). The first aspect is automatically adapted by the query engine (cf. Section 5.1), the second must be controlled by the execution control API, cf. Section 5.

4.4   "Optimize All the Time"—Adaptive Code Optimization

As argued above in Section 4.2 a separation of compilation/optimization from execution is an essential property of the AMAχoS virtual machine that allows it to be used for distributed query evaluation and Web querying where control over the queried data is not centralized.

This separation can be achieved partially by providing a unified evaluation algorithm (Section 4.3) that tunes itself, with the help of hints from the static optimization, to the available access methods and answer requirements.

However, separate compilation precludes optimizations based on intricate knowledge about the actual instances of the data to be queried (e.g., statistical information about selectivity, precise access paths, data clustering, etc.). This can, to some extent, be offset by *adaptive code optimization*. Adaptive query optimization is a technique sometimes employed in continuous query systems, where also the characteristic of the data instances to be queried is not known a priori, cf. [2].

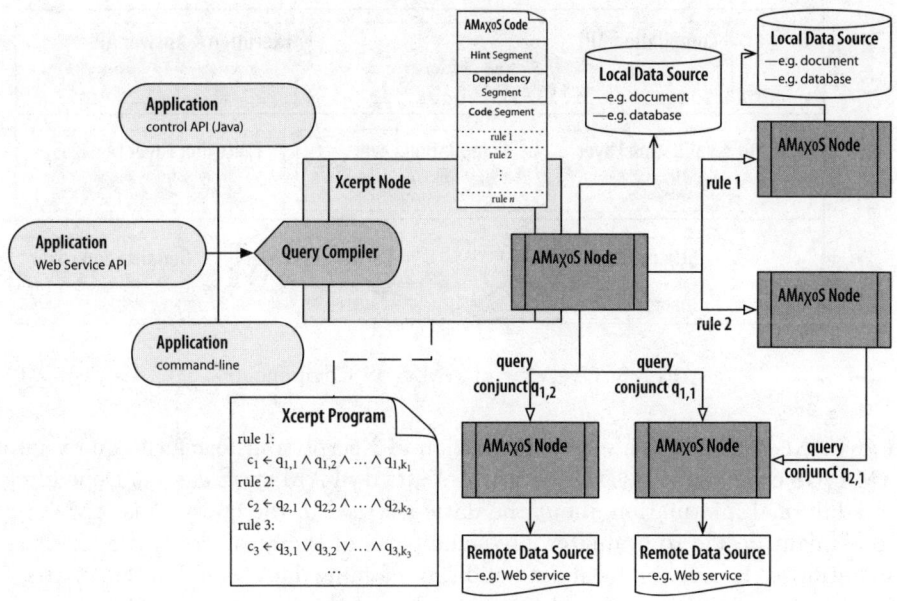

Fig. 2. Query Node Network

In the AMAχoS virtual machine we go a step further: Not only can the physical query plan expressed in the AMAχoS code continuously be adapted, but the result of the adaptation can be stored (and transmitted to other query nodes) as an AMAχoS program for further executions of the same query. Obviously, such adaptive code optimization is not for free and will most likely be useful in cases where the query is expected to be evaluated many times (e.g., when querying SOAP messages) or the amount of data is large enough that some slow-down for observation and adaption in the first part of the evaluation is offset by performance gains in later parts.

4.5 "Distribute Any Part"—Partial Query Evaluation

Once compilation and execution are separate, the possibility exists that one query node compiles the high-level Xcerpt program to AMAχoS code using knowledge about the query and possibly the schema of the data to optimize (globally) the query plan expressed in the AMAχoS code. The result of this translation can than be distributed among several query nodes, e.g., if these nodes have more efficient means to access the resources involved in the query.

Indeed, once at the level of AMAχoS code it is not only possible to distribute say entire rules or sets of rules, but even parts of rules (e.g., query conjuncts) or even smaller units. Figure 2 illustrates such a distributed query processing scenario with AMAχoS: Applications use one of the control APIs (obtaining, e.g., entire XML documents or separate variable bindings) to execute a query at

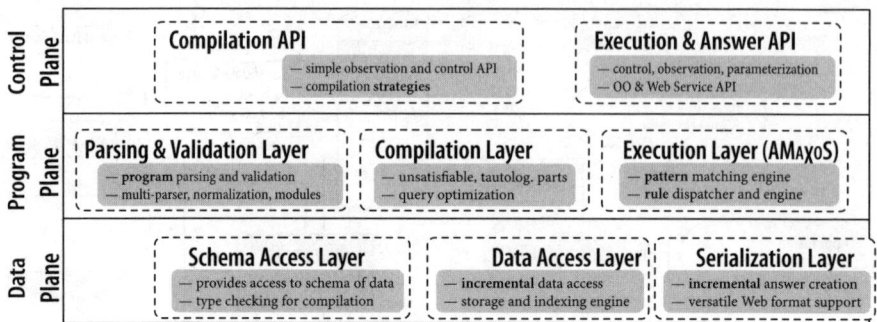

Fig. 3. Overview of AMAχoS Components

a given Xcerpt node. This implementation of Xcerpt transforms the query into AMAχoS code and hands this code over to its own AMAχoS engine. Depending on additional information about the data accessed in the query, this AMAχoS node might decide to evaluate only some parts of the query locally, e.g., those operating exclusively on local data and those joining data from different sources. All the remaining query may be send parts to other AMAχoS nodes that are likely to have more efficient access to the relevant data.

In contrast to distribution on the level of a high-level query language such as Xcerpt, distribution on the level of AMAχoS has two main advantages: the distributed query parts can be of finer granularity and the "controlling" node can have, by means of code transformation and hint sections, better control of the "slave" nodes.

Notice, that AMAχoS enables such query distribution, but does not by itself provide the necessary infrastructure (e.g., for registration and management of query nodes). It is assumed that this infrastructure is provided by outside means.

5 Architecture: Overview

The previous section illustrates the guiding principles in the development of AMAχoS. The remainder of this article focuses on how these principles are realized in its architecture and discusses several design choices regarding the architecture.

Notice, that only a small part of the full AMAχoS architecture as described here has been implemented so far. We have concentrated on the implementation on the execution and optimization layer, that are also described in more detail in Sections 5.1 and 5.2. Of the execution layer the core evaluation algorithm (pattern matching engine) is implemented as described in [8].

Figure 3 shows a high-level overview of AMAχoS and its components. The architecture separates the components in three planes:

Control Plane. The control plane enables outside control of the compilation, execution, and answer construction. Furthermore, it is responsible for observation and adaptive feedback during execution.

Program Plane. The program plane contains the core components of the architecture: the compilation and execution layer. It combines all processing that an Xcerpt program partakes when evaluated by an AMAχoS virtual machine. The first step is, naturally, parsing, validation, normalization, module expansion etc. These are realized as transformations on the layer of the Xcerpt language and the resulting normalized, validated, and expanded Xcerpt program can be accessed via the compilation API. However, usually the result becomes input for the compilation layer where the actual transformation into AMAχoS code takes place. The details of this layer are discussed below in Section 5.2. In the architecture overview, we chose to draw the compilation and execution layer as directly connected. However, it is also possible to access the resulting program (again via the compilation API) and execute it at a later time and even at a different place. Indeed, compilation and execution are properly separated with only one interface between them: the AMAχoS program that contains besides the expressions realizing individual rules in the Xcerpt program also supporting code segments that provide hints for the program execution and dependency information used in the rule dispatcher, cf. Section 5.1.

Data Plane. The architecture is completed by the data plane, wherein all access to data and schema of the data is encapsulated. During compilation, if at all, only the schema of the data is assumed to be available.

5.1 AMAχoS Core

The core of the AMAχoS virtual machine is formed by the query execution layer, or AMAχoS proper. Here, an AMAχoS program (generated separately in the compilation layer, cf. Section 5.2) is evaluated against data provided by the runtime data access layer resulting in answers that are serialized by the serialization API.

As shown in Figure 4, the query execution layer is divided in four main components: the rule engine, the construction engine, the static function library, and the storage manager. Once a program containing AMAχoS code is parsed information from the *hint segment* is used to parameterize storage manager and rule engine. These parameters address, e.g., the classification of the contained queries (tree vs. graph queries), the selection of access paths, filter expressions for document projection, the choice of in-memory representation (e.g., fast traversal vs. small memory footprint), etc. The rule dependency information is provided to the *rule dispatcher* who is responsible for combining the results of different rules and matching query conjuncts with rule heads. Each rule has a separate segment in the AMAχoS program containing code for pattern matching and for result construction. Intermediary result construction is avoided as much as possible, partially by rule unfolding, partially by propagating constraints on variables

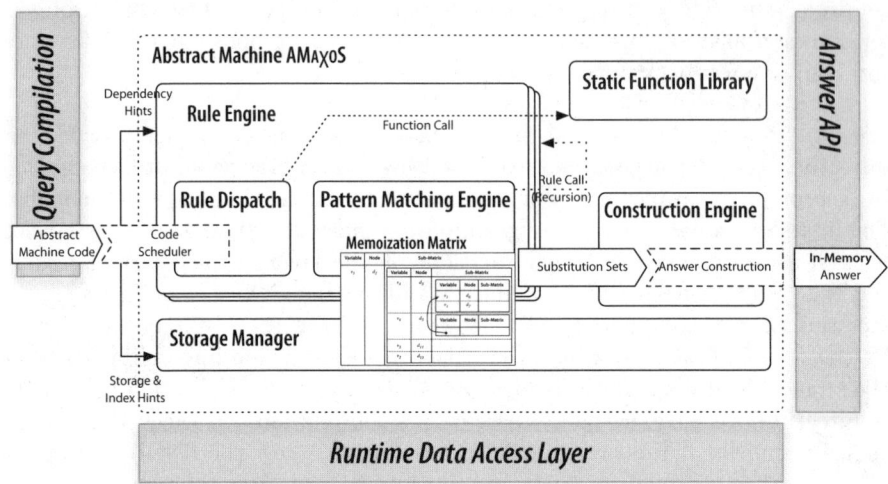

Fig. 4. Architecture of Core Query Engine AMAχoS

from rule heads into rule bodies. Only when aggregation or complex grouping expressions are involved, full intermediary construction is performed by the *construction engine*. The rule dispatcher uses the *pattern matching engine* for the actual evaluation of Xcerpt queries compiled into AMAχoS code. The pattern matching engine uses variants of the algorithms described in [8] that are based on the *memoization matrix* for storage and access to intermediary results. The rule engine also detects calls to external functions or Web services and routes such calls to the *static function library*, that provides a similar set of functions as [18] which are implemented directly in the host machine and not as AMAχoS code.

For each goal rule in the AMAχoS programs the resulting substitution sets are handed over to the *construction engine* (possibly incremental) which applies any construction expressions that apply for that goal and itself hands the result over to the serialization layer or to the answer API.

The most notable feature of the AMAχoS query engine is the separation in three core engines: the construction, the pattern matching, and the rule engine. Where the rule engine essentially glues the pattern matching and the construction engine together, these two are both very much separate. Indeed, at least on the level of AMAχoS code even programs containing only queries (i.e., expressions handled by the pattern matching engine) are allowed and can be executed by this architecture (the rule dispatcher and construction engine, in this case, merely forwarding their input).

5.2   Query Compiler

Aside from the execution engine, the query compilation layer deserves a closer look. Here, an Xcerpt program—represented by an abstract-syntax tree anno-

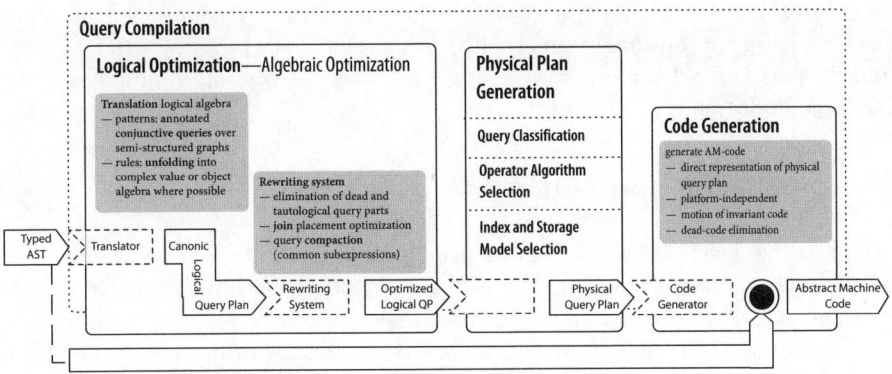

Fig. 5. Architecture of Query Compiler for AMAχoS

tated with type information—is transformed into AMAχoS code. It is assumed that the Xcerpt program is already validated, normalized, modules are expanded, and type information is added in the prior parsing layer. The query compilation is essentially divided in three steps: logical optimization, physical plan generation, and code generation.

Logical optimization is similar as in traditional database systems but additionally has to consider rules and rule dependencies: Xcerpt programs get translated into a logical algebra based on n-ary conjunctive queries over semi-structured graphs [8]. Expressions in this algebra are then optimized using various rewriting rules, including dead and tautological query part elimination, join placement optimization, and query compaction. Furthermore, where reasonable, rules are unfolded to avoid the construction of intermediary results during execution.

In contrast, *physical plan generation* differs notably, as the role of indices and storage model is inverted: In traditional databases these are given, whereas in the case of AMAχoS the query compiler generates code in the hint section indicating to execution engine and storage manager which storage model and indices (if any) to use. Essential for execution is also the classification of queries based on shape of the query and (static) selectivity estimates. E.g., a query with highly selective leaves but low selectivity in inner nodes is better evaluated in a bottom-up fashion, whereas a query with high selectivity in inner nodes profits most likely from a top-down evaluation strategy. Operator selection is rather basic, except that it is intended to implement also holistic operators for structural relations where entire paths or even sub-trees in the query are considered as parameter for a single holistic operator, cf., e.g., [5,21].

To conclude, the query compilation layer employs a mixture of traditional database and program compilation techniques to obtain an AMAχoS program from the Xcerpt input that implements the Xcerpt program and is, given the limited knowledge about the actual data instances, likely to perform well during execution. The compilation process is rather involved and expected to be time expensive if all stages are considered. A control API is provided to control the extent of the optimization and guide it, where possible. We believe that in many cases an extensive optimization is called for, as the query program can be reused and, in particular if remote data is accessed, query execution dominates by far query compilation.

6   Conclusion and Outlook

We present a brief overview over the principles and architecture of a novel kind of abstract or virtual machine, the AMAχoS virtual machine, designed for the efficient, distributed evaluation of Xcerpt query programs against Web data.

In particular, we show how the Web setting affects traditional assumptions about query compilation and execution and forces a rethinking of the conclusions drawn from these assumptions. The proposed principles and architecture reflect these changing assumptions

1. by emphasizing the *importance of a coherent and clearly specified execution environment* in form of an abstract machine for distributed query evaluation,
2. by *separating query compilation from query execution* (as in general programming language execution),
3. by employing a *unified query evaluation algorithm* for path, tree, and graph queries against tree and graph data, and
4. by emphasizing *adaptive optimization* as a means to ameliorate the loss of quality in predictive optimization due to lack of knowledge about remote or volatile data instances.

Implementation of the proposed architecture is still underway, first results on the implementation of the query engine have been reported in [8] and in [4], demonstrating the promise of the discussed method and architecture.

Acknowledgments.   This research has been funded by the European Commission and by the Swiss Federal Office for Education and Science within the 6th Framework Programme project REWERSE number 506779 (cf. `http://rewerse.net`).

References

1. D. J. Abadi, D. Carney, U. Çetintemel, *et al.* Aurora: a New Model and Architecture for Data Stream Management. *VLDB Journal*, 12(2):120–139, 2003.
2. R. Avnur and J. M. Hellerstein. Eddies: Continuously Adaptive Query Processing. In *Proc. ACM SIGMOD*, pages 261–272, 2000.
3. S. Babu and J. Widom. Continuous Queries over Data Streams. *SIGMOD Record*, 30(3):109–120, 2001.
4. S. Berger, F. Bry, T. Furche, *et al.* Beyond XML and RDF: The Versatile Web Query Language Xcerpt. In *Proc. Int'l. Conf. on World Wide Web*, 2006.
5. N. Bruno, N. Koudas, and D. Srivastava. Holistic Twig Joins: Optimal XML Pattern Matching. In *Proc. ACM SIGMOD*, pages 310–321, 2002.

6. F. Bry, F. Coskun, S. Durmaz, T. Furche, D. Olteanu, and M. Spannagel. The XML Stream Query Processor SPEX. In *Proc. ICDE*. 2005.

7. F. Bry, T. Furche, *et al.* Querying the Web Reconsidered: Design Principles for Versatile Web Query Languages. *J. of Semantic Web and Inf. Sys.*, 1(2), 2005.

8. F. Bry, A. Schroeder, T. Furche, and B. Linse. Efficient Evaluation of n-ary Queries over Trees and Graphs. Submitted for publication, 2006.

9. E. Bugnion, S. Devine, K. Govil, and M. Rosenblum. Disco: Running Commodity Operating Systems on Scalable Multiprocessors. *ACM TOCS*, 15(4):412–447, 1997.

10. B. Davis, A. Beatty, K. Casey, *et al.* The Case for Virtual Register Machines. In *Proc. Workshop on Interpreters, Virtual Machines and Emulators*, p. 41–49, 2003.

11. T. Garfinkel, B. Pfaff, J. Chow, *et al.* Terra: a Virtual Machine-based Platform for Trusted Computing. In *Proc. of ACM S. on Op. Sys. Princ.*, p. 193–206, 2003.

12. R. P. Goldberg. Survey of Virtual Machine Research. *Computer*, 7(6):34–45, 1974.

13. G. Gottlob, C. Koch, and K. U. Schulz. Conjunctive Queries over Trees. *J. of the ACM*, 53(2), 2006.

14. L. J. Groves and W. J. Rogers. The Design of a Virtual Machine for Ada. In *Proc. ACM Symposium on Ada Programming Language*, p. 223–234, 1980.

15. ISO/IEC. 23271, Common Language Infrastructure (CLI). Int'l. Standard, 2003.

16. T. Johnsson. Efficient Compilation of Lazy Evaluation. *SIGPLAN N.*, 19(6), 1984.

17. T. Lindholm and F. Yellin. *The Java Virtual Machine Specification*. Addison-Wesley Professional, 2nd edition, 1999.

18. A. Malhotra, J. Melton, and N. Walsh. XQuery 1.0 and XPath 2.0 Functions and Operators. Working draft, W3C, 2005.

19. A. Novoselsky. The Oracle XSLT Virtual Machine. In *XTech 2005*, 2005.

20. D. Olteanu, H. Meuss, T. Furche, and F. Bry. XPath: Looking Forward. In *Proc. EDBT Workshop on XML-Based Data Man.*, LNCS 2490, 2002.

21. P. O'Neil, E. O'Neil, S. Pal, *et al.* ORDPATHs: Insert-friendly XML Node Labels. In *Proc. ACM SIGMOD*, p. 903–908. 2004.

22. D. L. Overheu. An Abstract Machine for Symbolic Computation. *J. of the ACM*, 13(3):444–468, 1966.

23. S. Pemberton and M. Daniels. *Pascal Implementation: The P4 Compiler and Interpreter*. Ellis Horwood, 1982.

24. B. Randell and L. J. Russell. *ALGOL 60 Implementation*. Academic Press, 1964.

25. M. Rosenblum. The Reincarnation of Virtual Machines. *Queue*, 2(5):34–40, 2004.

26. K. Sagonas and T. Swift. An Abstract Machine for Tabled Execution of Fixed-order Stratified Logic Programs. *ACM TOPLAS*, 20(3), 1998.

27. S. Schaffert. *Xcerpt: A Rule-Based Query and Transformation Language for the Web*. Dissertation/Ph.D. thesis, University of Munich, 2004.

28. S. Schaffert and F. Bry. Querying the Web Reconsidered: A Practical Introduction to Xcerpt. In *Proc. Extreme Markup Languages*, 2004.

29. Y. Shi, D. Gregg, A. Beatty, and M. A. Ertl. Virtual Machine Showdown: Stack versus Registers. In *Proc. Int. Conf. on Virtual Execution Env.s*, p. 153–163, 2005.

30. D. H. D. Warren. An Abstract Prolog Instruction Set. Note 309, SRI Int'l., 1983.

Towards More Precise Typing Rules for Xcerpt

Włodzimierz Drabent

IPI PAN, ul. Ordona 21, PL – 01-237 Warszawa, Poland
IDA, Linköpings universitet, SE – 581 83 Linköping, Sweden
wdr@ida.liu.se

Abstract. In previous papers we presented a type system for a substantial fragment of the Web query language Xcerpt. It is a descriptive type system: the typing of a program is an approximation of its semantics. The type system was expressed by means of rules, which could be seen as a comprehensible abstraction of a typing algorithm. That system treats some query terms in a rather simplistic way. As a result the approximations produced for them are rather imprecise. In this paper we provide an improved type system, producing more precise results.

In previous papers [1, 2, 3, 8] we presented a type system for a substantial fragment of the Web query language Xcerpt [7, 6]. It is a descriptive type system: the typing of a program is an approximation of its semantics. In particular, types are sets (of data objects). The type system makes possible type derivation (computing an approximation of the set of the results of a program applied to data from a given set) and type checking (finding whether the results are included in a specified set of allowed results). The intended application is to help the programmer in finding errors in programs. A prototype implementation is presented in [8, 10].

The type system was expressed by means of rules, which could be seen as a comprehensible abstraction of a typing algorithm. That system treats some query terms in a rather simplistic way. As a result the approximations produced for them are rather imprecise. In the current paper we provide an improved type system, producing more precise results. The considered fragment of Xcerpt is the same as that dealt with in [1, 2]. It can be extended similarly as done in [8]. A preliminary version of a more precise type system appeared in [4], in a form of a rather complicated algorithm. Such a form of presentation was very difficult to understand and reason about.

The next section presents Xcerpt and the formalisms we use. The type system is introduced in Sect. 2 and proven correct in Sect. 3.

1 Preliminaries

To make the paper self-contained, we introduce here the underlying notions. We introduce data terms, which are our abstraction of XML documents, and a formalism of defining types (sets of data terms). We present the fragment of Xcerpt dealt with in this paper and define its formal semantics. This section is based on our former papers [9, 1, 2].

J.J. Alferes et al. (Eds.): PPSWR 2006, LNCS 4187, pp. 120–133, 2006.

1.1   Modelling XML Data

We model XML data using a formalism of data terms similar to that defined in [7]. Data terms can be seen as mixed trees which are labelled trees where children of a node are either linearly ordered or unordered. The content of an element is a sequence of other elements or **basic constants**. Basic constants are basic values such as attribute values and all "free" data appearing in an XML document (PCDATA). The set of basic constants will be denoted by $\mathcal{B}$. Tag names and attribute names of XML correspond to **labels** of data terms. The set of labels is denoted by $\mathcal{L}$.

Definition 1. *A* **data term** *is an expression defined inductively as follows:*

- *Any basic constant is a data term,*
- *If l is a label and $t_1, \ldots, t_n$ are $n \geq 0$ data terms, then $l[t_1, \ldots, t_n]$ and $l\{t_1, \ldots, t_n\}$ are data terms.*

The linear ordering of children of the node with label l is denoted by enclosing them by brackets $[\,]$, while unordered children are enclosed by braces $\{\}$.

A **subterm** of a data term t is defined inductively: t is a subterm of t, and any subterm of t_i $(1 \leq i \leq n)$ is a subterm of $l'[t_1, \ldots, t_n]$ and of $l'\{t_1, \ldots, t_n\}$. Data terms $t_1, \ldots, t_n$ will be sometimes called the arguments of l', or the **direct subterms** of $l'[t_1, \ldots, t_n]$ (and of $l'\{t_1, \ldots, t_n\}$). The **root** of a data term t, denoted $root(t)$, is defined as follows . If t is of the form $l[t_1, \ldots, t_n]$ or $l\{t_1, \ldots, t_n\}$ then $root(t) = l$; for t being a basic constant we assume that $root(t) = \$$.

1.2   Type Definitions

Here we introduce a formalism for specifying a class of decidable sets of data terms representing XML documents. First we specify a set of **type names** $\mathcal{T} = \mathcal{C} \cup \mathcal{S} \cup \mathcal{V}$ which consist of **type constants** from the alphabet $\mathcal{C}$, **enumeration type names** from the alphabet $\mathcal{S}$, and **type variables** from the alphabet $\mathcal{V}$. (In our former papers, enumeration type names were called special type names).

A type definition associates type names with sets of data terms. The set $[\![T]\!]$ associated with a type name T is called the **type** denoted by T. For T being a type constant or an enumeration type name, the elements of $[\![T]\!]$ are basic constants.

Type constants correspond to base types of XML schema languages. The set of type constants is fixed and finite; for each type constant $T \in \mathcal{C}$ the set $[\![T]\!] \subseteq \mathcal{B}$ is fixed.

We denote the empty string by ϵ. A *regular expression* over an alphabet Σ is ε, ϕ, any $a \in \Sigma$ and any $r_1 r_2$, $r_1 | r_2$ and r_1^*, where r_1, r_2 are regular expressions. A language $L(r)$ of strings over Σ is assigned to each regular expression r in a standard way: $L(\phi) = \emptyset$, $L(\varepsilon) = \{\epsilon\}$, $L(a) = \{a\}$, $L(r_1 r_2) = L(r_1)L(r_2)$, $L(r_1 | r_2) = L(r_1) \cup L(r_2)$, and $L(r_1^*) = L(r_1)^*$.

Definition 2. *A* **regular type expression** *is a regular expression over the alphabet of type names* $\mathcal{T}$. *We abbreviate a regular expression* $r^n|r^{n+1}|\cdots|r^m$, *where* $n \leq m$, *as* $r^{(n:m)}$, $r^n r^*$ *as* $r^{(n:\infty)}$, rr^* *as* r^+, *and* $r^{(0:1)}$ *as* $r^?$. *A regular type expression of the form*

$$T_1^{(n_{1,1}\,:\,n_{1,2})} \cdots T_k^{(n_{k,1}\,:\,n_{k,2})}$$

where $k \geq 0$, $0 \leq n_{i,1} \leq n_{i,2} \leq \infty$ *for* $i = 1,\ldots,k$, *and* $T_1,\ldots,T_k$ *are distinct type names, will be called a* **multiplicity list**.

Multiplicity lists will be used to specify multisets of type names. We use $types_D(r)$ to denote the set of all type names occurring in the regular expression r.

Definition 3. *A* **type definition** *is a set* D *of rules of the form*

$$T \rightarrow l[r], \quad T \rightarrow l\{s\}, \quad or \quad T' \rightarrow c_1 \mid \ldots \mid c_n,$$

where T *is a type variable,* T' *an enumeration type name,* l *a label,* r *a regular type expression,* s *a multiplicity list, and* $c_1,\ldots,c_n$ *are basic constants. A rule* $U \rightarrow G \in D$ *will be called a* **rule for** U *in* D. *We require that for any type name* $U \in \mathcal{V} \cup \mathcal{S}$ *occurring in* D *there is exactly one rule for* U *in* D.

If the rule for a type variable T *in* D *is as above then* l *will be called the* **label** *of* T *(in* D*) and denoted* $label_D(T) = l$. *For* T *being a type constant or an enumeration type name we define* $label_D(T) = \$$. *The regular expression in a rule for type variable* T *is called the* **content model** *of* T.

Type definitions are a kind of grammars, they define sets by means of derivations, where a type variable T is replaced by the right hand side of the rule for T and a regular expression r is replaced by a string from $L(r)$; if T is a type constant or an enumeration type name then it is replaced by a basic constant from respectively $[\![T]\!]$, or from the rule for T. This can be concisely formalized as follows (treating type definitions similarly to tree automata).

Definition 4. *Let* D *be a type definition. We will say that a data term* t *is* **derived** *in* D *from a type name* T *iff there exists a mapping* ν *from the subterms of* t *to type names such that* $\nu(t) = T$ *and for each subterm* u *of* t

- *if* u *is a basic constant then* $\nu(u) \in \mathcal{C}$ *and* $u \in [\![\nu(u)]\!]$ *or* $\nu(u) \in \mathcal{S}$ *and there exists a rule* $\nu(u) \rightarrow \cdots \mid u \mid \cdots$ *in* D.
- *otherwise* $\nu(u) = U \in \mathcal{V}$ *and*
  - *there is a rule* $U \leftarrow l[r] \in D$, $u = l[t_1,\ldots,t_n]$, *and* $\nu(t_1)\cdots\nu(t_n) \in L(r)$,
  - *or there is a rule* $U \leftarrow l\{r\} \in D$, $u = l\{t_1,\ldots,t_n\}$, *and* $\nu(t_1)\cdots\nu(t_n)$ *is a permutation of a string in* $L(r)$.

The set of the data terms derived in D *from a type name* T *will be denoted by* $[\![T]\!]_D$.

For examples see [1, 2]. Notice that if T is a type constant then $[\![T]\!]_D = [\![T]\!]$. If it is clear from the context which type definition is considered, we will often omit the subscript in the notation $[\![\ ]\!]_D$ and similar ones. For U being a set of type names $\{T_1, \ldots, T_n\}$, we define a set of data terms $[\![U]\!] = [\![T_1]\!] \cup \ldots \cup [\![T_n]\!]$. For a regular type expression r we define $[\![r]\!] = \{ d_1, \ldots, d_n \mid d_1 \in [\![T_1]\!], \ldots, d_n \in [\![T_n]\!]$ for some $T_1, \ldots, T_n \in L(r) \}$. Notice that if $D \subseteq D'$ are type definitions then $[\![T]\!]_D = [\![T]\!]_{D'}$ for any type name T occurring in D.

1.3   Xcerpt – Introduction

Xcerpt is a rule-based query and transformation language for XML [7, 6]. It employs patterns instead of paths to query XML and semistructured data. This approach stems from logic programming. A query term is matched against a data term from a database. A successful matching results in binding the variables in the query term to certain subterms of the data term. This operation is called simulation unification. In full Xcerpt simulation unification deals with data terms representing graphs. In the restricted version of Xcerpt considered in this paper, data terms are trees. Following [9] we provide a formal semantics for Xcerpt query terms. In this paper we are not interested in other constructs of Xcerpt.

Definition 5. Query terms *are inductively defined as follows:*

- *Any basic constant is a query term.*
- *A variable X is a query term.*
- *If q is a query term, then* desc q *is a query term.*
- *If X is a variable and q is a query term, then $X \rightsquigarrow q$ is a query term.*
- *If l is a label and $q_1, \ldots, q_n$ ($n \geq 0$) are query terms, then $l[q_1, \ldots, q_n]$, $l\{q_1, \ldots, q_n\}$, $l[[q_1, \ldots, q_n]]$ and $l\{\{q_1, \ldots, q_n\}\}$ are query terms (called* rooted *query terms).*

For a rooted query term $q = l\alpha q_1, \ldots, q_n\beta$, where $\alpha\beta$ are parentheses $[\,]$, $[[\,]]$, $\{\}$ or $\{\{\}\}$, $root(q) = l$ and $q_1, \ldots, q_n$ are the child subterms *of q. If q is a basic constant then $root(q) = \$$.*

We assume that a database is a data term or a multiset of data terms. To informally explain the role of query terms, consider a query term $q = l\alpha q_1, \ldots, q_m\beta$ and a data term $d = l'\alpha' d_1, \ldots, d_n\beta'$, where $\alpha, \beta, \alpha', \beta'$ are parentheses. In order to q match d it is necessary that $l = l'$. Moreover the child subterms $q_1, \ldots, q_m$ of q should match certain child subterms of d. Single parentheses in d ([or {}) mean that $m = n$ and each q_i should match some (distinct) d_j. Double parentheses mean that $m \leq n$ and $q_1, \ldots, q_m$ are matched against some m terms out of $d_1, \ldots, d_n$. Curly braces ({} or {{}}) in q mean that the order of the child subterms in d does not matter; square brackets in q mean that $q_1, \ldots, q_m$ should match (a subsequence of) $d_1, \ldots, d_n$ in the same order.

A variable matches any data term, desc q matches a data term d whenever q matches some subterm of d. A query term $X \rightsquigarrow q$ matches any data term matched by q. A side effect of a query term X or $X \rightsquigarrow q$ matching a data term d is that variable X obtains a value d.

Now we formally define which query terms match which data terms and what are the resulting assignments of data terms to variables. We do not follow the original definition of simulation unification. Instead we define a notion of answer substitution for a query term q and a data term d. As usually, by a *substitution* (of data terms for variables) we mean a set of pairs $\theta = \{\, X_1/d_1, \ldots, X_n/d_n \,\}$, where $X_1, \ldots, X_n$ are distinct variables and $d_1, \ldots, d_n$ are data terms; its domain $dom(\theta)$ is $\{X_1, \ldots, X_n\}$, its application to a (query) term is defined in a standard way.

Definition 6 ([9]). *A substitution θ is an* answer substitution *(shortly, an **answer**) for a query term q and a data term d if q and d are of one of the forms below and the corresponding condition holds. (In what follows $m, n \geq 0$, X is a variable, l is a label, $q, q_1, \ldots$ are query terms, and $d, d_1, \ldots$ data terms; set notation is used for multisets, for instance $\{d, d\}$ and $\{d\}$ are different multisets).*

q	d	condition on q and d
b	b	b is a basic constant
$l[q_1, \ldots, q_n]$	$l[d_1, \ldots, d_n]$	θ is an answer for q_i and d_i, for each $i = 1, \ldots, n$
$l[[q_1, \ldots, q_m]]$	$l[d_1, \ldots, d_n]$	for some subsequence $d_{i_1}, \ldots, d_{i_m}$ of $d_1, \ldots, d_n$ (i.e. $0 < i_1 < \ldots < i_m \leq n$) θ is an answer for q_j and d_{i_j}, for each $j = 1, \ldots, m$,
$l\{q_1, \ldots, q_n\}$	$l\{d_1, \ldots, d_n\}$ or $l[d_1 \cdots d_n]$	for some permutation $d_{i_1}, \ldots, d_{i_n}$ of $d_1, \ldots, d_n$ (i.e. $\{d_{i_1}, \ldots, d_{i_n}\} = \{d_1, \ldots, d_n\}$) θ is an answer for q_j and d_{i_j} for each $j = 1, \ldots, n$,
$l\{\{q_1, \ldots, q_m\}\}$	$l\{d_1, \ldots, d_n\}$ or $l[d_1, \ldots, d_n]$	for some $\{d_{i_1}, \ldots, d_{i_m}\} \subseteq \{d_1, \ldots, d_n\}$ θ is an answer for q_j and d_{i_j} for each $j = 1, \ldots, m$,
X	d	$X\theta = d$
$X \rightsquigarrow q$	d	$X\theta = d$ and θ is an answer for q and d
$\texttt{desc}\ q$	d	θ is an answer for q and some subterm d' of d

We say that q matches d if there exists an answer for q, d.

Thus if q is a rooted query term (or a basic constant) and $root(q) \neq root(d)$ then no answer for q, d exists. If $q = d$ then any θ is an answer for q, d. A query $l\{\{\}\}$ matches any data term with the label l. If θ, θ' are substitutions and $\theta \subseteq \theta'$ then if θ is an answer for q, d then θ' is an answer for q, d. If a variable X occurs in a query term q then queries $X \rightsquigarrow q$ and $X \rightsquigarrow \texttt{desc}\,q$ match no data term, provided that $q \neq X$ and q is not of the form $\texttt{desc} \cdots \texttt{desc}\,X$.

Example 1. Query term $q_1 = a[\,c\{\{d[\,],"e"\}\}, f[[g[\,], h\{"i"\}]]\,]$ matches data terms $a[\,c\{"e", d[\,], g[\,]\}, f[g[\,], l[\,], h["i"]]\,]$ and $a[\,c[d[\,], g[\,], "e"], f[g[\,], h["i"]]\,]$. In contrast, data terms $f[h["i"], g[\,]]$ and $f\{g[\,], h["i"]\}$ are not matched by $f[[g[\,], h\{"i"\}]]$. Query term $q_2 = \mathsf{desc}\, w\{\{\}\}$ matches data terms $a[b\{w[\,]\}]$ and $w\{"s"\}$. Query term $q_2 = a[[\,X_1 \leadsto c[[d\{\}]], X_2, "p"\,]]$ matches $a["s", c[d\{\}, "r"], h\{j[\,]\}, "p"]$, with an answer which binds X_1 to $c[d\{\}, "r"]$ and X_2 to $h\{j[\,]\}$.

Each answer for a query term q binds all the variables of the query to some data terms. For any such answer θ' (for q and d) there exists an answer $\theta \subseteq \theta'$ (for q and d) binding exactly these variables. We will call such answers *non redundant*. From Definition 6 one can derive an algorithm which produces non redundant answers for a given q and d. Construction of the algorithm is rather simple, we skip the details. Non redundant answers are actually those of interest; we consider a more general class of answers to simplify Definition 6.

1.4   Variable-Type Mappings

To represent (supersets of) the sets of answers to queries, we employ mappings from variables to certain expressions built of type names. In this section we assume a fixed type definition D and a fixed set V of variables (e.g. those occurring in the considered query). According to our convention, we will often skip the index $_D$.

We consider a set $\mathcal{E}$ of expressions; $\mathcal{E}$ contains 0, 1, the type names from D, and expressions of the form $T_1 \cap T_2$, where $T_1, T_2 \in \mathcal{E}$. Each expression E from $\mathcal{E}$ denotes a set $[\![E]\!]$ of data terms. For a type name T the set $[\![T]\!]$ is that defined by D, $[\![1]\!]$ denotes the set of all data terms, $[\![0]\!] = \emptyset$, and $[\![T_1 \cap T_2]\!] = [\![T_1]\!] \cap [\![T_2]\!]$. We will not distinguish expressions $T \cap 1$, $1 \cap T$ and T, and $T \cap 0$, $0 \cap T$ and 0 (where $T \in \mathcal{E}$).

A mapping $\Gamma : V \to \mathcal{E}$ will be called a *variable-type mapping*. The set of substitutions corresponding to Γ is

$$substitutions_D(\Gamma) = \{\, \theta \mid \forall_{X \in V}\, \theta X \in [\![\Gamma(X)]\!] \,\}.$$

Notice that if $\theta \in substitutions(\Gamma)$ then $V \subseteq dom(\theta)$ and if $\theta \subseteq \theta'$ then $\theta' \in substitutions(\Gamma)$. For a set Ψ of variable-type mappings we define $substitutions(\Psi) = \bigcup_{\Gamma \in \Psi} substitutions(\Gamma)$.

For $Y_1, \ldots, Y_k \in V$, $T_1, \ldots, T_k \in \mathcal{E}$, mapping $[Y_1 \mapsto T_1, \ldots, Y_k \mapsto T_k] : V \to \mathcal{E}$ is defined as

$$[Y_1 \mapsto T_1, \ldots, Y_k \mapsto T_k](X) = \begin{cases} T_i & \text{if } X = Y_i \\ 1 & \text{otherwise.} \end{cases}$$

Inclusion of types induces a pre-order $\sqsubseteq$ on the mappings from $V \to \mathcal{E}$, as follows. If Γ and Γ' are such mappings then $\Gamma \sqsubseteq \Gamma'$ iff $[\![\Gamma(X)]\!] \subseteq [\![\Gamma'(X)]\!]$ for each variable $X \in V$. Notice that $\Gamma \sqsubseteq \Gamma'$ is equivalent to $substitutions(\Gamma) \subseteq substitutions(\Gamma')$, provided that $[\![\Gamma(X)]\!] \neq \emptyset$ for each $X \in V$.

2   Typing Query Terms

Here we present a type system for Xcerpt query terms. Its purpose is to find (a superset of) the set of answers of a given query q applied to data terms from a given type $[\![T]\!]$. The type system is formulated as a set of derivation rules. Such a set of rules can be seen as a convenient abstraction of a (rather complicated) type inference algorithm.

The type system proposed in our previous papers treats query terms of the form $X \rightsquigarrow q$ in a simplistic way. The set of results of $X \rightsquigarrow q$ and that of X are both approximated by the same variable-type mapping (if X does not occur in q). Namely it is concluded that applying X, or $X \rightsquigarrow q$, to data from a type $[\![T]\!]$ may bind X to any term from $[\![T]\!]$. However $X \rightsquigarrow q$ can bind X only to such terms from $[\![T]\!]$ which are matched by q. So for each query term we need to find not only the type of results, as previously, but also (a superset of) the set data terms from the given type matched by the query term.

Our typing rules for query terms derive facts of the form $D \vdash q : T \triangleright (\Gamma, T')$, where D is a type definition, q is a query term, T, T' are type names, $[\![T']\!] \subseteq [\![T]\!]$, and Γ is a variable-type mapping. Intuitively such a fact means that query term q applied to a data term $d \in [\![T]\!]$ results in a substitution θ from $substitutions(\Gamma)$, moreover $d \in [\![T']\!]$. Formally, whenever q matches a $d \in [\![T]\!]$ with a result θ then a fact as above is derived, where $\theta \in substitutions(\Gamma)$ and $d \in [\![T']\!]$.[1] The previous type system derived facts of the form $D \vdash q : T \triangleright \Gamma$, not providing information which terms from $[\![T]\!]$ are matched by q.

The rule system has the following property. Whenever a variable-type mapping Γ can be obtained then any $\Gamma' \sqsubseteq \Gamma$ can be obtained too. (Formally, if $D \vdash q : T \triangleright (\Gamma, T')$ is derivable then $D \vdash q : T \triangleright (\Gamma', T')$ is derivable.) This makes it possible to abstract from computing the greatest lower bounds (glb's). For instance, we may require that for two query terms q_1, q_2 the same Γ is obtained, instead of explicitly computing the glb of mappings Γ_1, Γ_2 obtained for q_1, q_2.

Now we present the typing rules with informal explanation. A soundness proof is provided in the next section.

A query term which is a basic constant b matches a single data term b; we construct a type T' containing one element.

$$\frac{b \in [\![T]\!]}{D \vdash b : T \triangleright (\Gamma, T')} \qquad \text{(Constant)}$$

where $T' \to b \in D$ (and, according to Def. 3, $T' \in \mathcal{S}$).

A variable matches any data term (types T, T' are equal, as X can be bound to any element of type T).

$$\frac{\Gamma \sqsubseteq [X \mapsto T]}{D \vdash \mathsf{var}\ X : T \triangleright (\Gamma, T)} \qquad \text{(Var)}$$

---

[1] In practice we begin with a type definition $D_0 \subseteq D$ describing the type $[\![T]\!]_{D_0} = [\![T]\!]_D$ of the considered database. The rules of $D \setminus D_0$ are constructed according to the requirements of the typing rules.

A query $\text{var } X \rightsquigarrow q$ matches data terms that are matched by q. The resulting variable bindings are those given by q, but additionally X must be bound to the data term (from $[\![T']\!]$) that has been matched by q.

$$\frac{D \vdash q : T \triangleright (\Gamma, T') \qquad \Gamma \sqsubseteq [X \mapsto T']}{D \vdash \text{var } X \rightsquigarrow q : T \triangleright (\Gamma, T')} \tag{As}$$

Example 2. Consider a query $\text{var } X \rightsquigarrow \text{bb}$ applied to data terms from the type given by $T \to \text{aa} \mid \text{bb} \mid \text{cc} \in D$ (where aa, bb, cc are basic constants and $T \in \mathcal{S}$). For arbitrary Γ, from rule (CONSTANT) we obtain $D \vdash \text{bb} : T \triangleright (\Gamma, T')$, provided D contains $T' \to \text{bb}$. (Indeed, the query term bb matches only the data term bb.) Then $D \vdash \text{var } X \rightsquigarrow \text{bb} : T \triangleright (\Gamma, T')$ is obtained from rule (As), but only if $\Gamma \sqsubseteq [X \mapsto T']$. This shows that X can be bound only to the elements of $[\![T']\!] = \{\text{bb}\}$; for the same query the previous type system produces $\Gamma \sqsubseteq [X \mapsto T]$, giving $\{\text{aa}, \text{bb}, \text{cc}\}$ as the set of possible values of X.

Any term matched by a query q is matched by $\text{desc } q$:

$$\frac{D \vdash q : T \triangleright (\Gamma, T')}{D \vdash \text{desc } q : T \triangleright (\Gamma, T')} \tag{DESCENDANT}$$

Query $\text{desc } q$ matches a data term $d = l\alpha d_1, \ldots, d_n\beta$ if $\text{desc } q$ matches some subterm d_i.

$$\frac{D \vdash \text{desc } q : T_1 \triangleright (\Gamma, T_1')}{D \vdash \text{desc } q : T \triangleright (\Gamma, T')} \tag{DESCENDANT REC}$$

where $T \to l\alpha r\beta \in D$,
$\qquad T_1$ is a type name from r,
$\qquad L$ is the set of the strings from $L(r)$ containing the symbol T_1,
$\qquad r'$ is a regular expression for the language[2] $L' = \{\, [T_1/T_1'](w) \mid w \in L \,\}$,
$\qquad$ where $[T_1/T_1'](w)$ is the string obtained from w by replacing one occurrence of T_1 by T_1',
$\qquad T' \to l\alpha r'\beta \in D$.

The two rules for the $\text{desc } q$ queries are not sufficient. When T in D is defined recursively, they may produce an infinite set of approximations such that no finite subset of it is sufficient. (For each finite set S of derived facts there exists a data term $d \in [\![T]\!]$ matched by $\text{desc } q$ such that $d \notin [\![T']\!]$ for each fact $D \vdash \text{desc } q : T \triangleright (\Gamma, T')$ from S.)

Example 3. Consider a query $q = \text{desc } l[\,]$ and a rule $T \to l[T|A|\varepsilon] \in D$, where $l[\,]$ does not match any element of $[\![A]\!]$. The terms from $[\![T]\!]$ matched by q are

---

[2] To show that L' is regular, take a regular expression s for L and let s' be s with every T_1 replaced by $(T_1|T_1')$. Now L' is the intersection of $L(s')$ and the regular language of strings containing exactly one occurrence of T_1'.
    If $\alpha\beta = \{\}$ then we require that r' is a multiplicity list. Construction of such r' from the multiplicity list r is rather obvious.

$\{\, l^i[\,] \mid i > 0 \,\}$. From rule (PATTERN) below, $D \vdash l[\,] : T \triangleright (\Gamma, U_1)$ can be derived, where $U_1 \to l[\varepsilon] \in D$ and Γ is arbitrary. Now for $i = 1, 2, \dots$ we can derive $D \vdash \mathtt{desc}\, l[\,] : T \triangleright (\Gamma, U_i)$, where $U_{i+1} \to l[U_i] \in D$; these are all the facts concerning $\mathtt{desc}\, l[\,]$ that can be derived. Notice that $[\![U_i]\!] = \{l^i[\,]\}$. The union of $S = \{\, [\![U_i]\!] \mid i = 1, \dots \}$ contains all the terms matched by q, but no finite subset of S has this property.

Informally, the rules (DESCENDANT), (DESCENDANT REC) lead to infinite recursion, and the recursion should be terminated. For this purpose we introduce an additional rule, in which $T' = T$.

$$\frac{D \vdash q : T_1 \triangleright (\Gamma, U)}{D \vdash \mathtt{desc}\, q : T \triangleright (\Gamma, T)} \qquad \text{(DESCENDANT0)}$$

where T depends on T_1 in D. (T immediately depends on T' in D if the rule for T in D contains T'; if T_i immediately depends of T_{i+1} for $i = 1, \dots, n-1$ then T_1 depends on T_n.) [3]

Example 4. Applying rule (DESCENDANT0) to D, q, T from Example 3 results in $D \vdash \mathtt{desc}\, l[\,] : T \triangleright (\Gamma, T)$. Then applying (DESCENDANT REC) k times we obtain $D \vdash \mathtt{desc}\, l[\,] : T \triangleright (\Gamma, W_i)$, for $i = 1, \dots, k$, where D contains rules $W_1 \to l[T]$ and $W_{i+1} \to l[W_i]$, for $i = 1, \dots, k-1$. For each W_i we have $\{\, l^j[\,] \mid j > i \,\} \subseteq [\![W_i]\!]$.

Consider the facts $D \vdash \mathtt{desc}\, l[\,] : T \triangleright (\Gamma, T')$, where T' is $U_1, \dots, U_k, W_k$, derived in the previous and the current example. The union of types $[\![U_1]\!] \cup \cdots \cup [\![U_k]\!] \cup [\![W_k]\!]$ contains all the terms from $[\![T]\!]$ matched by q. (It also contains some other terms.) In contrast to Ex. 3 we deal here with a finite set of derived facts.

---

[3] Rule (DESCENDANT0) looses all information about which terms from $[\![T]\!]$ are matched by $\mathtt{desc}\, q$; it simply returns a fact with the last element T. We conjecture that more precise results can be obtained employing rules

$$\frac{D \vdash \mathtt{desc}\, q : T \triangleright (\Gamma, T') \;\; \vdash\!\!\!\!- \;\; D \vdash \mathtt{desc}\, q : T \triangleright (\Gamma, T')}{D \vdash \mathtt{desc}\, q : T \triangleright (\Gamma, T')} \qquad (1)$$

$$\frac{D \vdash q : T \triangleright (\Gamma, T_1') \qquad D \vdash q : T \triangleright (\Gamma, T_2')}{D \vdash q : T \triangleright (\Gamma, T')} \qquad (2)$$

where $[\![T_1']\!] \cup [\![T_2']\!] = [\![T']\!]$, and $\alpha \vdash\!\!\!\!- \beta$ means that fact β can be derived having assumed the fact α (and the derivation is nontrivial, i.e. at least one rule is applied). Rule (1) is similar to Hoare rule for correctness of recursive procedures (see e.g. [5]).

Using these rules should result in better approximations of the set of terms from $[\![T]\!]$ matched by $\mathtt{desc}\, q$. However it is unclear how to find such a $D \vdash \mathtt{desc}\, q : T \triangleright (\Gamma, T')$ for which (1) can be applied.

As an example take q, T from Ex. 3. Assuming a fact $F = D \vdash \mathtt{desc}\, l[\,] : T \triangleright (\Gamma, T')$, where $T' \to l[T'|\varepsilon] \in D$, and employing the already derived $D \vdash \mathtt{desc}\, l[\,] : T \triangleright (\Gamma, U_1)$, we can derive F. The used rules are (DESCENDANT REC) (producing T'', where $T'' \to l[T'] \in D$) and (2). Thus by (1) the fact F is concluded. It exactly describes the set of terms matched by q.

Taking a greater k results in a better approximation of the set of terms matched by q.

We will need to construct a multiplicity list which describes the union of the sets described by given n multiplicity lists. More formally, let $s_1 \cdots s_n$ be a concatenation of multiplicity lists ($n \geq 0$). In what follows $mult\_list(s_1 \cdots s_n)$ is a multiplicity list such that $perm(L(mult\_list(s_1 \cdots s_n))) = perm(L(s_1 \cdots s_n))$. (This means that the set of permutations of the strings from language $L(mult\_list(s_1 \cdots s_n))$ is the same as the set of permutations of the strings from language $L(s_1, \ldots, s_n)$.)

It remains to describe the set of variable bindings produced by a query of the form $l\,\alpha q_1 \cdots q_n \beta$ (where $\alpha\beta$ are [], [[]], {{}} or {}) and the set of terms from $[\![T]\!]$ matched by the query. If $l\,\alpha q_1 \cdots q_n \beta$ matches a data term d then d is of the form $l\alpha' d_1 \cdots d_m \beta'$ and queries $q_1, \ldots, q_n$ match certain data terms from $d_1 \cdots d_m$ (for details cf. Def. 6). From the definition of T given by D we determine the types $T_1, \ldots, T_n$ of data terms to which the queries $q_1, \ldots, q_n$ are respectively applied. From an assumption that q_i matches data terms from $[\![U_i]\!] \subseteq [\![T_i]\!]$ (for $i = 1, \ldots, n$) we construct a definition of a set containing the corresponding data terms matched by query $l\,\alpha q_1 \cdots q_n \beta$.

$$\frac{D \vdash q_1 : T_1 \triangleright (\Gamma, U_1) \quad \cdots \quad D \vdash q_n : T_n \triangleright (\Gamma, U_n)}{D \vdash l\,\alpha q_1, \cdots, q_n \beta : T \triangleright (\Gamma, U)} \qquad \text{(Pattern)}$$

where

the rule for T in D is $T \to l\alpha' r \beta'$,

if $\alpha\beta = [\,]$ then $\alpha'\beta' = [\,]$ and $T_1 \cdots T_n \in L(r)$ and $U \to l[U_1 \cdots U_n] \in D$,

if $\alpha\beta = [[\,]]$ then $\alpha'\beta' = [\,]$, $T_1 \cdots T_n$ is a subsequence of a string from $L(r)$ and $U \to l[r_2] \in D$, where

$$L(r_2) = L_2 = \{\, w_0 U_1 w_1 \cdots U_n w_n \mid w_0 T_1 w_1 \cdots T_n w_n \in L(r) \,\},$$

if $\alpha\beta = \{\}$ then $T_1 \cdots T_n$ is a permutation of a string $T_{i_1} \cdots T_{i_n} \in L(r)$ and $U \to l[U_{i_1} \cdots U_{i_n}] \in D$ if $\alpha'\beta' = [\,]$, and $U \to l\{mult\_list(U_{i_1} \cdots U_{i_n})\} \in D$ if $\alpha'\beta' = \{\}$,

if $\alpha\beta = \{\{\}\}$ and $\alpha'\beta' = [\,]$ then $T_1 \cdots T_n$ is a permutation of a string $T_{i_1} \cdots T_{i_n}$, which is a subsequence of a string from $L(r)$, and D contains a rule $U \to l[r_5]$ such that

$$L(r_5) = L_5 = \{\, w_0 U_{i_1} w_1 \cdots U_{i_n} w_n \mid w_0 T_{i_1} w_1 \cdots T_{i_n} w_n \in L(r) \,\},$$

if $\alpha\beta = \{\{\}\}$ and $\alpha'\beta' = \{\}$ then
let r be a multiplicity list $T_1'(l_1 : u_1) \cdots T_m'(l_m : u_m)$ and
y_j (for $j = 1, \ldots, m$) be the number of occurrences of T_j' in $T_1, \ldots, T_n$,
$y_1 + \ldots + y_m = n$ and $y_j \leq u_j$ for each $j = 1, \ldots, m$ (in other words a permutation of $T_1 \cdots T_n$ is a subsequence of a string from $L(r)$),
$U \to l\{\, mult\_list(\, U_1 \cdots U_n \, T_1(max(l_1 - y_1, 0) : u_1 - y_1)$
$\cdots T_m(max(l_m - y_m, 0) : u_m - y_m))\,)\,\} \in D.$

We have to show that the languages L_2, L_5 above are regular. Consider L_2, the reasoning for L_5 is similar. Let the type names occurring in r be $T'_1, \ldots, T'_m$. Notice that $\{T_1, \ldots, T_n\} \subseteq \{T'_1, \ldots, T'_m\}$. Consider two regular expressions $r_{All} = T'_1 | \cdots | T'_m$ and r' which is r with every type name T_i replaced by $T_i | U_i$, when $T_1, \ldots, T_n$ are distinct. In a general case, T_i is replaced by $T_i | U_{j_{i1}} | \cdots | U_{j_{ik_i}}$, where $T_{j_{i1}}, \ldots, T_{j_{ik_i}}$ are those elements of the sequence $T_1, \ldots, T_n$ which are equal to T_i ($i = 1, \ldots, n$, $k_i > 0$ and $j_{i1}, \ldots, j_{ik_i} \in \{1, \ldots, n\}$). Now L_2 is the intersection of regular languages:

$$L_2 = L(r_{All} U_1 r_{All} \cdots U_n r_{All}) \cap L(r').$$

Example 5. Let type T be defined by $T \to l[T_1(T_1|T_2)^*] \in D$. Assume that for queries q_1, q_2 facts $D \vdash q_1 : T_1 \triangleright (\Gamma, U_1)$ and $D \vdash q_2 : T_2 \triangleright (\Gamma, U_2)$ could be derived. Then for queries $l[q_1, q_2]$ and $l\{q_2, q_1\}$ rule (PATTERN) produces $D \vdash l[q_1, q_2] : T \triangleright (\Gamma, U)$ and $D \vdash l\{q_2, q_1\} : T \triangleright (\Gamma, U)$, provided that $U \to l[U_1 U_2] \in D$.

Notice that (from the facts on q_1, q_2 assumed above) we cannot obtain any facts on queries $l[q_2, q_1]$ or $l\{q_2\}$, as $T_2 T_1, T_2 \notin L(T_1(T_1|T_2)^*)$.

To apply rule (PATTERN) for a query term $l[[q_1, q_2]]$ one has to consider the set $L_2 = \{w_0 U_1 w_1 U_2 w_2 \mid w_0 T_1 w_1 T_2 w_2 \in L(T_1(T_1|T_2)^*)\}$. The strings of L_2 with empty w_0 are given by regular expression $r_{21} = U_1(T_1|T_2)^* U_2(T_1|T_2)^*$, and those with nonempty w_0 by $r_{22} = T_1(T_1|T_2)^* U_1(T_1|T_2)^* U_2(T_1|T_2)^*$. Hence rule (PATTERN) produces $D \vdash l[[q_1, q_2]] : T \triangleright (\Gamma, U)$, where $U \to l[r_{21}|r_{22}] \in D$.

Similarly, for $l\{\{q_2, q_1\}\}$ we obtain $D \vdash l\{\{q_2, q_1\}\} : T \triangleright (\Gamma, U)$, where $U \to l[r_{21}|r_{22}|r_{23}] \in D$ and $r_{23} = T_1(T_1|T_2)^* U_2(T_1|T_2)^* U_1(T_1|T_2)^*$.

Notice that there are cases in which the rule system cannot give exact results. Consider the type T from the last example and a query $l[XX]$. The query matches only data terms of the form $l[dd]$. The set of such terms from $[\![T]\!]$ cannot be defined by the formalism of type definitions, or any similar formalism. (In the author's opinion, it is not a regular set for any reasonable notion of regular sets of data terms.)

3   Soundness

Here we prove correctness of the presented rule system. We begin with a technical property.

Proposition 1. If $D \vdash q : T \triangleright (\Gamma, U)$ and $\Gamma' \sqsubseteq \Gamma$ then $D \vdash q : T \triangleright (\Gamma', U)$.
    If $D \vdash q : T \triangleright (\Gamma, U)$ and $D \subseteq D'$ then $D' \vdash q : T \triangleright (\Gamma, U)$

Soundness of the type system may be stated informally as follows. Whenever θ is an answer to a query term q and a data term d from the type specified by T then the type system produces a variable-type mapping Γ such that $\theta \in substitutions_{D'}(\Gamma)$. Moreover, it produces a type $[\![T']\!]$ containing d. Formally, we have:

Proposition 2. Let D be a type definition. If a query term q matches a data term $d \in [\![T]\!]_D$ with an answer substitution θ then there exists a type definition

$D' \supseteq D$, a variable-type mapping Γ and a type variable T' such that $D' \vdash q : T \triangleright (\Gamma, T')$, $\theta \in substitutions_{D'}(\Gamma)$ and $d \in [\![T']\!]_{D'} \subseteq [\![T]\!]_D$.

The proposition also holds if rule (DESCENDANT0) is removed. This property is too weak for our purposes. We require that a finite set of variable-type mappings (and a finite set of produced types) is sufficient for all the answers for q (when q is applied to data terms from the given type).

Theorem 1 (Soundness of the type system). Let q_0 be a query term, D a type definition, and T_0 a type name such that $[\![T_0]\!]_D \neq \emptyset$. Then there exists a type definition $D' \supseteq D$ and a finite set S of facts of the form $D' \vdash q_0 : T_0 \triangleright (\Gamma, T')$, derived by the rule system such that if q_0 matches a data term $d_0 \in [\![T_0]\!]_D$ with an answer substitution θ then S contains a $D' \vdash q_0 : T_0 \triangleright (\Gamma, T')$ where $d_0 \in [\![T']\!]_{D'} \subseteq [\![T_0]\!]_D$ and $\theta \in substitutions_{D'}(\Gamma)$.

Proof (outline). Formally, a fact can be derived by the rule system if it is the root of a derivation tree [5]. We describe how to construct the required set of facts. We construct derivation trees for these facts, starting from their roots. As D', Γ, T' are not known, we first construct skeletons of the trees; the nodes of the skeletons are of the form $\vdash q : T \triangleright (,)$. Formally, skeletons are derivation trees for the rules modified by removing from each fact the type definition, the variable-type mapping and the second type name.

A given $\vdash q : T \triangleright (,)$, where q is not of the form `desc` q', can be obtained from at most one rule. To generate a fact $\vdash$ `desc` q' : $T \triangleright (,)$, we either apply rules (DESCENDANT), (DESCENDANT REC), or rules (DESCENDANT), (DESCENDANT0). Under this restriction a given $\vdash q : T \triangleright (,)$ can be obtained from at most two rules. For each of the rules a finite set of premises (tuples of facts) can be used. (Only for rules (PATTERN), (DESCENDANT REC), (DESCENDANT0) the set contains more than one element.) If the applied rule is not (DESCENDANT REC) then each query term in the premises is a subterm of q. If the rule is (DESCENDANT REC) then $q =$ `desc` q' and the query term in the premise is q.

Assume that rule (DESCENDANT REC) is not used. Then the set of skeletons with a given root $\vdash q : T \triangleright (,)$ is finite. More generally, for a given $k \geq 0$ the set SS_k of skeletons with the root $\vdash q : T \triangleright (,)$ and with no more than k occurrences of rule (DESCENDANT REC) is finite.

Now we show how to construct a derivation tree out of a skeleton.

1. Consider the occurrences of the rules (CONSTANT), (DESCENDANT REC), and (PATTERN) in the skeleton. Each of them requires existence of a certain type definition rule in D'. D' can be constructed by adding the required rules to D. Notice that we can construct a single type definition D' for all the skeletons from SS_k (by adding to D the type definition rules required in all the skeletons).

2. Now the second type name in each node of the derivation tree is uniquely determined.

3. Consider all the conditions of the form $\Gamma \sqsubseteq [X \mapsto T']$ in the skeleton. Let $X_1, \ldots, X_n$ be the variables occurring in these conditions, and let $\Gamma \sqsubseteq [X_i \mapsto T_{i1}], \ldots, \Gamma \sqsubseteq [X_i \mapsto T_{im_i}]$ be the conditions involving the variable X_i. Let us take $\Gamma = [X_1 \mapsto U_1, \ldots, X_n \mapsto U_n]$, where each U_i is $T_{i1} \cap \ldots \cap T_{im_i}$. Such Γ satisfies all the conditions.

Thus from a skeleton with root $\vdash q_0 : T_0 \triangleright (\,,)$ we constructed a derivation tree for $D' \vdash q_0 : T_0 \triangleright (\Gamma, T')$. In this way from the set SS_k of skeletons a finite set TT of derivation trees is constructed.

It remains to show that if q_0 matches a data term $d_0 \in [\![T_0]\!]_D$ with an answer substitution θ then TT contains (a tree with the root) $D' \vdash q_0 : T_0 \triangleright (\Gamma, T')$ where $d_0 \in [\![T']\!]_{D'} \subseteq [\![T_0]\!]_D$ and $\theta \in \mathit{substitutions}_{D'}(\Gamma)$.

We iteratively label some facts in the trees of TT with data terms. If d labels a fact $D' \vdash q : T \triangleright (\Gamma, T')$ then q matches d and $d \in [\![T]\!]_{D'}$. Initially all the roots of TT are labelled with d_0.

1. If d labels the conclusion of an instance of rule (As) or (DESCENDANT) the premise of the instance is labelled with d, provided that the query term q in the premise matches d.

2. If d labels the conclusion $D' \vdash \mathtt{desc}\, q : T \triangleright (\Gamma, U)$ of an instance of (DESCENDANT0) and q matches some subterm d' of d then label with d' the premise $D' \vdash q : T_1 \triangleright (\Gamma, U)$ of the instance, provided that $d' \in [\![T_1]\!]_{D'}$.

3. (DESCENDANT REC) is treated similarly.

4. Assume that d labels the conclusion $D' \vdash l\alpha q_1, \ldots, q_n \beta : T \triangleright (\Gamma, U)$ of an instance of (PATTERN). Then $d = l\alpha' d_1, \ldots, d_m \beta'$ and $l\alpha q_1, \ldots, q_n \beta$ matches d. There are six similar cases to be considered. We discuss here the first one, where $\alpha\beta = \alpha'\beta' = [\,]$ and $m = n$. Each q_i matches d_i. If, for each premise $D' \vdash q_i : T_i \triangleright (\Gamma, U_i)$ of the instance, $d_i \in [\![T_i]\!]$ then label each premise with d_i, respectively.

Notice that the labelling process results in labelling of all the facts in at least one derivation tree Tr of TT. Also, $\theta \in \mathit{substitutions}(\Gamma)$, where Γ is the variable-type mapping from (each fact of) Tr.

Now by induction on the subtrees of Tr we obtain that if a data term d labels a fact $D' \vdash q : T \triangleright (\Gamma, U)$ then $d \in [\![U]\!]_{D'}$. This concludes the proof.   □

4   Typing Other Constructs of Xcerpt

The previous sections present typing rules for query terms. The rest of the typing system – the typing rules for queries, construct terms and query rules – remains the same as in [1, 2]. To connect the new and old part of the type system we need an additional rule

$$\frac{D \vdash q : T \triangleright (\Gamma, T')}{D \vdash q : T \triangleright \Gamma}$$

The rule transforms facts produced by the new rules into the form needed by the old rules for queries. It abandons the information on terms from $[\![T]\!]$ matched by q.

5   Conclusion

The "as" construct of Xcerpt ($\mathtt{var}\, X \rightsquigarrow q$) binds variable X to a data term, provided the data term is matched by query term q. To approximate the set of results of such construct, we need to maintain not only (an approximation of) the set of results of each query term, but also (an approximation of) the set of data terms matched by each query term. This paper adds dealing with the latter to the type system of our previous work. A new, more precise, type system is presented and proven correct.

The type system, similarly as the previous one, leads to algorithms which are inefficient for some cases [8, Sect. 4.4.1]. Practical needs for Xcerpt typing, and experience from using the previous type system should suggest how much of the presented type system should be implemented.

Acknowledgements. Earlier cooperation with Artur Wilk, Emmanuel Coquery and Sacha Berger on types for Xcerpt was crucial for this work.

This research has been partially funded by the European Commission and by the Swiss Federal Office for Education and Science within the 6th Framework Programme project REWERSE number 506779 (cf. http://rewerse.net).

References

[1] S. Berger, E. Coquery, W. Drabent, and A. Wilk. Descriptive typing rules for Xcerpt. In *International Workshop, PPSWR 2005, Dagstuhl Castle, Germany, September 2005, Proceedings*, number 3703 in LNCS, pages 85–100. Springer Verlag, 2005. http://www.springerlink.com/link.asp?id=8rejjqbwxbkydlwr.

[2] S. Berger, E. Coquery, W. Drabent, and A. Wilk. Descriptive typing rules for Xcerpt and their soundness. Technical Report REWERSE-TR-2005-01, REWERSE, 2005. http://rewerse.net/publications/#REWERSE-TR-2005-01.

[3] S. Berger, E. Coquery, W. Drabent, and A. Wilk. Errata to "Descriptive typing rules for Xcerpt". http://www.ida.liu.se/~wlodr/errata.LNCS3703.pdf, 2006.

[4] H. Cirstea, E. Coquery, W. Drabent, F. Fages, C. Kirchner, L. Liquori, B. Wack, and A. Wilk. Types for REWERSE reasoning and query languages. Deliverable I3-D4, REWERSE, 2005. http://rewerse.net/publications/#REWERSE-DEL-2005-I3-D4.

[5] H. R. Nielson and F. Nielson. *Semantics with Applications*. John Wiley and Sons, 1992. http://www.daimi.au.dk/~bra8130/Wiley_book/wiley.html.

[6] S. Schaffert. *Xcerpt: A Rule-Based Query and Transformation Language for the Web*. PhD thesis, University of Munich, Germany, 2004. http://www.wastl.net/download/dissertation/dissertation_schaffert.pdf.

[7] S. Schaffert and F. Bry. Querying the Web Reconsidered: A Practical Introduction to Xcerpt. In *Proceedings of Extreme Markup Languages 2004, Montreal*, 2004. http://rewerse.net/publications/#REWERSE-RP-2004-20.

[8] A. Wilk. Descriptive Types for XML Query Language Xcerpt. Licentiate thesis, Linköpings universitet, Sweden, 2006. http://www.ida.liu.se/~artwi/lic.pdf.

[9] A. Wilk and W. Drabent. On types for XML query language Xcerpt. In *International Workshop, PPSWR 2003, Mumbai, India, December 8, 2003, Proceedings*, number 2901 in LNCS, pages 128–145. Springer Verlag, 2003.

[10] A. Wilk and W. Drabent. A prototype of a descriptive type system for Xcerpt. In J. J. Alferes, J. Bailey, W. May, and U. Schwertel, editors, *Principles and Practice of Semantic Web Reasoning 2006*, LNCS 4187, p. 262. Springer-Verlag, 2006.

Extending an OWL Web Node with Reactive Behavior

Wolfgang May[1], Franz Schenk[1], and Elke von Lienen[2]

[1] Institut für Informatik, Universität Göttingen,
{may, schenk}@informatik.uni-goettingen.de
[2] Institut für Informatik, Technische Universität Clausthal,
elke.von.lienen@tu-clausthal.de

Abstract. We describe an extension of an OWL knowledge base using PostgreSQL, Jena, and Pellet with active rules in form of triggers. The triggers react on atomic events on the OWL level. In contrast to "simple" RDF triggers whose trigering events can directly be mapped on updates on RDF triples, the extension to RDFS and OWL requires to combine reactivity with OWL reasoning. For this, "direct", *pre-reasoning* triggers that react on *update operations* (often also providing support for the intended operation), and "indirect", *post-reasoning* triggers that react on *actual changes* have to be distinguished. The approach has been implemented in a prototype based on the Jena framework.

1 Introduction

The Semantic Web consists of application nodes (e.g., representing universities or airlines) that provide information and application-level functionality, and of infrastructure nodes that provide application-independent services that "talk about" the application-level issues. Application nodes often use any kind of knowledge base for storing persistent data. In such a scenario, triggers provide simple reactive behavior patterns in the style of *ECA (Event-Condition-Action)* rules: "ON event WHEN condition DO action", i.e., when a specified event occurs and a condition is satisfied, then execute a given action. Triggers that react on database updates are a common means for maintaining integrity, both wrt. general, data-model-immanent issues (such as e.g. referential integrity in databases), and for application-specific integrity. Additionally, they provide a base for application-specific behavior. Such triggers have been introduced for SQL, and also several proposals for triggers on XML or RDF data are around. Thus, there is a clear motivation to apply this concept also to OWL knowledge bases – which are significantly different from SQL, XML and RDF databases: they include *reasoning* that interferes with the basic trigger mechanisms.

The paper is structured as follows: next, we discuss the general situation about adding behavior to the Semantic Web. In Section 2, we discuss the notions of updates and events underlying triggers for a knowledge base in presence of OWL reasoning. The syntax and semantics of triggers on the OWL level of a knowledge base is investigated in Section 3. Section 4 describes the architecture

J.J. Alferes et al. (Eds.): PPSWR 2006, LNCS 4187, pp. 134–148, 2006.

of an OWL system based on the Jena [Jen] Semantic Web Framework that has been implemented in [Lie06]. It combines Jena with a PostgreSQL database, and uses Pellet [Pel] as external reasoner via the DIG interface [DIG]. Section 5 describes the actual event detection and handling of triggers in this setting, including the implemented solution and a discussion of alternative variants. A short conclusion completes the paper.

Evolution and Reactivity in the Semantic Web. In [MAB04], we proposed to follow the *ECA (Event-Condition-Action)* paradigm for describing and implementing behavior in the Semantic Web. ECA rules, in different expressiveness and complexity are appropriate for all levels, from the local behavior of individual nodes up to global cooperation and interaction of multiple nodes. In [MAA05b, MAA05a], we described a general, ontology-based approach for active behavior in the Semantic Web for the global level. The current paper now focuses on the local level of one such application node. Whereas the static concepts of the Semantic Web, i.e., RDF [RDF00], RDFS [RDF00], and OWL [OWL04] are assumed to be familiar to the reader, the dynamic concepts of events and actions are shortly reviewed: Events here are instantaneous happenings (e.g., the publication of a new book, a cancellation of a flight etc.) anywhere in the Web, also *composite* events (expressed by *event algebras*) that combine events at different nodes in the Web can be specified.

Atomic events can be regarded on different abstraction levels. Events on the data level of the node's knowledge base are expressed in terms of the database or knowledge base model. For SQL databases, these atomic events INSERT, UPDATE, DELETE *immediately* correspond to update operations.

This is not the case when RDFS or OWL models are considered: the basic events are still expressed on the data model level (in terms of statements), but they can be raised by syntactically different updates. E.g. an *event* CREATION OF INSTANCE OF person can be raised by an INSERT (scott_tiger, rdf:type, student) operation. Similarly, an event DELETION OF p OF INSTANCE OF CLASS c (deletion of property p of an object of class c) can be raised by a modification of the statement (y, q, x) (x and instance of c) to (y, q, z) where p is declared to be the inverse property to q.

As we will describe in more detail later, with a knowledge model where update operations and resulting changes are not the same (note that we already used "INSERT", "DELETE", and "ON CREATION" and "ON DELETION"), there will even be two slightly different kinds of triggers, *direct* ones that react upon the *operations*, and *indirect* ones that react on the *changes* of the model. This difference is a bit similar to SQLs BEFORE/AFTER vs. INSTEAD OF triggers that distinguish between base and derived relations (whereas in OWL any notion can be both base and derived).

On the application level, events can be fully *derived events*, e.g., the action "book a seat for Alice on flight LH0815 (from Frankfurt to Lisbon) on February 30th" can raise the events "Alice has been booked to seat 18A of ...", "flight LH0815 on Feb. 30th is fully booked", or "there are no more tickets on Feb.

30th from Germany to Lisbon". Application-level ECA rules can then react upon application-level events.

For this, (i) application-level events must be derived from low-level events in Semantic Web nodes, and (ii) there must be a communication of atomic events from the nodes where they occur to the engines that execute the ECA rules. The pure communication is done e.g. by *event brokers* based on the publish-subscribe communication pattern. The node where the event actually happens must only "provide" the event, i.e., information that the event happened. For this, the local triggers are used that "map" database updates (or, more correctly, changes) to events that are then signaled to the outside.

The Role of RDFS/OWL Triggers for Behavior in the Semantic Web.
The information flow between events and actions is depicted in Figure 1 and contains the following types of rules:

1. low-level ECA rules as triggers for local integrity maintenance in an RDF/OWL knowledge base,
2. ECE rules: derive and raise application-level events based on internal changes on the RDF/OWL level,
3. global ECA rules that use application-level events,
4. ACA mapping: map high-level actions to lower-level (e.g. INSTEAD OF triggers).

Amongst these, (1), (2), and partially also (4) are based on *database level and knowledge base level triggers*.

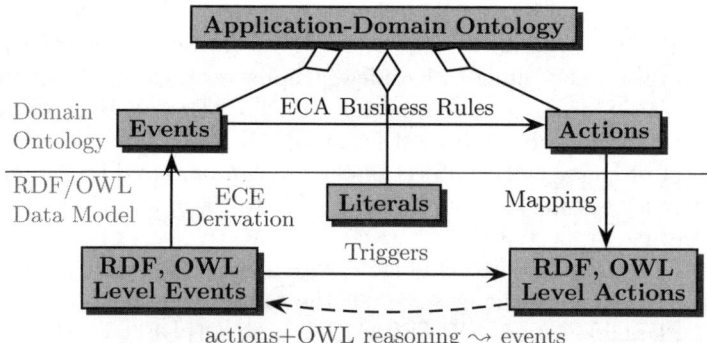

actions+OWL reasoning ⤳ events

Fig. 1. Interference of Events, Actions, and Rules

2   Triggers on the OWL Level

A simple form of active rules that is often provided by database systems, are *triggers*. Reacting directly to changes in the database, they provide the basic level of behavior. Triggers are simple rules on the *logical, (database) programming language and data structure level*. They follow a simple ECA pattern where the event is directly correlated with events in the database or knowledge base model, the conditions are given in the database query language and the action component is given in a simple, operational programming language. In SQL, triggers are of the form

ON database-update WHEN condition BEGIN pl/sql-fragment END .

In the Semantic Web, the data level is assumed to be in RDF format, equipped with RDFS and OWL semantics. RDF triples describe properties of a resource. RDFS [RDF00] and OWL [OWL04] data is also described by RDF, but RDFS and OWL add special predicates based on Description Logics [BCM+03] that allow and require *reasoning* to derive intensional knowledge from the RDF database. A proposal for RDF events and RDF triggers can be found in RDFTL [PPW03, PPW04].

2.1   Events and Updates in the Presence of OWL Reasoning

In contrast to SQL, XML, or RDF databases where the stored database is the "model", in an RDFS or OWL environment the "model" extends the materialized base facts with statements that can be derived by RDFS/OWL reasoning. RDFS/OWL triggers are expected to implement reactive behavior also on derived notions. Thus, for further investigations, we have first to analyze events and updates when working on the OWL level.

Events. While events on the data level in SQL, XML and RDF databases directly correspond to update operations, events on the OWL level can be *derived* events that result from some (syntactically different) update operation and RDFS/OWL reasoning. Thus, event detection can in general not be local to the database part, but must include the reasoning.

Before actually talking more detailed about events and triggers (in Section 3), the update operations have to be analyzed.

Updates. A closely related problem occurs with updates: due to the nature of the Description Logic reasoning underlying OWL, updates are not only *view updates*, but *theory updates*, i.e., intensional statements what should hold (or not hold any longer) afterwards. *View updates* are subject of investigations in databases, and intensional updates and theory updates are investigated in the contexts of knowledge representation. The OWL semantics and reasoning adds another issue in contrast to view definitions in classical databases: in classical databases, there is a clear dependency between a derived relation, and its underlying (mostly: base) relations. In OWL, every notion can be both materialized and derived (e.g., using inverseOf).

– adding data is simpler than for relational views: any data can be added as statements to the materialized knowledge base *without* the necessity to map views onto base relations, but

– deleting or modifying information that exists only as derived information requires to map it to base facts. Even more, since there may be redundant facts, "deleting" a fact from the materialized knowledge base may still not remove it when it is derivable from the remaining data. Thus, "deleting" from the materialized facts is different from *retracting* facts, i.e., asserting that something must not hold any longer.

2.2 OWL: Fact Base and Updates

An OWL-based node usually maintains a materialized (RDF) fact base (see also Section 4) and combines it with reasoning. We propose the following set of update actions on an OWL knowledge base node:

- DELETE(*statement*) from the fact base. This does not necessarily imply that the fact does not hold afterwards (e.g., deleting a redundant entry where a statement and its inverse are both materialized as shown below in Example 2). Here, one of the statements can be deleted without changing the knowledge base.

  Note that when deleting a reified statement from a fact base, statements about it should also be deleted.

- The stronger form is RETRACT(*statement*) which is an intensional update that (i) will delete *statement* from the facts (if present) and (ii) is considered to be executed successfully, if *statement* does not hold in the model afterwards (which will potentially require "help" by suitable (direct) triggers).

- INSERT(*statement*). This means to insert the statement explicitly into the fact base.

- ASSERT(*statement*). This means, if *statement* already holds, nothing has to be done. Otherwise, it has to be inserted into the fact base.

- UPDATE *statement* SET {SUBJECT|PREDICATE|OBJECT} = *resource*. Note that in case an inverse is materialized, it should be modified accordingly (which requires the help of appropriate triggers). In case of reified statements, the URI remains the same.

- DELETE(*resource*) deletes all statements concerning a given resource (cascading for reified statements),

- RENAME(*old, new*) replaces a URI by another in the whole factbase/model, (note that this is different from declaring sameAs($resource_{old}, resource_{new}$) since the old name becomes undefined and is free for other use afterwards).

- RENAME PROPERTY OF CLASS(*class, old, new*) replaces a URI by another wherever it occurs as a property name of an instance of class *class*.

2.3 Example Scenarios

We next motivate that a reactive OWL environment should provide to two kinds of triggers: direct ones in the style of SQL's INSTEAD OF-triggers that react upon the *update operation* before the reasoning is applied (i.e., their effect is already enforced before the reasoning), and indirect ones that react on *visible events*, i.e., *changes* after applying the reasoning on the model level.

For the following examples, it is sufficient to consider intuitive events as insertion, deletion, or modification of an RDF statement (*subject, predicate, object*), or the creation of a new class. As for SQL, events bind OLD and NEW variables that have components Subject, Property, Object, Class, Resource, referring to the modified items (as URIs), respectively.

Example 1 (Trigger Variables). A trigger reacting on MODIFICATION OF hasPresident OF INSTANCE OF company binds OLD.subject and NEW.subject to the company, and OLD.object and NEW.object to the old and new president, respectively.

Example 2. Consider a property hasHusband and a statement (hasHusband, inverseOf, hasWife). Given triples (Alice, hasHusband, Bob) and (Dan, hasWife, Carol), both (Bob, hasWife, Alice) and (Carol, hasHusband, Dan) are derived – both hasHusband and hasWife are as well derived as base "relations".

Consider now an RDF database that contains both (Emmy, hasHusband, Frank) and (Frank, hasWife, Emmy). Deleting *one* of them has no effect, since the reasoner will derive it from the other one. Thus, a *trigger* ON DELETE OF hasHusband DO BEGIN DELETE (OLD:object,hasWife,OLD:subject) END (and vice versa) would be suitable (and safe) to perform the intended update.

But: what does this trigger react upon? If it queries the model, it will neither react on DELETE (Emmy, hasHusband, Frank) nor on DELETE (Frank, hasWife, Emmy), because the model will not change at all after one of these operations. In contrast, these triggers must be triggered by the *action*.

Similar considerations hold for the cases where an update would violate consistency: then, a trigger that reacts on changes in the model would require to compute an inconsistent "model". Instead, integrity-preserving actions must be triggered *before* reasoning:

Example 3 (Unique President). Consider the following situation that describes that every company has a unique president. Assume $(c, \text{hasPresident}, x)$ and another person y. An operation INSERT $(c, \text{hasPresident}, y)$ would immediately cause an inconsistency since hasPresident is required to be functional. Here, a trigger that, when a new president becomes known, deletes the entry for the previous one would be required, e.g.:

ON INSERT OF hasPresident
WHERE {?c hasPresident ?x.} AND ?c = NEW.subject AND ?x <> NEW.object
DO BEGIN DELETE (?c, hasPresident, ?x) END

Thus, both cases show that an update of an OWL knowledge base is an *intensional* update whose materialization in the knowledge base must be done by suitable operations. In both cases, a trigger that reacts directly on the *operation* is required, to make the operation "complete" such that it will (i) actually induce a visible event (e.g., deletion) in the knowledge base, or (ii) maintain model-theoretic consistency.

We call such triggers *direct, pre-reasoning* triggers; the provide invisible, supporting reactive behavior. In contrast, *indirect, post-reasoning* triggers react only later on a *change* in the knowledge base as a theory (which in turn requires this theory to be consistent). They implement *visible* reactive behavior of an OWL node.

3   Triggers: Syntax and Semantics

The following proposal is based on our previous one for RDF triggers contained in [AAM05]. In some sense, the RDF triggers become the factbase-level *pre-reasoning* triggers whereas the *post-reasoning* triggers are concerned with RDFS and OWL semantics: event detection then also includes RDFS/OWL reasoning. As described above, triggers are of the form

ON *event* WHEN *condition* BEGIN *action* END .

- *event* is an event on the data model or knowledge base level. According to the distinction made above, direct, pre-reasoning and post-reasoning triggers react on different kinds of events (that will be described below).
- The *condition* part contains a query that can be used for obtaining additional information and also acts as a condition (expressed via join variables and predicates). In this work, the query is expressed as a conjunctive query in SPARQL [SPARQL] (that provides join variables) of the form

SELECT *variables* WHERE *condition*

against the local model. The test is considered to be true if at least one tuple of variable bindings is returned.
- The *action* part describes the action to be taken. The actions here can be update operations on the local database (e.g., for maintaining integrity conditions), sending a message, and raising events on a higher semantic level to the outside. The action part is executed for each tuple of variable bindings.

3.1   Direct, Pre-reasoning OWL Triggers

Direct, pre-reasoning triggers react *immediately* on *update operations*. Their task is to "support" the intended operation by performing appropriate updates on the underlying materialized data and obtain a consistent (wrt. the OWL model theory) state of the knowledge base. Direct triggers react on the following:

- ON {INSERT|UPDATE|RETRACT} OF *property* OF INSTANCE [OF *class*] is raised if a property is inserted for, updated or retracted from a resource (optionally: of the specified class).
- INSTEAD OF {ASSERT|UPDATE} OF *property* OF INSTANCE [OF *class*]   can be used for specifying how to execute an ASSERT or UPDATE instead of straightforwardly materializing the operation.

Since their task is only to support a required update operation, their actions are restricted to update operations on the database (i.e. external actions like sending messages or raising events are not allowed – such reactions are restricted to the post-reasoning triggers that react on actually visible changes).

Example 4. An OWL pre-reasoning trigger can be used in the situation of Example 2 for guaranteeing that a relationship is really removed:

Consider the user update RETRACT (Emmy, hasHusband, Frank) which immediately removes this tuple from the materialized RDF database. Still, (Frank, hasWife, Emmy) is contained in the RDF database and thus (Emmy, hasHusband, Frank) still exists as derived tuple – i.e. nothing visible changed. A pre-reasoning trigger ON RETRACT OF hasHusband DO BEGIN DELETE (OLD:object, hasWife, OLD:subject) END would remove the inverse tuple from the materialized database and thus "complete" the intended update. Then, the event DELETION OF hasHusband OF INSTANCE OF person is actually visible which is an event on which a post-reasoning trigger can react.

3.2   Post-reasoning OWL Triggers

Post-reasoning triggers react on actual changes of the model. Whereas the pre-reasoning triggers usually care for the OWL model-theoretic semantics, the post-reasoning triggers implement the actual application-specific reactive behavior. Post-reasoning triggers react on the following:

- ON {INSERTION|MODIFICATION|DELETION} OF *property* OF INSTANCE
  [OF *class*] is raised if a property is added to/updated/deleted from a resource (optionally: of the specified class).
- ON {CREATION|MODIFICATION|DELETION} OF INSTANCE OF *class* is raised if a resource of a given class is created, modified or deleted.
- ON NEW PROPERTY OF INSTANCE [OF *class*] is raised if a new property is added to an instance (optionally: to a specified class). This extends ON INSERTION OF *property* OF INSTANCE to properties that cannot be named (are unknown) during the rule design.
- ON NEW STATEMENT ABOUT INSTANCE [OF *class*] is raised, if a new statement is added to an instance (optionally: of a specified class). This extends ON NEW PROPERTY to the case that a new value for an already existing property is added that cannot be named (are unknown) during the rule design.

On the OWL level, also metadata changes are events:

- ON NEW CLASS is raised if a new class is introduced,
- ON NEW PROPERTY [OF *class*] is raised, if a new property (optionally: of a specified class) is introduced (in the metadata).

OWL post-reasoning triggers can then be used for (i) local updates (ECA rules) (ii) sending explicit messages or (iii) "raising" global events (ECE rules).

3.3   Example: Post-reasoning Triggers

Consider an OWL knowledge base about universities, researchers and publications, whose RDF Schema is described by triples of the form

(journal_publication, rdfs:subClassOf, publication)
(conference_publication, rdfs:subClassOf, publication)
(has_author, rdfs:domain, publication)
(has_author, rdfs:range, scientist)
(scientist, rdfs:subClassOf, foaf:person)
(works_at, rdfs:domain, foaf:person)
(works_at, rdfs:range, employer)
(university, subClassOf, employer)
(published, owl:inverseOf, has_author)
(is_employed, owl:inverseOf, works_at)

The instance level is given by appropriate triples, including e.g.

(john_doe, works_at, univ_stanford), (univ_stanford, rdf:type, university), and
(john_doe, name, "John Doe")

The knowledge base is e.g. maintained by inserting publications via a form where
the data is then transformed into RDF and added to the database, e.g.,

INSERT (jd-jacm-06, rdfs:type, journal_publication)
INSERT (jd-jacm-06, has_author, john_doe)

which now has –apart from the pure updates– several consequences, e.g.,

- -?(john_doe, published, jd-jacm-06) should now evaluate to true, and
- -?(john_doe, published, $X) should result in an answer set containing $X/jd-jacm-06.

Consider now that the database should also be able to list all publications that
have been published by university members when they are/were employed at a
given university. Note that this is different from

-? ($A, published, $P), ($A, works_at, $U), ($U, rdfs:type, university)

which would result in all publications *ever* published by a *current* member of the
university. In contrast, the intended knowledge is independent from the current
employer of the author, but assigns publications always to the employer at the
time of publication. Thus, it cannot be derived (except that the curriculum vitae
of persons is stored), but must be materialized. This can be done by a trigger:

```
ON INSERTION OF published OF INSTANCE OF person
  % (comes with parameters NEW.subject=author, NEW.property:=published,
  %    and NEW.object=publication)
WHERE {NEW.subject works_at $U.} AND {$U rdfs:type university.}
DO INSERT ($U, produced, NEW.object)
```

Note that the detection of the triggered event requires to derive (on the RDFS
level) that john_doe as an author is a scientist and thus a person.

Another application is raising a global event, where global ECA rules can
react upon. Such events are not to be materialized, but signaled to the outside,
using the outside's ontology instead of database level INSERT actions. E.g., the
event of hiring a new professor at a university can be signaled as

ON INSERTION OF is_employed OF INSTANCE OF university
WHERE {NEW.subject rdfs:type professor.}
RAISE EVENT professor_hired(NEW.object, NEW.subject)

where then other rules, e.g., a local newspaper that will write an article if the professor is very prominent, will react upon. Note that the latter rule is a global one that (i) "belongs to" the newspaper, (ii) reacts upon an event in the university (which must be communicated throughout the Semantic Web) and also has (iii) to use an ontology that defines "prominent".

4   Architecture of the Jena-Based Application Node

The application nodes (e.g., representing universities or airlines) that provide information and application-level functionality have to implement the domain ontologies, i.e., should be able to answer queries, make events visible to the Web, and to execute actions. This section describes an application node architecture supporting triggers based on the Jena framework that has been implemented in [Lie06].

The Jena [Jen] Framework provides an API for dealing with RDF and OWL data. In our architecture, Jena uses an external database (e.g. PostgreSQL) for storing base data. If Jena is used for RDFS or OWL data, an appropriate reasoner can be used. For this, Jena provides both a (restricted) internal reasoner and it can use a separate DL reasoner like or Pellet [Pel] via the DIG interface [DIG] conventions or via a Java API. Our RDF Web node is based on a service using the Jena framework with PostgreSQL and Pellet as shown in Figure 2.

The Jena node provides the OWL knowledge base functionality, i.e., storing models (that are distinguished internally by URIs) and querying them via SPARQL [SPARQL]. It is extended with update operations, further communication functionality and handling of triggers.

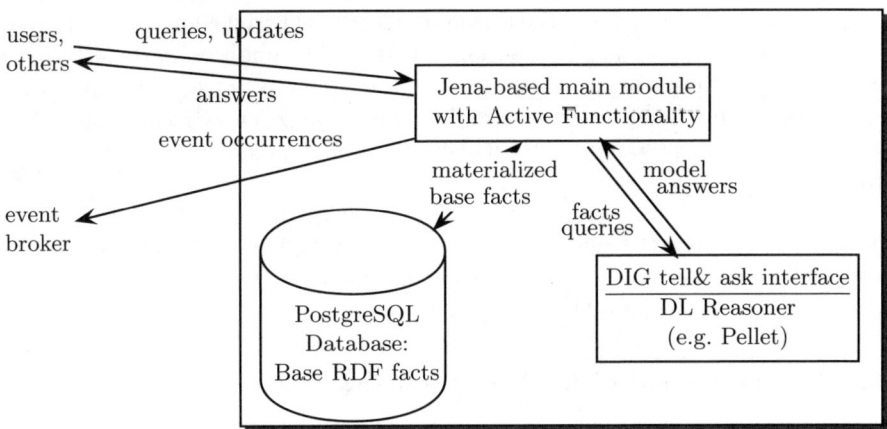

Fig. 2. Architecture of the Jena Node

Update Operations. SPARQL as a *query* language does not include any update statements. The implemented node provides methods (and a graphical interface) where *atomic updates* as given in Section 2.2 are supported.

Other Actions. Furthermore, the node is able to send HTTP messages to given URLs and to raise events (which are expected to be atomic events of the application domain according to the description in Section 1). Raised events are communicated to an external *event broker* "into the Semantic Web".

5   Algorithm for Firing Triggers in RDFS and OWL

As discussed above, there are *pre-reasoning* triggers for supporting update *operations* wrt. the underlying reasoning, and *post-reasoning* triggers that react upon visible *changes* in the model. For the first ones, "event detection" is rather simple: they are directly bound to the update operations. For the latter ones, changes in the model wrt. reasoning have to be detected.

5.1   Evaluating and Firing Pre-reasoning, Direct Triggers

Direct triggers serve for "completing" updates (e.g., by deleting also the inverse of a statement to be deleted), or enforcing OWL model-theoretic consistency. Concerning the latter situation, executing the original update operation alone may already lead to an inconsistent model (that should be cured by the trigger). Queries against inconsistent models are both theoretically and practically problematic (using Jena with an external reasoner allows for updating a model such that it becomes inconsistent, and allows to do further updates as long as the reasoner is not concerned, but causes problems when querying or exporting an inconsistent model). On the other hand, for the pre-reasoning triggers, the model is actually not needed at all:

Given an update operation *act* to be executed, the set Upd_{direct} is the set of updates that includes *act* and the actions of all (direct) triggers whose event part directly matches the action (i.e., action = event). All condition parts (which are in general very simple for direct triggers) of the respective triggers are evaluated against the model before executing any update. Computing Upd_{direct} thus does *not* require OWL reasoning. After its computation, Upd_{direct} it is executed as a whole.

Only after that, we require the model to be consistent wrt. the OWL semantics. Otherwise, the update is rejected and rolled back. If the fact base is consistent – as expected – the application-specific behavior is then implemented by post-reasoning triggers that react upon changes wrt. the original model.

5.2   Evaluating and Firing Post-reasoning Triggers

The actual *reaction* defined by the *post-reasoning* triggers is based on the *actually visible* changes of the derived model. Since we assume here the model to be consistent, the conditions can be evaluated against the current model.

During firing the post-reasoning triggers, all update operations are executed immediately, and all external actions, i.e., sending mails and raising events are put into a queue.

In case that the knowledge base becomes inconsistent after firing the post-reasoning triggers, or an operation is rejected (which can happen for RETRACT if the "supporting" direct triggers are not strong enough to actually remove the fact) the whole operation (including the initial update) is rejected and rolled back. Otherwise the queue of external actions is then also executed.

Below we first describe the difference-based algorithm that has been implemented and then discuss alternatives in Section 5.4.

5.3   Difference-Based Solution

A straightforward solution which is obviously correct, complete, and simple to implement can be characterized as a *difference-based* approach. It regards the database and the reasoner as external black boxes where the implementation should not interfere with, as provided by the Jena framework:

- before executing an update operation, export the whole model (including all derived statements) from the reasoner as beforemodel,
- execute the update and all direct triggers,
- export the whole model (including all derived statements) from the reasoner as aftermodel,
- compute the difference of both models (added and/or removed tuples),
- match each differing tuple (inserted, deleted, modified) against the event specifications in the post-reasoning triggers (note that modifications can be distinguished from deletions+insertions by forcing reification when a statement is modified and inspecting the statement's URI during the comparison).

The strategy is implemented by solely using classes of the Jena Framework:

```
// declarations
private static ModelRDB dbmodel;
private static OntModel ontmodel;
// create dbmodel and get a DIGReasoner
// create ontmodel by combining dbmodel and reasoner
OntModel ontmodel = ModelFactory.createOntologyModel(spec,dbmodel);
// prepare additional ontmodels for future before-after comparison
OntModel beforemodel;
OntModel aftermodel;
```

The class `ModelRDB` implements the RDF model materialized in a (relational) database, whereas the class `OntModel` implements models with ontological reasoning (combining an `ModelRDB` with an external reasoner via the DIG interface). `OntModel` provides all required methods for adding and deleting statements (and also maintains the underlying `ModelRDB`), SPARQL queries can be evaluated by generating a `QueryExecution` object for a given query and an `OntModel`, and then `execSelect`ing its result set.

For implementing the triggers, Jena's functionality to compute the difference between two `OntModel`s is used, which results in a list of statements that can be stored by an instance of the plain `Model` class (without any reasoning closure). The `Model` then provides an iterator over the difference statements (which usually are not too many after executing some simple updates). The basic strategy is as follows:

```
// loop invariant: aftermodel is a copy of the current ontmodel
beforemodel = aftermodel;
```

execute original update and direct triggers on ontmodel *as described above*
check if ontmodel *is consistent; if no, rollback and return*

```
aftermodel = ModelFactory.createOntologyModel();
aftermodel.add(ontmodel);
Model inserted = aftermodel.difference(beforemodel);
Model deleted = beforemodel.difference(aftermodel);
// simple Model does not include reasoning, it is just a list of statements
StmtIterator iter1 = deleted.listStatements();
StmtIterator iter2 = inserted.listStatements();
```

The iterators are then used for matching each tuple against the event specifications in the triggers. The latter are stored in a relational database (where the same PostgreSQL database is used that also stores the RDF database for Jena) with suitable indexes. Thus, the actual matching can be done efficiently.

The method can be criticized for the fact that it requires to export the whole model and to compute the whole difference twice (even if nothing actually happens). On the other hand, if the difference is small (which is in general the case), the remaining effort is small: every added/removed triple is matched with each of the trigger events, and the respective triggers are executed. We next discuss alternative approaches and show that the chosen solution is the preferable one:

- alternatives are algorithmically expensive, in general even incomplete,
- taking into account that the above method uses built-in operations of Jena which can be expected to be efficiently implemented and supported by internal structures of the `Model` and `OntModel` classes.

5.4   Discussion of Alternative Methods

Forward Reasoning. Another possibility is not to compare the models, but to reason about the effects of an update wrt. the current state of the database. This would mean to "simulate" the reasoner and anticipate what it will do. This can be done in two ways: based on the update statements on the RDF level, or based on the actual updates in the underlying SQL database: SQL triggers "raise" the appropriate RDF events.

In both cases, it is necessary to *derive* the actual events from some (syntactically different) update operation under consideration of other facts using RDFS/OWL reasoning. The approach amounts to the *view maintenance problem* since each view defined by one of the triple patterns used in triggering events must be monitored. In OWL (i.e., separately for each DL/OWL dialect), this problem has not been tackled so far. The process looks manageable – but, forward reasoning requires to know which facts to join for it, which requires SPARQL queries, computing transitive hulls etc. Considering the current architecture, it would mean to duplicate large parts of the reasoning.

Comparing Views. Instead of (i) comparing the whole models or (ii) maintaining the relevant views, each of the *views* that is relevant for the triggers can be computed before and after executing the model. For this, when registering a trigger, its event pattern has to be translated into an SPARQL query. The results of the query before and after executing the update can then be compared and the difference is used for firing the triggers.

Although, already for the most specific form of triggers, i.e., ON {INSERTION | MODIFICATION | DELETION} OF *property* [OF *class*], the whole extension of one property of a class is concerned. For ON {CREATION | MODIFICATION | DELETION} OF INSTANCE [OF *class*], the view contains the set of all instances of a class, and for ON NEW PROPERTY OF INSTANCE [OF *class*], the view consists of all pairs (*instance, property*). Having a large set of triggers, it is likely that parts of the views are computed several times. Here, *query containment* and *query rewriting* investigations could be used for optimization. Again, both are not yet investigated for OWL (and already for relational queries these problems are expensive).

Considering the fact that exporting the whole model and comparing models are built-in operations of Jena and the DIG interface, most probably the plain *difference-based* approach is more efficient than evaluating SPARQL queries two times and storing and comparing the answers.

6   Conclusion

Considering "event detection (derivation) in OWL knowledge bases", the complexity of the above algorithm is not necessarily the most efficient. But, considering the given architecture that uses the database and the reasoner as black boxes, the discussed alternatives that are theoretically more involved did not look promising. Having access to the reasoner, a more direct solution could be reasonable by reasoning about the updates. Theoretical research in this direction seems to be interesting. From a pragmatical point of view, partitioning of the database into reasoning-independent fragments can often reduce the amount of data to be compared for evaluating the triggers.

Further Work. The implementation was lead by a pragmatical motivation: to have a running active Jena-based OWL node for integration as a domain node

148   W. May, F. Schenk, and E. von Lienen

into the General ECA Framework [MAA05b], and as a testbed for further experiments with OWL. It showed that there are many (related) interesting theoretical issues that find an application in this scenario: DL and OWL theory updates, view maintenance, query containment.

Acknowledgements. This research has been funded by the European Commission within the 6th Framework Programme project REWERSE, no. 506779.

References

[AAM05]   J. J. Alferes, R. Amador, and W. May. A general language for Evolution and Reactivity in the Semantic Web. In *Principles and Practice of Semantic Web Reasoning (PPSWR)*, Springer LNCS 3703 pp. 101–115. 2005.

[BCM+03]   F. Baader, D. Calvanese, D. McGuinness, D. Nardi, and P. Patel-Schneider, editors. *The Description Logic Handbook*. Cambridge University Press, 2003.

[DIG]   Description Logic Implementation Group (DIG). http://dl.kr.org/dig/.

[Jen]   Jena: A Java Framework for Semantic Web Applications. http://jena.sourceforge.net.

[Lie06]   Elke von Lienen. Entwicklung eines RDF-Web-Services mit Trigger-Funktionalität. *Diplomarbeit*, TU Clausthal (in german), 2006.

[MAA05a]   W. May, J. J. Alferes, and R. Amador. Active Rules in the Semantic Web: Dealing with Language Heterogeneity. In *Rule Markup Languages (RuleML)*, Springer LNCS 3791, pp. 30–44. 2005.

[MAA05b]   W. May, J. J. Alferes, and R. Amador. An Ontology- and Resources-Based Approach to Evolution and Reactivity in the Semantic Web. In *Ontologies, Databases and Semantics (ODBASE)*, Springer LNCS 3761. 2005.

[MAB04]   W. May, J. J. Alferes, and F. Bry. Towards generic query, update, and event languages for the Semantic Web. In *Principles and Practice of Semantic Web Reasoning (PPSWR)*, Springer LNCS 3208, pp. 19–33. 2004.

[OWL04]   OWL Web Ontology Language. http://www.w3.org/TR/owl-features/, 2004.

[Pel]   Pellet: An OWL DL Reasoner. Maryland Information and Network Dynamics Lab, http://www.mindswap.org/2003/pellet.

[PPW03]   G. Papamarkos, A. Poulovassilis, and P. T. Wood. Event-Condition-Action Rule Languages for the Semantic Web. In *Workshop on Semantic Web and Databases (SWDB'03)*, 2003.

[PPW04]   G. Papamarkos, A. Poulovassilis, and P. T. Wood. RDFTL: An Event-Condition-Action Rule Language for RDF. In *Hellenic Data Management Symposium (HDMS'04)*, 2004.

[RDF00]   Resource Description Framework (RDF) Schema specification. http://www.w3.org/TR/rdf-schema/, 2000.

[SPARQL]   SPARQL Query Language for RDF. http://www.w3.org/TR/rdf-sparql-query/, 2006.

Supporting Open and Closed World Reasoning on the Web[*]

Carlos Viegas Damásio[1], Anastasia Analyti[2],
Grigoris Antoniou[2,3], and Gerd Wagner[4]

[1] Centro de Inteligência Artificial, Universidade Nova de Lisboa, Caparica, Portugal
[2] Institute of Computer Science, FORTH-ICS, Greece
[3] Department of Computer Science, University of Crete, Greece
[4] Institute of Informatics, Brandenburg Univ. of Technology at Cottbus Germany
`analyti@ics.forth.gr, antoniou@ics.forth.gr,`
`cd@di.fct.unl.pt, G.Wagner@tu-cottbus.de`

Abstract. In this paper general mechanisms and syntactic restrictions are explored in order to specify and merge rule bases in the Semantic Web. Rule bases are expressed by extended logic programs having two forms of negation, namely strong (or explicit) and weak (also known as default negation or *negation-as-failure*). The proposed mechanisms are defined by very simple modular program transformations, and integrate both open and closed world reasoning. These program transformations are shown to be appropriate for the two major semantics for extended logic programs: answer set semantics and well-founded semantics with explicit negation. Moreover, the results obtained by both semantics are compared.

1 Introduction

The Semantic Web [3] aims at defining formal languages, and corresponding tools, enabling automated processing and reasoning over (meta-)data available from the Web. Logic and knowledge representation play a central role, but the distributed and world-wide nature of the Web bring new interesting research problems. In particular, the widely recognized need of having rules in the Semantic Web [13,17] has restarted the discussion of the fundamentals of closed-world reasoning and the appropriate mechanisms to implement it in rule systems, such as the computational concept of *negation-as-failure*.

The classification if a predicate is completely represented or not is up to the owner of the knowledge base: the owner must know for which predicates there is complete information and for which there is not. Unfortunately, neither classical logic nor standard Prolog supports the distinction between "closed" and "open" predicates. Classical logic supports only open-world reasoning. On the contrary,

---

[*] This research has been partially funded by European Commission and by the Swiss Federal Office for Education and Science within the 6th Framework Programme project REWERSE number 506779 (cf. `http://rewerse.net`)

J.J. Alferes et al. (Eds.): PPSWR 2006, LNCS 4187, pp. 149–163, 2006.

most Prolog systems support only closed-world reasoning, as *negation-as-failure* is the only negation mechanism supported (a notable exception is XSB [18]). We resort to two major semantics of extended logic programs, namely *answer set semantics* [10], and *well-founded semantics with explicit negation* [15,1], which have two forms of negation: weak and strong. Weak negation is an appropriate rendering of the mechanism of nonmonotonic negation-as-failure, and strong negation allows the user to express negative knowledge and is monotonic. The combination of these two forms of negation allow the distinction between open and closed predicates, as will be illustrated by their application to the declaration and construction of rule bases in the Semantic Web.

The paper is organized as follows. In Section 2, the use of extended logic programming is explored to represent open and closed world reasoning, providing general mechanisms for achieving this. Section 3 defines new language mechanisms for sharing and integrating knowledge in the Semantics Web. In Section 4, the transformational semantics is provided for the constructs presented. The paper finishes with comparisons and conclusions.

2   Open and Closed World Assumption

Rule bases are sets of extended logic programming rules of the form

$$L_0 \leftarrow L_1, \ldots, L_m, \sim L_{m+1}, \ldots \sim L_n \tag{1}$$

where each L_i (with $0 \leq i \leq n$) is an objective literal, i.e. either an atom $A(\bar{t})$ or the strong negation of an atom $\neg A(\bar{t})$, where $\bar{t}$ is a sequence of terms. Variables are prefixed with a question mark symbol (**?**), therefore names for predicates, constants and function symbols can start with small and capital letters. It is assumed that a fixed first order logic alphabet is given, and only extended Herbrand interpretations are considered (sets of objective literals). In particular, a non-ground rule in an extended logic program stands for the set of ground rules obtained by instantiating logical variables with elements from the Herbrand universe. Notice that implicitly we are using a *domain closure assumption* which might not be acceptable in some situations. Without loss of generality, only ground programs are considered in the subsequent theoretical results. Furthermore, we restrict the discussion to DATALOG programs over a finite number of constants in order to guarantee decidability of reasoning. We define by $\mathcal{C}_{SEM}(P)$ the set of *objective literals* which are obtained from the extended logic program P under semantics SEM, where $SEM = WFSX$ or $SEM = AS$. Here we consider only sceptical answer set semantics [10], denoted by subscript $SEM = AS$, and well-founded semantics with explicit negation [15,1], denoted by subscript $SEM = WFSX$. For inconsistent programs, both these semantics adopt an explosive approach by letting $\mathcal{C}_{SEM}(P)$ be the set of all objective literals. The reader is referred to the literature for details.

Example 1. Consider the following program expressing immigration laws of an imaginary country. Notice that all the rules are objective, i.e. do not use weak negation.

```
Enter(?p) ← CountryEU(?c), citizenOf(?p,?c).
Enter(?p) ← ¬ CountryEU(?c), citizenOf(?p,?c), ¬ RequiresVisa(?c).
Enter(?p) ← ¬ CountryEU(?c), citizenOf(?p,?c),
            RequiresVisa(?c), HasVisa(?p).
```

Predicate `Enter/1` captures the following laws:

- A citizen of European Union can enter the country.
- A non European Union citizen can enter the country if a visa is not required.
- A non European Union citizen can enter the country if a visa is required and he/she has it.

These rules are complemented with the following knowledge, where it is assumed that the list of European Union countries is exhaustive:

```
CountryEU(Austria).                    ¬ RequiresVisa(Bulgaria).
  ⋮                                    ¬ RequiresVisa(?c) ← CountryEU(?c).
                                       RequiresVisa(China).

¬ CountryEU(China).
¬ CountryEU(Djibuti).
```

Some facts about Anne, Boris, Chen and Dil finish the program:

```
citizenOf(Anne,Austria).
citizenOf(Boris,Bulgaria).
citizenOf(Chen,China).        HasVisa(Chen).
citizenOf(Dil,Djibuti).       HasVisa(Dil).
```

The arbitrary uncontrolled use of weak negation in the Semantic Web is regarded problematic and unsafe. However, local closed world assumptions and *scoped negation-as-failure* have been identified as desirable and necessary for the Semantic Web [11,14,16,23,2]. The difficulty lies on the definition of simple mechanisms that can be easily explained to ordinary users, and have nice mathematical properties. For this reason, we propose a classification of predicates which cover the whole gamut of alternatives. The classes of *objective*, *open* and *closed* predicates impose some restrictions on the use of weak negation in the rules defining a predicate A in the Semantic Web, which are summarized in Figure 1. The top-half boxes contain the user's predicate definitions and are always sets of objective rules, i.e. rules which do not contain weak negation but might contain strongly negated literals, in particular the head of rules might be $A(\bar{t})$ or $\neg A(\bar{t})$. The bottom-half boxes contain special rules, added by the system, which characterize each type of predicate. Additionally, it is required that objective, open and closed predicates do not use (directly or indirectly) unrestricted predicates on their definitions. This prevents unintended use of weak negation in the Semantic Web. The unrestricted predicates are designated *normal* (or ordinary) predicates, adopting the usual logic programming accepted terminology.

Thus, objective predicates are defined by rules which do not contain weak negation at all. Since strong negation is monotonic, then these predicates can

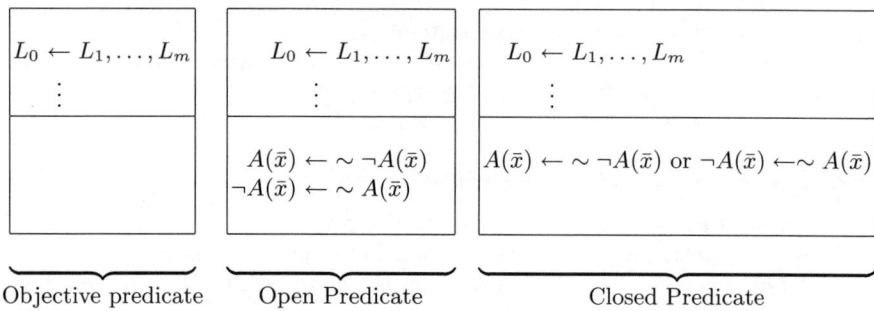

Fig. 1. Declarations for a predicate A (the predicate of L_0 is A)

be freely used in the Semantic Web without any restriction. These predicates are *partial* since it may be the case that neither $A(\bar{c})$ nor $\neg A(\bar{c})$ hold in a model (see [12,2] for more details), where $\bar{c}$ is a sequence of constants. On the other hand, open predicates have the following two additional rules, denoted by *openRules(A)*:

$$A(\overline{x}) \leftarrow\sim \neg A(\overline{x}) \qquad \neg A(\overline{x}) \leftarrow\sim A(\overline{x})$$

In answer set semantics, these specify that either $A(\bar{c})$ is true or $\neg A(\bar{c})$ is true in each model (answer set), thus forcing *totalness*.

Finally, closed predicates are complemented by one and only one of the previous two rules, called *default closure rules*, and denoted by *negClosure(A)* and *posClosure(A)*, respectively. This provides a mechanism for making closed world assumptions: either by making true what is not concluded false or by making false what is not concluded true.

Example 2. Returning to Example 1, start by assuming that all predicates are objective. The following conclusions are obtained from the original program, both with *AS* and *WFSX* semantics:

Enter(Anne)   Enter(Chen)

Interestingly, Enter(Boris) is not concluded because it is not known that Bulgaria is a European Union country and also it is not known that it is not a European Union country! One way to circumvent this situation is to state that predicate CountryEU/1 is open. Notice that it does not make sense to state that CountryEU/1 is closed since EU is evolving and new countries in the near future might integrate EU, namely Bulgaria[1]. By declaring CountryEU/1 open, the following two rules are added:

CountryEU(?c) ← ∼¬ CountryEU(?c)
¬ CountryEU(?c) ← ∼ CountryEU(?c)

From the new program and using AS semantics, it is concluded that Boris can enter the country. The argument is the following: if Bulgaria is a member

---

[1] This is a simple-minded solution to the problem of knowledge update.

of EU, then by the first rule Boris can enter the country; if Bulgaria is not a European Union country, since a Visa is not required for Bulgaria, then Boris can also enter the country. WFSX semantics is not capable of doing this case analysis and therefore this conclusion is not obtained.

Finally, consider the situation where `Enter/1` and `¬RequiresVisa/1` are exhaustive. These predicates can be closed, by introducing the following rules:

$$\neg\; \text{Enter(?p)} \;\leftarrow\; \sim \text{Enter(?p)}$$
$$\text{RequiresVisa(?c)} \;\leftarrow\; \sim \neg\; \text{RequiresVisa(?c)}$$

The first rule expresses that if by the immigration laws cannot be concluded that a person can enter the country, then that person cannot enter the country. The second rule states that the list of countries, for which it is not requested a Visa, is closed. This means that it is requested a Visa for the non-listed countries. Both under WFSX and AS semantics, it is now concluded that Dil can enter the country.

Notice that in the move from all predicates being objective to some being open and then closed, new conclusions might be obtained, as the following major Theorem shows:

Theorem 1. *Let A be an objective predicate in extended logic program P where all predicates are either objective or open. Then,*

- $\mathcal{C}_{SEM}(P) \subseteq \mathcal{C}_{SEM}(P \cup openRules(A))$
- $\mathcal{C}_{SEM}(P \cup openRules(A)) \subseteq \mathcal{C}_{SEM}(P \cup posClosure(A))$
- $\mathcal{C}_{SEM}(P \cup openRules(A)) \subseteq \mathcal{C}_{SEM}(P \cup negClosure(A))$

with $SEM = AS$ or $SEM = WFSX$.

For the case of $WFSX$ semantics the first containment is in fact an equality, i.e. $\mathcal{C}_{WFSX}(P) = \mathcal{C}_{WFSX}(P \cup openRules(A))$. The previous theorem cannot be generalized when some predicate is closed in P. This is expected due to the non-monotonic nature of weak negation under both AS semantics and WFSX semantics.

Example 3. Consider the original program of Example 1 but now `Enter/1` is declared closed with the rule:

$$\neg\; \text{Enter(?p)} \;\leftarrow\; \sim \text{Enter(?p)}$$

It can be concluded with WFSX and AS semantics that ¬ `Enter(Boris)` and ¬ `Enter(Dil)`. Now by declaring `CountryEU/1` open, ¬ `Enter(Dil)` is not concluded anymore with WFSX and AS. As previously, `Enter(Boris)` is concluded with AS but not with WFSX.

Notice that under WFSX no new objective conclusions are obtained by declaring predicates open. This is expected since entailment in WFSX can be computed in polynomial time, while entailment in AS is coNP-complete. This is the trade-off between expressivity and complexity of reasoning. However, WFSX and AS semantics are not unrelated:

Theorem 2. *[15] Let P be an extended logic program, then* $\mathcal{C}_{WFSX}(P) \subseteq \mathcal{C}_{AS}(P)$.

WFSX is a tractable semantics which approximates AS semantics, and therefore is a good candidate for defining the semantics of rule bases in the Semantic Web. However, the existence of an undefined truth-value in WFSX might affect the intuition in some particular cases, namely for closed predicates; this is the price to pay for guaranteeing tractability of reasoning. Aside that, both semantics assure the monotonicity of reasoning in the presence of only objective and open predicates:

Theorem 3. *Let P and Q be two extended logic programs where all predicates are either objective or open. Then,*

- $\mathcal{C}_{AS}(P) \subseteq \mathcal{C}_{AS}(P \cup Q)$
- $\mathcal{C}_{WFSX}(P) \subseteq \mathcal{C}_{WFSX}(P \cup Q)$

Obviously, the previous result does not hold whenever closed predicates are included in P or Q. The above theorems are explored in the next section for defining modular programming techniques to be used in the Semantic Web.

3   Modularity in the Semantic Web

In this section we study the mechanisms in order to be able to express the necessary context to use strong and weak negations safely in the Semantic Web environment. The discussion is abstract and independent of any rule engine. Currently, there is no notion of scope or context in the Semantic Web: all knowledge is global and all kinds of unexpected interactions can occur. The success of the Semantic Web is impossible without any form of modularity, encapsulation, information hiding and access control. The issue of modularity in logic programming has been actively investigated during the 90s, for a survey see [4]. Here we follow a typical approach similar to the import/export mechanisms of Prolog, but we will be concerned with the combination of open and closed world reasoning and other particularities of the Semantic Web. In particular, the following four levels of context and their interaction must be taken into account:

- The Semantic Web context;
- The application context, corresponding to the context where a user or Semantic Web agent loads, asserts or consumes the knowledge provided by rule bases in the Semantic Web;
- The rule base context, where the Semantic Web developer encapsulates a set of related rules and facts (predicates);
- The predicate context, which can be either global or local;

Rule bases are made available in the Semantic Web, and users or applications load or assert them explicitly into their application contexts. The connection to an external knowledge base should always be equivalent to loading it locally, but without the need to explicitly do that. When a user or application loads

DefinesDecl ::=
  [*RuleBaseIRI*] `"defines"` [*ScopeDecl*] *PredList* [`"visible to"` *RuleBaseList*] `"."`
UsesDecl ::= [*RuleBaseIRI*] `"uses"` *PredList* [`"from"` *RuleBaseList*] `"."`

ScopeDecl ::= `"global"` | `"local"` | `"internal"`
PredList ::= *PredicateDecl* (`","` *PredicateDecl*)*
RuleBaseList ::= *RuleBaseIRI* (`","` *RuleBaseIRI*)*
PredicateDecl ::= [`"objective"` | `"open"` | `"closed"` [`"¬"`] | `"normal"`] *PredicateInd*
PredicateInd ::= *AbsoluteIRI* [`"/"` Arity]
Arity ::= *Natural*
RuleBaseIRI ::= *AbsoluteIRI*

Fig. 2. The `defines` and `uses` declarations

or asserts knowledge, it may express that nonmonotonic reasoning forms may be rejected or allowed, or can force the deduction mechanisms to use only rules which extract safe knowledge in the Semantic Web context. The knowledge base programmer may use nonmonotonic constructs, knowing that these constructs might be inhibited or forbidden. The producer of knowledge might also express that the predicates he/she is declaring cannot be defined elsewhere, and may declare hidden predicates which are not visible in the Semantic Web. Furthermore, a knowledge base might use all the available knowledge in the application context, or get it explicitly from particularly loaded rule bases. By default, reasoning in the Semantic Web must be monotonic.

The challenge is to provide simple mechanisms in order to guarantee the fulfilment of the previous requirements. Obviously, the syntax of extended logic programs should be augmented with declarations to state the visibility of a predicate, its context, and whether it is normal (i.e. unrestricted), objective, open or closed. It is also necessary to express how external information to the knowledge base is incorporated into it. These can be attained with the declarations `defines` and `uses` with the syntax in BNF notation presented in Figure 2. The `defines` declaration specifies which predicates are defined (and exported) in the knowledge base, their scope and visibility, as well as type. The `uses` declaration describes which predicates are used (imported) from other rule bases or from the Semantic Web, and might change the original type of the predicate. Notice that predicates and rule bases are all identified by absolute IRIs (Internationalized Resource Identifiers [7]). When a predicate A is declared `closed` (resp. `closed` ¬) then the $posClosure(A)$ (resp. $negClosure(A)$) rule is implicitly added to the program. If the predicate is declared `open`, then both rules are added, as described in the previous section.

The scope plays a fundamental part, and describes what is the context of the predicate(s) and may take one of the following values, with the following corresponding limitations and meaning:

`"global"`: a predicate declared global is visible outside the knowledge base, and intends to capture predicates being defined in the Semantic Web. Moreover, the predicate can be defined elsewhere in other rule bases but it must be either objective or open[2]. Additionally, it can be optionally declared which rule bases can use the predicate; if omitted, it can be used everywhere.

"local": a local predicate can be used outside the rule base where it has been defined, but cannot be defined by any other knowledge base in the Semantic Web. A local predicate can be of any type (objective, open, closed and normal) and, as before, the user can state the rule bases where it can be used.

The rule base defines the scope for a closed predicate, and the closure rule may be inhibited by the consumer of the knowledge in the **uses** statement. If the predicate is normal, any form of negation can be used in its definition, and its use can be forbidden by the consumer of the knowledge, again with the **uses** statement.

"internal": predicate is internal to the rule base and cannot be used outside the rule base. Again, the rule base defines the scope for the evaluation of weak negation.

By default a predicate is global and open, and visible to any rule base in the Semantic Web. Also, all predicates in the RDF and RDFS vocabularies are global and open. Thus, the user doesn't have to state explicitly the scope and type of predicates in all rule bases. Furthermore, this guarantees monotonicity of reasoning. It is not practically possible to guarantee that a local predicate is not redefined multiple times in the Semantic Web. However, any implementation will not allow loading knowledge bases which define a local or global predicate defined local in another loaded rule base.

The visibility provides a basic security mechanism, but trust and authorization could be much improved, for instance using the PEERTRUST language [9]. These issues are orthogonal to present proposal but can be easily integrated due to the logical nature of our work. The **uses** declaration specifies the rule bases providing the definitions of global and local predicates that can be used by the importing rule base. The scope of the imported predicated is given by a corresponding **defines** statement in the rule base, whenever it exists. If the **from** list in the **uses** declaration (Fig. 2) is omitted then these predicates can be imported from any available knowledge base. Notice that the importer can specify what types of predicates (reasoning) he/she is willing to accept, and the default type is open. The exporter must provide the answers according to the cases specified in Table 1.

For instance, suppose that a rule base $< RB_A >$ **defines** a closed predicate P with: $< RB_A >$ **defines local closed** P.

However, the **uses** statement in rule base $< RB_B >$ declares that it is only willing to accept the conclusions obtained by opening the predicate P in $< RB_A >$: $< RB_B >$ **uses open** P **from** $< RB_A >$.

Rule base $< RB_A >$ should only provide answers to queries of P from $< RB_B >$ as if all closed predicates in $< RB_A >$ were open. If $< RB_B >$ **uses** predicate P of $< RB_A >$ in objective mode, then all predicates in rule base $< RB_A >$ are considered objective when computing the queries to P from

---

[2] For simplicity, this constraint is not enforced in the grammar.

Table 1. Combination of reasoning modes

uses (importer)	objective	open	closed	normal
normal	objective	open	closed	normal
closed	objective	open	closed	error
open	objective	open	open	error
objective	objective	objective	objective	error
	objective	open	closed	normal

defines (exporter)

$< RB_B >$. In other words, the reasoning mode should also be propagated to the predicates used in $< RB_A >$, whenever these predicates are necessary to answer the original query. Finally, we would like to note that there are subtle issues involved in the above mechanisms, namely the possibility of mutual dependencies between rule bases, which should be addressed in implementations. A runtime error is thrown when the exporter declares a local predicate normal but the importer uses one of the limited predicate reasoning forms: objective, open or closed. This behaviour corresponds to rejecting by the importer the uncontrolled use of weak negation in the Semantic Web. Note again that according to the results of the previous section, the default declarations guarantee that reasoning is monotonic.

A knowledge base might define and use the same predicate, but not all combinations are possible. The various allowed combinations are presented in Table 2.

Table 2. Defining and using the same predicate

defines	global	local	internal
global	allowed	error	error
local	error	error	error
internal	allowed	allowed	error
	global	local	internal

uses

Obviously, it is an error to globally or locally define a used local predicate; this goes against the notion that there is a sole provider for a local predicate. However, it is allowed to internally redefine a local predicate of a different rule base, since it is not made public. In particular, one might close an objective local predicate of a different provider since this is only for internal use.

The several combinations are illustrated with the next example.

Example 4. Consider the knowledge bases in the Semantic Web identified by IRIs <http://www.eu.int>, <http://gov.country> and <http://security.int>. We use the namespace prefixes eu, gov and sec to simplify writing of IRIs in the code of Figure 3.

The simpler rule base, identified by <http://www.eu.int>, defines the list of European Union countries, and this list is closed. Notice that this is a proper

```
<http://www.eu.int>
defines local closed eu:CountryEU/1.

eu:CountryEU(Austria).
:
eu:CountryEU(UnitedKingdom).
```

```
<http://security.int>

sec:citizenOf(Anne,Austria).
sec:citizenOf(Boris,Bulgaria).
sec:citizenOf(Chen,China).
sec:citizenOf(Dil,Djibuti).
```

```
<http://gov.country>
defines local closed gov:Enter/1.
defines internal objective gov:HasVisa/1.
defines internal closed ¬ gov:RequiresVisa/1.

defines internal open eu:CountryEU/1.
uses objective eu:CountryEU/1 from <http://www.eu.int>.

defines internal objective sec:citizenOf/2.
uses objective sec:citizenOf/2.
```
```
gov:Enter(?p) ← eu:CountryEU(?c), sec:citizenOf(?p,?c).
gov:Enter(?p) ← ¬ eu:CountryEU(?c), sec:citizenOf(?p,?c),
                ¬ gov:RequiresVisa(?c).
gov:Enter(?p) ← ¬ eu:CountryEU(?c), sec:citizenOf(?p,?c),
                gov:RequiresVisa(?c), gov:HasVisa(?p).

¬ gov:RequiresVisa(Bulgaria).
¬ gov:RequiresVisa(?c) ← eu:CountryEU(?c).
gov:RequiresVisa(China).

gov:HasVisa(Chen).
gov:HasVisa(Dil).

¬ eu:CountryEU(China).
¬ eu:CountryEU(Djibuti).
```

Fig. 3. Sharing of Knowledge in the Semantic Web

logical definition of the CWM [5] construct log:definitiveDocument. The second rule base, <http://security.int>, provides citizenship of people, and could be implemented in a ordinary relational database. Since no defines declaration is present, predicate sec:citizenOf/2 is a global and open predicate.

The third rule base defines the immigration policies of country <http://gov.country>, supported by the knowledge of the other two rule bases. The first three defines statements are according to the discussion in Example 1; it should be noticed the mechanism for closing negative instances in gov:RequiresVisa/1 with ¬. The country is not willing to accept the local closure of eu:CountryEU/1 performed in <http://www.eu.int>. Therefore, it uses the predicate forcing objective mode and, in this example, only facts are requested to `<http://www.eu.int>`. Furthermore, `eu:CountryEU` is made open, for use in this rule base; this can be done since the predicate is defined to be internal. Complementary additional facts to predicate `eu:CountryEU/1` are stated in the rule base. Predicate `sec:citizenOf` is used from any providers in the Semantics Web, but it is made objective for internal use only.

The code of the figure is unsatisfactory from a security point of view. In an additional rule base, it could be added a fact stating that, for instance, `sec:citizenOf(Chen,France)`. Since rule base `<http://gov.country>` is carelessly using `sec:citizenOf/2` from the Semantic Web it imports any existing available knowledge independently of the providing rule base. This can be corrected with the statement:

```
uses objective sec:citizenOf/2 from <http://security.int>.
```

If more sources are trusted, these can be added to the `from` list. Also, `<http://security.int>` is providing confidential information to any requester. This can also be improved by specifying the authorized consumers of this knowledge base in the `visible to` list, e.g.:

```
defines global open sec:citizenOf/2 visible to <http://gov.country>.
```

4   Transformational Semantics

In this section, we define a modular program transformation capturing the semantics of each of the proposed constructs described in the previous section. For capturing the intended semantics, a single extended logic program is constructed. In order to control visibility and scope of the predicates, predicate names are transformed into a pair containing the rule base IRI and the predicate IRI[3]. In our transformation, a rule will be translated into four rules, one for each possible reasoning mode: definite (objective), open, closed and normal. This permits a modular way of independently composing the several rule bases, i.e. adding the transformational rules corresponding to a rule base does not require changing the form of the transformational rules of already handled rule bases. Suppose that a rule base r contains the rule:

$$L_0 \leftarrow L_1, \ldots, L_m, \sim L_{m+1}, \ldots, \sim L_n. \tag{2}$$

Accordingly, the rule is translated into the following four rules:

$$r{:}d\_L_0 \leftarrow r{:}d\_L_1, \ldots, r{:}d\_L_m, \sim r{:}d\_L_{m+1}, \ldots, \sim r{:}d\_L_n.$$
$$r{:}o\_L_0 \leftarrow r{:}o\_L_1, \ldots, r{:}o\_L_m, \sim r{:}o\_L_{m+1}, \ldots, \sim r{:}o\_L_n.$$
$$r{:}c\_L_0 \leftarrow r{:}c\_L_1, \ldots, r{:}c\_L_m, \sim r{:}c\_L_{m+1}, \ldots, \sim r{:}c\_L_n.$$
$$r{:}n\_L_0 \leftarrow r{:}n\_L_1, \ldots, r{:}n\_L_m, \sim r{:}n\_L_{m+1}, \ldots, \sim r{:}n\_L_n.$$

where if $A(\bar{t})$ is an atom of the original rule base r, the literal $r{:}x\_\neg A(\bar{t})$ in the translated rules is replaced by $\neg r{:}x\_A(\bar{t})$ (for $x \in \{d, o, c, n\}$). The prefixes d, o, c and n are used to distinguish the reasoning mode for the rule, that is, definite,

---

[3] In order to avoid name clashes it is assumed that IRIs always appear between delimiters '<' and '>'.

open, closed, and normal, respectively. The meaning of a predicate A in a rule base r is always given by the instances of $r{:}n\_A(\bar{c})$ and $\neg r{:}n\_A(\bar{c})$ which are true in all intended model(s), under one of the adopted semantics $WFSX$ or AS. Recall that $WFSX$ is always an approximation of AS semantics, obtaining less conclusions.

Due to space limitations, our transformational semantics ignores errors, which should be syntactically treated a priori. For example, in the case that a predicate A in rule base r is defined as objective, open, or closed then for every rule (2) with $L_0 = A(\bar{t})$ or $L_0 = \neg A(\bar{t})$, it should hold $n = m$. All the syntactical restrictions are discussed in Section 3.

The **defines** declaration is translated according to the following. First, for global and local predicates the following rules are introduced. Notice that by declaring a predicate global or local, the rule base component of the name is removed and this makes the predicate accessible to the outside world.

$$
\begin{array}{ll}
d\_A(\bar{x}) \leftarrow r{:}d\_A(\bar{x}). & \neg d\_A(\bar{x}) \leftarrow \neg r{:}d\_A(\bar{x}). \\
o\_A(\bar{x}) \leftarrow r{:}o\_A(\bar{x}). & \neg o\_A(\bar{x}) \leftarrow \neg r{:}o\_A(\bar{x}). \\
c\_A(\bar{x}) \leftarrow r{:}c\_A(\bar{x}). & \neg c\_A(\bar{x}) \leftarrow \neg r{:}c\_A(\bar{x}). \\
n\_A(\bar{x}) \leftarrow r{:}n\_A(\bar{x}). & \neg n\_A(\bar{x}) \leftarrow \neg r{:}n\_A(\bar{x}).
\end{array}
$$

If predicate A is declared **open** in rule base r, the following rules are added (see column "open" of Table 1):

$$
\begin{array}{ll}
r{:}o\_A(\bar{x}) \leftarrow\sim \neg r{:}o\_A(\bar{x}). & \neg r{:}o\_A(\bar{x}) \leftarrow\sim r{:}o\_A(\bar{x}). \\
r{:}c\_A(\bar{x}) \leftarrow\sim \neg r{:}c\_A(\bar{x}). & \neg r{:}c\_A(\bar{x}) \leftarrow\sim r{:}c\_A(\bar{x}). \\
r{:}n\_A(\bar{x}) \leftarrow\sim \neg r{:}n\_A(\bar{x}). & \neg r{:}n\_A(\bar{x}) \leftarrow\sim r{:}n\_A(\bar{x}).
\end{array}
$$

Compare with the case when A is declared to be **closed** $\neg$ (negatively closed) or **closed** (positively closed) in rule base r (see column "closed" of Table 1):

$$
\begin{array}{llll}
r{:}o\_A(\bar{x}) \leftarrow\sim \neg r{:}o\_A(\bar{x}). & and & \neg r{:}o\_A(\bar{x}) \leftarrow\sim r{:}o\_A(\bar{x}). \\
r{:}c\_A(\bar{x}) \leftarrow\sim \neg r{:}c\_A(\bar{x}). & or & \neg r{:}c\_A(\bar{x}) \leftarrow\sim r{:}c\_A(\bar{x}). \\
r{:}n\_A(\bar{x}) \leftarrow\sim \neg r{:}n\_A(\bar{x}). & or & \neg r{:}n\_A(\bar{x}) \leftarrow\sim r{:}n\_A(\bar{x}).
\end{array}
$$

The rules in the first line make the predicate open, which corresponds to the case where the importing rule base forces open reasoning mode (see row "open" of Table 1). When the predicate is declared **objective** or **normal**, no additional rules are required.

The **uses** declaration is easier to treat, generating rules that also respect Table 1.

r **uses objective** A **from** s declaration:

$$
\begin{array}{ll}
r{:}d\_A(\bar{x}) \leftarrow s{:}d\_A(\bar{x}). & \neg r{:}d\_A(\bar{x}) \leftarrow \neg s{:}d\_A(\bar{x}). \\
r{:}o\_A(\bar{x}) \leftarrow s{:}d\_A(\bar{x}). & \neg r{:}o\_A(\bar{x}) \leftarrow \neg s{:}d\_A(\bar{x}). \\
r{:}c\_A(\bar{x}) \leftarrow s{:}d\_A(\bar{x}). & \neg r{:}c\_A(\bar{x}) \leftarrow \neg s{:}d\_A(\bar{x}). \\
r{:}n\_A(\bar{x}) \leftarrow s{:}d\_A(\bar{x}). & \neg r{:}n\_A(\bar{x}) \leftarrow \neg s{:}d\_A(\bar{x}).
\end{array}
$$

r uses open A from s declaration:

$$r{:}d\_A(\overline{x}) \leftarrow s{:}d\_A(\overline{x}). \qquad \neg r{:}d\_A(\overline{x}) \leftarrow \neg s{:}d\_A(\overline{x}).$$
$$r{:}o\_A(\overline{x}) \leftarrow s{:}o\_A(\overline{x}). \qquad \neg r{:}o\_A(\overline{x}) \leftarrow \neg s{:}o\_A(\overline{x}).$$
$$r{:}c\_A(\overline{x}) \leftarrow s{:}o\_A(\overline{x}). \qquad \neg r{:}c\_A(\overline{x}) \leftarrow \neg s{:}o\_A(\overline{x}).$$
$$r{:}n\_A(\overline{x}) \leftarrow s{:}o\_A(\overline{x}). \qquad \neg r{:}n\_A(\overline{x}) \leftarrow \neg s{:}o\_A(\overline{x}).$$

r uses closed A from s declaration:

$$r{:}d\_A(\overline{x}) \leftarrow s{:}d\_A(\overline{x}). \qquad \neg r{:}d\_A(\overline{x}) \leftarrow \neg s{:}d\_A(\overline{x}).$$
$$r{:}o\_A(\overline{x}) \leftarrow s{:}o\_A(\overline{x}). \qquad \neg r{:}o\_A(\overline{x}) \leftarrow \neg s{:}o\_A(\overline{x}).$$
$$r{:}c\_A(\overline{x}) \leftarrow s{:}c\_A(\overline{x}). \qquad \neg r{:}c\_A(\overline{x}) \leftarrow \neg s{:}c\_A(\overline{x}).$$
$$r{:}n\_A(\overline{x}) \leftarrow s{:}c\_A(\overline{x}). \qquad \neg r{:}n\_A(\overline{x}) \leftarrow \neg s{:}c\_A(\overline{x}).$$

r uses normal A from s declaration:

$$r{:}d\_A(\overline{x}) \leftarrow s{:}d\_A(\overline{x}). \qquad \neg r{:}d\_A(\overline{x}) \leftarrow \neg s{:}d\_A(\overline{x}).$$
$$r{:}o\_A(\overline{x}) \leftarrow s{:}o\_A(\overline{x}). \qquad \neg r{:}o\_A(\overline{x}) \leftarrow \neg s{:}o\_A(\overline{x}).$$
$$r{:}c\_A(\overline{x}) \leftarrow s{:}c\_A(\overline{x}). \qquad \neg r{:}c\_A(\overline{x}) \leftarrow \neg s{:}c\_A(\overline{x}).$$
$$r{:}n\_A(\overline{x}) \leftarrow s{:}n\_A(\overline{x}). \qquad \neg r{:}n\_A(\overline{x}) \leftarrow \neg s{:}n\_A(\overline{x}).$$

If the importing rule base list is absent from the uses declaration, then instead of $s{:}d\_A(\overline{x})$, $s{:}o\_A(\overline{x})$, $s{:}c\_A(\overline{x})$ and $s{:}n\_A(\overline{x})$ in the body of the previous rules, it should be used instead, respectively, $d\_A(\overline{x})$, $o\_A(\overline{x})$, $c\_A(\overline{x})$ and $n\_A(\overline{x})$. The effect is to import all the existing knowledge regarding the predicate and which is publicly available from the several rule bases (due to space limitations, here we ignore visibility issues).

The major issue remaining to be discussed is the scope of the weak negation operator. For simplicity of discussion, it is assumed that the variables of the transformational rules corresponding to a rule base r are instantiated according to the constants appearing in r. This is the mechanism that implements scoped negation-as-failure (for a possible implementation see for instance [8]). The syntax necessary to explicitly declare predicate domains will be described in a subsequent paper, but basically it gets translated to domain predicates in the bodies of rules in order to guarantee correct instantiation of variables in rules (e.g. by using rdf:type, rdf:domain and rdf:range properties).

5   Comparison and Conclusions

The notion of localized closed world assumptions has been proposed for instance in [11]. The idea is to have syntactic mechanisms in the Semantic Web languages (like DAML+OIL or OWL) to express that a predicate is closed, i.e. something which cannot be inferred can be assumed false: this is a usual assumption in logic programming (negation-as-failure, by default, or weak) and relational databases (the set difference operation of relational algebra). The major problem with the proposal of Heflin and Munoz-Avila is the use of a Clark's completion like approach, which is well-known to suffer from serious problems when applied to knowledge based systems [21,20], even without negation.

The notion of scoped negation-as-failure has also been suggested by several authors, see for instance [14,16], and systems like FLORA-2 [24] do support it. Both FLORA-2 and TRIPLE [22] support modularity constructions, which are essential for deployment of inference engines in the Semantic Web. Alternative proposals are already present in the `dlvhex` system [8], where the reader can find detailed discussion about applications to Semantic Web. This answer-set programming system has features like high-order atoms and external atoms which are very flexible. For instance, closure rules similar to our ones are expressed with high-order statements of the form

$$C'(X) \leftarrow o(X), concept(C), concept(C'), cwa(C, C'), \sim C(X)$$

where $concept(C)$ is a predicate which holds for all concepts C, $cwa(C, C')$ states that C' is the complement of C under the closed world assumption, and $o(X)$ is a predicate that holds for all individuals occurring in the knowledge base.

However, in contradistinction to the existing systems, we define the notion of objective, open and closed predicates, their semantically compatible definition, as well as languages constructs for controlling knowledge in the Semantic Web. The combination of open-world and closed-world reasoning in the same framework is also proposed in [2], where the ERDF stable model semantics of Extended RDF knowledge bases is developed, based on partial logic [12]. However, modularity issues are not considered there. The existence and combination of all our proposed mechanisms in a single language is a novelty, to the best of our knowledge.

The language is intuitive to use and gives absolute freedom to producers and consumers of knowledge in the Semantic Web. It can be implemented with the existing technology, and can support and integrate different inference engines ranging from relational databases to state-of-the-art inference engines, including description logic reasoners. Both tractable and more complex forms of inference are also easily syntactically identified and delimited. The semantics of the constructs can be defined via immediate program transformations, for which the rationale and corner-stone elements have been introduced in this paper.

There are still some important practical problems to be addressed at the implementation level for which solutions exist, but for lack of space cannot be presented in this work. Furthermore, the issue of contradiction is not addressed here, but the results of Section 2 can be adapted for existing paraconsistent semantics for extended logic programs, namely [1,6,19]. A prototypical implementation is underway, using immediate extensions to RuleML markup language [17].

References

1. J. J. Alferes, C. V. Damásio, and L. M. Pereira. A logic programming system for non-monotonic reasoning. *Journal of Automated Reasoning*, 14(1):93–147, 1995.
2. A. Analyti, G. Antoniou, C. V. Damásio, and G. Wagner. Stable Model Theory for Extended RDF Ontologies. In *4th Int. Semantic Web Conf.*, pages 21–36, 2005.
3. T. Berners-Lee, J. Hendler, and O. Lassila. The semantic web. *Scientific American*, May 2001.

4. M. Bugliesi, E. Lamma, and P. Mello. Modularity in logic programming. *Journal of Logic Programming*, 12(1), 1993.
5. CWM-closed world machine. (http://www.w3.org/2000/10/swap/doc/cwm.html).
6. C. V. Damásio and L. M. Pereira. A survey of paraconsistent semantics for logic programs. In D. Gabbay and P. Smets, editors, *Handbook of Defeasible Reasoning and Uncertainty Management Systems*, volume 2, pages 241–320. Kluwer, 1998.
7. Duerst and Suignard. Internationalized Resource Identifiers. RFC 3987, Jan. 2005.
8. T. Eiter, G. Ianni, R. Schindlauer, and H. Tompits. A uniform integration of higher-order reasoning and external evaluations in answer-set programming. In *Proc. of IJCAI'05*, pages 90–96. Professional Book Center, 2005.
9. R. Gavriloaie, W. Nejdl, D. Olmedilla, K. E. Seamons, and M. Winslett. No registration needed: How to use declarative policies and negotiation to access sensitive resources on the semantic web. In *Proc. of 1st ESWS-2004*, pages 342–356, 2004.
10. M. Gelfond and V. Lifschitz. Logic programs with classical negation. In Warren and Szeredi, editors, *Proc. of 7th ICLP*, pages 579–597. MIT Press, 1990.
11. J. Heflin and H. M. Avila. Lcw-based agent planning for the semantic web. In *Ontologies and the Semantic Web*, WS-02-11, pages 63–70. AAAI Press, 2002.
12. H. Herre, J. Jaspars, and G. Wagner. Partial Logics with Two Kinds of Negation as a Foundation of Knowledge-Based Reasoning. In D. M. Gabbay and H. Wansing, editors, *What Is Negation?* Kluwer Academic Publishers, 1999.
13. I. Horrocks, P. F. Patel-Schneider, H. Boley, S. Tabet, B. Grosof, and M. Dean. SWRL: A semantic web rule language combining OWL and RuleML. W3C Member Submission, 21 May 2004.
14. M. Kifer, J. de Bruijn, H. Boley, and D. Fensel. A realistic architecture for the semantic web. In *Proc. of RuleML 2005*, pages 17–29. Springer, November 2005.
15. L. M. Pereira and J. J. Alferes. Well founded semantics for logic programs with explicit negation. In B. Neumann, editor, *ECAI'92*, pages 102–106. John Wiley & Sons, 1992.
16. The rule interchange WG charter. (http://www.w3.org/2005/rules/wg/charter).
17. The Rule Markup Initiative (RuleML). Available at http://www.ruleml.org.
18. K. Sagonas, T. Swift, and D. S. Warren. XSB as an efficient deductive database engine. In *Proc. of SIGMOD 1994 Conference*. ACM, 1994.
19. C. Sakama and K. Inoue. Paraconsistent Stable Semantics for extended disjunctive programs. *Journal of Logic and Computation*, 5(3):265–285, 1995.
20. J. Shepherdson. Negation in logic programming for general logic programs. In J. Minker, editor, *Found. of Ded. Databases and Logic Programming*, pages 19–88. Morgan Kaufmann, 1988.
21. J. C. Shepherdson. Negation as failure: a comparison of Clark's completed data base and Reiter's CWA. *Journal of Logic Programming*, 1(1):51–79, 1984.
22. M. Sintek and S. Decker. TRIPLE - A Query, Inference, and Transformation Language for the Semantic Web. In *First International Semantic Web Conference on The Semantic Web (ISWC2002)*, pages 364–378. Springer-Verlag, 2002.
23. G. Wagner. Web Rules Need Two Kinds of Negation. In *Proc. of PPSWR'03*. Springer-Verlag, December 2003.
24. G. Yang, M. Kifer, and C. Zhao. Flora-2: A Rule-Based Know. Representation and Inference Infrastructure for the Sem. Web. In *ODBASE'03*, pages 671–688, 2003.

Reasoning with Temporal Constraints in RDF*

Carlos Hurtado[1] and Alejandro Vaisman[2]

[1] Universidad de Chile
churtado@dcc.uchile.cl
[2] Universidad de Buenos Aires
avaisman@dc.uba.ar

Abstract. Time management is a key feature needed in any query language for web and semistructured data. However, only recently this has been addressed by the Semantic Web community, through the study of temporal extensions to RDF (*Resource Description Framework*). In this paper we show that the ability of the RDF data model of handling unknown resources by means of blank nodes, naturally yields a rich framework for temporal reasoning in RDF. That is, even without knowing the interval of validity of some statements we can still entail useful knowledge from temporal RDF databases. To take advantage of this, we incorporate a class of temporal constraints over anonymous timestamps based on Allen's interval algebra. We show that testing entailment in temporal graphs with the constraints proposed reduces to closure computation and mapping discovery, that is, an extended form of the standard approach for testing entailment in non-temporal RDF graphs.

1 Introduction

The *Resource Description Framework (RDF)* [22] is a metadata model and language recommended by the W3C in order to create an infrastructure that will allow to build the so-called *Semantic Web*. In the RDF model, the universe to be modeled is a set of *resources*, essentially anything that can have a *universal resource identifier*, URI. The language to describe them is a set of binary predicates denoted *properties*. Descriptions are *statements* of the form subject-predicate-object. Both subject and object can be anonymous objects, known as *blank nodes*. In addition, the RDF specification includes a built-in vocabulary with a normative semantics (RDFS) [6]. This vocabulary deals with inheritance of classes and properties, as well as typing, among other features that allow describing the concepts and relationships that may exist in a community of people and software agents. The RDF specification can be seen as a graph where each subject-predicate-object triple is represented as a node-edge-node structure.

Time is present in almost any Web application. Thus, there is a clear need of applying temporal database concepts to RDF in order to be able to represent temporal knowledge. We illustrate this claim with the following motivating example, where RDF data is used to describe a collection of *web services*.

---

* This research was supported by Millennium Nucleus, Center for Web Research (P01-029-F), Mideplan, Chile. C. Hurtado was supported by FONDECYT 1030810, Chile.

J.J. Alferes et al. (Eds.): PPSWR 2006, LNCS 4187, pp. 164–178, 2006.

Web services are software applications that interact using web standards. The Semantic Web has been proposed as a tool for making applications able to automatically discover or invoke web services. In this way, *ontologies of services* could be used by service-seeking agents for representing a *service profile* (a mechanism for describing services offered by a web site). Our example is based on the web service ontology introduced by Antoniou *et al* [5] for a non-temporal RDF model. In order to keep track of the changes that can occur throughout the life cycle of the web service we introduce temporal features to a standard RDF graph representing the ontology, according to [17].

Figure 1 shows an example of an RDF representation of an evolving ontology for a web service denoted *Sport News*, first offered by the sports network ESPN, and later by another network, Fox Sports. The web site delivers up-to-date articles about sports. As input, the service receives a sports category and the customer's credit card number; it returns the requested articles. The arcs in the graph are labeled with their interval of validity. [1] The interval [0,3] over the edge between 'Sport News' and 'ESPN' means that the triple (Sports News, provided by, ESPN) is valid from time instant "0" to time instant "3". Analogously, the interval [3,Now] over the edge between 'Sport News' and 'ESPN' means that the triple (Sports News, provided by, Fox Sports) is valid from time instant "3" to the current time. For the sake of clarity, no temporal labels over an edge means that triple is valid in the interval [0,Now]. There is also an anonymous node (of type "service provider"), created at time "6". Anonymous (or blank) nodes are needed in an RDF graph when we do not know the global name for a node (or there is no name for it, no matter the reason why), and we need to write statements about this node. The impact of blank nodes in a temporal setting was given an in-depth study in [17,16].

1.1 Problem Statement

In former work we studied the problem of adding the time dimension to RDF documents, and we discussed the main problems and possibilities that arise when we address the problem of keeping track of the changes occurring over an RDF graph. We denoted this problem *Temporal RDF* [17,16]. The work was based on the theoretical framework provided by Gutierrez *et al* [15].

In a nutshell, a Temporal RDF graph is a set of temporal triples labeled with their interval of validity. These triples are of the form $(a, b, c) : [t_1, t_2]$. The graph in Figure 1 is an example of a Temporal RDF graph. We showed that temporal RDF can be implemented within the RDF specification, making use of a simple additional vocabulary. We also defined constructs that allow moving between point-based and interval-based representations in a discrete time dimension. An RDF graph can be regarded as a knowledge base from which new knowledge,

---

[1] Note that the standard graph(ical) representation of an RDF graph is not the most faithful to convey the idea of statements(triples) being labeled by a temporal element. Technically, temporal labels should be attached to a whole subgraph $u \xrightarrow{p} v$, and not only to an arc.

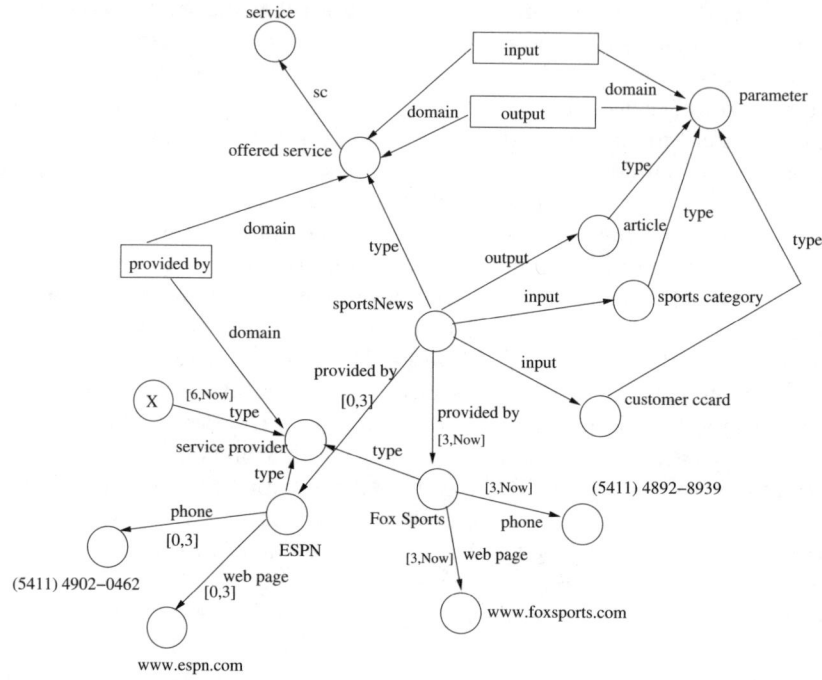

Fig. 1. An RDF graph for web services profiling of Sports networks

i.e., other graphs, may be entailed. In temporal RDF, entailment is slightly more involved. We studied this problem, and called it *temporal entailment*.

An important issue here is the treatment of blank nodes. Defining the semantics of temporal RDF in the presence of blank nodes turns out to be non-trivial, because we cannot consider the temporal database as the union of all its snapshots (a *snapshot* at time t of a temporal RDF graph G is the corresponding subgraph formed by triples labeled by an instant t). This means that even though two temporal graphs G_1 and G_2 are such that all snapshots of G_1 entail a snapshot of G_2, we cannot say that G_1 entails G_2.

The work in [16] also includes a first study of the problem of *anonymous time* in temporal RDF graphs, i.e., graphs containing temporal triples labeled with blanks. In this setting, we admit triples of the form $(a, b, c) : [X]$, where X is an anonymous timestamp stating that the triple (a, b, c) is valid in some time we do not exactly know yet (in [16] we called these graphs *general temporal graphs* to differentiate them from temporal graphs without blank timestamps). In our model, the sets of anonymous timestamps and blank nodes are disjoint, as we will explain later in the paper (actually they belong to different frameworks, namely time labels and triples, respectively).

Temporal blanks considerably extend the capabilities of the temporal RDF model by allowing representing incomplete temporal information [20]. In this paper we show that they also allow defining temporal constraints over the model. In this way, a richer treatment of time, along the lines of *constraint databases* [10] is possible (in relational constraint databases, the time of validity of a tuple can be defined by a formula Φ). There has been a substantial amount of work from the Artificial Intelligence community on temporal reasoning systems that use constraint propagation. Thus, adding constraints to temporal RDF allows reasoning about RDF graphs in order to infer useful knowledge. However, as Allen points out [2,3], the point-based representation of time cannot naturally capture some interval relationships used in reasoning about constraints. Thus, we also include intervals with anonymous starting and/or ending points (anonymous intervals) in in temporal RDF graphs.

Example 1. Consider the following extended temporal graph:

$$\{(a, \mathsf{sc}, b) : i_1, (b, \mathsf{sc}, c) : i_2, i_1 \text{ during } i_2\}.$$

here i_1 and i_2 are intervals whose endpoints are unknown. The temporal triple $(a, \mathsf{sc}, b) : i_1$ states that (a, sc, b) holds in all the timestamps inside the interval (which are infinite), and the constraint i_1 during i_2 states that the i_1 is inside i_2. Then, our approach allows inferring the graph $\{(a, \mathsf{sc}, c) : i_3\}$. Intuitively, this means that, given the original temporal graph, we can infer that in some unknown interval i_3, a was a subclass of c.

Relation	Meaning
$[l_1, l_2]$ before $[l_3, l_4]$	$l_2 < l_3$
$[l_1, l_2]$ meets $[l_3, l_4]$	$l_2 = l_3$
$[l_1, l_2]$ overlaps $[l_3, l_4]$	$l_3 < l_2 < l_4$ and $l_1 < l_3 < l_2$
$[l_1, l_2]$ starts $[l_3, l_4]$	$l_1 = l_3$ and $l_2 < l_4$
$[l_1, l_2]$ during $[l_3, l_4]$	$l_3 < l_1$ and $l_2 < l_4$
$[l_1, l_2]$ ends $[l_3, l_4]$	$l_1 > l_3$ and $l_2 = l_4$
$[l_1, l_2]$ equals $[l_3, l_4]$	$l_1 = l_3$ and $l_2 = l_4$

Fig. 2. Basic Interval Relations

The temporal RDF graphs with constraints and anonymous intervals we introduce in this paper (denoted *c-temporal graphs*), expand the expressive power of the temporal RDF data model, allowing to represent information about events occurring within some unknown intervals. Without this capability, this information could not be represented in a natural way, as the following example shows.

Example 2. Let us suppose that, in the example depicted in Figure 1, we are not certain about the time when 'Sport News' was transferred from ESPN to Fox Sports. A *c-temporal graph* for representing this situation is shown in Figure 3. The triple (Sports News, provided by, ESPN) is now labeled with an anonymous interval i_1. (instead of [0,2]). Analogously, (Sports News, provided by, Fox Sports) is labeled with an anonymous interval i_3 (instead of [3,Now]). We have

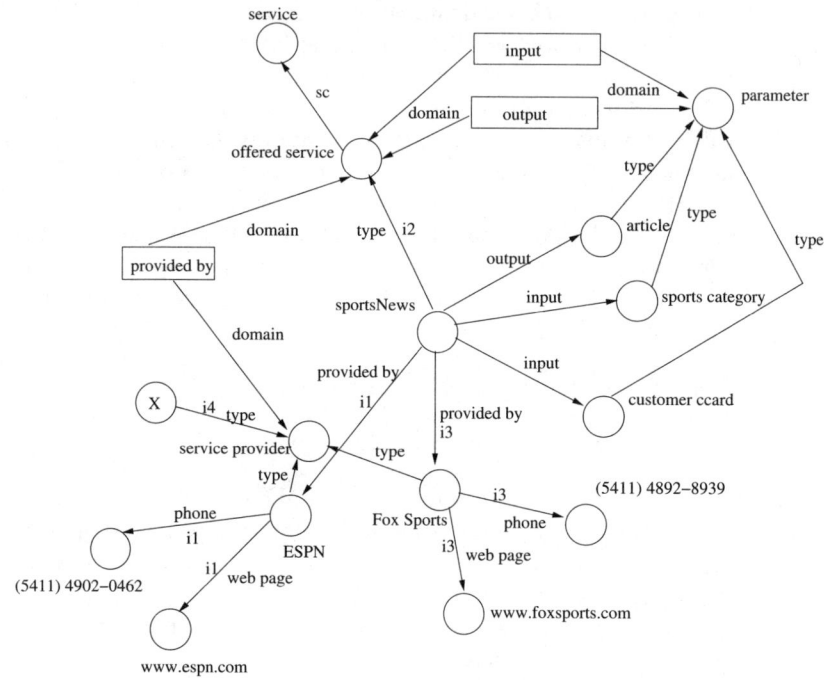

Fig. 3. The RDF graph of Figure 1 with Anonymous Time

also labeled with anonymous intervals the triples (Sports News, `type`, offered service), and (X,`type`, service provider) has been labeled with temporal blanks.

Now, we can use the basic Allen's interval relations [2] depicted in Figure 2 to place constraints over the anonymous intervals. As an example, we can use the constraint i_1 `meets` i_3 to state that Fox Sports started offering 'Sport News' immediately after ESPN stops offering it. We can also state that ESPN started offering the service at time 0 with the constraint i_1 `starts` $[0, Now]$. We can model that during interval i_1 the service was of type 'offered service' using the constraint i_1 `during` i_2.

Although the addition of anonymous time enriches the model, it introduces some problems that we study in the paper. Many of the results obtained in [16] do not work any more in the presence of temporal blank nodes and constraints. For example, the notion of slice closure must be modified. Consequently, testing temporal entailment must be modified accordingly, as well as the proofs that were obtained under the assumption that the temporal labels were only concrete time instants.

Even though our approach is close to temporal logics and constraint databases, temporal reasoning about RDF and RDFS ontologies introduces additional difficulties not present in the other settings. In this paper we study in detail *temporal graphs with constraints*, extending our previous results to these kinds of graphs.

1.2   Contributions and Outline

In this paper we incorporate temporal constraints and intervals (with unknown starting and/or ending time instants) to temporal RDF graphs, and denote the resulting graphs *c-temporal graphs*.

We extend temporal graphs in a stepwise manner. First, we include intervals and study the inference problem for temporal graphs with intervals. We consider intervals over a dense time domain, which allows a full treatment of intervals in temporal RDF.

Then, we generalize the former framework incorporating a fragment of Allen's interval algebra [2] for temporal constraints. We formalize c-temporal graphs, allowing modeling anonymous timestamps, anonymous intervals, and constraints over them. We define and study a notion of entailment for c-temporal graphs. Further, a new notion of closure is proposed for c-temporal graphs, and temporal entailment is characterized in terms of this notion of closure. In particular, we show that testing entailment for temporal graphs with the fragment of constraints studied, reduces to closure computation and mapping discovery, that is, an extended form of the standard approach for testing entailment in non-temporal RDF graphs. We also provide an algorithm for computing the slice closure of c-temporal graphs.

The remainder of the article is organized as follows. Section 2 reviews related work. Section 3 presents preliminary notation related to RDF and RDFS and temporal RDF graphs from previous work [15,17,16]. Section 4 studies temporal graphs with intervals. Section 5 introduces constraints to temporal graphs and their semantics, presents the notion closure, and characterizes entailment in terms of them. Finally, in Section 6 we conclude and outline some prospects for future work.

2   Related Work

The RDF model was introduced in 1998 by the World Wide Web Consortium (W3C) [22]. Formal work includes the study of formal aspects of RDF data and query languages [14,15,28], considering RDF features like entailment, the impact of blank nodes, reification, premises in queries, and the RDFS vocabulary with predefined semantics. Several query languages for RDF have been proposed and implemented. Some of them along the lines of traditional database query languages (e.g. SQL, OQL), others based on logic and rule languages. Good surveys are [18,21]. Temporal database management has been extensively studied, including data models, mostly based on the relational model and query languages [26], leading to the TSQL2 language [25]. Chomicki [10] provides a comprehensive survey of temporal query languages. Beyond the relational model, several works proposed temporal extensions for non-temporal models, like the semistructured data model and XML [9,4,12,13,24].

Regarding temporal extensions to RDF, Visser *et al* [27] proposed a temporal reasoning framework for the Semantic Web, which has been applied in BUSTER, an ontology-based prototype developed at the University of Bremen, supporting the so-called *concept@location in time* type of query. Bry *et al* [8,7], in the context of the REWERSE project [23], have stated the need of providing query languages and models for the web with temporal reasoning capabilities.

To the best of our knowledge, our previous work [17,16] constitutes the first formal study of temporality issues in RDF graphs and RDF query languages. In the present paper we continue this line of research with the study of Temporal RDF graphs with constraints and anonymous time.

3   Preliminaries

3.1   RDF Notation

The following is an excerpt of notation introduced in [6,15,19] that will be used subsequently in this paper.

In this paper we work with RDF graphs whith RDFS vocabulary. An RDF graph is a set of triples $(v_1, v_2, v_3) \in (U \cup B) \times U \times (U \cup B \cup L)$, where U is a set of URIs, B is a set of blank nodes, and L is a set of literals (the sets are pairwise disjoint). An *RDF term* is a URI, a blank, or a literal. We consider RDF graphs that can mention the RDFS vocabulary. The RDFS vocabulary defines *Classes* as sets of resources. Elements of a class are known as *instances* of that class. To state that a resource is an instance of a class, the property rdf:type may be used. The following are the most important classes (in brackets the name we will use in this paper) rdfs:Resource [res], rdfs:Class [class], rdfs:Literal [literal], rdfs:Datatype [datatype], rdf:XMLLiteral [xmlLit], rdf:Property [property]. *Properties* are binary relations between subject resources and object resources. The built-in properties are: rdfs:range [range], rdfs:domain [dom], rdf:type [type], rdfs: subClassOf [sc], rdfs:subPropertyOf [sp].

In this paper, we work with a characterization of entailment of RDF graphs in term of the notions of map and closure.

A *map* is a function $\mu : (U \cup B \cup L) \rightarrow (U \cup B \cup L)$ preserving URIs and literals, i.e., $\mu(u) = u$ and $\mu(l) = l$ for all $u \in U$ and $l \in L$. Given a graph G, we define $\mu(G)$ as the set of all $(\mu(s), \mu(p), \mu(o))$ such that $(s, p, o) \in G$. We will overload the meaning of map and speak of a *map* $\mu : G_1 \rightarrow G_2$ if there is a map μ such that $\mu(G_1)$ is a subgraph of G_2. A map μ is *consistent* with G if $\mu(G)$ is an RDF graph, *i.e.*, if s is the subject of a triple, then $\mu(s) \in U \cup B$, and if p is the predicate of a triple, then $\mu(p) \in U$. In this case, we say that the graph $\mu(G)$ is an *instance* of the graph G. An instance of G is *ground* if $\mu(G)$ does not mention blanks.

In this paper, we use a working characterization of the standard notion of entailment between RDF graphs (cf. [19]), which will be denoted by $\models$. We use the known notion of *closure* of a RDFS graph G, denoted cl(G), which is the maximal graph that can be derived from the set of inference rules given in [19,15].

Theorem 1 (cf. [19,15]). $G_1 \models G_2$ *if and only if there is a map from G_2 to the* closure *of G_1.*

3.2   Temporal Graphs

In this section, we present in a compressed form relevant notation and results for temporal graph from previous work [17,16].

A *temporal triple* is an RDF triple (a, b, c) with a temporal timestamp t, which is a positive rational number. We will use the notation $(a, b, c) : [t]$. The *snapshot* of a temporal graph G at t, is defined as the graph $G(t) = \{(a, b, c) \mid (a, b, c) : [t] \in G\}$. Usually for a temporal graph G we will apply the same notions used for standard RDF graphs, for example, we will say "G is ground" meaning that $u(G)$ is ground, write $\mu(G)$ for $\{(\mu(a), \mu(b), \mu(c)) : [t] \mid (a, b, c) : [t] \in G\}$, and so on.

Definition 1 (Entailment (c.f. [16])). *Let G_1, G_2 be RDF temporal graphs. (1) For ground temporal RDF graphs G_1, G_2 define $G_1 \models_\tau G_2$ if and only if $G_1(t) \models G_2(t)$ for each t; (2) For temporal RDF graphs, define $G_1 \models_\tau G_2$ if and only if for every ground instance $\mu_1(G_1)$ there exists a ground instance $\mu_2(G_2)$ such that $\mu_1(G_1) \models_\tau \mu_2(G_2)$.*

Temporal entailment can be characterized in terms of a notion of clousure of temporal graphs, denoted *slice closure*.

For an RDF graph H and a time stamp t, define H^t as the temporalization of all its triples by a temporal mark t, that is, $H^t = \{(a, b, c) : [t] \mid (a, b, c) \in H\}$. The *slice closure* of G, denoted $\mathrm{scl}(G)$, is a temporal graph defined by the expression $\bigcup_t (\mathrm{cl}(G(t)))^t$, where $\mathrm{cl}(G(t))$ is any closure of the RDF graph $G(t)$.

Theorem 2 (c.f. [17]). *Let G_1, G_2 be temporal RDF graphs. Then $G_1 \models_\tau G_2$ if and only if there is a map from G_2 to $\mathrm{scl}(G_1)$.*

This result yields an algorithm for testing temporal entailment. Indeed, the slice closure can be obtained by computing the closures of the snapshots of the temporal graph.

4   Temporal Graphs with Time Intervals

In this section we extend temporal graphs introduced in Section 3.2 to model time intervals defined by timestamps, that is, intervals whose extremes are positive rational numbers.

4.1   Basic Definitions

We extend *temporal triples* to triples of the form $(a, b, c) : i$, where $i = [t_1, t_2]$ is an interval defined by the timestamps (positive rational numbers) $t_1, t_2, t_1 \leq t_2$, yielding *temporal graphs with intervals*. For the case where $t_1 = t_2$ a triple $(a, b, c) : [t_1, t_2]$ is equivalent to temporal triple $(a, b, c) : [t_1]$, as defined in Section 3.2, therefore temporal graphs with intervals subsume temporal graphs. Given a temporal graph with intervals G, we denote by $I(G)$ the intervals mentioned in G, and denote by $T(G)$ the set of timestamps that appear as bounds in the intervals in $I(G)$. Two timestamps $t_1, t_2 \in T(G)$ are *consecutive* if there is no timestamp $t' \in T(G)$, such that $t_1 < t' < t_2$. Given an interval $i \in I(G)$, we denote by $G(i)$, the set containing RDF triples (a, b, c) such that $(a, b, c) : i \in G$.

A temporal graph with intervals represents a (possibly infinite) temporal graph, that is, each triple $p : [t_1, t_2]$ represents the set of temporal triples $\{p : [t] \mid t_1 \leq t \leq t_2\}$. Given a temporal graph with intervals G, we denote by G^+ the temporal graph that represents G. In this form, the notion of entailment from Definition 1 can be naturally extended to temporal graph with intervals. Formally, we write $G \models_\tau H$ iff $G^+ \models_\tau H^+$.

4.2   Reasoning

Theorem 2 also characterizes entailment for temporal graphs with intervals (just consider the underlying temporal graphs involved). However, the theorem has no practical application, since underlying graphs (and therefore mappings) may be infinite. In this section, we give a characterization of entailment that yields a procedure for the testing entailment of temporal graphs with intervals.

Given two intervals $[t_1, t_2], [t_3, t_4]$, we write that $[t_1, t_2]$ contains $[t_3, t_4]$ iff $t_1 \leq t_3$ and $t_4 \leq t_2$. Given an interval i and a set of intervals S, we denote by CoverSet(i, S) the set containing intervals $i' \in S$ such that i' contains i.

The following definition extends the notion of slice closure (Section 3.2) to temporal graphs with intervals.

Definition 2. *Let G be a temporal graph with intervals. The slice closure of G, denoted $H = \texttt{iscl}(G)$, is defined as follows:*

1. *Let H' be the following temporal graph with intervals: for each pair of timestamps $t_1, t_2 \in T(G)$, $H'([t_1, t_2]) = \text{cl}(\bigcup_{i \in \texttt{CoverSet}([t_1, t_2], I(G))} G(i))$.*
2. *Then, for each set of consecutive timestamps $t_1, t_2, t_3, \ldots, t_{n-1}, t_n$ in $T(G)$, we have $H([t_1, t_n]) = \bigcap_{[t_i, t_{j+1}] \in S} H'([t_j, t_{j+1}])$.*

Example 3. Consider the temporal graph with constraints $G = \{(a, \texttt{sc}, b) : [1, 3], (b, \texttt{sc}, c) : [2, 4], (a, \texttt{sc}, c) : [3, 5]\}$. First, we illustrate condition 1 of Definition 2. As an example, consider the two timestamps $2, 3 \in T(G)$. Then CoverSet$([2, 3], I(G)) = \{[1, 3], [2, 4]\}$. Therefore, $H'([2, 3]) = \text{cl}((a, \texttt{sc}, b), (b, \texttt{sc}, c))$, which is $\{(a, \texttt{sc}, b), (b, \texttt{sc}, c), (a, \texttt{sc}, c)\}$. Now, in order to explain condition 2 of Definition 2, consider the set of consecutive timestamps $2, 3, 4, 5$ in $T(G)$. Then, $H([2, 5]) = H'([2, 3]) \cap H'([3, 4]) \cap H'([4, 5])$, which is $\{(a, \texttt{sc}, c)\}$.

For simplicity, the previous example use only the subclass property (sc). The example could be easily turned much more complex if we include in the graphs other RDFS built-in-properties.

Observe that $G \subseteq \texttt{iscl}(G)$. The following lemma states other important properties of the slice closure.

Lemma 1. *Let G be a temporal graph with intervals.*
(1) $\texttt{scl}(G^+) = (\texttt{iscl}(G))^+$.
(2) $G \equiv_\tau \texttt{iscl}(G)$.

(3) If there is a triple $(a, b, c) \in \mathrm{scl}(G^+)(t)$ for all timestamps t in some arbitrary interval i, then there is an interval $i' \in I(\mathrm{iscl}(G))$ such that i' contains *i and $(a, b, c) : i' \in \mathrm{iscl}(G)$.*

We define *interval mappings* as follows. Given two sets of intervals S, S' an interval mapping is a function $\gamma : S \to S'$, such that for each interval $i \in S$, $i' = \gamma(i)$ should satisfy i' contains i. When we apply an interval mapping to a temporal graph with intervals G, we obtain the temporal graph with interval G' containing the triples $(a, b, c) : \gamma(i)$ such that $(a, b, c) : i \in G$. In addition, we extend maps between temporal graphs (see Section 3.2) to maps between temporal graphs with intervals.

Theorem 3. *Let G, H be temporal RDF graphs with intervals. Then $G \models_\tau H$ if and only if there is an interval mapping $\gamma : I(H) \to I(G)$, and a mapping μ from $\gamma(H)$ to $\mathrm{iscl}(G)$.*

Theorem 3 yields a two-steps procedure for testing implication for temporal graphs with intervals, which requires to first compute a slice closure and then an interval mapping. In Section 5.4, we study the complexity of testing entailment.

5   Temporal Graphs with Temporal Constraints

In this section, we define *temporal graphs with temporal constraints* (c-temporal graphs in short), which generalize temporal graphs with intervals introduced in Section 4.

5.1   Temporal Constraints

In this paper, we focus on a basic fragment of the known Allen's interval algebra [2]. The temporal primitive here is an interval $[l_i, l_f]$ which is an ordered pair of *time labels* l_i, l_f. Time labels may be timestamps (positive rational numbers) or anonymous timestamps, which are temporal variables. In our model RDF terms and temporal labels belong to different frameworks: time labels and triples, and are therefore disjoint. Temporal labels are interpreted as points in the temporal domain, which is the set of positive rational numbers. So we assume a dense temporal domain.

The algebra considers one of the seven relationships depicted in Figure 2 to state relationships between intervals. By a *temporal constraint* we refer to an expression of the form $l_i \ \omega \ l_j$, where ω is one of the seven relationships of Allen's algebra.

Given a set of temporal constraints Σ we denote $I(\Sigma)$ the intervals in Σ and by $L(\Sigma)$ the temporal labels that appears in intervals in $I(\Sigma)$. A map for a set of temporal constraints Σ is a function γ from $I(\Sigma)$ to ground intervals (intervals whose limits are timestamps) preserving timestamps. We denote by $\gamma(\Sigma)$ the set of constraints resulting from Σ by replacing each interval i by $\gamma(i)$.

An *instance* for a set of temporal constraints $\Sigma = \{\alpha_1, \ldots, \alpha_n\}$ is a map μ such that $\mu(\Sigma)$ is ground (i.e., mentions only timestamps) and each $\gamma(\alpha_i)$ holds in the temporal domain. If Σ is empty the empty set is its unique ground instance. Σ is *consistent* iff it has at least one instance. Notice that an empty set of constraints is consistent. Given two sets of temporal constraints Σ_1, Σ_2, define $\Sigma_1 \models_{constr} \Sigma_2$ if and only if for each instance γ of Σ_1, there is also an instance of $\gamma(\Sigma_2)$.

Testing entailment and consistency for the class of temporal constraints considered can be done in polynomial time. Following standard results in inequality constraints (e.g. [3,1]), we can represent the fragment we presented in a point based algebra, by building the *inequality graph* for the labels in the constraints (which is a particular case of a temporal constraint network [11]), that is, a directed graph with a node for each temporal label in $L(\Sigma)$, and edges (l_i, l_j) labeled with the arithmetic comparisons $=, <, \leq$, that models Allen's relationships in Σ. As an example, the constraint $[l_1, l_2]$ during $[l_3, l_4]$ yields $l_1 \leq l_2, l_3 \leq l_4, l_3 < l_1$, and $l_2 < l_4$. The graph has also edges that capture the natural ordering between timestamps mentioned in the constraints and between each pair of time labels that mark the bound of an interval. The arithmetic constraint in the inequality graph can be propagated by simple transitive closure computation, yielding the closed inequality graph, which can be used for implementing an efficient testing of entailment and consistency of a set of constraints. We refer the reader to e.g., [3,1,11] for further details.

In this paper we consider constraints Σ whose inequality graph is totally ordered (modulo renaming time labels that are entailed to be equal). Therefore, even though the intervals themselves may be unknown, the relationship between any two of them is fully determined by the constraints, that is for all $i, i' \in I(\Sigma)$ we have $\Sigma \models_{constr} i \; \omega \; i'$ (or the inverse $i' \; \omega \; i$) for some interval relation ω.

5.2   Basic Definitions

We extend the notion of temporal graph to handle anonymous labels in timestamps and interval. So we consider a temporal triple to be an element of the form $p : i$, where p is an RDF triple and i is an interval.

Definition 3. *A temporal graph with temporal constraints (subsequently called a c-temporal graph) is a pair $C = (G, \Sigma)$, where G is a graph with temporal triples and Σ is a set of temporal constraints over the intervals of G.*

For simplicity, we sometimes write the temporal constraints and the temporal triples in a single set. Given a c-temporal graph $C = (G, \Sigma)$, we denote by $I(C)$ and $L(C)$ the intervals and time labels that appear in the triples in G.

Interval maps defined in Section 4 can be naturally extended to consider intervals defined with temporal labels. If we apply an interval map ν to a c-temporal graph C, we obtain another c-temporal graph, denoted $\nu(C)$, by renaming each interval r with $\nu(r)$. A time-ground instance of a c-temporal graph $C = (G, H)$ is a temporal graph with intervals $\nu(C)$ (i.e., ν maps each interval to an interval defined by timestamps) such that $\nu(\Sigma)$ is consistent.

Definition 4 (Entailment). *Let $C_1 = (G_1, \Sigma_1)$ and $C_2 = (G_2, \Sigma_2)$ be c-temporal graphs. Define $C_1 \models_{\tau(constr)} C_2$ if and only if for each time-ground instance $\nu_1(C_1)$ of C_1 there is a time ground instance $\nu_2(C_2)$ of C_2 such that $\nu_1(C_1) \models_\tau \nu_2(C_2)$.*

Example 4. Let C_1 be the c-temporal graph

$$\{(a, \mathsf{sc}, b) : i_1, (b, \mathsf{sc}, c) : i_2, i_1 \text{ during } i_2, i_1 \text{ starts } [3, now]\}.$$

The following entailment holds: $C_1 \models_{\tau(constr)} \{(a, \mathsf{sc}, c) : i_3, i_3 \text{ starts } [3, now]\}.$

The following lemma can be easily verified.

Lemma 2. *Let $C_1 = (G_1, \Sigma_1)$ and $C_2 = (G_2, \Sigma_2)$ be c-temporal graphs. If $C_1 \models_{\tau(constr)} C_2$, then $C_1 \models_{\tau(constr)} (G_2, \emptyset).$*

5.3   Reasoning

First, we extend the interval containment relationship of Section 4.2 to intervals over anonymous timestamps restricted by constraints. Given a set of intervals S, and an interval i, we denote by $\mathsf{CoverSet}_\Sigma(i, S)$ the set of intervals $i' \in S$ that can be entailed from Σ to contain i.

The following definition extends the notion of slice closure (Definition 2) to c-temporal graphs.

Definition 5. *Let $C = (E, \Sigma)$ be a c-temporal graph. The slice closure of C, denoted $H = \mathsf{cscl}(C)$, is a c-temporal graph (F, Σ), where F is defined as follows:*

1. *Let F' be the following c-temporal graph. For each pair of labels $l_1, l_2 \in L(C)$,*
   $$F'([l_1, l_2]) = \mathsf{cl}(\bigcup_{i \in \mathsf{CoverSet}_\Sigma([l_1, l_2], I(C))} C(i)).$$
2. *Then, for each set of consecutive labels $l_1, l_2, l_3, \ldots, l_{n-1}, l_n$ in $L(C)$, we have*
   $$F([l_1, l_n]) = \bigcap_{[l_j, l_{j+1}] \in S} F'[l_j, l_{j+1}].$$

Lemma 3. *Let $C = (G, \Sigma)$ be a c-temporal graph.*
(1) For each time-ground instance $\gamma(C)$ of C, $\gamma(\mathsf{cscl}(C)) = \mathsf{iscl}(\gamma(C))$.
(2) $\mathsf{cscl}(C) \equiv_{\tau(constr)} C$.

A c-temporal graph is consistent if it has at least one temporal-ground instance. Since we can entail anything from a inconsistent c-temporal graph, we will study entailment from consistent graphs. In order to simplify the presentation, we subsequently assume that c-temporal graphs $C = (G, \Sigma)$ are consistent.

We define interval mappings between c-temporal graphs. Let $C_1 = (G_1, \Sigma_1)$ and $C_2 = (G_2, \Sigma_2)$ be two independent c-temporal graphs. An interval mapping from C_2 to C_1 is a function $\mu : I(C_2) \to I(C_1)$, which satisfies $\Sigma_1 \models_{constr} (\Sigma_2 \cup \Sigma_u)$, where Σ_u is the following set of constraints $\{l_3 \leq l_1, l_2 \leq l_4 : \mu([l_1, l_2]) = [l_3, l_4]\}$.

Theorem 4. *Let $C_1 = (G_1, \Sigma_1), C_2 = (G_2, \Sigma_2)$ be c-temporal RDF graphs. Then $C_1 \models_{\tau(constr)} C_2$ if and only if there exist an interval map γ from C_2 to C_1 and a map μ from $\gamma(C_2)$ to $\mathsf{cscl}(C_1)$.*

5.4   Algorithm and Complexity

Theorem 4 yields an algorithm for testing the entailment $C_1 \models_{\tau(constr)} C_2$, which consists of the following two steps: (i) compute the slice closure $\texttt{cscl}(C_1)$ by applying rules (1) and (2) of Definition 5; and (ii) find an interval map γ from C_2 to C_1 and a map μ from $\gamma(C_2)$ to $\texttt{cscl}(C_1)$. Step (ii) is similar to finding a mapping between non-temporal graphs [15]. In the remaining of this section we study the complexity of the two steps of the algorithm.

A standard result regarding RDFS entailment is that the closure $\text{cl}(G)$ of an RDF G graph is of polynomial size in $|G|$; computing the closure also takes polynomial time (an upper bound for both is $O(n^3)$, where n is the number of RDF terms mentioned in G). We consider a polynomial $p(|G|)$ that bounds the size of the closure and the time it takes to compute it. We also consider a polynomial $q(|\Sigma|)$ that bounds the time of computing an implication of temporal constraints.

Lemma 4. *Let $C = (G, \Sigma)$ be a temporal graph with intervals and let $(E, \Sigma) = \texttt{cscl}(C)$. (1) The graph E is of size $O(N^2 p(|G|))$, where $N = |L(C)|$. (2) The slice closure $\texttt{cscl}(C)$ can be computed in time $O(N^4(q(|\Sigma| + p(|G|)))$.*

Better complexity bounds for computing the slice closure could be certainly obtained by developing more efficient algorithms, an issue we do not address in this paper. We next show that the decision problem of entailment for c-temporal graphs is NP-complete, thus maintaining the complexity of temporal graphs (and also of the non-temporal case).

Theorem 5. *(1) Given two temporal c-temporal graphs C_1, C_2, the problem of deciding whether $C_1 \models_{\tau(constr)} C_2$ is NP-complete. (1) Given two temporal graphs with intervals G_1, G_2, the problem of deciding whether $G_1 \models_{\tau} G_2$ is NP-complete.*

As stated previously, for testing whether $C_1 \models_{\tau(constr)} C_2$, Theorem 4 requires the inequality graph of Σ_1 to yield a total ordering of time labels. However, if this is not the case, the condition can be adapted to be required by each topological ordering of the inequality graph. So, testing entailment for graphs with few topological orderings still does not add extra complexity to RDF entailment. Further techniques can be used to make this case of entailment more efficient. As an example, if the graph has connected components it is enough to consider combinations of topological orderings inside each component, while keeping a fixed ordering for the components themselves, thus reducing significantly the processing. We left this problem for future work.

6   Conclusion

In this paper we have extended temporal RDF graphs with a class of temporal constraints over intervals. In this way, temporal reasoning about these constructs is enabled. First, taking advantage of the support of blank nodes in RDF, we introduced intervals such that boundaries may be anonymous timestamps. We developed a notion of closure for temporal RDF graphs with intervals.

Then, we introduced c-temporal graphs (temporal graphs with constraints and the intervals previously defined), and gave a notion of closure for these temporal graphs. We also proved that entailment from such graphs reduces to finding mappings to the "closed" version of the graphs. These results show that query processing for temporal graphs with constraints also reduces to computing a matching between the query and the closed graphs.

We left as future work the study of entailment for more expressive classes of constraints based either in Allen's interval algebra or point algebras [10]. In particular, we plan to study entailment for the case where the constraints do not entail a total ordering of anonymous timestamps. We are also beginning to work on an implementation of the theoretical framework presented here.

References

1. F. Afrati, C. Li, and P. Mitra. On containment of conjunctive queries with arithmetic comparisons. In *UCIISC Technical Report*, 2003.
2. J. Allen. Maintaining knowledge about temporal intervals. *Communications of the ACM 26(11)*, pages 832–843, 1983.
3. J. Allen. Time and time again: The many ways to represent time. *International Journal of Intelligent Systems, 6(4)*, pages 341–355, 1990.
4. T. Amagasa, M. Yoshikawa, and S. Uemura. A temporal data model for XML documents. In *Proceedings of DEXA Conference*, pages 334–344, 2000.
5. G. Antoniou and F. van Harme. *A Semantic Web Primer*. MIT Press, London, England, 2004.
6. D. Brickley and R.V.(Eds.) Guha. RDF vocabulary description language 1.0: RDF schema. *W3C Recommendation, 10 February 2004*.
7. F. Bry, B. Lorenz, H.J. Ohlbach, and S. Spranger. On reasoning on time and location on the web. In *Proceedings of ICLP03*, Mumbai, India, 2003.
8. F. Bry and S. Spranger. Temporal constructs for a web language. In *Proceedings of the 4 Workshop on Interval Temporal Logics and Duration Calculi, ESSLLI'03*, Austria, 2003.
9. S. Chawathe, S. Abiteboul, and J. Widom. Managing historical semistructured data. In *Theory and Practice of Object Systems, Vol 5(3)*, pages 143–162, 1999.
10. J. Chomicki. Temporal query languages: a survey. In *Proceedings of First International Conference on Temporal Logic. Lecture Notes in Artificial Intelligence 827*, Springer-Verlag, Bonn, Germany, 1994.
11. R. Dechter, I. Meiri, and J. Pearl. Temporal constraint networks. In *Artificial Intelligence 40:61*, pages 49: 61–95, 1991.
12. C.E. Dyreson. Observing transaction-time semantics with TTXPath. In *Proceedings of WISE 2001*, pages 193–202, 2001.
13. C. Gao and R. Snodgrass. Temporal slicing in the evaluation of XML queries. In *Proceedings of the 29th International Conference on Very Large Data Bases*, pages 632–643, Berlin, Germany, 2003.
14. C. Gutierrez, C. Hurtado, and A.O. Mendelzon. Formal aspects of querying RDF databases. In *Proceedings of SWDB*, pages 293–307, 2003.

15. C. Gutierrez, C. Hurtado, and A.O. Mendelzon. Foundations of semantic web databases. In *23rd. Symposium on Principles of Database Systems (PODS'04)*, pages 95–106, 2004.
16. C. Gutierrez, C. Hurtado, and A. Vaisman. Introducing time into RDF. In *(to appear) IEEE Transactions on Knowledge and Data Engineering, Special Issue on Knowledge and Data Engineering in the Semantic Web Era, 2007.*
17. C. Gutierrez, C. Hurtado, and A. Vaisman. Temporal RDF. In *European Conference on the Semantic Web (ECSW'05) (Best paper award)*, pages 93–107, 2005.
18. P. Haase, J. Broekstra, A. Eberhart, and R. Volz. A comparison of RDF query languages. In *International Semantic Web Conference*, 2004.
19. Patrick Hayes(Ed.). RDF semantics. *W3C Recommendation, 10 February 2004.*
20. M. Koubarakis. Temporal query languages: a survey. *Information Systems, 19(2):141-174,* 1993.
21. A. Magkanaraki, G. Karvounarakis, T.T. Anh, V. Christophides, and D. Plexousakis. Ontology storage and querying. *Technical Report No. 308 Foundation for Research and Technology Hellas, Institute of Computer Science, Information System Laboratory,* 2002.
22. F. Mannola and E.(Eds.) Miller. Rdf primer. *W3C Recommendation, 10 February 2004.*
23. The REWERSE Project. http://www.rewerse.net.
24. F. Rizzolo, A.O. Mendelzon, and A. Vaisman. Indexing temporal XML documents. In *Proceedings of the 30th International Conference on Very Large Databases*, pages 216–227, Toronto, Canada, 2004.
25. Richard Snodgrass. *The TSQL2 Temporal Query Language.* Kluwer Academic Publishers, 1995.
26. A. Tansel, J. Clifford, and S. Gadia (eds.). *Temporal Databases: Theory, Design and Implementation.* Benjamin/Cummings, 1993.
27. U. Visser. Intelligent information integration for the semantic web. *Lecture Notes in Artificial Intelligence (3159),* 2004.
28. G. Yang and M. Kifer. On the semantics of anonymous identity and reification. In *Proceedings of the First International Conference on Ontologies, Databases and Applications of Semantics (ODBASE)*, pages 1047–1066, 2002.

Bidirectional Mapping Between OWL DL and Attempto Controlled English

Kaarel Kaljurand[1] and Norbert E. Fuchs[2]

[1] University of Zurich, University of Tartu
kalju@ifi.unizh.ch
[2] University of Zurich
fuchs@ifi.unizh.ch

Abstract. We describe ongoing work on a bidirectional mapping between Attempto Controlled English (ACE) and OWL DL. ACE is a well-studied controlled natural language, with a parser that converts ACE texts into Discourse Representation Structures (DRS). We show how ACE can be translated into OWL DL (by using the DRS as interlingua) and how OWL DL can be verbalized in ACE. This mapping renders ACE an interesting companion to existing OWL front-ends.

1 Introduction

The Web Ontology Language OWL in all its versions (Lite, DL, Full) has a normative syntax which is based on RDF and XML which both are inherently difficult to read and write. OWL can be alternatively expressed in the OWL Abstract Syntax notation ([16]) which is concise and easier to use, but the main problem still remains — the user is required to possess a large knowledge of Descriptions Logics (DL) to work with OWL. In order to enable wide adoption of OWL on the web, the users are encouraged to use front-end tools. Such tools (Protégé[1], SWOOP[2], etc) are user-friendly graphical editors, but for complex class descriptions they revert to using a DL-like syntax and thus fail to hide the complexities of OWL. E.g. [17] list the problems that users encounter when working with OWL DL and express the need for a "pedantic but explicit" paraphrase language.

To answer this need, we envision a text-based ontology editing environment that allows the users to express the ontologies in the most natural way — in natural language. Such an environment would provide a natural syntax for logical constructs such as disjointness or transitivity, i.e. it would not use keywords but instead a syntactic structure to represent those complex concepts. It would tightly integrate an OWL DL reasoner, but the output of the reasoner (if expressed in OWL DL as a modification of the ontology) would again be verbalized in natural language, so that all user interaction takes place in natural language and the central role during the ontology editing is carried by plain text.

---

[1] http://protege.stanford.edu
[2] http://www.mindswap.org/2004/SWOOP/

J.J. Alferes et al. (Eds.): PPSWR 2006, LNCS 4187, pp. 179–189, 2006.

As a basis of the natural language, we have chosen Attempto Controlled English (ACE), a subset of English that can be converted into Discourse Representation Structures (DRS) — a syntactical variant of first-order logic — and automatically reasoned about (see [5,1] for more information). The current version of ACE offers language constructs like countable and mass nouns; collective and distributive plurals; generalized quantifiers; indefinite pronouns; negation, conjunction and disjunction of noun phrases, verb phrases and sentences; and anaphoric references to noun phrases through proper names, definite noun phrases, pronouns, and variables. The intention behind ACE is to minimize the number of syntax and interpretation rules needed to predict the resulting DRS, or for the end-user, the reasoning results. At the same time, the expressivity and naturalness of ACE must not suffer. The small number of ACE function words have a clear and predictable meaning and the remaining content words are classified only as verbs, nouns, adjectives and adverbs. Still, ACE has a relatively complex syntax compared to the OWL representation e.g. in the OWL Abstract Syntax specification ([16]), but as ACE is based on English, its grammar rules are intuitive (already known to English speakers) and experience shows that ACE can be learned in a few days. [2] show also that users are likely to prefer ACE to visibly formal languages such as SQL.

Our work towards using ACE as a front-end to OWL DL addresses the following issues:

1. Show that there is a mapping from a subset of ACE (which we call OWL ACE) into a syntactic subset of OWL DL (i.e. a subset which does not use all the syntactic constructs in OWL DL but is still capable of expressing everything that OWL DL can express). This mapping uses the DRS as interlingua.
2. Show that the two involved subsets and the mapping from one to the other are easy to explain to the users. This means that the entailment and consistency results given by the OWL DL reasoners "make sense" on the ACE level.
3. Show that there is a mapping from the syntactic subset of OWL DL into OWL ACE (possibly using the DRS as interlingua). This mapping (which can be called a verbalization) must, again, be easily explainable.
4. Implement a converter from OWL DL to the chosen syntactic subset of OWL DL. By this, we will be able to handle all OWL DL ontologies on the web.
5. If needed, extend ACE to provide a more natural syntax or more syntactic variety for expressing the OWL DL constructs.
6. Extend the verbalization process to target a richer syntactic subset of OWL ACE.
7. Extend all the aspects of this work in order to be compatible with future standards of OWL DL, e.g. OWL 1.1 ([15]) or extensions of it, e.g. SWRL ([11]).

So far, we have focused on the first 3 steps. In the following, we describe a mapping from OWL ACE to OWL DL (in RDF/XML syntax)[3], the problems encountered, the OWL ACE subset and the verbalization of OWL DL.

---

[3] A preliminary implementation of this mapping is available among the Attempto tools at http://www.ifi.unizh.ch/attempto/tools

2 From ACE to OWL

The following figure shows the DRS corresponding to the ACE text

> Bill who is a man likes himself. Bill is not John. Every businessman who is richer than at least 3 things is a self-made-man or employs a programmer who knows Bill.

(Note that the example is somewhat artificial to demonstrate concisely the features of OWL DL as expressed in ACE.)

```
[A, B, C, D, E, F]
object(A, atomic, named_entity, person, cardinality, count_unit, eq, 1)
named(A, Bill)
object(C, atomic, man, person, cardinality, count_unit, eq, 1)
predicate(E, state, be, A, C)
predicate(B, unspecified, like, A, A)
object(D, atomic, named_entity, person, cardinality, count_unit, eq, 1)
named(D, John)

    NOT
    [F]
    predicate(F, state, be, A, D)

    [G, H, I, J]
    object(H, atomic, businessman, person, cardinality, count_unit, eq, 1)
    predicate(J, state, be, H, I)
    property(I, richer_than, G)
    object(G, group, thing, object, cardinality, count_unit, geq, 3)
    =>
    []
        [K, L]
        object(K, atomic, self-made-man, person, cardinality, count_unit, eq, 1)
        predicate(L, state, be, H, K)
        v
        [M, N, O]
        object(M, atomic, programmer, person, cardinality, count_unit, eq, 1)
        predicate(N, unspecified, know, M, A)
        predicate(O, unspecified, employ, H, M)
```

The DRS (see [3] for a complete overview of the DRS language used to represent ACE texts) makes use of a small number of predicates, most importantly object derived from nouns and predicate derived from verbs. The predicates share information by means of discourse referents (denoted by capital letters) and are further grouped by embedded DRS-boxes, that represent implication (derived from 'every' or 'if... then...'), negation (derived from various forms of English negation), and disjunction (derived from 'or'). Conjunction — derived from relative clauses, explicit 'and', or the sentence end symbol — is represented by the co-occurrence in the same DRS-box.

The mapping to OWL DL does not modify the existing DRS construction algorithm but only the interpretation of the DRS. It considers everything in the toplevel DRS to denote individuals (typed to belong to a certain class), or to denote relations between individuals. Individuals are introduced by nouns, so that propernames ('Bill', 'John') map to individuals with type *owl:Thing* and common nouns to an anonymous individual with the type derived from the corresponding noun (e.g. class *Man*). Properties are derived from transitive verbs ('likes') and transitive adjectives. Special meaning is assigned to the copula 'be' which introduces an identity (or difference, if negated) between individuals.

An embedded implication-box introduces a *subClassOf*-relation between class descriptions — the left-hand side of the implication maps to a class description, the right-hand side to its superclass description. Transitive verbs ('employ', 'know') and transitive adjectives ('richer than') introduce a property restriction with *someValuesFrom* a class denoted by the object of the verb or adjective, and the copula introduces a class restriction. Co-occurrence of predicates maps to *intersectionOf*. Negation and disjunction boxes introduce *complementOf* and *unionOf*, respectively. Any embedding of them is allowed. The plural form of the word 'thing' and the usage of numbers and generalized quantifiers ('more than', 'less than', 'at least', 'at most') allow to define cardinality restrictions. Thus our DRS has the following meaning (in DL notation):

$$\text{bill} \in \top$$
$$\text{m1} \in \text{Man}$$
$$\text{bill} = \text{m1}$$
$$\text{likes(bill, bill)}$$
$$\text{john} \in \top$$
$$\text{bill} \neq \text{john}$$

$$(\text{Businessman} \sqcap \geq 3 \text{ isRicherThan}) \sqsubseteq$$
$$(\text{SelfMadeMan} \sqcup (\exists \text{ employs } (\text{Programmer} \sqcap (\exists \text{ knows } \{\text{bill}\}))))$$

Note that in full English, the sentence "A man who owns a dog likes an animal." is ambiguous between a reading relating individuals (a man, a dog, an animal), and a reading relating classes (men who own dogs, things that like animals). In ACE, however, this sentence is unambiguous, describing relationships between individuals and not classes. To express the class reading, in ACE one would have to use "Every man who owns a dog likes an animal."

The mapping to OWL DL allows also to describe properties. A superproperty (e.g. 'likes') for a given property (e.g. 'loves') can be defined as:

Everybody who loves somebody likes him/her.

Describing the transitivity of properties and inverse properties is quite "mathematical" in ACE, but there does not seem to be a better way in natural languages, unless one defines keywords such as 'transitive' or 'inverseOf' which then have to be explained to the average users. Consider e.g.

If something A is taller than something B and B is taller than something C then A is taller than C.

If something A is taller than something B then B is shorter than A. If something A is shorter than something B then B is taller than A.

Note that property definitions can make use of indefinite pronouns ('everybody', 'somebody', 'everything', 'something') or a noun 'thing', which all map to *owl:Thing*.

The current mapping does not target all the syntactic variety defined in the OWL DL specification, e.g. elements like *disjointWith* or *equivalentProperty* cannot be directly expressed in ACE, but their semantically equivalent constructs can be generated.

3 Problems and Missing Features

Now we look at some of the problems that we have encountered when implementing the mapping from ACE to OWL DL. On the one hand, some expressions that can be concisely handled in OWL DL do not have an elegant counterpart in ACE. This calls for an extension of the grammar of ACE. On the other hand, some DRS structures cannot be directly mapped into OWL DL syntax which differs from DRS syntax by being heavily influenced by the standard Description Logics' syntax. This calls for a preprocessing of the DRS structures.

The biggest problem that we have encountered is that *allValuesFrom* cannot be expressed in ACE in the most natural way, i.e. by using words like 'only', 'nothing but' or 'nothing else than'. Note that existing approaches to verbalizing *allValuesFrom* tend to use 'only' (see [17,19]) and 'always' (see [8]). ACE has excluded 'only' even as a general adverb, in order to reduce the possible ambiguity that this word might introduce. Therefore a concise form to express e.g. the statement $Carnivore \equiv \forall eat.Meat$ is missing in ACE.

*Every carnivore eats nothing but meat.
*Everything that eats nothing but meat is a carnivore.

In order to express this meaning, the ACE user can choose double negation (essentially using the equivalence $\forall R.C \equiv \neg \exists R.\neg C$) or an *if-then* construction (essentially using the mapping ϕ to first-order logic syntax $\phi_{\forall R.C}(x) = \forall y.R(x,y) \rightarrow \phi_C(y)$). E.g. the DL statement $Carnivore \sqsubseteq \forall eat.Meat$ can be expressed in ACE in the following ways (the equality sign points to a different formulation that gives exactly the same DRS representation).

No carnivore eats something that is not a meat.
(= If there is a carnivore then it does not eat something that is not a meat.)
Everything that a carnivore eats is a meat.
(= If a carnivore eats something then it is a meat.)
For every carnivore everything that it eats is a meat.
(= If there is a carnivore then everything that it eats is a meat.)

The opposite direction, i.e. the DL statement $\forall eat.Meat \sqsubseteq Carnivore$ can be expressed in ACE as

> If there is something X that does not eat something that is not a meat then X is a carnivore.
> If there is something and everything that it eats is a meat then it is a carnivore.

Some of those constructions might even be acceptable in verbalizations of existing ontologies or paraphrases of existing ACE texts (i.e. they might be suitable for reading and confirmation), but they are unacceptable as the only way to express *allValuesFrom* in ACE.

Some problems emerge from the difference of the Description Logics' syntax and the DRS syntax. E.g. complex class descriptions as arguments to *someValuesFrom* are difficult to map to OWL DL, since the DRS representation resembles more a rule language than a DL-style property restriction.

The mapping of ACE's negation into the DRS language generates a negation-box that does not match OWL DL's representation of negation as implication. Therefore, when mapping a sentence like "No man is a woman." to OWL DL, we first convert the negation-box into an implication-box which contains the subject of the sentence in the *if*-part and the rest of the predicates in a negated *then*-part.

Some OWL DL features are missing altogether. Currently, there is no support for enumerations (*oneOf*). One possibility would be to extend ACE with noun phrase disjunction.

> *Every student is John or Mary or Bill.
> *Everybody likes John or Mary or likes John or Bill.
> *Everybody who is John or Bill is a man and is a student.

Also, at this point, ACE has no support for datatype properties. One could imagine using ACE's *of*-construction (or Saxon genitive) for that purpose, e.g.

> John's age is more than 21 years.
> If a person drinks a beer then the age of the person is more than 21 years.

And finally, metalevel constructions such as URIs, imports, annotation properties, versioning, etc, which essentially make OWL DL a Semantic Web language cannot be cleanly expressed in ACE.

4   Explaining OWL ACE

As is the case with full ACE, in order to be successful, OWL ACE must be easy to use for the average users. This means that the users can quickly learn to resolve the syntactic and semantic errors that they encounter when inputing an OWL ACE text. Assuming that full ACE has achieved the required simplicity, we now look at the various restrictions to OWL ACE as compared to full ACE.

Some of those restrictions apply on the level of words, phrases and sentence types, and are thus easy to explain: there is no support for intransitive and ditransitive verbs, prepositional phrases, adverbs, intransitive adjectives, and most forms of plurals. Also, query sentences (e.g. "Who employs Bill?") are not allowed in OWL ACE.

Other restrictions apply to the finer details of the syntactic structure of sentences, e.g. disjunction is not allowed to occur at the toplevel DRS ("John sees Mary or Bill likes Ann.") and implication must be rephrasable as an *every*-sentence which makes anaphoric references only to propernames and other toplevel objects (i.e. individuals). E.g. the definition of *home-worker*, "If somebody lives-at a place X and works-at the place X then he/she is a home-worker." cannot be expressed in OWL DL due to argument sharing between predicates (see [6]). Although one can express it in ACE by an *every*-sentence, "Everybody who lives-at a place that he/she works-at is a home-worker.", the anaphoric reference 'he/she' still remains and therefore this sentence does not qualify as an OWL ACE sentence. *Every*-sentences can express complex structures via relative clauses (which can be conjoined, disjoined or negated using verb phrase conjunction, disjunction or negation, respectively). At the same time, they put a natural restriction on how the subjects and objects can be used in the sentence.

5   From OWL to ACE

The mapping in the opposite direction must handle all OWL DL constructs, some of which the ACE-to-OWL mapping does not produce. A bigger issue is raised by the naming conventions used for OWL classes and properties. Those names are not under the control of current OWL editing tools and the user is guided only by informal style-guides, which mainly discuss the capitalization of names (see e.g. [10]). OWL ACE would prefer classes to be named by singular nouns, properties by transitive verbs or adjectives, and individuals by singular nouns or propernames. Real-world OWL ontologies, however, can contain class names like *SpicyPizza*, *MotherWith3Children*, property names like *account-Name*, *brotherOf*, *isWrittenBy*, and individual names like *red*, *married*. Still, [14] analyze the linguistic nature of class and property names in real-world OWL ontologies and find that those names fall, in most cases, quite well into the categories of nouns and verbs, respectively, with only a small overlap in linguistic patterns used. (They do not study the morphological features of names of individuals.)

Mapping from OWL to ACE also involves parsing RDF/XML, which is the normative syntax for OWL DL. So far, we have implemented a simple prototype in XSLT, which generates ACE from the XML Presentation Syntax of OWL [9] and hope that more OWL tools will support this syntax as an alternative output format. The current mapping directly generates ACE. An alternative would target the DRS instead, and use an existing general mapping from the DRS to a canonical Core ACE form (see [4]).

Currently, the ACE representation ends up being quite repetitive and unordered. For large ontologies this might become a problem and a more complex strategy is needed. Consider e.g. the following sentences.

Every wine which originates-from France is a french-wine.
Everything which is a wine and which originates-from France is something which is a french-wine.
If there is a wine and it originates-from France then the wine is a french-wine.
If there is a wine W and W originates-from France then W is a french-wine.

Those sentences are equivalent, as far as the mapping to OWL DL is concerned. Still, some of those sentences are more readable than others, e.g. one could argue that the *every*-construction with a relative clause is more readable than the *if-then* construction with full clauses. On the other hand, relative clauses in ACE cannot express certain predicate-argument structures, e.g. if the predicates don't share any arguments, or, the opposite, if they are too much interlinked. A flexible ACE generation system could use relative clauses in case they allow to correctly express all the references in the DRS and revert to using *if-then* sentences in case a more flexible reference system is needed. It might turn out that the expressivity provided by *every*-sentences (using relative clauses) is enough to verbalize OWL DL.

Note also, that a variety of different verbalizations can be achieved by changing the input ontology with a reasoner which restructures the ontology and/or modifies it by adding/removing certain (possibly redundant) information. I.e. we could provide a relatively direct OWL-to-ACE mapping, but use a reasoner to customize the verbalization procedure for our needs.

6   Related Work

Some existing results show the potential and the need for a natural language based interface to OWL, and to the Semantic Web in general. [12] discusses the so-called "people axis" of the Semantic Web, i.e. technologies which would make the Semantic Web accessible to the widest possible audience. He describes Pseudo Natural Language which provides an interface to RDF, and points to the need for a dedicated natural interface to extensions of RDF, such as OWL. [18] proposes writing OWL ontologies in a controlled language, but does not provide a natural syntax for writing terminological statements (i.e. TBoxes). [19] extends this work to cover also the terminological statements using *if-then* sentences and describes a bidirectional mapping to the OWL Abstract Syntax. The details of this mapping as well as a working prototype are not presented. TRANSLATOR[4] (TRANSlator from LAnguage TO Rules) is a tool which maps the DRS

---

[4] http://www.ruleml.org/translator/

representation of ACE sentences into RuleML syntax, covering full ACE. Its goal is to allow non-experts to write facts and rules in formal representation for use on the Semantic Web.

There is more work on the verbalization of OWL ontologies, although not in controlled languages, i.e. such verbalization cannot be edited and parsed back into a standard OWL representation. [13] discuss inferences (so called *natural language directed inference*) to be applied on the ontology which are necessary to make the verbalization of the ontology linguistically more acceptable, e.g. the verbalization must not violate the Gricean maxims. [8] paraphrase OWL class hierarchies and use a part-of-speech tagger to analyze the linguistic nature of class names and then split the names apart to form more readable sentences. [7] extends this work to OWL individuals and their properties.

7 Future Work

The current mapping lacks support for datatype properties and enumerations. Also, *allValuesFrom* cannot be directly generated, but its semantics can be captured by using double negation. We will add support of those constructs along with support of proposed extensions to the current version of OWL DL, such as qualified cardinality and local reflexivity restrictions. Some of those changes require modification of the existing ACE syntax. ACE also needs support for URIs and namespaces, at least on the tokenizer level.

The ACE parser uses a large lexicon of content words to know which words belong to which word class. ACE texts containing domain specific words cannot be parsed unless the built-in general-purpose lexicon is updated to contain knowledge about these words. This makes parsing faster and allows us to point out spelling mistakes. On the other hand, the dependency on the lexicon can make the system less convenient to use. The restrictions that the OWL ACE subset of ACE sets on ACE syntax, might be strong enough, so that the word class information could be unambiguously derived from the context (e.g. a determiner such as 'every' or 'a' signals that the following word is a singular noun). We are thus in search for a lexicon-independent subset of ACE and explore its relation to OWL ACE.

Our long term goal is to develop ACE into a Semantic Web language which can capture both ontology languages and rule languages in a uniform syntax and thus hide the sometimes artificial distinction between those paradigms.

Acknowledgment

This research has been funded by the European Commission and by the Swiss State Secretariat for Education and Research within the 6th Framework Programme project REWERSE number 506779 (cf. http://rewerse.net).

The authors would like to thank the anonymous reviewers and the participants of PPSWR'06 for their valuable feed-back.

References

1. Attempto project. Attempto website, 2006. http://www.ifi.unizh.ch/attempto.
2. Abraham Bernstein, Esther Kaufmann, Anne Göhring, and Christoph Kiefer. Querying Ontologies: A Controlled English Interface for End-users. In *4th International Semantic Web Conference*, pages 112–126, November 2005.
3. Norbert E. Fuchs, Stefan Höfler, Kaarel Kaljurand, Gerold Schneider, and Uta Schwertel. Extended Discourse Representation Structures in Attempto Controlled English. Technical Report ifi-2005.08, Department of Informatics, University of Zurich, Zurich, Switzerland, 2005.
4. Norbert E. Fuchs, Kaarel Kaljurand, and Gerold Schneider. Deliverable I2-D5. Verbalising Formal Languages in Attempto Controlled English I. Technical report, REWERSE, 2005. http://rewerse.net/deliverables.html.
5. Norbert E. Fuchs, Kaarel Kaljurand, and Gerold Schneider. Attempto Controlled English Meets the Challenges of Knowledge Representation, Reasoning, Interoperability and User Interfaces. In *FLAIRS 2006*, Melbourne Beach, Florida, May 11–13th 2006.
6. Benjamin N. Grosof, Ian Horrocks, Raphael Volz, and Stefan Decker. Description logic programs: Combining logic programs with description logic. In *Twelfth International World Wide Web Conference (WWW 2003)*, pages 48–57, Budapest, Hungary, May 20–24th 2003.
7. Christian Halaschek-Wiener, Jennifer Golbeck, Bijan Parsia, Vladimir Kolovski, and Jim Hendler. Image browsing and natural language paraphrases of semantic web annotations. In *First International Workshop on Semantic Web Annotations for Multimedia (SWAMM)*, Edinburgh, Scotland, May 22nd 2006.
8. Daniel Hewlett, Aditya Kalyanpur, Vladamir Kovlovski, and Chris Halaschek-Wiener. Effective Natural Language Paraphrasing of Ontologies on the Semantic Web. In *End User Semantic Web Interaction Workshop (ISWC 2005)*, 2005.
9. Masahiro Hori, Jérôme Euzenat, and Peter F. Patel-Schneider. OWL Web Ontology Language XML Presentation Syntax. W3C Note 11 June 2003. Technical report, W3C, June 11th 2003. http://www.w3.org/TR/owl-xmlsyntax/.
10. Matthew Horridge, Holger Knublauch, Alan Rector, Robert Stevens, and Chris Wroe. A Practical Guide To Building OWL Ontologies Using The Protégé-OWL Plugin and CO-ODE Tools. Edition 1.0. Technical report, The University Of Manchester, 2004. http://www.co-ode.org/resources/tutorials/.
11. Ian Horrocks, Peter F. Patel-Schneider, Harold Boley, Said Tabet, Benjamin Grosof, and Mike Dean. SWRL: A Semantic Web Rule Language Combining OWL and RuleML. W3C Member Submission 21 May 2004. Technical report, W3C, 2004. http://www.w3.org/Submission/2004/SUBM-SWRL-20040521/.
12. Massimo Marchiori. Towards a People's Web: Metalog. Technical report, W3C, 2004.
13. Chris Mellish and Xiantang Sun. Natural Language Directed Inference in the Presentation of Ontologies. In *10th European Workshop on Natural Language Generation*, Aberdeen, Scotland, August 8–10th 2005.
14. Chris Mellish and Xiantang Sun. The Semantic Web as a Linguistic Resource. In *Twenty-sixth SGAI International Conference on Innovative Techniques and Applications of Artificial Intelligence*, Peterhouse College, Cambridge, UK, December 12–14th 2005.
15. Peter F. Patel-Schneider. The OWL 1.1 Extension to the W3C OWL Web Ontology Language. Editor's Draft of 14 June 2006. Technical report, 2006. http://www-db.research.bell-labs.com/user/pfps/owl/overview.html.

16. Peter F. Patel-Schneider, Patrick Hayes, and Ian Horrocks. OWL Web Ontology Language Semantics and Abstract Syntax. W3C Recommendation 10 February 2004. Technical report, W3C, 2004. http://www.w3.org/TR/owl-semantics/.

17. Alan L. Rector, Nick Drummond, Matthew Horridge, Jeremy Rogers, Holger Knublauch, Robert Stevens, Hai Wang, and Chris Wroe. OWL Pizzas: Practical Experience of Teaching OWL-DL: Common Errors & Common Patterns. In Enrico Motta, Nigel Shadbolt, Arthur Stutt, and Nicholas Gibbins, editors, *Engineering Knowledge in the Age of the Semantic Web, 14th International Conference, EKAW 2004*, volume 3257 of *Lecture Notes in Computer Science*, pages 63–81. Springer, October 5–8th 2004.

18. Rolf Schwitter. Controlled Natural Language as Interface Language to the Semantic Web. In *2nd Indian International Conference on Artificial Intelligence (IICAI-05)*, Pune, India, December 20–22nd 2005.

19. Rolf Schwitter and Marc Tilbrook. Let's Talk in Description Logic via Controlled Natural Language. In *Logic and Engineering of Natural Language Semantics 2006, (LENLS2006)*, Tokyo, Japan, June 5–6th 2006.

XML Querying Using Ontological Information

Hans Eric Svensson and Artur Wilk

Dept. of Computer and Information Science,
Linköping University, S 581 83 Linköping, Sweden
{x05erisv, artwi}@ida.liu.se

Abstract. The paper addresses the problem of using semantic annotations in XML documents for better querying XML data. We assume
that the annotations refer to an ontology defined in OWL (Web Ontology Language). The intention is then to combine syntactic querying
techniques on XML documents with OWL ontology reasoning to filter
out semantically irrelevant answers. The solution presented in this paper
is an extension of the declarative rule-based XML query and transformation language Xcerpt. The extension allows to interface an ontology
reasoner from Xcerpt rules. This makes it possible to use Xcerpt to filter extracted XML data using ontological information. Additionally it
allows to retrieve ontological information by sending semantic queries to
a reasoner. The prototype implementation uses DIG (Description Logic
interface) for communication with the OWL reasoner RacerPro where
the ontology queries are answered.

1   Introduction

XML, designed by W3C[1], is increasingly used for representing semistructured
data on the Web. XML is considered a basic layer in the W3C Semantic Web
initiative initiated by Tim Berners-Lee. As stated by Antoniou and van Harmelen [2] the objective of the initiative is "to represent Web content in a form
that is more easily machine-processable and to use intelligent techniques to take
advantage of these representations". The intention is not to build a new Web
from scratch, but to stimulate gradual evolvement of the existing Web in the
above-mentioned direction.

   Another layer of the Semantic Web is the so-called ontology layer. Ontologies
provide information about concepts, roles and individuals in a given application
domain. Thus an ontology gives a common vocabulary to be understood in the
same way by various applications in the domain. For example the concept *tree*
in graph theory applications is understood to be a special kind of the concept
graph. The same concept would be understood to be a special kind of the concept
plant in a botanical vocabulary. The roles defined by an ontology are binary
relations on concepts. The Web Ontology Language OWL [1], recommended by
the W3C, is used for specifying Web ontologies. Formally the language is based
on a Description Logic. An OWL ontology can thus be seen as a set of logical

---

[1] http://www.w3.org/

J.J. Alferes et al. (Eds.): PPSWR 2006, LNCS 4187, pp. 190–203, 2006.
© Springer-Verlag Berlin Heidelberg 2006

axioms. Querying a given ontology is done by reasoning in the underlying logic. For example, if the graph ontology states that the individual t is a *tree* it can be concluded that t is a *graph*.

XML is supported by query languages, including the W3C Candidate Recommendation XQuery [4]. Querying of XML data in such languages relies on the structure of the queried XML data: a query identifies a (possibly empty) set of fragments of given XML data. The structure-based querying of XML data is thus based on the syntax of the data. XML data may include semantic annotations, referring to concepts defined by ontologies. However, XML query languages do not provide ontology reasoning capabilities. The objective of this paper is to show how structure-based querying can be combined with ontology reasoning. For this we combine the XML query language Xcerpt [10,9] with ontology queries. Xcerpt is being developed by the EU Network of Excellence REWERSE [2] in the 6th Framework Programme. It differs from most other XML query languages in that it is deductive and rule based. This makes it more suitable for integration with ontology queries.

As already stated, the objective of our work is to enhance structural querying of XML data with ontology reasoning. We assume that XML data contains annotations referring to an ontology defined in OWL. We would like to filter XML documents returned by a structural query by reasoning on semantic annotations included therein. This can be illustrated by the following example. Assume that an XML database of culinary recipes is given. Each recipe indicates ingredients (like flour, salt, sugar etc.). We assume that the names of the ingredients are defined by a standard ontology, accessible separately on the web and providing also some classification. For example, the standard may specify disjoint classes of gluten-containing and gluten-free ingredients (see Figure 1). Thus, the names of ingredients in the XML recipe can be seen as semantic annotations. To prepare dinner we would query the XML database for recipes. To check if the ingredients of a chosen recipe are gluten-free we have additionally to query the ontology.

Thus, the problem outlined above can be seen as the problem of interfacing of an XML query language with an ontology reasoner. We decided to choose Xcerpt as the query language as variables of Xcerpt can naturally be used for passing semantic annotations from results of Xcerpt queries to an ontology reasoner. Also we had access to the source code of the Xcerpt implementation which made it possible to implement our solution by modification of this code. The prototype implementation uses DIG (Description Logic interface [3]) for communication with the OWL reasoner RacerPro[3] where the ontology queries are answered.

The prototype implements two ways of interfacing a reasoner from Xcerpt. One of them involves boolean ontology queries, which are used to filter out irrelevant answers. Another one allows arbitrary DIG queries to retrieve ontological information from the reasoner. Such information can be further used by other rules in an Xcerpt program.

---

[2] http://www.rewerse.net/

[3] http://www.racer-systems.com/

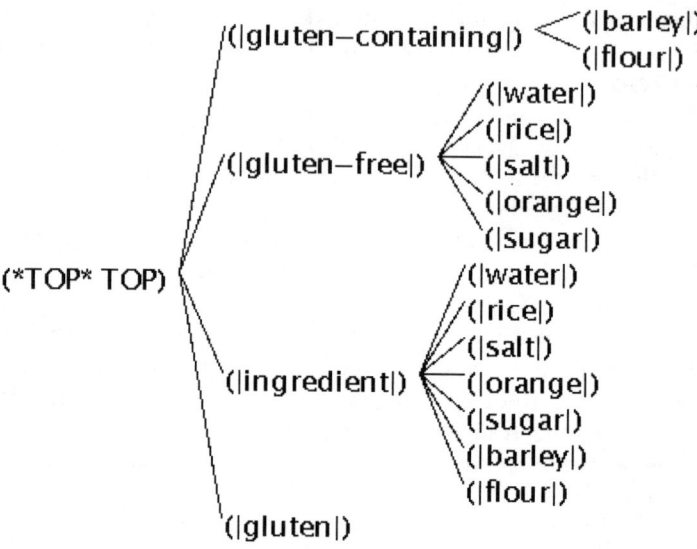

Fig. 1. Recipe ontology graph (generated by RacerPorter - a graphical user interface of RacerPro)

The rest of the paper is organised as follows. Section 2 briefly introduces the query language Xcerpt and gives some background information on the DIG interface. Section 3 presents an extension of Xcerpt allowing querying XML using ontological information. It also presents a prototype implementing new constructs in Xcerpt. Finally, Section 4 provides some conclusions.

2   Preliminaries

This section gives a brief introduction to the XML query and transformation language Xcerpt and the DIG Interface. These are basic techniques applied in the presented work.

2.1   Xcerpt

An Xcerpt program is a set of rules consisting of a body and of a head. The body of a rule is a query intended to match data terms. If the query contains variables such matching results in answer substitutions for variables. The head uses the results of matching to construct new data terms. The queried data is either specified in the body or is produced by rules of the program. There are two kinds of rules: goal rules produce the final output of the program, while construct rules produce intermediate data, which can be further queried by other rules.

Their syntax is as follows:

GOAL	CONSTRUCT
head	*head*
FROM	FROM
body	*body*
END	END

Sometimes, we will denote the rules as *head* ← *body* neglecting distinction between goal and construct rules.

XML data is represented in Xcerpt as **data terms**. Data terms are built from basic constants and labels using two kinds of parentheses: brackets [ ] and braces { }. Basic constants represent basic values such as attribute values and character data (called PCDATA). A label represents an XML element name. The parentheses following a label include a sequence of data terms (its direct subterms). Brackets are used to indicate that the direct subterms are ordered (in the order of their occurrence in the sequence), while braces indicate that the direct subterms are unordered. The latter alternative is used to encode attributes of an XML element by a data term of the form $attr\{l_1[v_1], \ldots, l_n[v_n]\}$ where l_i are names of the attributes and v_i are their respective values.

Example 1. This is an XML element and the corresponding data term.

```
<CD price="9.90">              CD[ attr{ price["9.90"] },
  <title>Empire</title>            title[ "Empire" ],
  <artist>Bob Dylan</artist>       artist["Bob Dylan"],
  <country>USA</country>           country["USA"]
</CD>                          ]
```

There are two other kinds of terms in Xcerpt: query terms and construct terms.

Query terms are (possibly incomplete) patterns which are used in a rule body (query) to match data terms. In particular, every data term is a query term. Generally query terms may include variables so that a successful matching binds variables of a query term to data terms. Such bindings are called answer substitutions. A result of a query term matching a data term is a set of answer substitutions. For example a query term $a[b[], \text{var } X]$ matches a data term $a[b[], c[]]$ resulting in answer substitution set $\{X/c[]\}$. Query terms can be ordered or unordered patterns, denoted, respectively, by brackets and braces. For example a query term $a[c[], b[]]$ is an ordered pattern and it does not match a data term $a[b[], c[]]$ but a query term $a\{c[], b[]\}$, which is an unordered pattern, matches $a[b[], c[]]$. Query terms with double brackets or braces are incomplete patterns. For example a query term $a[[b[], d[]]]$ is an incomplete pattern which matches a data term $a[b[], c[], d[]]$. As the query term uses brackets the matching subterms of the data term must occur in the same order as in the pattern. Thus the query term $a[[b[], d[]]]$ does not match a data term $a[d[], b[], c[]]$. In contrast a query term $a\{\{b[], d[]\}\}$ matches $a[d[], b[], c[]]$. To specify subterms

at arbitrary depth a keyword desc is used e.g. a query term desc $d[\,]$ matches a
data term $a[\,b[\,d[\,]\,],c[\,]\,]$.

A query term q in a rule body may be associated with a resource r storing
XML data or data terms. This is done by a construction of the form $\text{in}[r,q]$.
The meaning of this construction is that q is to be matched against data in r.
Query terms in the body of a rule which have no associated resource are matched
against data generated by rules of the Xcerpt program.

Rule bodies are constructed from query terms (possibly with indicated resources) using logical connectives such as or, and, and not.

Construct terms are used in rule heads to construct new data terms. They
are similar to data terms, but may contain variables which act as place holders
for data selected in a query. They may also use a grouping construct all which
is used to collect all instances that result from different variable bindings.

A construct term c in a goal rule head may be associated with a resource r
to which the goal results are written. This is done by a construction of the form
$\text{out}[r,c]$. If a head of a goal rule is a construct term which is not associated with
a resource the results of the rule are directed to the standard output.

Example 2. Consider a document *catalogue.xcerpt* containing a data term:

```
catalogue[
   cd[ title["Empire"], artist["Bob Dylan"], year["1985"] ],
   cd[ title["Hide your heart"], artist["Bonnie Tyler"], year["1988"] ],
   cd[ title["Stop"], artist["Sam Brown"], year[ "1988"] ]
]
```

Here is an Xcerpt rule which queries the document and extracts titles and artists
of the CD's issued in 1988 and presents the results in a changed form (title as
name and artist as author).

```
GOAL
   results [
      all result[ name[ var TITLE ], author[ var ARTIST ] ]
]
FROM
   in[ "file:catalogue.xcerpt",
      catalogue{{
         cd{ title[ var TITLE ], artist[ var ARTIST ], year[ "1988" ] }
      }}
   ]
END
```

The result returned by the rule is:

```
results[ result[ name[ "Hide your heart" ], author[ "Bonnie Tyler" ] ],
         result[ name[ "Stop" ], author[ "Sam Brown" ] ] ]
```

Xcerpt rules may be chained to form complex query programs, i.e. rules may
query the results of other rules.

2.2   DIG Interface

Ontologies provide information about concepts, roles and individuals in a given application domain. Thus an ontology gives a common vocabulary to be understood in the same way by various applications in the domain. A main language used to defined ontologies is OWL developed by W3C. OWL is based on description logics.

An OWL file representing an ontology is just an encoding of a set of axioms. To make use of the axioms one needs an ontology reasoner. Using an ontology reasoner it is possible to draw conclusions from the set of axioms such as discovering implicit subclass relationships and discovering class equivalence. In the presented work we use the ontology reasoner RacerPro. To allow Xcerpt programs to communicate with the reasoner we need to use a reasoner interface. For this purpose we have chosen DIG (Description Logic interface [3]) which is supported by RacerPro.

The DIG interface is an API for a general description logic system. It is capable of expressing class and property expressions common to most description logics. Using DIG, clients can communicate with a reasoner through the use of HTTP POST requests. The request is an XML encoded message of one of the following types: management, ask or tell. Management requests are used e.g. to identify the reasoner along with its capabilities or to allocate a new knowledge base and return its unique identifier. Tell requests, expressed in the *Tell* language, are used to make assertions into the reasoner's knowledge base. Ask requests, expressed in the *Ask* language, are used to query the knowledge base. Replies to ask requests are provided with the *Response* language. Tell, Ask and Response languages use expressions from the *Concept* language which is used to define classes, properties, declare individuals etc. Here we present an extract of expressions from the Concept language:

- Primitive concepts, roles and individuals:
  - `<top/>` - the universal concept (like owl:Thing)
  - `<bottom/>` - the empty concept (like owl:Nothing)
  - `<catom name="`CN`"/>` - a concept (i.e. class) CN
  - `<ratom val="`RN`"/>` - a role (i.e. property) RN
  - `<individual name="`IN`"/>` - introduces an individual IN
- Boolean operators:
  - `<and>`$C_1 \ldots C_n$`</and>` - intersection of concept expressions $C_1, \ldots, C_n$
  - `<or>`$C_1 \ldots C_n$`</or>` - union of concept expressions $C_1, \ldots, C_n$
  - `<not>`C`</not>` - complement of a concept expression C

This is an excerpt from the Ask language (C, C_1, C_2 are concept expressions):

- satisfiability queries for which the response is a boolean value
  - `<satisfiable>`C`</satisfiable>`
  - `<subsumes>`$C_1 \, C_2$`</subsumes>`
  - `<disjoint>`$C_1 \, C_2$`</disjoint>`
- concept retrieval queries for which the response is a set of concepts

- `<allConceptNames/>`
- `<parents>`C`</parents>`
- `<children>`C`</children>`
- `<descendants>`C`</descendants>`
- `<equivalents>`C`</equivalents>`

3 Extended Xcerpt

This section presents a way for extending Xcerpt to enable it to interface with an ontology reasoner while querying XML data. First we present a kind of a filter used in Xcerpt rules to filter out semantically irrelevant answers. Then, we propose a more general way for interfacing an ontology reasoner with Xcerpt.

In order not to confuse keywords from Xcerpt like or, and etc., with similar keywords used in DIG, we precede them with the character '!'. Thus, for example, !or in Extended Xcerpt is equivalent to or in Xcerpt. Also, the character '!' is used to denote a label of a data term representing attributes (!*attr*).

3.1 Answer Filtering

Here we present a new Xcerpt construction called *filter*. Such a filter can be used between a body and a head of an Extended Xcerpt rule to filter out semantically irrelevant answers:

GOAL	CONSTRUCT
head	*head*
FILTER	FILTER
filter	*filter*
FROM	FROM
body	*body*
END	END

A *filter* is an expression !dig[U_{RL}, *cterm*], where U_{RL} is an URL of an ontology reasoner answering DIG queries and *cterm* is a construct term used to produce a DIG query. Evaluation of a body of a rule results in a set Ψ of answer substitutions. The substitutions are then used by the construct term *cterm* to build a data term $asks[a_1, \ldots, a_n]$ where $a_1, \ldots, a_n$ are expressions from the DIG's Ask language for which boolean answers can be given. The data term $asks[a_1, \ldots, a_n]$ corresponds to a result of an Xcerpt rule *cterm* ← *body*. The data term is transformed into an XML document and sent to an ontology reasoner specified by U_{RL}. The XML document sent to the reasoner additionally contains a header with DIG namespace declarations and unique identifiers for the elements corresponding to $a_1, \ldots, a_n$. The reasoner replies with a boolean answer for each ask expression. If the answer for the query a_i is 'false' the answer substitutions used to construct a_i are discarded[4]; otherwise they are retained. As a result we obtain a subset Ψ' of the set of answer substitutions Ψ. Only the substitutions from Ψ' are used then to build the results of the initial rule.

---

[4] As *cterm* may contain grouping constructs a_i may originate from more than one answer substitution.

Our prototype of Extended Xcerpt implements this method of filtering. However, the present version of the prototype is somewhat restricted. It only allows filters in goal rules and forbids use of grouping constructs such as !all in filters. As the grouping constructs are forbidden there is no need to use explicitly a common label *asks* for ask expressions in the filter. Thus a construct term *cterm* in a filter !dig[U_{RL}, *cterm*] is used to build a separate ask expression a_i for each answer substitution from Ψ. Then a data term $asks[a_1, \ldots, a_n]$ is built automatically; it is translated into XML and sent to a reasoner. In order to be able to further query the results of goal rules with filters the Xcerpt implementation has been altered in such way that the files produced by goal rules can be queried by other goal rules. The goal rules are evaluated in the order they appear in a program.

Usage of the filter is illustrated on the following example which can be run on the prototype. Consider an XML document *recipes.xml*, which is a collection of culinary recipes. The document is represented by the data term:

```
recipes[
 recipe[
   name[ "Recipe1" ],
   ingredients[
     ingr[ name[ "sugar" ], amount [ !attr{ unit[ "tbsp" ] }, 3 ] ],
     ingr[ name[ "orange" ], amount[ !attr{ unit[ "unit" ] }, 1 ] ]
   ]
 ],
 recipe[
   name[ "Recipe2" ],
   ingredients[
     ingr[ name[ "flour" ], amount[ !attr{ unit[ "dl" ] }, 3 ] ],
     ingr[ name[ "salt" ], amount[ !attr{ unit[ "krm" ] }, 1 ] ]
   ]
 ],
 recipe[
   name [ "Recipe3" ],
   ingredients[
     ingr[ name[ "barley" ], amount[ !attr{ unit[ "dl" ] }, 1 ] ],
     ingr[ name[ "salt" ], amount[ !attr{ unit[ "dl" ] }, 2 ] ]
   ]
 ]
]
```

Also consider the culinary ingredients ontology from introduction (Figure 1). We assume that the ontology is loaded into an ontology reasoner which is accessible via the URL http://localhost:14159/. We also assume that the names of the ingredients used in the XML document are defined by the ontology. Thus, names of ingredients in the XML document can be seen as semantic annotations. We want to find all the recipes in the XML document which are gluten-free. This can be achieved using the following program with two goal rules, one of them with a filter:

```
GOAL
  !out [
    !resource [ "file:bad-recipes.xcerpt" ],
    bad-recipe-names [ !all name [ var R ] ] ]
FILTER
  !dig [ "http://localhost:14159/",
      subsumes [
        catom [ !attr { name [ "gluten-containing" ] } ],
        catom [ !attr { name [ var N ] } ] ] ]
FROM
  !in [ !resource [ "file:recipes.xml" ],
    recipes [[
      recipe [[
        name [ var R ],
        ingredients [[ ingredient [[ name [ var N ] ]] ]] ]] ]] ]
END

GOAL
    recipes [ !all name [ var R ] ]
FROM
  and[
    !in [ !resource [ "file:recipes.xml"],
      recipes [[ recipe [[ name [ var R ] ]] ]] ],
    !in [ !resource [ "file:bad-recipes.xcerpt"],
      not bad-recipe-names [[ name [ var R ] ]] ]
  ]
END
```

Evaluation of the program starts from the first goal rule. Evaluation of the body of the rule results in the set of answer substitutions $\Psi = \{\{R/"Recipe1", N/"sugar"\}, \{R/"Recipe1", N/"orange"\}, \{R/"Recipe2", N/"flour"\}, \{R/"Recipe2", N/"salt"\}, \{R/"Recipe3", N/"barley"\}, \{R/"Recipe3", N/"salt"\}\}$. Then the substitution set Ψ is used in construct term from the filter to build data terms representing ask expressions. A separate ask expression is built for each substitution from Ψ. The obtained ask expressions are grouped together under a common label *asks*:

```
asks[
  subsumes[
    catom[ attr{ name [ "gluten-containing" ] } ],
    catom[ attr{ name [ "sugar" ] } ] ],
  subsumes[
    catom[ attr{ name [ "gluten-containing" ] } ],
    catom[ attr{ name [ "orange" ] } ] ],
  subsumes[
    catom[ attr{ name [ "gluten-containing" ] } ],
    catom[ attr{ name [ "flour" ] } ] ],
  subsumes[
    catom[ attr{ name [ "gluten-containing" ] } ],
    catom[ attr{ name [ "salt" ] } ] ],
  subsumes[
```

```
    catom[ attr{ name [ "gluten-containing" ] } ],
    catom[ attr{ name [ "barley" ] } ] ],
  subsumes[
    catom[ attr{ name [ "gluten-containing" ] } ],
    catom[ attr{ name [ "salt" ] } ] ] ]
```

The *asks* data term is sent to a reasoner. The reasoner replies with a positive answer for the third and the fifth ask expressions as only flour and barley contain gluten wrt. the ontology. As the answers for the remaining ask expressions are negative the substitutions used to build them are discarded. Thus, the obtained set of substitutions used to build the final result of the rule is $\Psi' = \{\{R/"Recipe2", N/"flour"\}, \{R/"Recipe3", N/"barley"\}\}$. Hence, the final result written by the first goal rule into the file *bad-recipes.xcerpt* is:

```
bad-recipe-names[ name["Recipe 2"], name ["Recipe 3"] ]
```

The second goal rule returns those names of recipes from *recipes.xml* which are not in *bad-recipes.xcerpt*. Thus the final result of the program returned by the second goal rule is

```
recipes[ name["Recipe 1"] ]
```

The kind of queries which can be sent to a reasoner is limited due to the DIG interface which is often not sufficiently expressive. It lacks e.g. logical operators such as *and* and *or* (keywords *and* and *or* are used in DIG to denote intersection and union of concepts, respectively). This is a reason why we had to use two goal rules instead of one rule in the example above. To obtain the same result using a program with only one rule we need to be able to use grouping constructs in a filter and e.g. conjunction in the ask expression constructed by the filter. The latter would be needed to assure that each ingredient of a recipe is subsumed by the concept *gluten-free*.

3.2   DIG Rules - Querying Ontology Reasoner with Xcerpt

In the previous section we introduced a filter which sends boolean queries to an ontology reasoner and based on the reasoner replies, filters out irrelevant answers. However, we can take more general approach where the queries sent to a reasoner are arbitrary DIG ask expressions (not only boolean). An ordinary Xcerpt rule, say ask rule, can be used to produce such an ask expression which is sent to a reasoner. Then another Xcerpt rule, say response rule, captures the response received from the reasoner and transforms it to a desired format.

This can be reflected by a higher level rule called e.g. a DIG rule. A DIG rule can be denoted as $(h_R \leftarrow b_R) \leftarrowtail (h_A \leftarrow b_A)$, where $h_A \leftarrow b_A$ is an ask rule and $h_R \leftarrow b_R$ is a response rule. Thus h_A is a construct term of the form $asks[\ldots]$ and b_R a query term of the form e.g. $responses\{\{\ldots\}\}$. DIG rules could be handled by an external application which executes relevant Xcerpt programs and communicates with a reasoner. Another solution is extending Xcerpt itself with DIG rules so it interfaces an ontology reasoner. Beside ordinary rules (i.e.

Xcerpt query rules) such an extended Xcerpt could use response and ask rules, respectively, of the forms:

```
CONSTRUCT                    CONSTRUCT
     hR                          !out[!dig[ URL], hA]
FROM                         FROM
     !in[ !dig[ URL], bR ]        bA
END                          END
```

To implement this idea based on backward rule chaining we need to assure that a response rule invokes a relevant ask rule, the result of the ask rule is sent to a reasoner, and the reasoner response is queried by the initial response rule.

We can consider a special, simple case of a DIG rule $(h_R \leftarrow b_R) \leftarrowtail (h_A \leftarrow b_A)$, where its body, the ask rule, is of the form $h_A \leftarrow$!and[ ]. Thus the ask rule is equivalent to a data term h_A which represents fixed ask expressions i.e. h_A is a data term $asks[\ldots]$. Such a simple DIG rule can be denoted as $(h_R \leftarrow b_R) \leftarrowtail h_A$. The prototype of Extended Xcerpt is restricted to such simple DIG rules. DIG rules $(h_R \leftarrow b_R) \leftarrowtail h_A$ are incorporated into Xcerpt goal rules which are of the form:

```
GOAL
     hR
FROM
     !in[ !dig[ URL, hA ], bR ]
END
```

h_A is a data term $asks[a_1, \ldots, a_n]$ containing ask expressions $a_1, \ldots, a_n$ or a data term $tells[t_1, \ldots, t_n]$ containing tell expressions $t_1, \ldots, t_n$. Alternatively, h_A can be a URI of an XML file storing an ask or tell expression. The ask expressions $a_1, \ldots, a_n$ (and tell expressions) must contain unique identifiers to be able to relate reasoner responses with them. As the programmer handles the reasoner responses by himself/herself this time the identifiers cannot be added automatically. The rule is evaluated in the following way. The data term h_A is transformed into an XML document to which a header containing DIG namespace declarations is added. Such a document is sent to the reasoner specified by URL. The response returned by the reasoner is queried by the query b_R. Then the resulting answer substitutions are applied to a construct term h_R and a rule result is returned.

Consider the following example. We want to query the ingredients ontology to build a document containing gluten-free ingredients. We use the following rule:

```
GOAL
  results [ !all var C ]
FROM
 !in [
   !dig [ "http://localhost:14159/",
     asks [
       descendants [
```

```
          !attr{ id [ "q1" ] },
          catom [[ !attr { name [ "gluten-free" ]} ]],
        ]
      ]
    ],
    responses {{
      conceptSet {{
        !attr { id [ "q1" ] },
        synonyms [[
          catom [[ !attr { name [ var C ] } ]]
        ]]
      }}
    }}
  ]
```

The result returned by the rule is

```
results [
    "water",
    "rice",
    "salt",
    "orange",
    "sugar"
]
```

Although the approach using DIG rules is in some sense more general than answer filtering presented in the previous section, it cannot be used directly for answer filtering. This is because a response rule can only query a response of the reasoner and does not have access to the answers of the body of the ask rule. Thus the answers cannot be filtered based on the reasoner responses. However, a workaround for achieving the same goal as with answer filtering is possible. First, the needed ontological information could be captured by a DIG rule. Then an ordinary Xcerpt rule could query both an XML document and the ontological data obtained from a reasoner. In this way the irrelevant (wrt. the ontology) XML data could be filtered out.

4   Conclusions

The paper addresses the problem of how to use ontological information in the context of querying XML data. The solution proposed in this paper extends the XML query language Xcerpt by allowing the combination of XML queries with ontology queries. The extension allows Xcerpt rules to communicate with an ontology reasoner using the DIG interface. We presented two ways of extension. The first of them is a kind of a filter used in between the body and the head of an Xcerpt rule to filter out semantically irrelevant answers. Another approach, which is more general in some sense, allows interfacing an ontology reasoner with arbitrary DIG queries.

A restricted version of the presented techniques of interfacing an ontology reasoner is implemented in a prototype of Extended Xcerpt. The prototype requires further development. Allowing grouping constructs in filters, filters in construct rules and unrestricted DIG rules would substantially increase the functionality of the prototype.

The problem of combination of XML queries with ontology queries seems to be important for achieving the Semantic Web but it is not sufficiently covered in literature. Previous related work addresses mostly integration of the logic programming language Datalog with Description Logics. Early work of this kind is represented by AL-log [5] and CARIN [7], where Datalog rule bodies are extended with queries to a given ontology (DL axioms). The authors discuss theoretical foundations as well as implementation of such an integration, but do not consider the context of the Semantic Web. More recently, Eiter et al. [6] extend Datalog with so-called DL-queries which make it possible to query locally modified DL axioms thus allowing information flow in both directions between rules and ontologies. A theoretical study of integration of logic programming rules and DL ontologies is presented by Rosati [8] (see also references therein for other related work). In contrast to the above mentioned papers our rules are not Datalog clauses but Xcerpt queries.

Acknowledgments

We would like to thank Professor Jan Małuszyński for his interesting ideas initiating this work.

This research has been funded by the European Commission and by the Swiss State Secretariat for Education and Research within the 6th Framework Programme project REWERSE number 506779 (cf. http://rewerse.net).

In the work presented here the RacerPro Software was used under a free educational license from Racer Systems GmbH & Co. KG[5] for ontology reasoning.

References

1. OWL Web Ontology Language Overview. February 2004. W3C Recommendation. http://www.w3.org/TR/owl-features/.
2. G. Antoniou and F.van Harmelen. *A Semantic Web Primer*. The MIT Press, 2004.
3. S. Bechhofer. The DIG Description Logic Interface: DIG/1.1. In *Proceedings of DL2003 Workshop*, Rome, 2003.
4. W3 Consortium. XQuery 1.0: An XML Query Language. http://www.w3.org/TR/2005/WD-xquery-20050915/.
5. F. Donini, M. Lenzerini, D. Nardi, and A. Schaerf. Al-log: integrating datalog and description logics. *J. of Intelligent and Cooperative Information Systems*, 10:227–252, 1998.
6. T. Eiter, T. Lukasiewicz, R. Schindlauer, and H. Tompits. Combining answer set programming with description logics for the semantic web. In *International Conference of Knowledge Representation and Reasoning*, 2004.

---

[5] http://www.racer-systems.com/

7. Alon Y. Levy and Marie-Christine Rousset. CARIN: A Representation Language Combining Horn Rules and Description Logics. In *European Conference on Artificial Intelligence*, pages 323–327, 1996.
8. R. Rosati. Semantic and computational advantages of the safe integration of ontologies and rules. In *International Workshop, PPSWR 2005, Dagstuhl Castle, Germany, September 2005, Proceedings*, volume 3703, pages 50–64, 2005.
9. S. Schaffert. *Xcerpt: A Rule-Based Query and Transformation Language for the Web*. PhD thesis, University of Munich, Germany, 2004.
10. S. Schaffert and F. Bry. Querying the Web Reconsidered: A Practical Introduction to Xcerpt. In *Proceedings of Extreme Markup Languages 2004, Montreal, Quebec, Canada (2nd–6th August 2004)*, 2004.

Semantic Web Reasoning Using a Blackboard System

Craig McKenzie, Alun Preece, and Peter Gray

University of Aberdeen, Department of Computing Science
Aberdeen AB24 3UE, UK
{cmckenzie, apreece, pgray}@csd.abdn.ac.uk

Abstract. In this paper, we discuss the need for a hybrid reasoning approach to handing Semantic Web (SW) data and explain why we believe that the Blackboard Architecture is particularly suitable. We describe how we have utilised it for coordinating a combination of ontological inference, rules and constraint based reasoning within a SW context.

After describing the metaphor on which the Blackboard Architecture is based we introduce its key components: the blackboard Panels containing the solution space facts and problem related goals and sub-goals; the differing behaviours of the associated Knowledge Sources and how they interact with the blackboard; and, finally, the Controller and how it manages and focuses the problem solving effort.

To help clarify, we use our test-bed system, the AKTive Workgroup Builder and Blackboard (AWB+B) to explain some of the issues and problems encountered when implementing a SW Blackboard System in a problem oriented context.

1 Introduction and Motivation

The W3C Semantic Web Activity Group[1] describes the Semantic Web (SW) as providing *"...a common framework that allows data to be shared and reused across application, enterprise, and community boundaries."* Unfortunately, since this machine processable information is essentially a "symbolic" version of the current web, the drawback is that there is no regulation over the proffered content, creating many complicating factors and making the task of utilising (and reasoning against) "open web" data far from trivial. Because the Logic Layer of the SW architecture means not only the use of logic to enrich data but also the application of logic to "do something" with the data [12], our research interest lies in exploring the suitability of a Blackboard System to utilise incomplete, SW information in a closed world, problem oriented context, i.e. using SW data to create a (finite domain) Constraint Satisfaction Problem (CSP) before attempting to solve it.

An interesting starting domain was within the context of the CS AKTive Space[2] [16], namely the Computing Science (CS) community in the UK. Our

---

[1] http://www.w3.org/2001/sw/
[2] http://cs.aktivespace.org

J.J. Alferes et al. (Eds.): PPSWR 2006, LNCS 4187, pp. 204–218, 2006.

demo application, the AKTive Workgroup Builder and Blackboard (AWB+B), is a SW application that attempts to construct one or more working groups of people from a pool of known individuals. Workgroup composition must adhere to a set of user defined constraints, e.g. "the workgroup must contain between 5 and 10 individuals" or "at least half the members of the workgroup must have a research interest of *Agents*".

Since our problem combines ontological inference, rules and constraint based reasoning, we believe that a combination of reasoning methods are necessary. The "one size fits all" reasoning theory was questioned in [17] when a DL based reasoner was compared to a First-Order prover. The final conclusion was that when dealing with a very expressive OWL DL ontology a combination of both is necessary because there was no known single reasoning algorithm able to adequately cope with the full expressivity possible with the OWL DL language. They also flagged slow performance speed as a potential hurdle. Therefore, for this to be efficient, a hybrid reasoning [2] approach is required.

Once this necessity for hybrid reasoning was identified, we realised that there is nothing in the architecture of the Semantic Web for coordinating this effort. We believe the Blackboard architecture is appropriate as it meets our requirements – supporting the use of distributed Knowledge Sources (KSs) responding to a central, shared knowledge base via a control mechanism [15,3].

The paper is organised as follows: Section 2 introduces our test-bed application, the AWB+B, and explains the process of building workgroups; Section 3 describes the blackboard analogy before comparing the traditional approach to our Semantic Web based approach; Section 4 describes the role of the Knowledge Sources and discusses their individual attributes; Section 5 describes the controlling mechanism of the blackboard; Section 6 describes the planned direction of our future work; and Section 7 provides discussion and our conclusions.

2   Building Workgroups

The AKTive Workgroup Builder and Blackboard (AWB+B) is a new incarnation of our earlier version of the system (AWB [13]) that did not use the blackboard architecture. Like its predecessor, the AWB+B is a web-based application that tackles the problem of assembling a workshop containing one or more workgroups from a pool of known people. Since the user is not expected to have knowledge about the lower level operations of the blackboard, we assume that all the necessary RDF information resources (describing the people, constraints, derivation rules, etc) to be included are known to the user (via URIs). This allows the blackboard to be initialised and the KSs to be dynamically created and registered with the blackboard "behind the scenes".

The RDF data processed by the AWB+B contains information about each individual's research interests, publications and projects they have been involved in. The detail of this information will vary depending upon what is published by a particular data source. Ideally, this information will need to be reasoned against in order to infer additional facts that may not have been explicitly stated

– for example projects that a person has worked on or papers that they have published can imply additional research interests.

3   The Blackboard Analogy

The concept of a Blackboard System is based upon a metaphor whereby a group of people, each with differing expertise and knowledge, are all standing around a blackboard deliberating over a problem that has been written up on it. Everyone understands that the ultimate goal is to solve the problem and that they will know the solution when they see it but, at this point in time, no single individual can derive the final solution on their own. The process begins when one person looks at the problem description on the board and realises that he/she can make a small relevant contribution. They write their finding onto the blackboard for the others to see. This inspires another person to a further idea, which they also write on the blackboard. This scenario continues until eventually a solution is reached via these incremental, cooperative steps (for a fuller description see [15]). No-one is allowed to communicate directly, everything must be done through the blackboard which becomes a shared "thinking space" for all the participants. We must also consider the protocol of how everyone writes on the blackboard. For example, if there is only one piece of chalk, how is the decision made as to whom gets to use it (and when) to write on the blackboard? Potentially, this could be by having someone act as a *controller*. In computing terms, the architecture of a Blackboard System has the "blackboard" as a shared Knowledge Base, and the "people" as various Knowledge Sources – we discuss KSs in more detail in Section 4.

3.1   Traditional Approach

The pioneering blackboard systems (Hearsay-II [6], HASP/SIAP [8], CRYSALIS [5] and OPM [11]) maintained the blackboard as a shared data repository representing a communal work area or "solution space" of potential solution components. The associated KSs were able to view the contents of the blackboard and react by indicating what they could contribute. They were only allowed to modify the contents of the blackboard if/when requested to do so by the Controller. For this to work efficiently, the data held on the blackboard must be structured hierarchically into Abstraction Levels (see Figure 1); multiple distinct hierarchies were referred to as Panels.

This organisation served two purposes. Firstly, it aided each KS to check if it can contribute (i.e. the KS was activated, or *triggered*, by the propagation of information onto an abstraction level that it was monitoring). Secondly, it helped focus the search for the solution. As the name suggests, each layer is an abstraction using concepts that hide the detail on the layer below it. To clarify, using the domain of speech understanding, suppose the lowest abstraction level could be the phonetic sounds accepted by the system; the level above could be potential combinations of these sounds into letter groups; the next level being single words; the next level could be phrases; with, finally, the topmost level

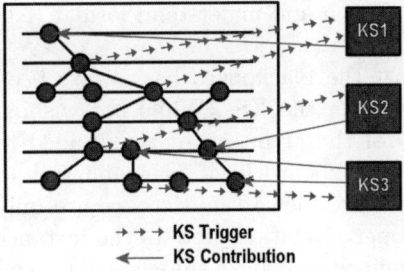

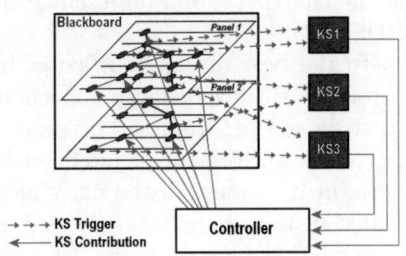

Fig. 1. Each Knowledge Source (KS) can view the Abstraction Levels within a Blackboard Panel. A KS can be *triggered* by any of the items on blackboard, allowing it to *contribute* something at any of the abstraction levels.

Fig. 2. The core architectural components of a Blackboard System. Each KS can view the contents of the Blackboard Panels, but it is the Controller that decides which KS(s) are allowed to contribute to the Blackboard.

consisting of potential whole sentences. A word-dictionary KS would examine the phonetic letter groups and combine these to form words, which (controller permitting) it would then post onto the level above.

The nature of each abstraction level and the actual entries within each level, can vary from implementation to implementation depending upon the nature of the problem attempted. Instead of the bottom-up approach used in the example, a top-down approach may be required, so the first abstraction level is vague with later ones becoming more refined. Likewise a KS's trigger could span multiple layers with a contribution also affecting one or more layers (see Figure 2).

As mentioned already, the decision of what is (or is not) placed on the blackboard is made by the controller, and the complexity of the solving strategy adopted can vary from a simplistic "just action everything" approach to a more complex goal driven algorithm. The key point is that it directs the solving process, via goals and sub-goals, that each of the KSs can be triggered by. This also helps to ensure that only *relevant* information is added. Since the triggering action can be dependent upon information added by a different KS, this results in an opportunistic solving paradigm. A blackboard system is fundamentally backward chaining – it is goal driven. In our case, the initial goal placed on the blackboard is to find a solution to a specified workgroup problem.

3.2 Semantic Web Approach

Our *Semantic Web Blackboard* maintains all the principles of the *traditional* blackboards but improves upon them by incorporating some of the concepts of the Semantic Web. The notion of Abstraction Levels aligns itself well to the hierarchical, structured nature of an ontology. In our test-bed system, AWB+B (discussed later), the information represented on blackboard is stored as an RDF graph. This also has the advantage that the contents of the blackboard can be easily serialised into textual form – either for debugging purposes or propagation of the contents – and represented in a well known and understood format (e.g. RDF, N3).

To the best of our knowledge, in the past the blackboard has always been passive with any deductive mechanism placed in the KSs. While not wishing to stray too far from the original concepts of the architecture, we decided to introduce an element of intelligence to the blackboard itself by enabling it to perform reasoning on the class hierarchy being added to it. Here we are only materialising all the transitive sub-class/property relations and all the instance type relations. For example, if a class C_1 is defined as being a sub-class of C_2 and C_2 is a sub-class of C_3 then the blackboard would assert that C_1 is a sub-class of C_3. The blackboard also has the ability to assert new `<rdf:type>` statements about individuals. Continuing the previous example, if X is an instance of C_1 and C_1 is a sub-class of C_2 then we can assert that X is also an instance of C_2.

We elected to only perform this type of reasoning and not a richer type of classification that is possible within OWL (e.g. using property domain and ranges) since this is such a common operation that having it done by the blackboard eliminates the need for frequent call outs to KS that would perform the same function. Unfortunately, enabling the Blackboard to make inferences about itself must be treated with caution. Since reasoning is both difficult and time consuming, it would be undesirable if the actual blackboard became a bottleneck while it attempted to fully reason about itself and denied all KSs from contributing – hence we have not increased the blackboard's inference ability any further. The problem is that there is absolutely no guarantee of decidability w.r.t. information placed on the blackboard. In ontological terms, a KS could contribute triples that make the blackboard contents OWL Full (meaning that it could not be fully reasoned against anyway). To prevent this, we inhibit the statements placed by the KSs to be OWL Lite. We can guarantee decidability by ensuring all contributed statements are based upon a known URIs which can be checked to classify its OWL species. This can be done in one of two ways: the underlying ontology is checked against a register of known OWL Lite Ontologies; or, providing it is not too computationally expensive, the OWL species can be checked with an existing validator (e.g. Pellet[3], WonderWeb[4], BBN[5]).

4   Behaviours of Knowledge Sources

The KSs represent the problem solving knowledge of the system. Each KS can be regarded as being an *independent* domain expert with information *relevant* to the problem at hand. The key point is that no assumptions should be made about the capabilities of a KS – conceptually it should be regarded as a black box. Due to the tightly coupled nature of the KSs and the Blackboard, all KSs must be "registered" so that they can view the blackboard contents and inform the Controller of any potential contributions.

---

[3] http://www.mindswap.org/2003/pellet/species.shtml
[4] http://phoebus.cs.man.ac.uk:9999/OWL/Validator
[5] http://owl.bbn.com/validator/

KSs can access the blackboard and continually check to see if they can contribute. Each one has a precondition (or event trigger) and an action (*what* it can add to the blackboard). The blackboard is monotonic, facts are only ever added by the KSs, never retracted. This mechanism is usually overseen by a controller that monitors changes to the blackboard and delegates actions accordingly. The whole process is driven by the posting of goals which a KS either offers a direct solution to, or breaks down further into sub-goals, indicating that more knowledge is required.

The following sub-sections describe the main types of KS currently implemented within the AWB+B system based on their behaviours w.r.t. the blackboard. This is by no means an exhaustive list of all the possible types of KS and it should be noted that future KSs could combine some of these behaviours, but we have not explored this yet. Since our interest lies in rule and constraint based reasoning, we discuss the KSs relating to these areas in greater depth.

4.1 User (Human) KS

While this may not be immediately obvious, the user of the system can be regarded as a type of KS. This represents "human" knowledge which is entered via the web-based user interface. In AWB+B terms this would be a user specifying the problem parameters, e.g. the number of workgroups to be built, the size of each workgroup, any associated compositional constraints etc. Once all the necessary information for the CSP has been entered, the KS transforms it into the starting goals for the system which are then posted onto the blackboard. Each starting goal is a skeletal instance of the Workgroup class containing only those properties that describe its composition and constraints. There are no hasMember properties implying its membership. It is the posting of these goals onto the blackboard that kick-starts the whole process.

In the current AWB+B implementation this interaction is minimal, merely the problem definition. However, there is nothing to prevent a more "interactive" human KS. Another variation of a User KS could, for example, continually check the blackboard for inconsistencies and when one is found present the user with pop-up windows asking them to offer a possible resolution, i.e. it gives the user a "view" of inconsistencies found on the blackboard.

4.2 Instance Based KS

This type of KS contains instance data corresponding to an ontology but not the actual schema itself. This could either be from a simple RDF file, a Web Service or data held in an RDF datastore. This KS contributes in the following way:

i) Try to add a "solution" to a posted (sub-)goal by adding instance data for classes and/or properties defined on the blackboard.
ii) Try to add a "solution" to classify any property's *direct* subject and/or object which the blackboard does not have a class definition for.

For example, if the ontological class Professor is defined on the blackboard and this KS has instances of that class then, as per (i), the offered solution is all the

`Professor` instances that it knows about. Property definitions work in the same way, but are slightly more complex. As per (i), when this KS responds to the property based goal `worksFor` the KS would offer the statement:

        <ex:john>   <ont:worksFor> <ex:abdnUni>   .

However, this gives no information about the subject or the object of that triple. This is not an issue if they are already instantiated on the blackboard, but if they are not (and assuming the object is not a literal) then subsequently, as per (ii), the KS could also offer the following:

        <ex:john>   <rdf:type>   <ont:Lecturer>   .
        <ex:abdnUni> <tdf:type>   <ont:University> .

Since this KS does not know the underlying schema, it cannot contribute class definition information about the `Lecturer` or `University` classes.

If this KS is a repository of RDF triples (e.g. 3Store [9]) then no reasoning ability is assumed. We require a wrapper for this KS, allowing us to communicate with the datastore via its API. In the case of the 3Store, it uses a `http` interface that accepts SPARQL[6] queries. We transform any blackboard goal into a query, the result of which can be transformed into triples and asserted onto the blackboard.

Since this type of repository can contain a vast amount of information, this raises the issue of the state which that information is in. Since access to the data is via a query mechanism, we are still effectively querying an RDF graph for which we have no means of knowing whether all, some or no additional entailments have been inferred. For example, while an ontology describes a `Professor` as a sub-class of `Academic` and the datastore contains instances of `Professor` for this schema, it might not actually contain the triples saying that `Professor` instances are also `Academics`. Consequently, a SPARQL query for Academics would not return the Professors as it does not follow sub-class links. The only way around this is to query for all the sub-classes; which will eventually occur, as the Schema based KS (described next) will post the sub-classes as sub-goals prompting more refined queries.

4.3   Schema Based KS

This represents a KS that only contains information at an ontological schema level. Since the blackboard initially contains no ontological structure (i.e. it does not contain any RDFS/OWL statements for the domain), it is the job of this KS to help facilitate the construction of the relevant ontological parts on the blackboard. This type of KS attempts to contribute in the following ways:

i) Try to add new sub-goals to the blackboard by looking for:
   - Ontological sub-classes of a class defined on the blackboard.
   - Ontological sub-properties of property defined on the blackboard.

---

[6] SPARQL (SPARQL Protocol And RDF Query Language), is documented at: http://www.w3.org/TR/rdf-sparql-query/

ii) Try to improve the (limited) reasoning ability of the blackboard by adding and inferring:
- subClassOf statements connecting classes already defined on the black-board.
- subPropertyOf statements connecting properties already defined on the blackboard.

Note: Statements are only added for *direct* sub-class/sub-property relations.

iii) Try to add new sub-goals for any property's subject and/or object on the blackboard that does not have a class definition. The sub-goals, in this case, being the missing class definitions.

In (i) and (ii) super-classes/properties are never added to the blackboard as these are deemed irrelevant and would widen the scope of the blackboard contents too much. Likewise, we need to be careful in (iii), as we do not just want to use the *domain* and *range* values of a property because they might (intentionally) be set very open. Continuing our previous example from section 4.3, let us suppose that when the ontology was first authored, the worksFor property was assigned a domain of Person and a range of <owl:Thing>. This was because the author believed that only a Person is capable of working, but what it is they actually work for could either be another *Person* or an *Organisation*. Therefore, for simplicity, they just widened the domain to encompass as many classes as possible. If we were to use these domain and range values, we would introduce a sub-goal asking for all instances of <owl:Thing> which would end up with each KS offering every instance it has. Therefore, in an attempt to narrow the search space as much as possible, only the class definitions of instances with the worksFor property are added as sub-goals (in this case Lecturer and University respectively).

4.4   Rule Based KS

A Rule KS, like all the other KS types, can be viewed as a black box, encapsulating its rules and keeping them private. The ability to derive new information through rules is an extremely important and powerful asset. Since we assume that these rules come from the open SW, we use SWRL[7] for expressing them as it is currently the dominant representation. This KS works by examining the contents of the blackboard to determine if any of the rules that it knows about are required and then attempts to contribute. A rule is required *only* if any of the elements in the consequent (head) are present on the blackboard[8]. The KS attempts to contribute to the blackboard in the following ways:

i) Try to add a "solution" by firing the rule against instances already on the blackboard and asserting the appropriate triples.

ii) Try to add new sub-goals to the blackboard by looking for:

---

[7] SWRL: A Semantic Web Rule Language Combining OWL and RuleML, W3C Member submission, http://www.w3.org/Submission/SWRL/

[8] The reason why this is "any head element" is because SWRL allows the consequent to contain a conjunction of atoms.

- Any ontological classes that are antecedents of the rule and that have not been defined on the blackboard.
- Any ontological properties that are antecedents of the rule and that have not been defined on the blackboard.

The sub-goals in this case are the ontological class or property definitions.

We need to be careful here, remembering that we want to keep the blackboard contents relevant to the problem at hand and not introduce superfluous classes or properties. The following example illustrates one way a Rule Based KS can comply with this relevancy criteria of the blackboard:

"*If a person is known to be an author of a book and that book has a topic then this implies that the person is an expert on that particular topic.*"

In informal SWRL syntax, where $?x$ denotes a variable, this can be written as:

(1) Person($?p$) $\wedge$ Book($?b$) $\wedge$ hasTopic($?b,?t$) $\wedge$ authorOf($?p,?b$)
     $\Rightarrow$ PublishedAuthor($?p$) $\wedge$ expertOn($?p,?t$)

Here Person, Book and PublishedAuthor are predicates denoting ontological classes and hasTopic, authorOf and expertOn are predicates relating properties to classes. If a rule has a conjunctive consequent it can be split into separate rules for each head atom. This means that if a consequent is not needed, that rule will not be considered avoiding the placement of unnecessary sub-goals (i.e. class/property definitions) onto the blackboard that could, subsequently, cause other KSs to add irrelevant information relating to these (either solution instances or sub-class/property sub-goals). Because of the conjunction in the consequent, this can be split up and re-written as 2 separate rules:

(2) Person($?p$) $\wedge$ Book($?b$) $\wedge$ authorOf($?p,?b$) $\Rightarrow$ PublishedAuthor($?p$)
(3) Person($?p$) $\wedge$ Book($?b$) $\wedge$ hasTopic($?b,?t$) $\wedge$ authorOf($?p,?b$)
      $\Rightarrow$ expertOn($?p,?t$)

Using rule (1) from the above example, if the blackboard only contains the property expertOn then we apply the equivalent of rule (3) to the blackboard and since (2) is not needed, it will not be considered – we only want to add new expertOn properties and ignore instances of the class PublishedAuthor.

Now if PublishedAuthor does exist on the blackboard and we assume no new antecedent information has been placed on the blackboard between cycles, the first cycle would involve adding all values of PublishedAuthor as per rule (2). In the 2nd cycle, it would see that no new instance data for PublishedAuthor can be added and, iteratively, move onto the next consequent item (expertOn) to see if it can contribute as per rule (3) – which it can. Finally, in the 3rd cycle, the rule would check both (2) and (3) and find that no new data can be added, so it would respond by saying it cannot contribute.

The current implementation of the AWB+B rewrites each rule into SPARQL queries, which it places against the blackboard contents to determine if any new triples can be asserted – essentially this is a *brute force*, forward chaining approach to deriving new entailments. The query results are then added to the blackboard. From the previous example, using rule (3) to determine the expertOn property, we can create the following query, where `rdf` is the RDF namespace, and `ont` is the appropriate ontology namespace:

```
SELECT ?p, ?t
WHERE { ?p  rdf:type      ont:Person .
        ?b  rdf:type      ont:Book   .
        ?b  ont:hasTopic  ?t         . }
```

The result set of this query contains value pairs of *Person* URI and *Topic* URI which are asserted onto the blackboard as the new triples of the form:

```
?p  <ont:expertOn>  ?t .
```

We avoid adding duplicate instance values by checking the query results and only adding new values. Since multiple rules could be applied, with new antecedent instances added at any time by any of the KSs, this is an iterative process with the entire sequence repeated until no new entailments are generated.

While this may not be the most efficient implementation, it does reflect the opportunistic nature of a blackboard system. The current implementation only has one starting rule per Rule KS (it can be split as per the above example), but we plan to extend this to allow multiple, different rules within one KS. This also allows for the interdependency between each of the rules within a KS as well as rule chaining.

From the Blackboard's perspective, all the KSs are goal oriented (backward chaining). When a rule based KS posts a sub-goal it is understood that it (the KS) has concluded that, by backward chaining, a solution can be posted once this sub-goal has been achieved. However, internally it could be forward chaining. Suppose the KS in question is an efficient implementation of a RETE forward chaining algorithm. The KS works by constantly monitoring the blackboard's contents and, within its own Knowledge Base, duplicates all elements it requires to forward chain using its known rules. Once all the processing has completed, it then offers those newly derived facts as solutions to goals posted on the blackboard. In this scenario the KS might never post a single sub-goal onto the blackboard, merely offering solutions to blackboard goals.

In our future work we wish to further investigate the trade-off between opportunism and relevancy of the blackboard data, specifically by examining the effect that *Rule Chaining*, with its inter-dependent antecedents, will have on the posting of sub-goals onto the blackboard. If a KS encapsulates its rule's antecedents then these will never be placed upon the blackboard as sub-goals. Our main concern is how this will effect the reasoning process. Since the other KSs are not aware of these potential sub-goals (which they may have instances of, and hence solutions too) they will never make a relevant contribution. Therefore, the overall potential solving ability of the system decreases, due to this unnecessary curtailment of the solution space. Conversely, it might be the case that these intermediate antecedents are not actually required/relevant at all and so by placing them as sub-goals on the blackboard a whole raft of irrelevant instance data (and consequential sub-goals) would placed upon the blackboard. This would be detrimental to the solving process as effort could be expended on non-relevant data.

4.5   CSP Solver KS

This KS allows us to perform constraint-based reasoning and attempts to solve the CSP goal posted on the blackboard. The constraints for the workgroup(s) are expressed using CIF/SWRL [13] – our Constraint Interchange Format (CIF), which is an RDF based extension of SWRL that allows us to express fully quantified constraints. These constraints are placed on the blackboard by the User KS when the workgroup is first defined. Since the goal of the AWB+B is to form workgroups that adhere to these specified constraints, this KS has the trigger:

i) Try to add a "solution" by using instance data already on the blackboard to perform CSP solving and assert the appropriate `hasMember` triples to the corresponding instance of the `Workgroup` class.

The triggering mechanism of this KS requires it to continually monitor the blackboard contents and attempt to provide a solution to the CSP. To improve efficiency, we decided that rather than attempting full blown CSP solving each cycle, the solver should perform the faster check of each of the constraints individually and only if they can all be satisfied, should it attempt the more difficult task of solving them combinatorially. If no solution can be found then this KS will simply not offer a contribution.

In our implementation the CSP solver is unique, in that it is the only KS that can post a solution to the `Workgroup` goal, initially posted onto the blackboard by the User KS. However, there is no restriction on the number of CSP solver KSs that could be used within the system. In our future work there is also the possibility of greater user interaction (via the User KS) w.r.t to acceptance or rejection of a solution. Here the user could ask the CSP Solver KS to contribute again (provided there are alternate solutions) or accept the current one.

5   The Controller

As the name suggests, the role of the Controller is to oversee the running of the system as a whole. In the initial blackboard systems, one of the main problems was the lack of direction or a statement of goals to focus the solving effort. The BB1 system [10] extended the blackboard architecture by adding a second blackboard to control the state of the problem, and so better direct the solving. So far we have talked about the contents of the blackboard as merely containing the solution. In actual fact, like BB1, the AWB+B blackboard is divided into two panels. The first panel is the Data Panel which holds the solution related information. In order to inhibit the actions of the KSs accessing this panel, there are a couple of safeguards in place. The Controller will not allow the goal of "instances of `<owl:Thing>`" to be placed onto the blackboard since this is *the* OWL super-class, this would result in *all* class (and sub-class) instances known by a KS being added onto the blackboard.

The second panel is the Tasklist Panel and is used, primarily, by the Controller to coordinate the actions of each KS by storing information about *what* each knowledge source can contribute, based on the current state of the black-board. Like the Data Panel, this is visible to all the KSs however, unlike the Data Panel, the KSs are allowed to add to this panel directly (but not remove items from it). The KSs add `TasklistItems` that describe the nature of any contribution they could offer. The Controller looks at the items on the Tasklist Panel and determines which KS is allowed to contribute. Once a `TasklistItem` has been actioned, the Controller removes it from the panel. This "request for contribution" and "make your contribution" sequence is applied using a Java interface, which each registered KS must implement and consists of the two method calls: `canContribute` and `makeContribution`. When a KS's `canContribute` method is called it first determines *what* it can contribute (as per the steps previously outlined) and then checks, in the following order, that its "current" proposed contribution is not on the blackboard already; has not been contributed previously by itself; and is not already on the Tasklist, i.e. already proposed by another KS. Only then is a `TasklistItem` created and added to the Tasklist Panel.

In our current implementation the Controller is relatively simple. After all the KSs have been registered, the system "cycles" over each one asking it to populate the Tasklist Panel. Next, the Controller examines the contents of the Tasklist and decides which items to action (by calling the appropriate `makeContribution` method of a KS). After actioning the appropriate `TasklistItems` on the Tasklist Panel, the Controller has the option of retaining tasks that have not been actioned, or removing any remaining items from the Tasklist completely. This is purely a housekeeping measure as it prevents redundant or "out of date" items remaining on the Tasklist Panel. Then the cycle begins again. If nothing new has been added to the Tasklist Panel after a complete cycle, it is assumed that none of the KSs can contribute further and so the CSP Solver KS is activated and attempts to find a solution. While this is relatively straightforward to implement, it is far from optimised. We plan to increase the intelligence of the Controller to further focus the problem solving, which should improve performance.

6   Future Direction

Currently, the CSP solver adopts a closed world reasoning model. Since the Semantic Web is open world, it seems logical to investigate the influencing and enabling factors for performing effective open world reasoning based upon closed world reasoners as well as the analysis and combination of constraints to solve the CSP. The importance of negation and negative information is argued by Analyti and Wagner in [1]. The difficulty here is that negation is only partially supported in OWL DL (via disjunction) but not at all in OWL Lite. This would require either the extension of OWL at the language level in much the same way as the RDF(s) extension suggested in [1]; or through the application of rules to explicitly state negative information (as described in [14]).

We plan to incorporate the *Local Closed World Assumption* (LCWA) [7,4] into the AWB+B, since this can be thought of as a compromise between both the open and closed world assumptions. The LCWA means that a query placed against a

Knowledge Base (KB) can be answered with *true, false* or *unknown*. For example, if we posed the query "Is *Person(x)* also a *Professor?*" against our KB, what answer would we get? With both assumptions, if the result *Professor(x)* or ¬*Professor(x)* exists in the knowledge base (either explicitly or via some derived means) then the result would be *true* or *false* as appropriate. However, if there is no explicit statement describing *x* as a *Professor* then in the open world assumption, the result would be *unknown* since we cannot prove this definitively either way. In the case of a closed world the result would be *false* – the assumption being made that if we do not know a fact for definite, then it is always regarded as *false*. Now, suppose we do know that there is only one *Professor* in the world – *Professor(y)* and, therefore it is not *Person(x)*. How could we guarantee that our query correctly returns *false*? With the closed world assumption this would already be the case, however with the open world assumption we would still have the value *unknown*. The only way to correct this error would be to state the fact ¬*Professor(?)* for the (potentially infinite) set of everything else in the world. The LCWA overcomes this problem by maintaining two databases of world information. The first contains the known facts describing the world. The second one contains metadata indicating what sets of facts in the first database can be regarded as closed (since it would be impossible to store a potentially infinite set of non-members). So, using our example above, the first database would contain the fact *Professor(y)* and the second one would contain *ClosedWorld(Professor)*. Using the query mechanism of the LCWA we could extend how data is contained within each KS and on the blackboard, whereby the result of a query is either *true, false* or *unknown*. This allows the option of creating a specific goal as an attempt at resolving an *unknown* that would otherwise have been regarded as a *false*.

This process should stop when we believe that the closed world problem is now complete enough to enable realistic problem solving. A closed collection of values is crucial since the problem solving we are attempting is that of a Finite Domain CSP. When a generated workgroup is "released" back onto the open Semantic Web, the composition will need some explanation as to the assumptions used in its creation (i.e. it has been created using negation as failure). Therefore we require an appropriate representation that would better enable someone else to reuse the data and to reason against further. For example, if a published workgroup is constrained to only contain *Students* but, on closer examination, one member is actually a *Lecturer* then this is a contradiction. By annotating the composition such that it is clear that it was constructed using a closed world, negation as failure, approach, a consumer may be more forgiving as their assumption would be the *Lecturer* was simply misclassified at the time of construction due to a lack of data.

7   Discussion and Conclusion

In this paper we have explained why we believe the blackboard architecture aligns itself well with the hybrid reasoning approach necessary for reasoning with Semantic Web data. An important issue we encountered was the inefficiency of the two stage "trigger" and "action" approach to KS interaction with the blackboard. The work involved for a KS to know if it is "triggerable" is comparable to that of making the actual contribution itself, which it may never be called upon by the controller to do. However, we believe the benefits of the blackboard architecture outweigh this shortcoming since the paradigm allows us to perform a mix of reasoning methods on instance data and we would argue that performance could be improved by committing more time to the development of the AWB+B to further optimise the triggering conditions.

There are also complexity issues to be considered with the Blackboard framework giving us a number of options on how to explore these in our future work. For example, what if a KS starts to perform reasoning that could take hours or days to complete? The architecture supports the addition or removal of KSs from the system with the only adverse effect being on quality of the results and so guards against the inefficiency of KSs – the overall process of controlling the problem solving remains with the Controller. For example, had we implemented an asynchronous version of the application, then a time-out mechanism could be added to the Controller, so if a KS takes an inordinate amount of time to respond it could just be ignored, allowing the rest of the system to continue.

We have also highlighted the importance of ensuring only *relevant* items are placed on the blackboard and how this effects the opportunism of the system. Since the blackboard system is attempting to centralise distributed SW data it does not want *all* the data available from each of the KSs; it is only interested in as small a subset of this as is possible in order to solve the CSP problem. It is the job of the Controller to ensure that this is the case, otherwise it may become intractable. Since we place a great deal of importance upon relevancy, the high level strategy of the controller is that of a goal driven (backward chaining) approach – in our case, the initial goal placed on the blackboard is to find a solution to a specified workgroup problem. In our future work there is the possibility of adopting a forward chaining approach, overseen by a suitable controlling strategy. We also believe there is scope for further investigation of complexity and scalability trade-offs (e.g. using multiple ontologies that require mapping, increasing the size of the dataset, etc) as well as the modification of the Controller strategy to enhance performance.

Acknowledgements. This work is supported under the Advanced Knowledge Technologies (AKT) IRC (EPSRC grant no. GR/N15764/01) comprising Aberdeen, Edinburgh, Sheffield, Southampton and the Open Universities. http://www.aktors.org

References

1. C. V. D. Anastasia Analyti, Grigoris Antoniou and G. Wagner. Negation and Negative Information in the W3C Resource Description Framework. *Annals of Mathematics, Computing & Teleinfomatics*, 1(2):25–34, 2004.
2. R. Brachman, V. Gilbert, and H. Levesque. An Essential Hybrid Reasoning System: Knowledge and Symbol Level Accounts of KRYPTON. In *The Ninth International Joint Conference on Artificial Intelligence (IJCAI-85)*, pages 532–539, Los Angeles, California, USA, 1985.

3. N. Carver and V. Lesser. The Evolution of Blackboard Control Architectures. CMPSCI Technical Report 92-71, Computer Science Department, Southern Illinois University, 1992.

4. P. Doherty, W. Lukaszewicz, and A. Szalas. Efficient Reasoning using the Local Closed-World Assumption. In *9th International Conference on Artificial Intelligence: Mehtodology, Systems, Applications*, 2000.

5. R. S. Engelmore and A. Terry. Structure and Function of the CRYSALIS System. In *The Sixth International Joint Conference on Artificial Intelligence (IJCAI79)*, pages 250–256, Tokyo, Japan, August 20-23 1979.

6. L. D. Erman, F. Hayes-Roth, V. R. Lesser, and D. R. Reddy. The Hearsay-II Speech-Understanding System: Integrating Knowledge to Resolve Uncertainty. *ACM Computing Surveys*, 12(2):213–253, 1980.

7. O. Etzioni, K. Golden, and D. Weld. Sound and Efficient Closed-World Reasoning for Planning. *Artificial Intelligence*, 89(1-2):113–148, January 1997.

8. E. A. Feigenbaum, H. P. Nii, J. J. Anton, and A. J. Rockmore. Signal-to-signal Transformation: HASP/SIAP Case Study. *AI Magazine*, 3(2):23–35, 1982.

9. S. Harris and N. Gibbins. 3store: Efficient Bulk RDF Storage. In *1st International Workshop on Practical and Scalable Semantic Systems (PSSS'03)*, pages 1–20, 2003.

10. B. Hayes-Roth. A Blackboard Architecture for Control. *Artificial Intelligence*, 26(3):251–321, 1985.

11. B. Hayes-Roth, F. Hayes-Roth, F. Rosenschien, and S. Cammarata. Modelling Planning as an Incremental, Opportunistic Process. In *The Sixth International Joint Conference on Artificial Intelligence (IJCAI79)*, pages 375–383, Tokyo, Japan, August 20-23 1979.

12. J. Hendler. Agents and the Semantic Web. *IEEE Intelligent Systems*, 16(2):30–37, March/April 2001.

13. C. McKenzie, A. Preece, and P. Gray. Extending SWRL to Express Fully-Quantified Constraints. In G. Antoniou and H. Boley, editors, *Rules and Rule Markup Languages for the Semantic Web (RuleML 2004)*, LNCS 3323, pages 139–154, Hiroshima, Japan, November 2004. Springer.

14. J. Mei, S. Liu, A. Yue, and Z. Lin. An Extension to OWL with General Rules. In G. Antoniou and H. Boley, editors, *Rules and Rule Markup Languages for the Semantic Web (RuleML 2004)*, LNCS 3323, pages 155–169, Hiroshima, Japan, November 2004. Springer.

15. H. P. Nii. Blackboard Systems: The Blackboard Model of Problem Solving and the Evolution of Blackboard Architectures. *AI Magazine*, 7(2):38–53, 1986.

16. N. Shadbolt, N. Gibbins, H. Glaser, S. Harris, and m. schraefel. CS AKTive Space, or How We Learned to Stop Worrying and Love the Semantic Web. *IEEE Intelligent Systems*, 19(3):41–47, 2004.

17. D. Tsarkov and I. Horrocks. DL Reasoner vs. First-Order Prover. In *2003 Description Logic Workshop (DL 2003)*, volume 81, pages 152–159. CEUR (http://ceur-ws.org/), 2003.

Effective and Efficient Data Access in the Versatile Web Query Language Xcerpt

Sacha Berger, François Bry, Tim Furche, Benedikt Linse,
and Andreas Schroeder

Institute for Informatics,University of Munich,
Oettingenstraße 67, 80538 München, Germany
http://pms.ifi.lmu.de/

Abstract. Access to Web data has become an integral part of many applications and services. In the past, such data has usually been accessed through human-tailored HTML interfaces. Nowadays, rich client interfaces in desktop applications or, increasingly, in browser-based clients ease data access and allow more complex client processing based on XML or RDF data retrieved through Web service interfaces. Convenient specifications of the data processing on the client and flexible, expressive service interfaces for data access become essential in this context. Web query languages such as XQuery, XSLT, SPARQL, or Xcerpt have been tailored specifically for such a setting: declarative and efficient access and processing of Web data. Xcerpt stands apart among these languages by its versatility, i.e., its ability to access not just one Web format but many. In this demonstration, two aspects of Xcerpt are illustrated in detail: The first part of the demonstration focuses on Xcerpt's pattern matching constructs and rules to enable effective and versatile data access. It uses a concrete practical use case from bibliography management to illustrate these language features. Xcerpt's visual companion language visXcerpt is used to provide an intuitive interface to both data and queries. The second part of the demonstration shows recent advancements in Xcerpt's implementation focusing on experimental evaluation of recent complexity results and optimization techniques, as well as scalability over a number of usage scenarios and input sizes.

1 Introduction

Web querying has received considerable attention from academia and industry culminating in the recent development of the W3C Web query languages XQuery and SPARQL. These main-stream languages, however, focus only on one of the different data formats available on the Web. Integration of data from different sources and in different formats becomes a daunting task that requires knowledge of several query languages and to overcome the impedance mismatch between the query paradigms in the different languages. Xcerpt [10,11] addresses this issue by garnering the entire language towards versatility in format, representation, and schema of the data, cf. [6]. It is a *semi-structured query language*, but very much unique among such languages (for an overview see [1]):

(1) In its use of a *graph data model*, it stands more closely to semi-structured query languages like Lorel than to recent mainstream XML query languages.

J.J. Alferes et al. (Eds.): PPSWR 2006, LNCS 4187, pp. 219–224, 2006.

(2) In its aim to address all *specificities of XML*, it resembles more mainstream XML query languages such as XSLT or XQuery.

(3) In using (slightly enriched) *patterns* (or templates or examples) of the sought-for data for querying, it resembles more the "query-by-example" para-digm [12] than mainstream XML query languages using navigational access.

(4) In offering a *consistent extension of XML*, it is able to incorporate access to data represented in richer data representation formats. Instances of such features are element content, where the order is irrelevant, and non-hierarchical relations.

(5) In providing (syntactical) extensions for querying, among others, RDF, Xcerpt becomes a *versatile query language*, cf. [6]. These extensions are currently under development and not implemented in the demonstration.

(6) In its strict separation of querying and construction in *rules*, it makes programs more readable and optimization over intermediary results feasible.

visXcerpt [3] is Xcerpt's visual companion language related to it in an unusual way: visXcerpt is a *visual* query language obtained by mere rendering of Xcerpt without changing the language constructs or the runtime system for query eval-uation. This rendering is mainly achieved via CSS styling of Xcerpt's constructs. The authors believe that this approach is promising, as it makes those languages easy to learn—and easy to develop. An extension of CSS useful for this kind of visual language design is illustrated in [7].

This demonstration is split in two parts: first the novel language constructs for versatile pattern matching and rule-based data integration are illustrated along a practical demonstrator application using visXcerpt. Xcerpt's core fea-tures, especially the pattern-oriented queries and answer-constructors, its rules or views, and its specific language constructs for incomplete specifications are emphasized in this application. It is demonstrated (a) how incomplete specifi-cations are essential for retrieving semi-structured data, (b) how access to both Web and Semantic Web data in the same query program is achieved and (c) how visXcerpt complements and integrates with Xcerpt. Special emphasis is placed on recent advancements in language constructs and concepts.

The second part of this demonstration focuses on the evaluation and opti-mization of Xcerpt queries. In particular, it shows experimental confirmation of recent complexity results for various Xcerpt subsets. Furthermore, an impres-sion of the effects of recent optimizations of complex queries involving negated or optional subterms is given.

The demonstration is based on and in the first part most similar to a previous demonstration of Xcerpt [2].

2   Part I: Language Features and visXcerpt

Setting of the Demonstrator

Excerpts from DBLP[1] and from a computer science taxonomy form the base for the scenario considered in the application. DBLP is a collection of bibliographic

---

[1] http://www.informatik.uni-trier.de/~ley/db/

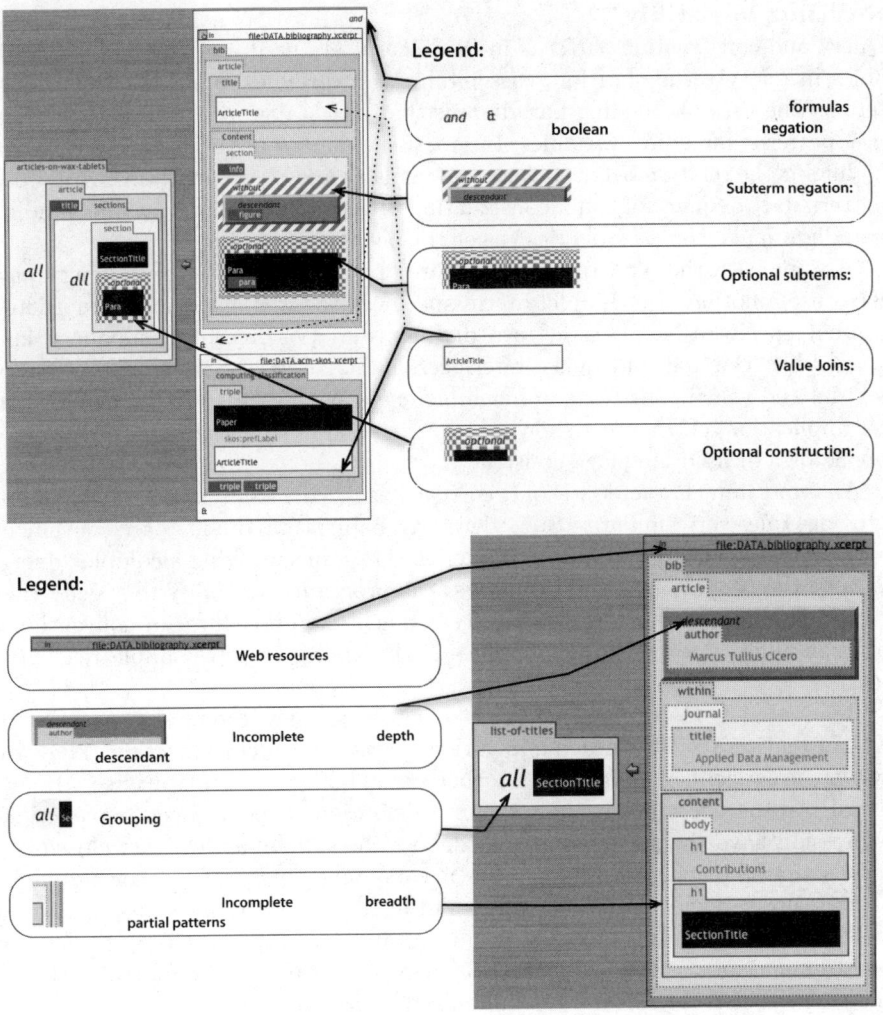

Fig. 1. Exemplary visXcerpt Query Patterns

entries for articles, books, etc. in the field of Computer Science. DBLP data is a
representative for standard Web data using a mixture of rather regular XML content combined with free form, HTML-like information. A small Computer Science
taxonomy has been built for the purpose of this demonstration. Very much in the
spirit of SKOS, this is a lightweight ontology based on RDF and RDFS. Combining such an ontology as metadata with the XML data of DBLP is a foundation for
applications such as community based classification and analysis of bibliographic
information using interrelations between researchers and research fields. Realizing
such applications is eased by using the integrated Web and semantic Web query
language (vis)Xcerpt that also allows reasoning using rules.

Realizing Versatility

Query and construction *patterns* in (vis)Xcerpt are used, both for binding variables in query terms and for reassembling the variables in so-called construct terms. The variable binding paradigm is that of Datalog: the programmer specifies patterns including variables. Interactive behavior of variables in visXcerpt highlights the relation between variables in query and construct terms. Arguably, pattern based querying and constructing together with the variable binding paradigm make complex queries easier to specify and read.

To cope with the semistructured nature of Web data, (vis)Xcerpt query patterns use a notion of incomplete term specifications with optional or unordered content specification. This feature distinguishes (vis)Xcerpt from query languages like Datalog and query interfaces like QBE [12]. Simple, yet powerful textual and visual constructs of incompleteness are presented in the demonstrator application, cf. Figure 1 showing two exemplary visual query patterns and a breakdown of used language constructs.

An important characteristic of (vis)Xcerpt is its rule-based nature: (vis)Xcerpt provides rules very similar to SQL views. Arguably, rules or views are convenient for a logical structuring of complex queries. Thus, in specifying a complex query, it eases the programming and improves the program readability to specify (abstract) rules as intermediate steps—very much like procedures in conventional programming. Another aspect of rules is the ability to solve simple reasoning tasks.

Referential transparency and answer closedness are essential properties of Xcerpt and visXcerpt, surfacing in various parts of the demonstration. They are two precisely defined traits of the rather vague notion of "declarativity". Referential transparency means that within a definition scope all occurrences of an expression have the same value, i.e., denote the same data. Answer-closedness means that replacing a sub-query in a compound query by a possible single answer always yields a syntactically valid query. Referentially transparent and answer-closed programs are easy to understand (and therefore easy to develop and to maintain), as the unavoidable shift in syntax from the data sought for to the query specifying this data is minimized.

3 Part II: Effectiveness and Efficiency

Currently, two main threads are considered in the Xcerpt project: (1) A careful review of language constructs is underway that aims at an improved effectiveness for query authoring, cf. [8]. Related is a better support for RDF, including proper handling of b-nodes in results and incomplete data specifications. Furthermore, a type system [4] for Xcerpt is under development that eases error detection and recovery. (2) Novel evaluation methods for Xcerpt, enabled by high-level query constructs, are being investigated. Xcerpt's pattern matching is based on simulation unification. An efficient algorithm of simulation unification that is competitive with current main-stream Web query languages both in worst-case complexity and practical performance is described in [5]. The demon-

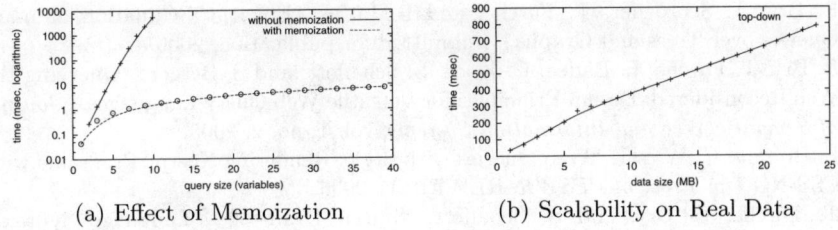

(a) Effect of Memoization   (b) Scalability on Real Data

Fig. 2. Experimental Evaluation of "Memoization Matrix" Approach

stration shows that the employed evaluation algorithm, called "memoization matrix" scales over a large set of query scenarios, empirically confirming the theoretical complexity derived in [5]. Figure 2 shows on the left hand the effect of the memoization on query evaluation time. The right hand side illustrates that the algorithm scales quite nicely over large amounts of data, assuming realistic queries and data (here the Nasa XML dataset from the University of Washington XML Repository[2] is used). Furthermore, the scalability of basic pattern queries over a broad range of data sizes is illustrated. Finally, the effect of several advanced query constructs is investigated. It is shown that constructs such as `optional` or qualified descendant do not only make queries easier to express and understand, but in many practical cases also more efficient to evaluate. Effects of optionality, injectivity, order, totality, and subterm negation are shown in detailed evaluations.

In further work, optimizations of the rule chaining algorithm are investigated, partially based on dependency analysis provided by the above mentioned type system. Furthermore, rule unfolding and algebraic optimization beyond intermediary construction similar to optimization of nested construction in languages such as XQuery is investigated, cf. [9] for details on the relation of the two.

Acknowledgments. This research has been funded by the European Commission and by the Swiss Federal Office for Education and Science within the 6th Framework Programme project REWERSE number 506779 (cf. `http://rewerse.net`).

References

1. J. Bailey, F. Bry, T. Furche, and S. Schaffert, "Web and Semantic Web Query Languages: A Survey," in *Reasoning Web Summer School 2005*, J. Maluszinsky and N. Eisinger, Eds. Springer-Verlag, 2005.
2. S. Berger, F. Bry, and T. Furche, "Xcerpt and visXcerpt: Integrating Web Querying," in *Proc. Plan-X*. 2006.
3. S. Berger, F. Bry, and S. Schaffert, "A Visual Language for Web Querying and Reasoning," in *Proc. PPSWR*, LNCS, vol. 2901. Springer-Verlag, 2003.
4. S. Berger, E. Coquery, W. Drabent, and A. Wilk, "Descriptive Typing Rules for Xcerpt," in *Proc. of PPSWR*. REWERSE, 2005.

---

[2] `http://www.cs.washington.edu/research/xmldatasets/`

5. F. Bry, A. Schroeder, T. Furche, and B. Linse, "Efficient Evaluation of n-ary Queries over Trees and Graphs," Submitted for publication, 2006.
6. F. Bry, T. Furche, L. Badea, C. Koch, S. Schaffert, and S. Berger, "Querying the Web Reconsidered: Design Principles for Versatile Web Query Languages," *Journal of Semantic Web and Information Systems*, vol. 1, no. 2, 2005.
7. F. Bry and C. Wieser, "Web Queries with Style: Rendering Xcerpt Programs with CSS-NG," in *Proc. of PPSWR*. REWERSE, 2006.
8. T. Furche, F. Bry, and S. Schaffert, "Initial Draft of a Language Syntax," REWERSE, Deliverable I4-D6, 2006.
9. B. Linse, "Automatic Translation between XQuery and Xcerpt," Diplomarbeit/Master thesis, Institute for Informatics, University of Munich, 2006.
10. S. Schaffert, "Xcerpt: A Rule-Based Query and Transformation Language for the Web," Dissertation/Ph.D. thesis, University of Munich, 2004.
11. S. Schaffert and F. Bry, "Querying the Web Reconsidered: A Practical Introduction to Xcerpt," in *Proc. Extreme Markup Languages*, 2004.
12. M. M. Zloof, "Query By Example: A Data Base Language," *IBM Systems Journal*, vol. 16, no. 4, pp. 324–343, 1977.

Web Queries with Style:
Rendering Xcerpt Programs with CSS^{NG}

François Bry and Christoph Wieser

University of Munich, Institute for Informatics
Oettingenstr. 67, 80538 München, Germany
bry@pms.ifi.lmu.de, wieser@cip.ifi.lmu.de
http://www.pms.ifi.lmu.de

Abstract. Styling and formatting of XML documents for various target media is often specified with the Cascading Style Sheet (CSS) language. An appealing feature of CSS is that it specifies formatting instructions using rather simple guarded rules. A limitation of CSS is that it focuses on *static* formatting rules. As a consequence scripting languages such as ECMA Script are used in practice for dynamic adaptation of formatting. CSS^{NG} is a novel extension of CSS 3, the newest version of CSS, introducing just a few rules for a dynamic rendering and for markup visualization. This limited extension of CSS 3 turns out to make possible a rather advanced visualization of programs. This article (1) introduces into the extensions of CSS^{NG} with respect to CSS 3, (2) describes a proof-of-concept prototype implementation of CSS^{NG}, and (3) demonstrates CSS^{NG} on Xcerpt query programs.

1   Introduction

CSS style sheets in the currently implemented version CSS 2.1 [6] have gained in importance, since the Web has become a mass medium. This language is used for a sophisticated rendering of semi-structured data especially expressed in XML [7]. CSS 3 [5], the newest version of CSS, is about to receive the status of a W3C recommendation, which is in fact a standard.

With the emerging trend from static to dynamic Web pages, the expressive power of the dynamic document rendering features in CSS 2.1 and in CSS 3 are not any longer sufficient. Sub-menus, for instance, which can be superimposed on a mouse click, are widespread on Web pages. They cannot be specified in CSS 3. Furthermore, CSS 2.1 and CSS 3 are often insufficient for a user-friendly rendering of XML documents with complex structures.

In practice, scripting languages supporting the DOM [12] interface to XML documents like ECMA Script [10] are used to obtain dynamic rendering features. In XHTML documents, for instance, scripts are rather often invoked in the context of an XHTML element by XHTML *intrinsic event* [1] attributes like onclick. As a consequence the styling specification is not separated from content like in CSS. That means that

J.J. Alferes et al. (Eds.): PPSWR 2006, LNCS 4187, pp. 225–236, 2006.

- dynamic styling via scripting is relatively complicated,
- the maintenance of styling programs is expensive, and
- applying dynamic styling to multiple documents is rather difficult

CSS^{NG} [16] is an extension of CSS 3. The strengths of this extension are the visualization of query languages like Xcerpt [14] as well as the visualization of RDF [13] graphs such as FOAF [8] definitions (see [16] for details on such Semantic Web applications). CSS^{NG} is a rather limited and conservative extension. Nonetheless CSS^{NG} makes it possible

- to specify dynamic styling,
- to generalize markup visualization, and
- to integrate the keyboard as input device.

The extension of CSS^{NG} allows for a *declarative* and, therefore, concise and quite simple specification of dynamic document rendering by comparison to query languages like XSLT [15] or scripting languages like ECMA Script [10].

2   CSS 3: A Brief Introduction

CSS 3 and its predecessors have been developed to simplify changes of the content as well as of the presentation of HTML and XML documents by separating content from presentation. The following rule (see Fig. 1) demonstrates a well-known *static* styling feature already introduced in CSS 1:

```
a          { text-decoration: underline; }
```

Fig. 1. Example: static rule (CSS 1)

The left-hand *head* of the CSS rule, a, selects HTML anchors. The so-called *declaration* on the right-hand side assigns the styling parameter to XML elements selected by the head of a CSS rule. In the example above it specifies that anchors are presented underlined as customary in Web pages to mark hyperlinks.

Also *dynamic* styling features are offered in CSS 3. The background color of an HTML anchor can be switched to yellow while the mouse cursor is hovering (:hover) over it:

```
a:hover  { background-color: yellow; }
```

Fig. 2. Example: dynamic rule (CSS 2)

3   How CSS^{NG} Extends CSS 3

Markup especially in XML documents often conveys application relevant information. Therefore, it might be useful to visualize it. However, CSS 2.1 and CSS 3 offer quite limited means for markup visualization. The following subsections 3.1 to 3.3 briefly introduce novel static CSS^{NG} rules mainly aiming at visualizing XML markup. Finally Section 3.4 introduces the rule-based interface for dynamic document styling. Full details on how CSS^{NG} extends CSS 3 can be found in [16].

CSS^{NG} rules such as specified in a file can be linked in an XML document via a so-called processing instructions (PI) or in the header of an XHTML document. Note that CSS^{NG} extensions introduced for XML elements apply also to XHTML elements.

3.1   Markup Insertion

CSS 3 allows the insertion of plain text specified in a CSS style sheet. The *pseudo-elements* ::before and ::after cause insertion of text before and after a selected XML or HTML element.

CSS^{NG} extends these pseudo-elements of CSS 3. In addition to inserting plain text in CSS 3, the CSS^{NG} functions element(NAME,ATTRIBUTES, VALUE) and attribute(NAME,VALUE) provide also inserting XML elements and attributes before and after XML elements. The following example inserts tabs (see Fig. 6) inscribed with element before each element in an XML document (The CSS^{NG} function element(NAME,VALUE) has only two arguments, if there are no attributes.):

```
<a title="Tab">elem</a>
                        is inserted before each XML element by the rule
*::before { content: element("a",
                             attribute("title","Tab"),
                             "elem") }
```

Fig. 3. Markup Insertion (CSS^{NG})

3.2   Markup Querying

CSS 3 provides the function attr(X) for querying the content of a known XML attribute X of an XML element. The name of an XML element and its XML attributes can not be queried. Implementing the markup visualization in Fig. 4 without generalized markup querying would mean one rule for every XML type like bib.

CSS^{NG} adds the function element-name() yielding the name of the currently selected XML element. Furthermore, one XML element can host several XML attributes. Therefore, CSS^{NG} offers *attribute rules* selecting XML

XML source   **Presentation**

1	`<bib>`
2	`  <book year="1994" id="42">`
3	`    <title>`
4	`      TCP/IP Illustrated`
5	`    </title>`
6	`    <author>`

```
bib
 book
  year 1994  id 42
   title
    TCP/IP Illustrated
   author
```

Fig. 4. XML document (left side) and rendering using CSS^{NG} (right side)

attributes instead of XML elements. The CSS^{NG} functions `attribute-name()` and `attribute-value()` query XML attribute names and values in the context of a selected XML element. The example in Fig. 5 implements a tab in front of each XML element listing the XML element name and all of the XML elements' attributes including their values as shown in Fig. 4.

XML source (see Fig. 4)

```
1   ... <book year ="1994" id ="42"> ... </book> ...
```

CSS^{NG} style sheet

```
1   *::before { content:
2     element("span",          element("span", element-name())
3                   *  { element("span", attribute-name() " "
4                                        attribute-value() )
5                   } )
6   }
```

intermediate representation

```
1   ... <span>
2         <span>book<span>
3           <span> year  1994</span>
4           <span> id  42</span>
5         </span>
6         <book year="1994" id="42"> ... </book> ...
```

Fig. 5. Generation of tabs. The presentation in Fig. 4 is obtained by rendering the intermediate representation using further CSS 3 means.

3.3   Depth-Dependent Styling

Styling depending on breadth is planned in CSS 3 [5]. Tables, for instance, can be styled using alternating background colors for each line. CSS^{NG} additionally offers styling depending on the depth of an XML element in an XML document: The pseudo-class `:nth-descendant(an+b)` restricts selections to XML elements having $an + b$ ancestors.

Fig. 6 demonstrates the visualization of a highly nested XML document with colors repeating on every sixth level. On the left side this rendering is realized using CSS^{NG} and alternatively using CSS 3. Thanks to its depth-dependent styling features, the upper CSS^{NG} style sheet needs only six rules. The CSS 3 style sheet below needs one rule for every level. Hence, styling in CSS 3 is possible up to a certain depth only as shown on the right side of Fig. 6 using the CSS 3 style sheet on the lower right side of Fig. 6. Such a styling would also be useful for applications such as the visualization of threads in a discussion forum.

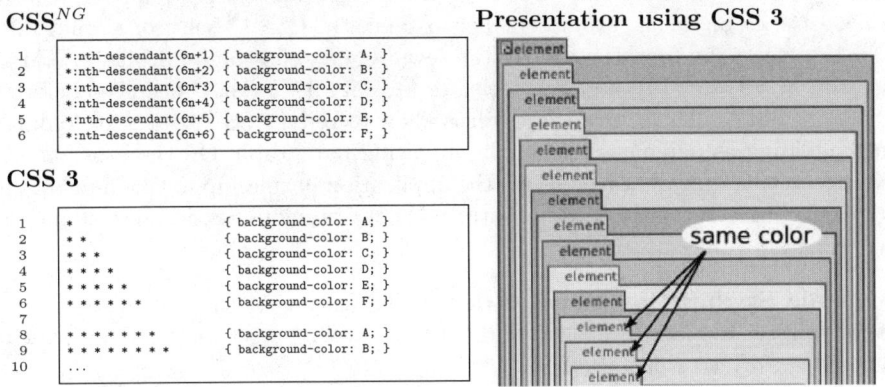

Fig. 6. Comparing Depth-dependent Styling using CSS^{NG} and CSS 3

3.4 Dynamic Styling Generalized

Dynamic styling in CSS 3 is limited to the dynamic pseudo-class `:hover`. This construct allows dynamic styling in the local context of the mouse cursor only as demonstrated in Section 2. This is not sufficient to implement a behavior like folding a tab as demonstrated in Section 8: when the mouse cursor moves away, the cursor does no longer hover over the selected XML element, and its tab would be automatically unfolded.

CSS^{NG} introduces dynamic pseudo-classes for *all* HTML intrinsic events [1] such as `onclick` or `onkeypress` (see [16] for sample applications). Instead of using HTML intrinsic event attributes like for scripting languages, CSS^{NG} allows a standalone specification of dynamic styling in separate CSS^{NG} files that can be applied for multiple documents. The following example in Fig. 7 shows a rather simple dynamic CSS^{NG} rule.

The rule in Fig. 7 implements an adaptive hyperlink. After 10 clicks on the hyperlink the background color changes to green meaning that the hyperlink on the Web page is frequented by the user.

```
a:onclick(10) { background-color: green; }
```

Fig. 7. Dynamic Styling (CSS^{NG})

This extension makes it possible to apply dynamic styling on different sections of an XML document at the same time. For instance if two hyperlinks were clicked ten times in a Web page, both will be presented with different background colors.

Similar extensions using HTML intrinsic events have been already proposed by the W3C (see Section 7). The following paragraphs introduce to novel capabilities of CSS^{NG}:

Recurrence Patterns. All CSS^{NG} dynamic pseudo classes support *recurrence patterns*, an+b, as parameters. For instance the CSS^{NG} selector *:onclick (3n+1) detects the first, the fourth, the seventh, etc. click on an arbitrary XML element. More generally, a CSS^{NG} selector fires, if $an + b$ events occurred before.

On one hand such recurrence patterns allow to reuse CSS^{NG} rules for folding and unfolding as demonstrated in the following paragraph. On the other hand recurrence patterns allow to "delay" the application of rules up until a number of events, for instance clicks, as demonstrated in the previous Section (see adaptive hyperlink above).

Dynamic Styling Combined. A noticeable feature of the (novel) dynamic pseudo-classes of CSS^{NG} is their compatibility with CSS 3 *combinators*, which allow to specify tree patterns.

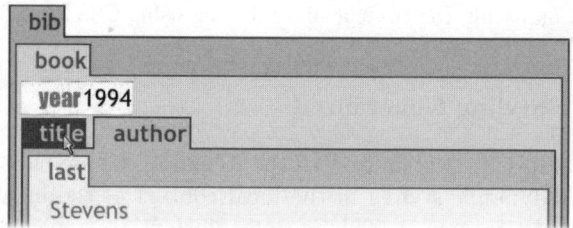

Fig. 8. Folded visualization of an XML element `title`. The corresponding unfolded example is shown in Fig. 4.

A CSS 3 selector is an alternating sequence of so-called *simple selectors* (already informally introduced in Section 2) and combinators. For instance, the combinator + means that the simple selector on its left side must be a preceding sibling of the simple selector on the righthand side. The CSS declaration (in curly braces) is only applied to the XML element matched by the right simple selector.

The following example (see Fig. 9) implements *alternating folding and unfolding* for the visualization of arbitrary (simple selector *) XML elements (see

Fig. 8). A click on a tab of a visualized XML element like $\boxed{\texttt{title}}$ folds its visualization. Another click on a tab unfolds it (see $\boxed{\texttt{title}}$ in Fig. 4):

1	`tab:onclick(2n+1) + * {display:none}`	*Fold on odd number of clicks.*
2	`tab:onclick(2n+2) + * {display:block}`	*Unfold on even number of clicks.*

Fig. 9. Combined dynamic styling in CSS^{NG} (rendering in Fig. 8)

In the example above, the lefthand *selector* of the first CSS^{NG} rule above is composed of the two *simple selectors* `tab:onclick(2n+1)` and `*` combined with the CSS 3 combinator, `+`. The visualization of an XML element matched by the simple selector `*` disappears, if a mouse click was performed on its preceding sibling XML element, while its tab stays visible.

Structure-Independent Styling. A static CSS 3 styling rule is applied to all XML elements matching its selector. A dynamic CSS 3 styling rule is applied only to XML elements being in the context of an input device such as an XML element laying under the mouse cursor. CSS^{NG} abolishes this restriction and allows (novel) so-called *monorama* and *panorama* selections as demonstrated in Fig. 14. The `Author` element on the left side is highlighted, while the mouse cursor is hovering over the `Author` element on the right side (see Fig. 10).

1	`Author                 { background-color: black; }`
2	`Author:hover ? Author { background-color: white; }`

Fig. 10. Highlighting of Xcerpt variables

The CSS 3 rule in line 1 defines the standard background black for XML `Author` elements. In line 2 the CSS^{NG} combinator `?`, called *if*, is applied as follows: If an XML `Author` element is hovered in an XML document, set the background color of all XML `Author` elements to white.

4   System Architecture of the Prototype

The CSS^{NG} extension of CSS 3 is planned and implemented for proving the concept of CSS^{NG}. Therefore we draw on established components for getting a transparent and easily scalable prototype instead of implementing a high-performance extension of a single Web browser.

This system compiles XHTML as well as XML 'Input Documents' according to rules in 'CSS^{NG} style sheets' for rendering in standard Web browsers such as Mozilla Firefox[1] or MS Internet Explorer[2].

---

[1] http://www.mozilla.com/firefox/

[2] http://www.microsoft.com/windows/ie/default.mspx

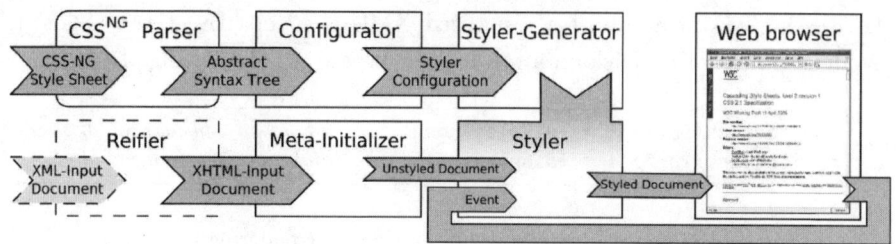

Fig. 11. CSS^{NG} styling of an X(HT)ML document and rendering

The upper row in Fig. 11 manages the compilation of an input 'CSS^{NG} Style Sheet' to a 'Styler' (see Section 4.1 for details). On the lower row, this 'Styler' is responsible for compiling a preprocessed (see Input Preprocessing below) 'XML input document' to a 'Styled Document' that can be rendered by the Web browser. All further *dynamic* styling activities such as triggered by mouse clicks in a Web browser window update meta-data of the 'Styled Document'. Changes on these meta-data are evaluated by the 'Styler' and are finally rendered by a Web browser.

4.1 Styler Generation

On the upper row (see Fig. 11), the 'CSS^{NG} style sheet' is parsed resulting in an 'Abstract Syntax Tree' (AST), which is based on a slightly extended Grammar of CSS 2.1 [6]. In a next step the 'Configurator' condenses the 'AST' to a human readable 'Styler Configuration'. Finally, this configuration is implemented by a 'Styler-Generator' yielding the 'Styler'.

4.2 Input Preprocessing

Since many of the current Web browsers do not offer standard event APIs for XML documents, we transform 'XML Input Documents' to get 'XHTML Input Documents'[3] as demonstrated in the following table (see Fig. 12). The XML markup on the left side is expressed using XHTML markup exclusively on the right side. (**XHTML input documents** can be initialized directly without reification.)

Source XML:	XML as XHTML:

`<workshop>`
`  PPSWR 2006`
`</workshop>`
	`<div>`
	`  <span class="element">workshop</span>`
	`  PPSWR 2006`
	`</div>`

Fig. 12. Expressing XML (left side) using XHTML (right side)

The 'Meta-Initializer' installs listeners as well as histories for relevant XHTML elements. An XHTML element is called dynamically relevant with respect to the **CSS^{NG} Style Sheet**, if a dynamic rule (see Dynamic Styling) defines its styling.

---

[3] This transformation is called reification.

5 Proof-of-Concept Implementation

The main principles of the proof-of-concept implementation are

- drawing on Web standards for
- gaining platform independency and
- reducing implementation effort.

Therefore all data formats and transformations (see Fig. 11) except **CSS^{NG} Parser** are based on W3C standards. Since the CSS 2.1 grammar [6] is specified in extended Yacc and Flex syntax, the Yacc parser and the Flex lexical scanner are used to transform **CSS^{NG} style sheets** into XML format (there are no W3C standards for this kind of transformation). All other transformations are implemented as XSL Transformations [15].

The **Styler** is the heart of the system. It processes all XHTML elements in the document tree of an **(Un)styled Document** recursively. Each XHTML element passes through one test for each CSS^{NG} rule in a CSS^{NG} style sheet. If a test succeeds, the XHTML `style` attribute of the current XHTML element is modified. The tests are implemented in XPath [9]. Since tests are executed from the perspective of each XML element, CSS^{NG} selectors need to be translated to XPath selecting XML elements in reverse direction as demonstrated in the following example (see Fig. 13):

CSS^{NG}   **XPath**

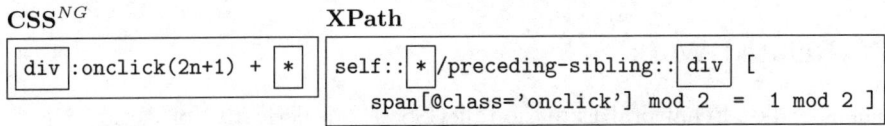

Fig. 13. Translation of CSS Selectos in XPath (CSS^{NG})

6 Proof-of-Concept Application: Rendering of Xcerpt Programs

CSS^{NG} can be applied to implement query visualization as textual query rendering as shown in Fig. 14. Here, the viewer of the visual interface visXcerpt [3] [4] for the XML query and transformation language Xcerpt [14] is re-implemented by only a few CSS^{NG} rules (131 lines of code). It is worth stressing that

- the original implementation of visXcerpt (ECMA Script, XSLT, and Python) is much longer (2060 lines of code) and much more complex,
- CSS^{NG} is a high level styling language applicable not only to visualize Xcerpt programs but more generally any XML document,
- specifying advanced visual features using CSS^{NG} does not require programming skills as required by ECMA script
- but instead offers much more limited programming capabilities sufficient for styling using CSS.

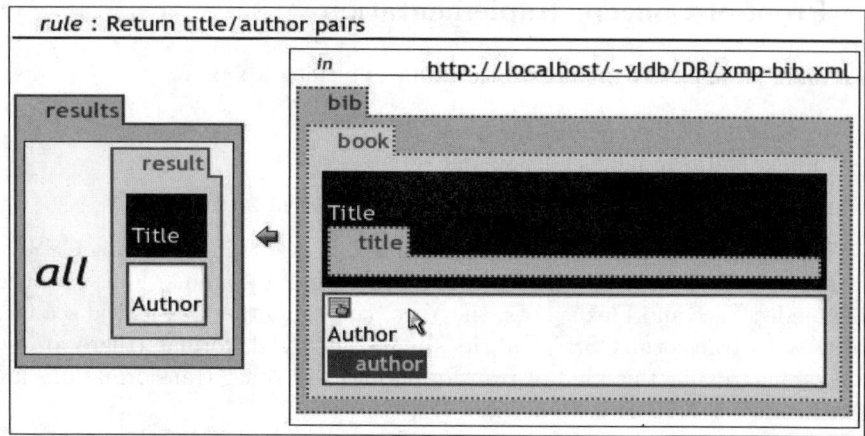

Fig. 14. Query Visualization as Textual Query Rendering. All occurrences (*panorama*) of `Author` are highlighted by white background color.

The example above demonstrates highlighting of Xcerpt variables having the same name: All occurrences of the Xcerpt variable `Author` are highlighted because the mouse cursor is hovering over one occurrence, while Xcerpt variables named `Title` stay black. We refer to [16] for further examples of CSS^{NG} applications.

7   Related Work

The so-called Behavioral Extension of CSS [11], a derivative of Action Sheets [2], is a proposal for extending CSS toward dynamic styling features. The main idea is to separate scripts from content using the selector mechanism of CSS. The approach draws on scripting languages for implementing dynamic styling. The Behavioral Extension of CSS specifies events in the declaration of the rule.

Behavioral Extension of CSS   **CSS**^{NG}

```
1    .Rollover {
2       border      : thin solid blue;
3       onmouseover: "this.src=
4          this.getAttribute('oversrc');
5          this.style.borderColor= 'red';
6          statusText.data=
7             this.getAttribute('status');"
8       onmouseout : "this.src=
9          this.getAttribute('outsrc');
10         this.style.borderColor= 'blue';
11         statusText.data= '';" }
```

```
1    .Rollover {
2       border:thin solid blue;}
3    .Rollover:onmouseover {
4       borderColor:red; }
5    .Rollover:onmouseout {
6       borderColor:blue; }
```

Fig. 15. Comparison of the Behavioral Extension of CSS and CSS^{NG}

Rather simple dynamic tree patterns of CSS^{NG}, as demonstrated in Section 3.4, can only be simulated in the Behavioral Extension of CSS using rather complicated scripts. The following use case (see Fig. 15) of Behavioral Extension of CSS is taken from the working draft of the W3C:

The right side of the example above shows a CSS^{NG} style sheet that re-implements the style sheet implemented with the Behavioral Extension of CSS on the left side. This example demonstrates how scripting, which is also possible in CSS^{NG} via insertion of markup, can be avoided in many use cases (see [16] for more use cases).

8   Conclusion

In this article we presented how CSS^{NG} extends CSS 3 toward dynamic styling features and markup visualization. As shown in Section 6, CSS^{NG} allows program visualization of Xcerpt programs as textual program rendering. However we believe that CSS^{NG} allows generic visualizations of programming languages. Such visualizations realized as textual document rendering (see Fig. 14) could help making visual programming more widespread than today because the huge quantity of tools for textual programming languages can still be used. To the best of our knowledge further approaches of visual languages never allow visual and textual programming as well.

Acknowledgments

This research has been funded by the European Commission and by the Swiss Federal Office for Education and Science within the 6th Framework Programme project REWERSE number 506779 (cf. http://rewerse.net).

References

1. S. Adler, A. Berglund, J. Caruso, S. Deach, T. Graham, P. Grosso, E. Gutentag, A. Milowski, S. Parnell, J. Richman, and S. Zilles. *HTML 4.01*. W3C, 1999.
2. V. Apparao, B. Eich, R. Guha, and N. Ranjan. *Action Sheets: A Modular Way of Defining Behavior for XML and HTML*. W3C, 1998.
3. S. Berger. Conception of a Graphical Interface for Querying XML. Diploma thesis, Institute for Informatics, LMU, Munich, 2003.
4. S. Berger, F. Bry, S. Schaffert, and C. Wieser. Xcerpt and visXcerpt: From Pattern-Based to Visual Querying of XML and Semistructured Data. In *Proceedings of 29th Intl. Conference on Very Large Databases*, 2003.
5. B. Bos. *Cascading Style Sheets Under Construction*. W3C, 2005.
6. B. Bos, H. W. Lie, C. Lilley, and I. Jacobs. *Cascading Style Sheets*. W3C, 1998.
7. T. Bray, J. Paoli, C. M. Sperberg-McQueen, and E. Maler. *Extensible Markup Language (XML) 1.0, 2nd Edition*. W3C, 2000.
8. D. Brickley and L. Miller. FOAF Vocabulary Specification, 2005.
9. J. Clark and S. DeRose. *XML Path Language (XPath) Version 1.0*. W3C, 1999.

10. ECMA. *Standard ECMA-262, ECMAScript Language Specification*, 1999.
11. V. A. et al. *Behavioral Extensions to CSS*. W3C, 1999.
12. A. L. Hors, P. L. Hégaret, L. Wood, G. Nicol, J. Robie, M. Champion, and S. Byrne. *Document Object Model (DOM) Level 2 Core Specification*. W3C, 2000.
13. O. Lassila and R. R. Swick. *Resource Description Framework (RDF)*. W3C, 1999.
14. S. Schaffert and F. Bry. Querying the Web Reconsidered: A Practical Introduction to Xcerpt. In *Proc. of Extreme Markup Languages*, 2004.
15. W3C. *Extensible Stylesheet Language (XSL) 1.0*, 2001.
16. C. Wieser. CSS^{NG}: An Extension of the Cascading Styles Sheets Language (CSS) with Dynamic Document Rendering Features. Diploma thesis, Institute for Informatics, LMU, Munich, 2006. http://www.pms.ifi.lmu.de/publikationen/.

Information Gathering in a Dynamic World

Thomas Hornung, Kai Simon, and Georg Lausen

Institute of Computer Science, Albert-Ludwigs University Freiburg, Germany
{hornungt, ksimon, lausen}@informatik.uni-freiburg.de

Abstract. Web resources with constantly fluctuating content, such as virtual market places, are becoming more and more relevant as information resources. Classic search engines, unfortunately, crawl and index the Web in sporadic intervals and therefore rely on outdated information. In this paper we present OntoGather, a framework based on ontology-driven inferences on dynamically gathered annotated instances from the Web, which consists of two main components: the Web data-extraction and annotation system ViPER and the deductive object-oriented database system Florid.

1 Introduction

Classic search engines (e.g. Google) crawl the Web in intervals and build up indexes from vast amounts of data to be able to answer user queries within a reasonable time frame. This was (and still is) well-suited for static Web pages that remain stable for a longer period of time, but today many resources on the Web are in constant flux. Prominent examples for this are virtual market places or real-time information systems, e.g. stock-exchange price services. The underlying volatile nature of the aforementioned domains necessitates a dynamic approach to support user queries of the form *what is the cheapest price for an IXUS digital camera (at the moment)?*

To solve this problem we propose an approach that relies on dynamic integration of information sources which are accessed at query time. The core of our system is Florid [1], a deductive object-oriented database system based on F-Logic [2], which operates on top of a domain-specific background ontology. It serves as inference engine used for Web resource selection and evaluates a user query on up-to-the-minute information. In this paper we deal with information extracted from HTML pages with the aid of a wrapper tool. Web resources that can be accessed via Web Service interfaces, such as WSDL APIs or RSS feeds have not been considered yet, but can be easily integrated into our system. Wrapper tools range from semi-automatic approaches, such as LIXTO [3], to fully-automatic. In our scenario a fully-automatic approach is most suitable, because the wrapper generation and maintenance effort is negligible, which suits the requirements of our dynamic world scenario best. Therefore we use our fully-automatic extraction system ViPER [4], that is able to extract up-to-date information from arbitrary HTML pages consisting of data records, which have a similar structure.

J.J. Alferes et al. (Eds.): PPSWR 2006, LNCS 4187, pp. 237–241, 2006.

The paper is structured as follows: In section 2 we present our extraction and integration system ViPER. Next we describe the underlying background ontology in section 3. The section 4 presents the main components by an example. Finally we conclude in section 5 and give an outlook in section 6.

2   Information Integration

Aiming at a robust, fast and extensible information system we opt for our fully-automatic wrapper extraction tool named ViPER (**Vi**sual **P**erception-based **E**xtraction of **R**ecords). ViPER is able to extract and discriminate with high accuracy the relevance of different repetitive Web information content with respect to the user's *visual* perception of a single Web page. After ViPER has identified the most relevant *data region* the tool generates a *pattern* (extraction rule), matching similar *data records*. These data records can usually be found in static Web catalogs as well as dynamic Web pages. Since these sites are often filled with information from back-end databases by predefined templates or server-side scripts, the extraction process can be seen as reverse engineering on the basis of materialized database views which have been published in HTML pages.

3   Resource Ontology

In the OntoGather system, we expect our information sources to be organized in a domain-specific ontology. This ontology initially contains meta-information about accessible Web resources, which can be referenced by unique resource ids resolved by ViPER into Web URLs. The ontology in principle could be given in any kind of formalism, e.g. OWL. Since we are particularly interested in answering queries, we have chosen F-Logic where we can specify the background ontology and the queries themselves in the same language. To further illustrate this point, we use the following running example:

```
top[resourceID⇒integer; name⇒string].
product :: top[price⇒float].
...
digital_camera :: product[model⇒string; resolution⇒integer].    (3.1)
ixus :: digital_camera[name•↠"IXUS"; resourceID↠{23, 42}].
canon :: digital_camera[name•↠"CANON"; resourceID↠{12, 23}].
```

Example (3.1) shows an excerpt of a simple product ontology. The first expression defines the concept `top` with the *multi-valued* method `resourceID` and the *functional* method `name` via their signatures. These signature definitions are inherited to every instance and subclass. The second expression declares `product` to be a *subclass* of top with the additional functional method `price`. The third expression introduces the class `digital_camera` which has `ixus` and `canon` as subclasses (expression four and five), that provide an implementation of the methods `name` and `resourceID`. The method `name` has been declared to be inheritable, therefore all instances of `ixus` and `canon` will have the result of the method `name` set to "IXUS" or "CANON", respectively.

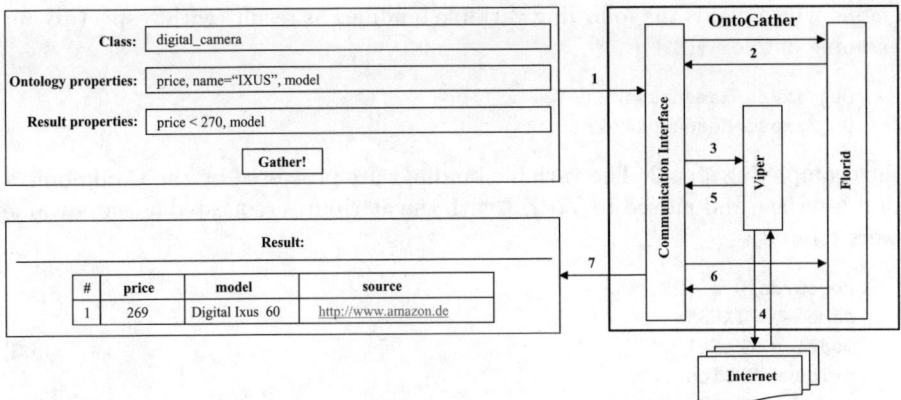

Fig. 1. OntoGather system overview

4   OntoGather by Example

Our framework is depicted in figure 1, which describes the processing of a query in seven steps. On the upper left part we see the user interface, which offers three form fields to specify a request: the field entitled "Class" narrows down the search area to a specific subpart of the ontology. The "Ontology properties" field selects the required attributes the class of interest has to provide, where it is possible to select a value (for instance name="IXUS") to further restrict possible candidates. The "Result properties" field lists the desired output attributes with the constraints that have to hold. The request in figure 1 asks for products falling in the digital camera subpart of the ontology, which provide information on price, model and name, where name has to be "IXUS". Finally the result is restricted to all models having a price lower than 270. To allow most users an intuitive use of the system the interface is held simple, but support for automatic inference of remaining possible attributes and graphical selection of subparts of the graph are envisioned. Furthermore we are looking into ways to allow for more complex queries, e.g. where attributes of two distinct classes (analog and digital cameras for instance) can be requested.

After the user starts her request, the contents of the form fields are sent to the Communication Interface, that acts as a negotiation layer translating requests between ViPER and Florid (step 1). The Communication Interface generates a Florid query based on the the provided information, asking for all resources that can contribute to the answer:

$$
\text{Obj :: digital\_camera[price} \Rightarrow \text{\_Price; model} \Rightarrow \text{\_Model;} \\
\text{name} \bullet \rightarrow \text{"IXUS"; resourceID} \rightarrow\!\!\!\rightarrow \text{Resources].} \tag{4.1}
$$

In query (4.1) strings starting with a capital letter are treated as variables, where strings preceded by an underscore are anonymous variables, whose bindings are not returned in the answer. The result value for the method **name** is used as restriction on the possible answer set. We forward this request to the Florid engine which yields the following variable bindings as result (with respect to our example ontology (3.1)):

```
Obj/ixus, Resources/23
Obj/ixus, Resources/42
```
(4.2)

thus completing step 2. The variable bindings are processed by the Communication Interface and passed to ViPER with the attributes requested as name-value pairs (step 3):

```
resourceID = {23, 42}
name = !"IXUS"
model = ?Model
price = ?Price
resource = ?Resource
```
(4.3)

Every string that occurs in the input is marked with an exclamation mark (!), to indicate ViPER that it can be used for query generation to fill out search forms. On the other side, variables marked with a question mark (?) indicate the annotated data items we are interested in. ViPER internally resolves the resource ids to valid Web URLs and extracts the desired data records. With a new extension of ViPER we are also able to annotate these data records according to our background ontology (step 4). The resulting bindings are returned to the Communication Interface with the resource ids resolved to URLs (step 5):

```
[resourceID = 23
 resource = "http://www.amazon.de",
 name = "IXUS",
 model = "Digital Ixus 60",
 price = 269],
[resourceID = 42
 resource = "http://www.mediaonline.de",
 name = "IXUS",
 model = "Digital Ixus 700",
 price = 295]
```
(4.4)

In listing (4.4) each resource only contributes one result, but generally multiple results per resource are usual. These results are converted to F-Logic facts and inserted into our ontology.

```
...
ixus[name→"IXUS"; resourceID↠{23, 42}].
ixus_1 : ixus[model→"Digital Ixus 60"; price→269;
              resource→"http://www.amazon.de"].
ixus_2 : ixus[model→"Digital Ixus 700"; price→295;
              resource→"http://www.mediaonline.de"].
```
(4.5)

Listing (4.5) shows the final state of our ontology instantiated with the extracted data items. The new instances have been inserted into the fact base as instances of the respective class, i.e. ixus, inheriting the name attribute from it with the value set to "IXUS". The instances could either be stored for later time series analysis or the ontology will be reset to its initial state after having finished the query.

Now we are able to select the attributes of interest, taking into account the information from the "Result properties" form field in figure 1, resulting in the following F-Logic query (step 6):

$$\_Obj:ixus[price\rightarrow Price;\ model\rightarrow Model;$$
$$name\rightarrow"IXUS";\ resource\rightarrow\!\!\!\rightarrow Resources],\ Price\ <\ 270. \tag{4.6}$$

The Florid results are shown in listing (4.7) and are finally transformed into a tabular HTML representation, were we additionally list the resources that provided the data items (step 7).

$$Resources/http://www.amazon.de\,,$$
$$Price/269\,, \tag{4.7}$$
$$Model/"Digital\ Ixus\ 60"$$

5   Conclusion

We presented the OntoGather system, an ontology-based dynamic Web resource querying engine, that is geared towards the requirements of a dynamic world. Because of our resource preselection mechanism we are able to process a user query from a pool of different resources that we decide on at runtime. This is made possible by our fully-automatic Web data extraction system ViPER. Our main contributions are twofold: first the selection of the query-relevant resources and second the reasoning on fresh data items extracted and annotated by ViPER, which both happens at query time.

6   Outlook

Our future goals include time series analysis, which is explicitly supported by our object-centered approach, by aggregating the results of several user queries. This could be realized by introducing a method time_stamp to indicate the freshness of the information. Additionally including ECA rules might be an interesting topic while monitoring specific dynamic resources over a given time frame for an invariant query.

References

1. Frohn, J., Himmeröder, R., Kandzia, P.T., Lausen, G., Schlepphorst, C.: FLORID: A Prototype for F-Logic. In: ICDE'97, IEEE Computer Society (1997) 583
2. Kifer, M., Lausen, G., Wu, J.: Logical Foundations of Object-Oriented and Frame-Based Languages. J. ACM **42** (1995) 741–843
3. Baumgartner, R., Flesca, S., Gottlob, G.: Visual Web Information Extraction with Lixto. In: VLDB. (2001) 119–128
4. Simon, K., Lausen, G.: ViPER: Augmenting Automatic Information Extraction with Visual Perceptions. In: ACM CIKM'05, Bremen, GERMANY, ACM Press (2005) 381–388

Practice of Inductive Reasoning
on the Semantic Web:
A System for Semantic Web Mining

Francesca A. Lisi

Dipartimento di Informatica, Università degli Studi di Bari,
Via E. Orabona 4, I-70125 Bari, Italy
lisi@di.uniba.it

Abstract. Mining the layers of ontologies and rules provides an interesting testbed for inductive reasoning on the Semantic Web. Systems based on Inductive Logic Programming (ILP) could serve the purpose if they were more compliant with the standards of representation for ontologies and rules in the Semantic Web and/or interoperable with well-established tools for Ontological Engineering (OE) that support these standards. In this paper we present a middleware, $\mathcal{SW}$ING, that integrates the ILP system $\mathcal{AL}$-QuIn and the OE tool Protégé-2000 in order to enable Semantic Web Mining applications of $\mathcal{AL}$-QuIn. This showcase highlights practical issues of performing induction on the Semantic Web.

1 Introduction

Most of the effort spent by the community of Knowledge Representation and Reasoning (KR&R) in the Semantic Web area is currently concentrated on the *logical* layer. Indeed, whereas the mark-up language OWL for *ontologies* is already undergoing the standardization process at W3C, the debate around a unified language for *rules* is still ongoing. Proposals like SWRL[1] extend OWL with constructs inspired to Horn clauses in order to meet the primary requirement of the logical layer: 'to build rules on top of ontologies'. Since the design of OWL has been based on Description Logics (DLs) [2] (more precisely on the DL $\mathcal{SHIQ}$ [11]), SWRL is intended to bridge the notorious expressiveness gap between DLs and Horn clausal logic [5] in a way that is similar in the spirit to hybridization in KR&R systems such as $\mathcal{AL}$-log [7]. In fact, $\mathcal{AL}$-log has been very recently mentioned as the blueprint for *well-founded* Semantic Web rule mark-up languages because its underlying form of integration (called *safe*) assures semantic and computational advantages that SWRL - though more expressive than $\mathcal{AL}$-log - currently can not assure [26]. Also it has been adopted as the KR&R setting in a framework for learning Semantic Web rules [17] that resorts to the methodological apparatus of Inductive Logic Programming (ILP) [24]. The framework is general in the sense that it does not depend on the scope of induction (prediction/description). The ILP system $\mathcal{AL}$-QuIn [19,18] (a previous version is

---

[1] http://www.w3.org/Submission/SWRL/

J.J. Alferes et al. (Eds.): PPSWR 2006, LNCS 4187, pp. 242–256, 2006.

described in [20]) implements the framework in the case of characteristic induction, i.e. description. More precisely it supports a variant of the data mining task of frequent pattern discovery [23].

Semantic Web Mining [3] is a new application area which aims at combining the two areas of Semantic Web [4] and Web Mining [15] from a twofold perspective. On one hand, the new semantic structures in the Web can be exploited to improve the results of Web Mining. On the other hand, the results of Web Mining can be used for building the Semantic Web. Most work in Semantic Web Mining simply extends previous work to the new application context. E.g., Maedche and Staab [21] apply a well-known algorithm for association rule mining to discover conceptual relations from text. Also there is an increasing amount of work on mining the RDF/RDFSchema layer. E.g., Maedche and Zacharias [22] propose distance measures to cluster RDF-based metadata descriptions. Mining the layers of ontologies and rules provides an interesting testbed for inductive reasoning on the Semantic Web. ILP systems could serve the purpose if they were more compliant with the standards of representation for ontologies and rules in the Semantic Web and/or interoperable with well-established tools for Ontological Engineering (OE) [9], e.g. Protégé-2000 [25], that support these standards.

In this paper we present a middleware, $\mathcal{SWING}$, that integrates $\mathcal{AL}$-QuIn and Protégé-2000 in order to enable Semantic Web Mining applications of $\mathcal{AL}$-QuIn. This showcase highlights practical issues of performing induction on the Semantic Web.

The paper is structured as follows. Section 2 and 3 briefly introduce $\mathcal{AL}$-QuIn and Protégé-2000 respectively. Section 4 presents the middleware $\mathcal{SWING}$. Section 5 draws conclusions and outlines directions of future work.

2   The ILP System $\mathcal{AL}$-QuIn

In data mining a *pattern* is considered as an intensional description (expressed in a given language $\mathcal{L}$) of a subset of $\mathbf{r}$. The *support* of a pattern is the relative frequency of the pattern within $\mathbf{r}$ and is computed with the evaluation function *supp*. The task of *frequent pattern discovery* aims at the extraction of all *frequent* patterns, i.e. all patterns whose support exceeds a user-defined threshold of *minimum support*. The blueprint of most algorithms for frequent pattern discovery is the *levelwise search* [23]. It is based on the following assumption: If a generality order $\succeq$ for the language $\mathcal{L}$ of patterns can be found such that $\succeq$ is monotonic w.r.t. *supp*, then the resulting space $(\mathcal{L}, \succeq)$ can be searched breadth-first starting from the most general pattern in $\mathcal{L}$ and by alternating *candidate generation* and *candidate evaluation* phases. In particular, candidate generation consists of a refinement step followed by a pruning step. The former derives candidates for the current search level from patterns found frequent in the previous search level. The latter allows some infrequent patterns to be detected and discarded prior to evaluation thanks to the monotonicity of $\succeq$.

The ILP system $\mathcal{AL}$-QuIn ($\mathcal{AL}$-log QuEry INduction) [19,18] solves a variant of the frequent pattern discovery problem which takes concept hierarchies into

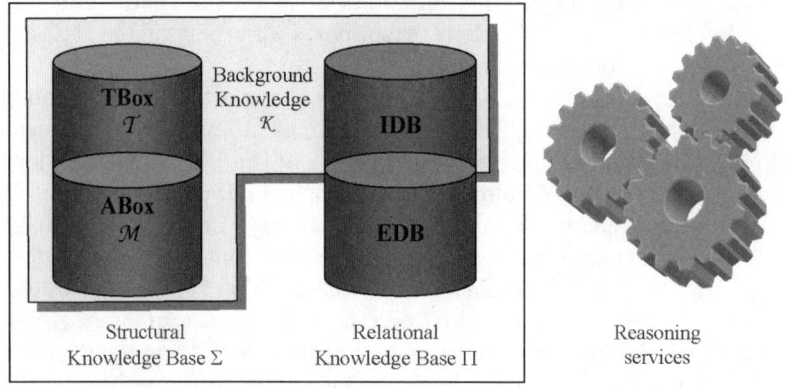

$\mathcal{AL}$-log Knowledge Base $\mathcal{B}$

Fig. 1. Organization of the hybrid knowledge bases used in $\mathcal{AL}$-QuIn

account during the discovery process, thus yielding descriptions of a data set **r** at multiple granularity levels up to a maximum level $maxG$. More formally, given

- a data set **r** including a taxonomy $\mathcal{T}$ where a reference concept C_{ref} and task-relevant concepts are designated,
- a multi-grained language $\{\mathcal{L}^l\}_{1 \leq l \leq maxG}$ of patterns
- a set $\{minsup^l\}_{1 \leq l \leq maxG}$ of minimum support thresholds

the problem of *frequent pattern discovery at l levels of description granularity*, $1 \leq l \leq maxG$, is to find the set $\mathcal{F}$ of all the patterns $P \in \mathcal{L}^l$ frequent in **r**, namely P's with support s such that (i) $s \geq minsup^l$ and (ii) all ancestors of P w.r.t. $\mathcal{T}$ are frequent. Note that a pattern Q is considered to be an ancestor of P if it is a coarser-grained version of P.

In $\mathcal{AL}$-QuIn the data set **r** is represented as an $\mathcal{AL}$-log knowledge base $\mathcal{B}$ and structured as illustrated in Figure 1. The structural subsystem Σ is based on $\mathcal{ALC}$ [27] and allows for the specification of knowledge in terms of classes (*concepts*), binary relations between classes (*roles*), and instances (*individuals*). In particular, the TBox $\mathcal{T}$ contains is-a relations between concepts (*axioms*) whereas the ABox $\mathcal{M}$ contains instance-of relations between individuals (resp. couples of individuals) and concepts (resp. roles) (*assertions*). The relational subsystem Π is based on an extended form of DATALOG [6] that is obtained by using $\mathcal{ALC}$ concept assertions essentially as type constraints on variables. The portion $\mathcal{K}$ of $\mathcal{B}$ which encompasses the whole Σ and the intensional part (IDB) of Π is considered as *background knowledge*. The extensional part of Π is partitioned into portions $\mathcal{A}_i$ each of which refers to an individual a_i of C_{ref}. The link between $\mathcal{A}_i$ and a_i is represented with the DATALOG literal $q(a_i)$. The pair $(q(a_i), \mathcal{A}_i)$ is called *observation*.

The language $\mathcal{L} = \{\mathcal{L}^l\}_{1 \leq l \leq maxG}$ of patterns allows for the generation of $\mathcal{AL}$-log unary conjunctive queries, called $\mathcal{O}$-queries. Given a reference concept

C_{ref}, an $\mathcal{O}$-query Q to an $\mathcal{AL}$-log knowledge base $\mathcal{B}$ is a (linked and connected)[2] constrained DATALOG clause of the form

$$Q = q(X) \leftarrow \alpha_1, \ldots, \alpha_m \& X : C_{ref}, \gamma_1, \ldots, \gamma_n$$

where X is the *distinguished variable* and the remaining variables occurring in the body of Q are the *existential variables*. Note that α_j, $1 \leq j \leq m$, is a DATALOG literal whereas γ_k, $1 \leq k \leq n$, is an assertion that constrains a variable already appearing in any of the α_j's to vary in the range of individuals of a concept defined in $\mathcal{B}$. The $\mathcal{O}$-query

$$Q_t = q(X) \leftarrow \& X : C_{ref}$$

is called *trivial* for $\mathcal{L}$ because it only contains the constraint for the *distinguished variable* X. Furthermore the language $\mathcal{L}$ is *multi-grained*, i.e. it contains expressions at multiple levels of description granularity. Indeed it is implicitly defined by a *declarative bias specification* which consists of a finite alphabet $\mathcal{A}$ of DATALOG predicate names and finite alphabets Γ^l (one for each level l of description granularity) of $\mathcal{ALC}$ concept names. Note that the α_i's are taken from $\mathcal{A}$ and γ_j's are taken from Γ^l. We impose $\mathcal{L}$ to be finite by specifying some bounds, mainly $maxD$ for the maximum depth of search and $maxG$ for the maximum level of granularity.

The *support* of an $\mathcal{O}$-query $Q \in \mathcal{L}^l$ w.r.t an $\mathcal{AL}$-log knowledge base $\mathcal{B}$ is defined as

$$supp(Q, \mathcal{B}) = |\ answerset(Q, \mathcal{B})\ |\ /\ |\ answerset(Q_t, \mathcal{B})\ |$$

where Q_t is the trivial $\mathcal{O}$-query for $\mathcal{L}$. The computation of support relies on query answering in $\mathcal{AL}$-log. Indeed, an *answer* to an $\mathcal{O}$-query Q is a ground substitution θ for the distinguished variable of Q. An answer θ to an $\mathcal{O}$-query Q is a *correct (resp. computed) answer* w.r.t. an $\mathcal{AL}$-log knowledge base $\mathcal{B}$ if there exists at least one correct (resp. computed) answer to $body(Q)\theta$ w.r.t. $\mathcal{B}$. Therefore proving that an $\mathcal{O}$-query Q covers an observation $(q(a_i), \mathcal{A}_i)$ w.r.t. $\mathcal{K}$ equals to proving that $\theta_i = \{X/a_i\}$ is a correct answer to Q w.r.t. $\mathcal{B}_i = \mathcal{K} \cup \mathcal{A}_i$.

The system $\mathcal{AL}$-QuIN implements the aforementioned levelwise search method for frequent pattern discovery. In particular, candidate patterns of a certain level k (called k-*patterns*) are obtained by refinement of the frequent patterns discovered at level $k - 1$. In $\mathcal{AL}$-QuIN patterns are ordered according to $\mathcal{B}$-subsumption (which has been proved to fulfill the abovementioned condition of monotonicity [20]). The search starts from the most general pattern in $\mathcal{L}$ and iterates through the generation-evaluation cycle for a number of times that is bounded with respect to both the granularity level l ($maxG$) and the depth level k ($maxD$).

Since $\mathcal{AL}$-QuIN is implemented with Prolog, the internal representation language in $\mathcal{AL}$-QuIN is a kind of DATALOG^{OI} [28], i.e. the subset of DATALOG$^{\neq}$ equipped with an equational theory that consists of the axioms of Clark's Equality Theory augmented with one rewriting rule that adds *inequality atoms* $s \neq t$ to

---

[2] For the definition of linkedness and connectedness see [24].

any $P \in \mathcal{L}$ for each pair (s, t) of distinct terms occurring in P. Note that concept assertions are rendered as *membership atoms*, e.g. $a : C$ becomes $c\_C(a)$.

3   The OE Tool Protégé-2000

Protégé-2000[3] [8] is the latest version of the Protégé line of tools, created by the Stanford Medical Informatics (SMI) group at Stanford University, USA. It has a community of thousands of users. Although the development of Protégé has historically been mainly driven by biomedical applications, the system is domain-independent and has been successfully used for many other application areas as well. Protégé-2000 is a Java-based standalone application to be installed and run in a local computer. The core of this application is the ontology editor. Like most other modeling tools, the architecture of Protégé-2000 is cleanly separated into a model part and a view part. Protégé-2000's model is the internal representation mechanism for ontologies and knowledge bases. Protégé-2000's view components provide a Graphical User Interface (GUI) to display and manipulate the underlying model.

Protégé-2000's model is based on a simple yet flexible metamodel [25], which is comparable to object-oriented and frame-based systems. It basically can represent ontologies consisting of classes, properties (*slots*), property characteristics (*facets* and *constraints*), and instances. Protégé-2000 provides an open Java API to query and manipulate models. An important strength of Protégé-2000 is that the Protégé-2000 metamodel itself is a Protégé-2000 ontology, with classes that represent classes, properties, and so on. For example, the default class in the Protege base system is called :STANDARD-CLASS, and has properties such as :NAME and :DIRECT-SUPERCLASSES. This structure of the metamodel enables easy extension and adaption to other representations.

Using the views of Protégé-2000's GUI, ontology designers basically create classes, assign properties to the classes, and then restrict the properties facets at certain classes. Using the resulting ontologies, Protégé-2000 is able to automatically generate user interfaces that support the creation of individuals (instances). For each class in the ontology, the system creates one form with editing components (*widgets*) for each property of the class. For example, for properties that can take single string values, the system would by default provide a text field widget. The generated forms can be further customized with Protégé-2000's form editor, where users can select alternative user interface widgets for their project. The user interface consists of panels (*tabs*) for editing classes, properties, forms and instances.

Protégé-2000 has an extensible architecture, i.e. an architecture that allows special-purpose extensions (aka *plug-ins*) to be easily integrated. These extensions usually perform functions not provided by the Protégé-2000 standard distribution (other types of visualization, new import and export formats, etc.), implement applications that use Protégé-2000 ontologies, or allow configuring

---

[3] The distribution of interest to this work is 3.0 (February 2005), freely available at http://protege.stanford.edu/ under the Mozilla open-source license.

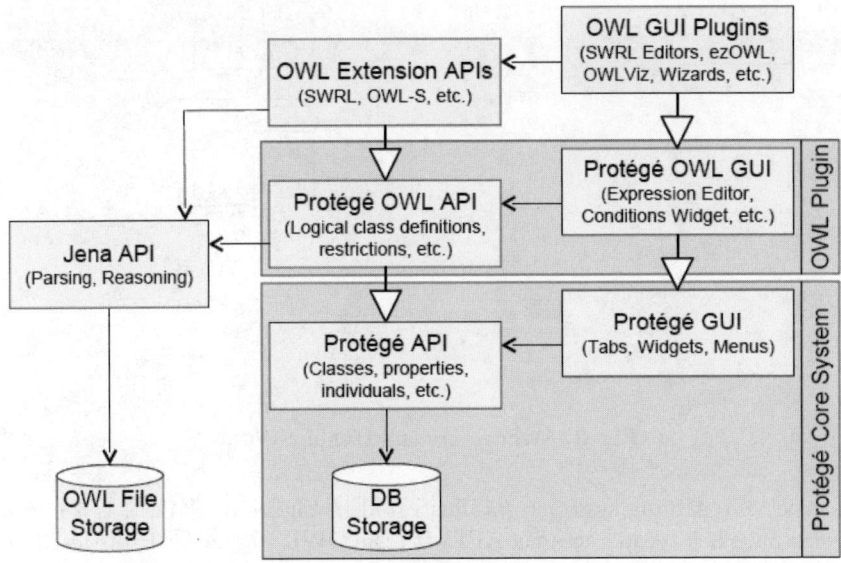

Fig. 2. Architecture of the OWL Plugin for Protégé-2000

the ontology editor. Most of these plug-ins are available in the Protégé-2000 Plug-in Library, where contributions from many different research groups can be found. One of the most popular in this library is the OWL Plugin [14].

As illustrated in Figure 2, the **OWL Plugin** extends the Protégé-2000 model and its API with classes to represent the OWL specification. In particular it supports RDF(S), OWL Lite, OWL DL (except for anonymous global class axioms, which need to be given a name by the user) and significant parts of OWL Full (including metaclasses). The OWL API basically encapsulates the internal mapping and thus shields the user from error-prone low-level access. Furthermore the OWL Plugin provides a comprehensive mapping between its extended API and the standard OWL parsing library Jena[4]. The presence of a secondary representation of an OWL ontology in terms of Jena objects means that the user is able to invoke arbitrary Jena-based services such as interfaces to classifiers, query languages, or visualization tools permanently. Based on the above mentioned metamodel and API extensions, the OWL Plugin provides several custom-tailored GUI components for OWL. Also it can directly access DL reasoners such as RACER [10]. Finally it can be further extended, e.g. to support OWL-based languages like SWRL.

4   The Middleware $\mathcal{SW}$ing

To enable Semantic Web Mining applications of $\mathcal{AL}$-QUIN we have developed a software component, $\mathcal{SW}$ING, that assists users of $\mathcal{AL}$-QUIN in the design of

---
[4] http://jena.sourceforge.net

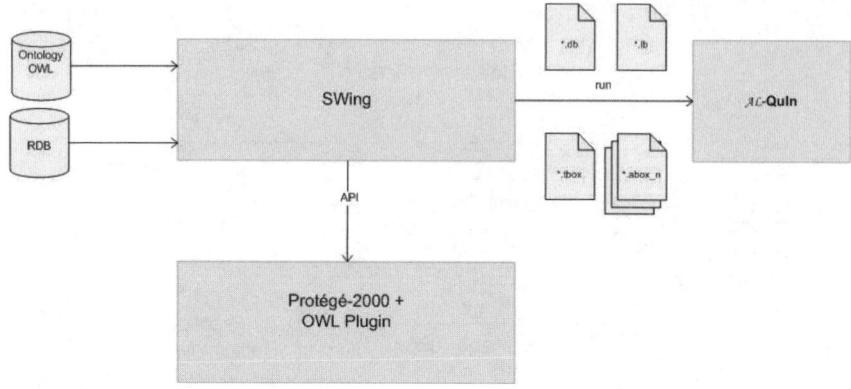

Fig. 3. Architecture and I/O of $\mathcal{SW}$ING

Semantic Web Mining sessions. As illustrated in Figure 3, $\mathcal{SW}$ING is a middle-ware because it interoperates via API with the OWL Plugin for Protégé-2000 to benefit from its facilities for browsing and reasoning on OWL ontologies.

Example 1. The screenshots reported in Figure 4, 5, 6 and 7 refer to a Semantic Web Mining session with $\mathcal{SW}$ING for the task of finding frequent patterns in the on-line CIA World Fact Book[5] (data set) that describe Middle East countries (reference concept) w.r.t. the religions believed and the languages spoken (task-relevant concepts) at three levels of granularity ($maxG = 3$). To this aim we define $\mathcal{L}_{\text{CIA}}$ as the set of $\mathcal{O}$-queries with $C_{ref} = \texttt{MiddleEastCountry}$ that can be generated from the alphabet $\mathcal{A} = \{\texttt{believes/2}, \texttt{speaks/2}\}$ of DATALOG binary predicate names, and the alphabets

$\Gamma^1 = \{\texttt{Language}, \texttt{Religion}\}$
$\Gamma^2 = \{\texttt{IndoEuropeanLanguage}, \ldots, \texttt{MonotheisticReligion}, \ldots\}$
$\Gamma^3 = \{\texttt{IndoIranianLanguage}, \ldots, \texttt{MuslimReligion}, \ldots\}$

of $\mathcal{ALC}$ concept names for $1 \leq l \leq 3$, up to $maxD = 5$. Examples of $\mathcal{O}$-queries in $\mathcal{L}_{\text{CIA}}$ are:

$Q_t = \texttt{q(X)} \leftarrow \texttt{\&} \; \texttt{X:MiddleEastCountry}$
$Q_1 = \texttt{q(X)} \leftarrow \texttt{speaks(X,Y)} \; \texttt{\&} \; \texttt{X:MiddleEastCountry, Y:Language}$
$Q_2 = \texttt{q(X)} \leftarrow \texttt{speaks(X,Y)} \; \texttt{\&} \; \texttt{X:MiddleEastCountry, Y:IndoEuropeanLanguage}$
$Q_3 = \texttt{q(X)} \leftarrow \texttt{believes(X,Y)} \texttt{\&} \; \texttt{X:MiddleEastCountry, Y:MuslimReligion}$

where Q_t is the trivial $\mathcal{O}$-query for $\mathcal{L}_{\text{CIA}}$, $Q_1 \in \mathcal{L}_{\text{CIA}}^1$, $Q_2 \in \mathcal{L}_{\text{CIA}}^2$, and $Q_3 \in \mathcal{L}_{\text{CIA}}^3$. Note that Q_1 is an ancestor of Q_2.

Minimum support thresholds are set to the following values: $minsup^1 = 20\%$, $minsup^2 = 13\%$, and $minsup^3 = 10\%$. After $maxD = 5$ search stages, $\mathcal{AL}$-QUIN returns 53 frequent patterns out of 99 candidate patterns compliant with the parameter settings. One of these findings is the pattern Q_2 which turns out to

---

[5] http://www.odci.gov/cia/publications/factbook/

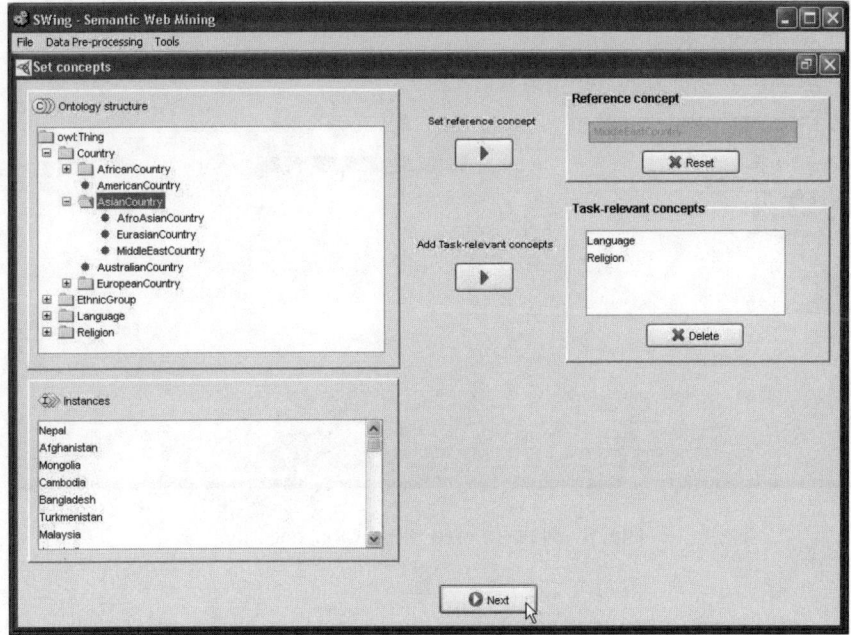

Fig. 4. $\mathcal{SW}$ING: step of concept selection

be frequent because it has support $supp(Q_2, \mathcal{B}_{\text{CIA}}) = 13\%$ ($\geq minsup^2$). This has to be read as '13 % of Middle East countries speak an Indoeuropean language'.

A wizard provides guidance for the selection of the (hybrid) data set to be mined, the selection of the reference concept and the task-relevant concepts (see Figure 4), the selection of the relations - among the ones appearing in the relational component of the data set chosen or derived from them - with which the task-relevant concepts can be linked to the reference concept in the patterns to be discovered (see Figure 5 and 6), the setting of minimum support thresholds for each level of description granularity and of several other parameters required by $\mathcal{AL}$-QuIn. These user preferences are collected in a file (see ouput file *.lb in Figure 3) that is shown in preview to the user at the end of the assisted procedure for confirmation (see Figure 7).

4.1   A Closer Look to the I/O

The input to $\mathcal{SW}$ING is a hybrid knowledge base that consists of an ontological data source - expressed as a OWL file - and a relational data source - also available on the Web - integrated with each other.

Example 2. The knowledge base $\mathcal{B}_{\text{CIA}}$ for the Semantic Web Mining session of Example 1 integrates an OWL ontology (file `cia_exp1.owl`) with a DATALOG

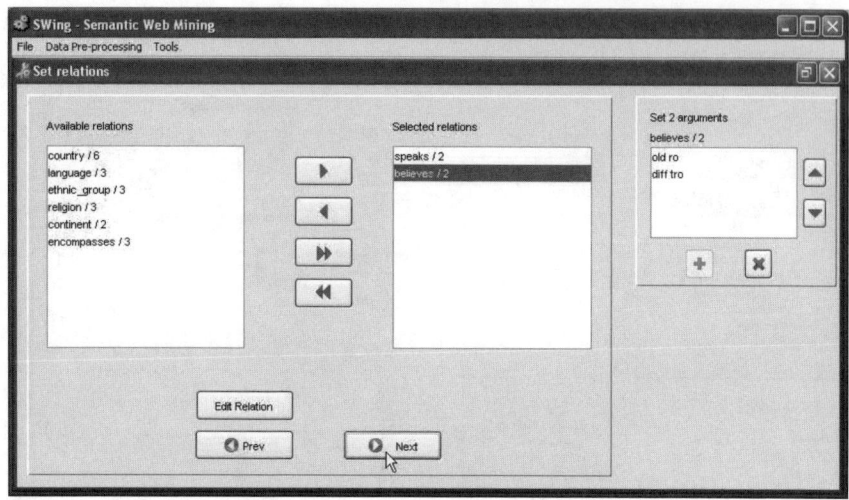

Fig. 5. $\mathcal{SW}$ING: step of relation selection

database (file `cia_exp1.edb`) containing facts [6] extracted from the on-line 1996 CIA World Fact Book. The OWL ontology[7] contains axioms such as

```
AsianCountry ⊑ Country.
MiddleEastEthnicGroup ⊑ EthnicGroup.
MiddleEastCountry ≡ AsianCountry ⊓ ∃Hosts.MiddleEastEthnicGroup.
IndoEuropeanLanguage ⊑ Language.
IndoIranianLanguage ⊑ IndoEuropeanLanguage.
MonotheisticReligion ⊑ Religion.
MuslimReligion ⊑ MonotheisticReligion.
```

and membership assertions such as

```
'IR':AsianCountry.
'Arab':MiddleEastEthnicGroup.
<'IR','Arab'>:Hosts.
'Persian':IndoIranianLanguage.
'ShiaMuslim':MuslimReligion.
'SunniMuslim':MuslimReligion.
```

that define taxonomies for the concepts `Country`, `EthnicGroup`, `Language` and `Religion`. Note that Middle East countries (concept `MiddleEastCountry`) have been defined as Asian countries that host at least one Middle Eastern ethnic group. In particular, Iran (`'IR'`) is classified as Middle East country.

---

[6] http://www.dbis.informatik.uni-goettingen.de/Mondial/mondial-rel-facts.flp

[7] In the following we shall use the corresponding DL notation.

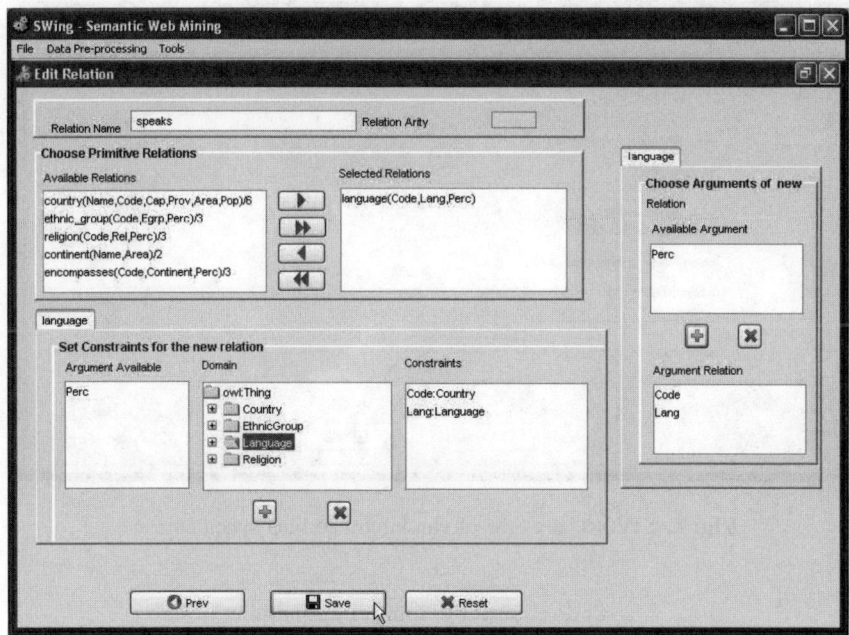

Fig. 6. SWING: editing of derived relations

Since C_{ref}=MiddleEastCountry, the DATALOG database is partitioned according to the individuals of MiddleEastCountry. In particular, the observation $(q('IR'), \mathcal{A}_{IR})$ contains DATALOG facts such as

```
language('IR','Persian',58).
religion('IR','ShiaMuslim',89).
religion('IR','SunniMuslim',10).
```

concerning the individual 'IR'.

The output file *.db contains the input DATALOG database eventually enriched with an intensional part. The editing of derived relations (see Figure 6) is accessible from the step of relation selection (see Figure 5).

Example 3. The output DATALOG database cia_exp1.db for Example 1 enriches the input DATALOG database cia_exp1.edb with the following two clauses:

```
speaks(Code, Lang)← language(Code,Lang,Perc),
                    c_Country(Code), c_Language(Lang).
believes(Code, Rel)←religion(Code,Rel,Perc),
                    c_Country(Code), c_Religion(Rel).
```

that define views on the relations language and religion respectively. Note that they correspond to the constrained DATALOG clauses

```
speaks(Code, Lang)← language(Code,Lang,Perc) &
```

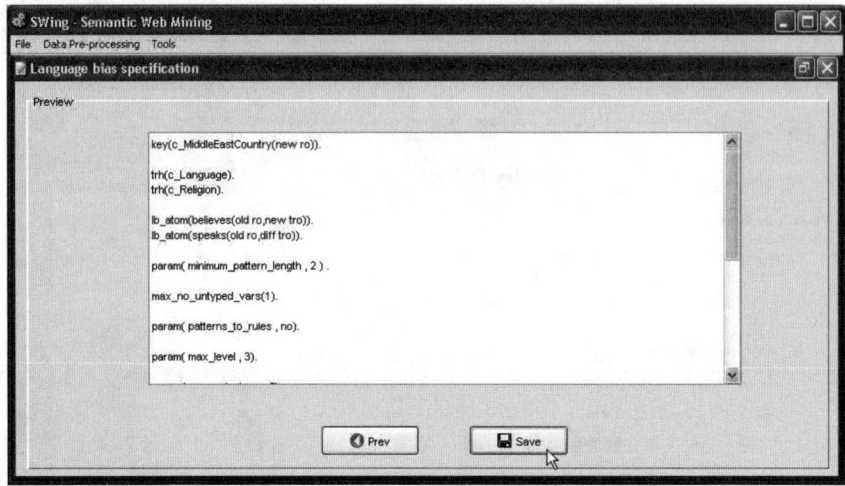

Fig. 7. $\mathcal{SW}$ING: preview of the language bias specification

$$\text{Code:Country, Lang:Language.}$$
$$\text{believes(Code, Rel)} \leftarrow \text{religion(Code,Rel,Perc)} \ \&$$
$$\text{Code:Country, Rel:Religion.}$$

and represent the intensional part of Π_{CIA}.

The output file *.lb* contains the declarative bias specification for the language of patterns and other directives.

Example 4. With reference to Example 1, the content of `cia_exp1.lb` (see Figure 7) defines - among the other things - the language $\mathcal{L}_{\text{CIA}}$ of patterns. In particular the first 5 directives define the reference concept, the task-relevant concepts and and the relations between concepts.

The output files *.abox_n* and *.tbox* are the side effect of the step of concept selection as illustrated in the next section. Note that these files together with the intensional part of the *.db* file form the background knowledge $\mathcal{K}$ for $\mathcal{AL}$-QUIN.

4.2   A Look Inside the Step of Concept Selection

The step of concept selection deserves further remarks because it actually exploits the services offered by Protégé-2000. Indeed it also triggers some supplementary computation aimed at making a OWL background knowledge Σ usable by $\mathcal{AL}$-QUIN. To achieve this goal, it supplies the following functionalities:

- levelwise retrieval w.r.t. Σ
- translation of both (asserted and derived) concept assertions and subsumption axioms of Σ to DATALOG^{OI} facts

The latter relies on the former, meaning that the results of the levelwise retrieval are exported to DATALOG^{OI} (see output files *.abox_n and *.tbox in Figure 3). The *retrieval* problem is known in DLs literature as the problem of retrieving all the individuals of a concept C [2]. Here, the retrieval is called *levelwise* because it follows the layering of T: individuals of concepts belonging to the l-th layer T^l of T are retrieved all together.

Example 5. The DATALOG^{OI} rewriting of the concept assertions derived for T^2 produces facts like:

```
c_AfroAsiaticLanguage('Arabic').
...
c_IndoEuropeanLanguage('Persian').
...
c_UralAltaicLanguage('Kazak').
...
c_MonotheisticReligion('ShiaMuslim').
c_MonotheisticReligion('SunniMuslim').
...
c_PolytheisticReligion('Druze').
...
```

that are stored in the file cia_exp1.abox_2.

The file cia_exp1.tbox contains a DATALOG^{OI} rewriting of the taxonomic relations of T such as:

```
hierarchy(c_Language,1,null,[c_Language]).
hierarchy(c_Religion,1,null,[c_Religion]).
```

for the layer T^1 and

```
hierarchy(c_Language,2,c_Language,
        [c_AfroAsiaticLanguage, c_IndoEuropeanLanguage, ...]).
hierarchy(c_Religion,2,c_Religion,
        [c_MonotheisticReligion, c_PolytheisticReligion]).
```

for the layer T^2 and

```
hierarchy(c_Language,3,c_AfroAsiaticLanguage,[c_AfroAsiaticLanguage]).
...
hierarchy(c_Language,3,c_IndoEuropeanLanguage,
        [c_IndoIranianLanguage, c_SlavicLanguage]).
hierarchy(c_Language,3,c_UralAltaicLanguage,[c_TurkicLanguage]).
hierarchy(c_Religion,3,c_MonotheisticReligion,
        [c_ChristianReligion, c_JewishReligion, c_MuslimReligion]).
```

for the layer T^3.

Note that the translation from OWL to DATALOG^{OI} is possible because we assume that *all* the concepts are named. This means that an equivalence axiom is required for each complex concept in the knowledge base. Equivalence axioms help keeping concept names (used within constrained DATALOG clauses) independent from concept definitions.

5   Conclusions and Future Work

The middleware $\mathcal{SWING}$ represents a practical step towards Semantic Web Mining considered as a testbed for inductive reasoning on the Semantic Web. It follows engineering principles because it promotes:

- the reuse of existing systems ($\mathcal{AL}$-QuIn and Protégé-2000)
- the adherence to standards (either normative - see OWL for the Semantic Web - or *de facto* - see Prolog for ILP)

Furthermore the resulting artifact overcomes the capabilities of the two systems when considered stand-alone. In particular, $\mathcal{AL}$-QuIn was originally conceived to deal with $\mathcal{ALC}$ ontologies. Since OWL is equivalent to $\mathcal{SHIQ}$ and $\mathcal{ALC}$ is a fragment of $\mathcal{SHIQ}$, the middleware $\mathcal{SWING}$ allows $\mathcal{AL}$-QuIn to deal with more expressive ontological background knowlege.

The middleware $\mathcal{SWING}$ supplies several facilities to $\mathcal{AL}$-QuIn, primarily facilities for compiling DL-based background knowledge down to the usual DATALOG-like formalisms of ILP systems. In this respect, the pre-processing method proposed by Kietz [13] to enable legacy ILP systems to work within the framework of the hybrid KR&R system CARIN [16] is related to ours but it lacks an application. Analogously, the method proposed in [12] for translating OWL to disjunctive DATALOG is far too general with respect to the specific needs of our application. Rather, the proposal of interfacing existing reasoners to combine ontologies and rules [1] is more similar to ours in the spirit.

For the future we plan to extend $\mathcal{SWING}$ with facilities for extracting information from semantic portals and for presenting patterns generated by $\mathcal{AL}$-QuIn.

References

1. U. Assmann, J. Henriksson, and J. Maluszynski. Combining safe rules and ontologies by interfacing of reasoners. To appear in J.J. Alferes, J. Bailey, W. May, and U. Schwertel, editors, *Principles and Practice of Semantic Web Reasoning*, volume ? of *Lecture Notes in Computer Science*, pages ?-?. Springer, 2006.
2. F. Baader, D. Calvanese, D. McGuinness, D. Nardi, and P.F. Patel-Schneider, editors. *The Description Logic Handbook: Theory, Implementation and Applications*. Cambridge University Press, 2003.
3. B. Berendt, A. Hotho, and G. Stumme. Towards semantic web mining. In I. Horrocks and J.A. Hendler, editors, *International Semantic Web Conference*, volume 2342 of *Lecture Notes in Computer Science*, pages 264–278. Springer, 2002.
4. T. Berners-Lee, J. Hendler, and O. Lassila. The Semantic Web. *Scientific American*, May, 2001.
5. A. Borgida. On the relative expressiveness of description logics and predicate logics. *Artificial Intelligence*, 82(1–2):353–367, 1996.
6. S. Ceri, G. Gottlob, and L. Tanca. *Logic Programming and Databases*. Springer, 1990.
7. F.M. Donini, M. Lenzerini, D. Nardi, and A. Schaerf. $\mathcal{AL}$-log: Integrating Datalog and Description Logics. *Journal of Intelligent Information Systems*, 10(3):227–252, 1998.

8. J.H. Gennari, M.A. Musen, R.W. Fergerson, W.E. Grosso, M. Crubézy, H. Eriksson, N. Fridman Noy, and S. W. Tu. The evolution of Protégé: An environment for knowledge-based systems development. *International Journal of Human-Computer Studies*, 58(1):89–123, 2003.

9. A. Gómez-Pérez, M. Fernández-López, and O. Corcho. *Ontological Engineering*. Springer, 2004.

10. V. Haarslev and R. Möller. Description of the RACER System and its Applications. In C.A. Goble, D.L. McGuinness, R. Möller, and P.F. Patel-Schneider, editors, *Working Notes of the 2001 International Description Logics Workshop (DL-2001)*, volume 49 of *CEUR Workshop Proceedings*, 2001.

11. I. Horrocks, P.F. Patel-Schneider, and F. van Harmelen. From $\mathcal{SHIQ}$ and RDF to OWL: The making of a web ontology language. *Journal of Web Semantics*, 1(1):7–26, 2003.

12. U. Hustadt, B. Motik, and U. Sattler. Reducing $\mathcal{SHIQ}$-description logic to disjunctive datalog programs. In D. Dubois, C.A. Welty, and M.-A. Williams, editors, *Principles of Knowledge Representation and Reasoning: Proceedings of the Ninth International Conference (KR2004)*, pages 152–162. AAAI Press, 2004.

13. J.-U. Kietz. Learnability of description logic programs. In S. Matwin and C. Sammut, editors, *Inductive Logic Programming*, volume 2583 of *Lecture Notes in Artificial Intelligence*, pages 117–132. Springer, 2003.

14. H. Knublauch, M.A. Musen, and A.L. Rector. Editing Description Logic Ontologies with the Protégé OWL Plugin. In V. Haarslev and R. Möller, editors, *Proceedings of the 2004 International Workshop on Description Logics (DL2004)*, volume 104 of *CEUR Workshop Proceedings*, 2004.

15. R. Kosala and H. Blockeel. Web Mining Research: A Survey. *SIGKDD: SIGKDD Explorations: Newsletter of the Special Interest Group (SIG) on Knowledge Discovery & Data Mining, ACM*, 2, 2000.

16. A.Y. Levy and M.-C. Rousset. Combining Horn rules and description logics in CARIN. *Artificial Intelligence*, 104:165–209, 1998.

17. F.A. Lisi. Principles of Inductive Reasoning on the Semantic Web: A Framework for Learning in $\mathcal{AL}$-log. In F. Fages and S. Soliman, editors, *Principles and Practice of Semantic Web Reasoning*, volume 3703 of *Lecture Notes in Computer Science*, pages 118–132. Springer, 2005.

18. F.A. Lisi and F. Esposito. Efficient Evaluation of Candidate Hypotheses in $\mathcal{AL}$-log. In R. Camacho, R. King, and A. Srinivasan, editors, *Inductive Logic Programming*, volume 3194 of *Lecture Notes in Artificial Intelligence*, pages 216–233. Springer, 2004.

19. F.A. Lisi and D. Malerba. Ideal Refinement of Descriptions in $\mathcal{AL}$-log. In T. Horvath and A. Yamamoto, editors, *Inductive Logic Programming*, volume 2835 of *Lecture Notes in Artificial Intelligence*, pages 215–232. Springer, 2003.

20. F.A. Lisi and D. Malerba. Inducing Multi-Level Association Rules from Multiple Relations. *Machine Learning*, 55:175–210, 2004.

21. A. Maedche and S. Staab. Discovering Conceptual Relations from Text. In W. Horn, editor, *Proceedings of the 14th European Conference on Artificial Intelligence*, pages 321–325. IOS Press, 2000.

22. A. Maedche and V. Zacharias. Clustering Ontology-Based Metadata in the Semantic Web. In T. Elomaa, H. Mannila, and H. Toivonen, editors, *Principles of Data Mining and Knowledge Discovery*, volume 2431 of *Lecture Notes in Computer Science*, pages 348–360. Springer, 2002.

23. H. Mannila and H. Toivonen. Levelwise search and borders of theories in knowledge discovery. *Data Mining and Knowledge Discovery*, 1(3):241–258, 1997.

24. S.-H. Nienhuys-Cheng and R. de Wolf. *Foundations of Inductive Logic Programming*, volume 1228 of *Lecture Notes in Artificial Intelligence*. Springer, 1997.
25. N. Fridman Noy, R.W. Fergerson, and M.A. Musen. The Knowledge Model of Protégé-2000: Combining Interoperability and Flexibility. In R. Dieng and O. Corby, editors, *Knowledge Acquisition, Modeling and Management*, volume 1937 of *Lecture Notes in Computer Science*, pages 17–32. Springer, 2000.
26. R. Rosati. On the decidability and complexity of integrating ontologies and rules. *Journal of Web Semantics*, 3(1), 2005.
27. M. Schmidt-Schauss and G. Smolka. Attributive concept descriptions with complements. *Artificial Intelligence*, 48(1):1–26, 1991.
28. G. Semeraro, F. Esposito, D. Malerba, N. Fanizzi, and S. Ferilli. A logic framework for the incremental inductive synthesis of Datalog theories. In N.E. Fuchs, editor, *Proceedings of 7th International Workshop on Logic Program Synthesis and Transformation*, volume 1463 of *Lecture Notes in Computer Science*, pages 300–321. Springer, 1998.

Fuzzy Time Intervals System
Description of the FuTI–Library

Hans Jürgen Ohlbach

Institut für Informatik, Universität München
ohlbach@lmu.de

Abstract. The FuTI–library is a collection of classes and methods for
representing and manipulating fuzzy time intervals. Fuzzy time intervals
are represented as polygons over integer coordinates. FuTI is an open
source C++ library with many advanced operations and highly optimised
algorithms. Version 1.0 is now available from the URL
http://www.pms.ifi.lmu.de/CTTN/FuTI.

1 Fuzzy Time Intervals

Many temporal notions used in everyday life have a deliberate imprecise meaning.
For example, if I say in the morning "tonight I'll go to the disco", and somebody asks
me "will you go to the disco at 8 pm?" I may neither want to say "yes" nor may I want
to say "no". As another example, consider a database with, say, a cinema timetable.
If you query the timetable "give me all performances ending *before* midnight", do
you really want to exclude a performance ending just one minute after midnight?
I think, not. One could solve this problem by giving the 'before' relation a fuzzy
meaning, such that performances ending before midnight get a fuzzy value 1, and
performances ending after midnight get a fuzzy value which decreases the later the
performance ends. In the CTTN system [1] (Computational Treatment of Temporal
Notions) which is currently under development, one can define such relations. One
of the key modules in this system is the FuTI libraray.

Fuzzy Intervals are usually defined through their membership functions. A
membership function maps a base set to a real number between 0 and 1. This
"fuzzy value" denotes a kind of degree of membership to a fuzzy set S. The base
set for fuzzy time intervals is the time axis. In FuTI it is represented by the set $\mathbb{R}$
of real numbers. Real numbers allow us to model the continuous time flow which
we perceive in our life. A fuzzy time interval in FuTI is now a fuzzy subset of
the real numbers.

A typical fuzzy interval may look like:

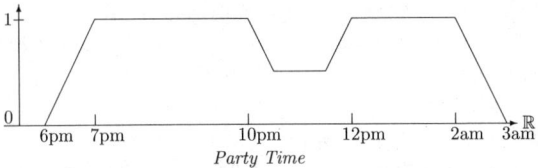

Party Time

J.J. Alferes et al. (Eds.): PPSWR 2006, LNCS 4187, pp. 257–261, 2006.

This set may represent a particular party time, where the first guests arrive at 6 pm. At 7 pm all guests are there. Half of them disappear between 10 and 12 pm (because they go to the pub next door to watch an important soccer game). Between 12 pm and 2 am all of them are back. At 2 am the first ones go home, and finally at 3 am all are gone. The fuzzy value indicates in this case the number of people at the party.

Fuzzy intervals in FuTI may be infinite, but the membership must be constant from certain time onwards.

2   Data Structures and Algorithms

There are four basic data types: time points, fuzzy values, fuzzy temporal intervals and y-functions.

Time Points. The time points are points on the $\mathbb{R}$-axis. Arbitrary real numbers cannot be represented on computers. The choice is therefore between floating point numbers and integers as representation of time points. The range of floating point numbers is much higher than the range of integers. Unfortunately, algorithms operating on floating point numbers are prone to uncontrollable rounding errors. Therefore the FuTI–library *represents time with integer coordinates*. There is no assumption about the meaning of these integers. They may be years, seconds, picoseconds or even cycles of the Caesium 133 light. The system can use two types of integers, 64 bit long integers, and multiple precision integers from the GMP library (http://www.swox.com/gmp).

Fuzzy Values. Fuzzy values are usually real numbers between 0 and 1. A first choice would therefore be to use floating point numbers for the fuzzy values. Again, floating point numbers are prone to rounding errors. Moreover, computation with floating point numbers is more expensive than computation with integers. Therefore FuTI uses again integers instead of floating point numbers. This means of course that one cannot represent the fuzzy value 1 as the integer 1. We could then use just 0 and 1 and no other fuzzy value. Instead one better represents the fuzzy value 1 as a suitable unsigned integer of a certain bit size. Since fuzzy values are estimates only anyway, 16 bit unsigned integer (unsigned short int in C) are precise enough for fuzzy values.

Fuzzy Time Intervals. Fuzzy intervals are usually implemented by a representation of their membership functions. Arbitrary membership functions are almost impossible to represent precisely on a computer. A natural choice for realizing approximated fuzzy time intervals over integer time and integer fuzzy values is the representation with *envelope polygons* over integer coordinates. This has a number of advantages: the representation is compact and can nevertheless approximate the membership functions very well; simple structures, like crisp intervals, have a simple representation; we can use ideas and algorithms from Computational Geometry, there are very efficient algorithms for most of the problems, and it is clear where rounding errors can occur, and where not.

3   The Class Hierarchy

The data structures are organised in the following hierarchy:

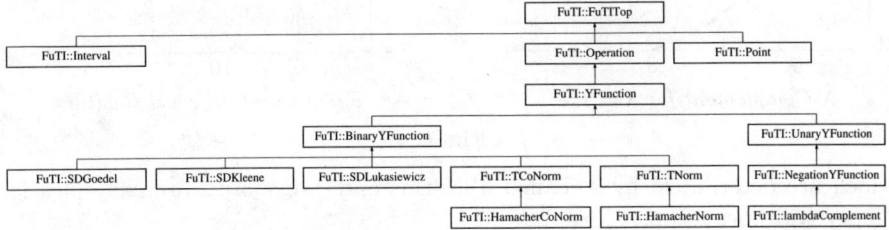

3.1   Point

The class 'Point' represents 2D points with integer coordinates. These points form the vertices of the envelope polygons for fuzzy sets. Since two points determine a line segment, all the algorithms for line segments are also contained in 'Point'. The algorithms range from simple 'leftturn' tests up to integration over two multiplied linear functions, where the linear functions are determined by two lines.

3.2   Interval

This is the most important class in the FuTI–library. It contains the representation of fuzzy intervals as polygons. There are two types of operations on these polygons. The first type consists of some dozens of 'hardwired' operations which transform the fuzzy sets in a certain way. Computing three different types of hulls (monotone, convex and crisp hull) is an example. Multiplying a crisp or fuzzy interval with a linear or Gaussian distribution is another example. Further operations are, for example, normalised integrations over the membership functions, from past to future and the other way round.

The second type are parameterised operations on fuzzy intervals where the parameters themselves are operations on membership functions (called Y-functions in FuTI).

An example for a *unary* transformation of a fuzzy interval is the complement operation, which is defined by a negation function on the membership function. The so-called λ-complement $n_\lambda(y) \overset{\text{def}}{=} \frac{1-y}{1+\lambda y}$ function can be used for this purpose. The function n_λ is then a parameter to a 'unary-transformation' operation (left picture in Fig. 1).

More complex combinations of these transformation functions can compute, for example, a fuzzified point–interval 'before' relation (right picture in Fig. 1). $F(I)$ (the dotted line in this picture) is a fuzzified and extended version of the interval I where a Gaussian distribution is multiplied with I. C is a complement operation. The result, $C(F(I))$ gives for every time point t the fuzzy value for 't is before I'.

Besides unary transformations, there is also a function 'binary-transformation' on intervals, which is parameterised by a function that takes two fuzzy values as input and computes a new fuzzy value. Set operations like union or intersection,

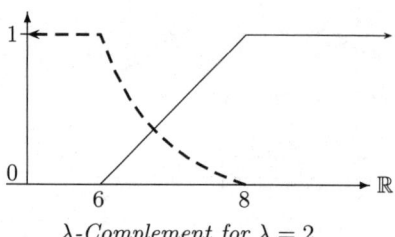
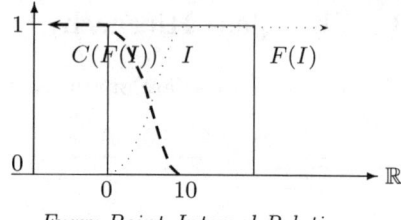

λ-Complement for λ = 2   *Fuzzy Point–Interval Relation*

Fig. 1.

which are determined by so-called T-Norms and T-Conorms are examples for binary transformations.

A particular binary transformation is the (normalised) integration over multiplied membership functions. A definition of a fuzzy interval–interval 'before' relation as the weighted average over the point–interval 'before' relation $B(J)$ could be $before_B(I, J) \stackrel{\text{def}}{=} \int I(t) \cdot B(J)(t) \, dt / |I|$ which is computed by a suitable binary transformation function. $B(J)$ could be a fuzzy interval where for each point t, $B(J)(t)$ indicates the degree of 'beforeness' between t and the interval J. Some of the transformations are non-linear, i.e. they turn straight lines into curves. The algorithms in FuTI approximate the curves automatically with sufficiently dense polygons.

3.3   Operation

This class is the top class for all unary and binary Y-functions and other operations on intervals. The subclasses of 'Operation' implement a standard repertoire of Y-functions. New Y-functions can easily be added by adding further subclasses of the class 'YFunction'. The classes 'SDGoedel', 'SDKleene' and 'SD-Lukasiewicz' implement binary Y-functions which realise three different types of fuzzy set difference operations.

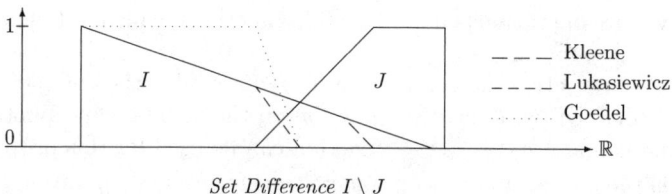

Set Difference $I \setminus J$

The classes 'TCoNorm' and 'TNorm', with their subclasses 'HamacherCoNorm' and 'HamacherNorm' are used for realising fuzzy union and intersection operations. The picture below illustrates the operations. The class 'UnaryYFunction' has, so far, only subclasses for standard and *lambda*-complement.

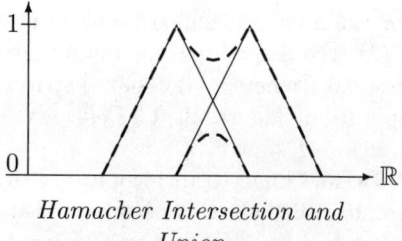

Hamacher Intersection and Union

4 Summary

The FuTI-library is a component of the CTTN-system (Computational Treatment of Temporal Notions) [1], a program for evaluating temporal expressions like 'three weeks after Easter'. CTTN is currently under development. CTTN contains in particular the specification language GeTS for specifying and working with temporal notions [3]. Many of the language primitives in GeTS are the operations of the FuTI–library. Other language primitives in GeTS use the PartLib–library for representing periodical temporal notions [4]. GeTS is in particular suitable for specifying fuzzy relations between fuzzy time intervals [5,2]. Therefore FuTI is only one piece in a bigger mosaic, which is to be used as a geotemporal background theory in Semantic Web applications, in particular query languages and ontology formalisms. Some of the design decisions in FuTI are motivated by the needs of the GeTS language. Nevertheless the API for FuTI is general enough to be useful also for other applications.

Acknowledgements

This research has been funded by the European Commission and by the Swiss Federal Office for Education and Science within the 6th Framework Programme project REWERSE number 506779 (cf. http://rewerse.net).

References

1. Hans Jüergen Ohlbach.   Computational treatement of temporal notions – the CTTN system.   In François Fages, editor, *Proceedings of PPSWR 2005*, Lecture Notes in Computer Science, pages 137–150, 2005.   see also URL: http://www.pms.ifi.lmu.de/publikationen/#PMS-FB-2005-30.
2. Hans Jürgen Ohlbach. Relations between fuzzy time intervals. In *Proceedings of 11th International Symposium on TEMPORAL REPRESENTATION AND REASONING, Tatihoui, Normandie, France (1st–3rd July 2004)*, pages 44–51. IEEE Computer Society, 2004. See also http://www.pms.ifi.lmu.de/publikationen/#PMS-FB-2004-33.
3. Hans Jürgen Ohlbach. GeTS – a specification language for geo-temporal notions. Research Report PMS-FB-2005-29, Inst. für Informatik, LFE PMS, University of Munich, June 2005.   URL: http://www.pms.ifi.lmu.de/publikationen/#PMS-FB-2005-29.
4. Hans Jürgen Ohlbach.   Modelling periodic temporal notions by labelled partitionings of the real numbers – the PartLib library.   Research Report PMS-FB-2005-28, Inst. für Informatik, LFE PMS, University of Munich, June 2005. URL: http://www.pms.ifi.lmu.de/publikationen/#PMS-FB-2005-28.
5. Hans Jürgen Ohlbach. Relations between fuzzy time intervals. Research Report PMS-FB-2005-27, Inst. für Informatik, LFE PMS, University of Munich, June 2005. URL: http://www.pms.ifi.lmu.de/publikationen/#PMS-FB-2005-27.

A Prototype of a Descriptive Type System
for Xcerpt

Artur Wilk[1] and Włodzimierz Drabent[1,2]

[1] Dept. of Computer and Information Science,
Linköping University, S 581 83 Linköping, Sweden
[2] Institute of Computer Science, Polish Academy of Sciences,
ul. Ordona 21, Pl – 01-237 Warszawa, Poland
{artwi, wlodr}@ida.liu.se

Abstract. The paper presents a prototype implementation of a descriptive type system for the XML query language Xcerpt. Its intended application is finding (a certain kind of) errors in programs. The implementation is able to check correctness of an Xcerpt program with respect to a type specification. A type specification describes a set of possible data bases to which the program is to be applied and an expected set of results. Program correctness means that all its results are in the expected set. Failure of a correctness check suggests an error in the program. Under certain conditions such failure indeed means that the program is incorrect.

Current implementation works for a restricted, but interesting subset of Xcerpt. The system provides (approximations of) the set of program results and the sets of values of program variables; this information is useful for programmers (and is produced even when the specification of the expected set of results is not given).

1 Introduction

This paper presents a prototype implementation of a descriptive type system for XML query language Xcerpt [6,5]. The type system has been presented in [8,1,2,7]. The prototype, called here *typechecker*, implements a method for computing the type of results of an Xcerpt program given a type of documents which are queried. If additionally a user provides a specification of an expected result type of a program, the typechecker can prove the program correctness wrt. the specification or warn about a possible error. Similarly as in Xcerpt we use data terms as an abstraction of XML data. In our approach types are sets of data terms. To specify types we use a formalism of Type Definitions [1]. Additionally, our typechecker supports type specifications given by DTD's [9] which are translated into Type Definitions.

The prototype is restricted to the fragment of Xcerpt covered by our type system described in [7]. It is still under development and the goal is to extend it towards the full Xcerpt. The simplified version of Xcerpt handled by the typechecker deals with basic and the most important Xcerpt constructs. An important simplification is that our data terms represent trees while in full Xcerpt

J.J. Alferes et al. (Eds.): PPSWR 2006, LNCS 4187, pp. 262–275, 2006.

terms are used to represent graphs (by adding unique identifiers to some tree nodes and introducing nodes which are references to these identifiers). Other neglected Xcerpt features in respect to the Xcerpt version described in [6,5] are: functions and aggregations, non-pattern conditions, optional subterms, position specifications, negation, regular expressions and label variables. Moreover, our typechecker is restricted to Xcerpt programs consisting only of one query rule.

The typechecker has been added as an extension to the Xcerpt prototype, written in the functional language Haskell. Xcerpt together with the typechecker can be accessed online via the link http://www.ida.liu.se/~artwi/XcerptT. The website contains also some examples illustrating usage of the type system.

To fully understand this paper, some familiarity with Xcerpt and with the formalism of type definition is needed; see [6] and [1] for an introduction. The rest of the paper is organized as follows. Section 2 describes usage of the prototype. Section 3 presents possible application of the type system together with simple scenario examples. Finally, Section 4 discusses directions for future work.

2   Usage of the Prototype

This section uses notation where square brackets [ ] and strings enclosed by triangle parentheses <...> belong to a metalanguage: [ ] represents optional part and <...> is a nonterminal which can be replaced with a string without spaces.

The typechecker is invoked like the standard Xcerpt run-time system (i.e. executing xcerpt or xcerpt.exe). To perform type checking (or type inference) of a program a parameter -t is used:

xcerpt -t <program file> [<type specification>]

The typing mechanism can also be invoked using the interactive Xcerpt command mode with the command:

:type <program file> [<type specification>]

In the abovementioned commands <program file> is a name of a file containing an Xcerpt program consisting of one query rule and <type specification> is a name of a text file specifying the types of resources[1] which are queried and the types of expected results. A <type specification> file may contain:

− a Type Definition i.e. rules defining types,
− one or more input type specifications,
− one output type specification.

The input type specification has the syntax:

```
Input::
  [ resource = <resource URI> ]
  [ typedef  = <typedef location> ]
  typename = <type name>
```

---

[1] A resource corresponds to a database db in a targeted query term $\mathbf{in}(db, q)$ [1].

and the output type specification has the syntax:

$$
\text{Output}::
$$
$$
[\ \texttt{typedef}\ \ =\ <typedef\ location>]
$$
$$
\texttt{typename} = <type\ name>
$$

where

- *<resource URI>* is an URI of the resource being queried whose type we specify. If the parameter `resource` is omitted the input type specification specifies a type of every resource occurring in the *<program file>* whose type was not specified (overridden) by other input type specification. A *<type specification>* file can contain at most one input type specification without the parameter `resource`.
- *<typedef location>* is a URI of an external file containing a Type Definition (or DTD). If the the parameter `typedef` is omitted the input or output type specification refers to the local Type Definition i.e. specified in the current *<type specification>* file.
- *<type name>*, if used in an input type specification, is a type name specifying the type of the resource the specification refers to. If it is used in an output type specification it is a type name specifying the result type of the program. It can be the most general type `Top` or a type name which is defined in the Type Definition or the DTD the input or output type specification refers to. If the specification refers to a DTD then a type name can be one of the element names declared in the DTD.

A syntax of Type Definitions in the typechecker is slightly different than the one used in [8,1,7]. The difference is that the rules defining types do not use quotation marks to denote basic constants [1].

Example 1. This is an example of a <type specification> file *books.xts*:

```
Books -> books[ Book* ]
Book -> book[ Title Author+ Editor+ ]
Title -> title[ Text ]
Author -> author[ P ]
Editor -> editor[ P' ]
P -> person[ S ]
P' -> person[ F? S? ]
Person -> person[ F+ S ]
F -> firstname[ Text ]
S -> surname[ Text ]
Result -> result[ Person+ ]

Input::
  resource = file:books.xml
  typename = Books
Output::
  typename = Result
```

For instance, the first rule of the Type Definition above states that the elements of type Books are data terms of the form $books[d_1, \ldots, d_n]$, where $n \geq 0$ and $d_1, \ldots, d_n$ are members of type Book. Such a data term corresponds to an XML element named books, whose content is a sequence of elements corresponding to data terms $d_1, \ldots, d_n$. For more details see e.g. [1].

Invoking the typing mechanism (e.g. with command xcerpt -t <*program file*> <*type specification*>) starts the process of type inference for the query rule. The type inference is done using the types of resources given by input type specifications. If the type of a resource is not specified by any input type specification, it is assumed to be the most general type *Top* (which can be seen as a default type of a resource). After the type of results for the query rule has been inferred, it is checked whether it is included in the output type (specified by the output type specification). If the output type is *Top* then type checking is needless i.e. only type inference is performed. If the output type specification is missing then the specified output type is assumed to be *Top*. Invoking the typing mechanism without <*type specification*> parameter has the same effect as invoking it with an empty <*type specification*> file.

As a result of typing an Xcerpt program we get a printout containing:

- information whether type checking or only type inference was performed with the result of type checking (if it was performed),
- the inferred result type,
- variable-type mappings for variables occurring in the query rule,
- a Type Definition defining the inferred type, the specified result type and types of resources.

For types being intersections of other types their content models are provided by Deterministic Finite Automata (DFA's) instead of regular type expressions. (Regular expressions and DFA's are equivalent formalisms [4].) The intersection of regular languages is computed by constructing a product automaton of DFA's representing the languages. Transformation of a DFA to a regular expression is of exponential time complexity, and the resulting expression is often complicated and hard to understand. That is why we decided not to perform this transformation.

A DFA representing an intersection of regular languages is presented by descriptions of all its states. Each such a description is of the form $S_i => a_1 > S_{k_{i1}}$ $\ldots a_n > S_{k_{in}}$, where S_i is the number of the state being described, $a_1, \ldots, a_n$ are the symbols of the input alphabet of the DFA, and each $S_{k_{ij}}$ is the number of the state reached from the state S_i by reading the symbol a_j. Additionally, the number of the state being described may be preceded by the character '>' which denotes the initial state or it may be followed by the character '!' which denotes a final state. This is an example of a DFA defining the same language as the regular expression AF^*:

```
0  => A>0 F>0
>1 => A>2 F>0
2! => A>0 F>2
```

A name given by the system to a type being the intersection of types T_1, T_2 is $T_1 \char`^ T_2$. The type checker also invents type names for newly inferred types. The devised new type names are the labels of the corresponding construct terms occurring in heads of query rules. If such name has already been used, the new type name is augmented with an index i.e. a number added at the end of the type name (underscore separated). If a type name with a given index already exists the new type name has the index increased by 1.

Example 2. Here we present the result of typing the following Xcerpt program:

```
CONSTRUCT
  result [ all var X ]
FROM
  in {
    resource { "file:books.xml" },
    books {{
      book {{
        author [ var X ],
        editor [ var X ]
      }}
    }}
  }
END
```

The rule queries the document *books.xml* and extracts those book authors who are also editors (of the same book). More precisely, it is checked whether the main symbol of the document (viewed as a data term) is books and one of its arguments, with the main symbol book, has within its arguments data terms of the form author$[d_1]$, editor$[d_2]$ (in arbitrary order). Variable X is bound both to d_1 and to d_2, hence $d_1 = d_2$. All such values of X are collected into the argument list of symbol result, building a data term which is returned by the rule. For more details see [6].

A type specification for the program is given by *books.xts* file from the previous example. Typing of the program results in:

```
==================================================
Type checking ... FAILED
--------------------------------------------------
Result type: result (not a subset of Result)


--------------------------------------------------
Variable-type mappings:
--------------------------------------------------
X->P^P'


==================================================
Type Definition:
```

```
----------------------------------------------------
result -> result[ P^P'+ ]
Books -> books[ Book* ]
Book -> book[ Title Author+ Editor+ ]
Title -> title[ Text ]
Author -> author[ P ]
Editor -> editor[ P' ]
P -> person[ S ]
P' -> person[ F? S? ]
Person -> person[ F+ S ]
F -> firstname[ Text ]
S -> surname[ Text ]
Result -> result[ Person+ ]
P^P' -> person[
 0  => S>0
>1  => S>2
 2! => S>0
 ]
====================================================
```

The printout points out that the type *result* is not a subset of the type *Result*. This is because the type P^P' (defined, equivalently, by rule P^P'->person[S]) is not a subset of the type *Person* (defined by Person->person[F+ S]).

The typechecker can be used online, at http://www.ida.liu.se/~artwi/ XcerptT. Figure 1 presents a screen shot of the online user interface which can be used more conveniently than the presented command line interface. The online interface includes two main text areas which are used to edit an Xcerpt program and a type specification. The typechecker can be executed by pressing the button *Type Program*. Then a printout containing a result of typing appears at the bottom of the screen in the section *Result of last Evaluation*.

3   Application of the Type System

This section describes main purposes of the type system. Then we present two simple scenarios illustrating the way the presented type system can be helpful for programmers using Xcerpt for querying Web data. The main purposes for which the type system can be used are:

- **Type inference.** An approximation (a superset) of the set of program results can be computed given a type for each database to which the program refers. These are the ways it can be helpful for a user:
  - A programmer can check manually if the inferred result type conforms to his/her expectations. He/she may also check if the inferred types of variables are as expected.
  - Emptiness of the inferred result type of a program suggests an error as the program will never give any results.

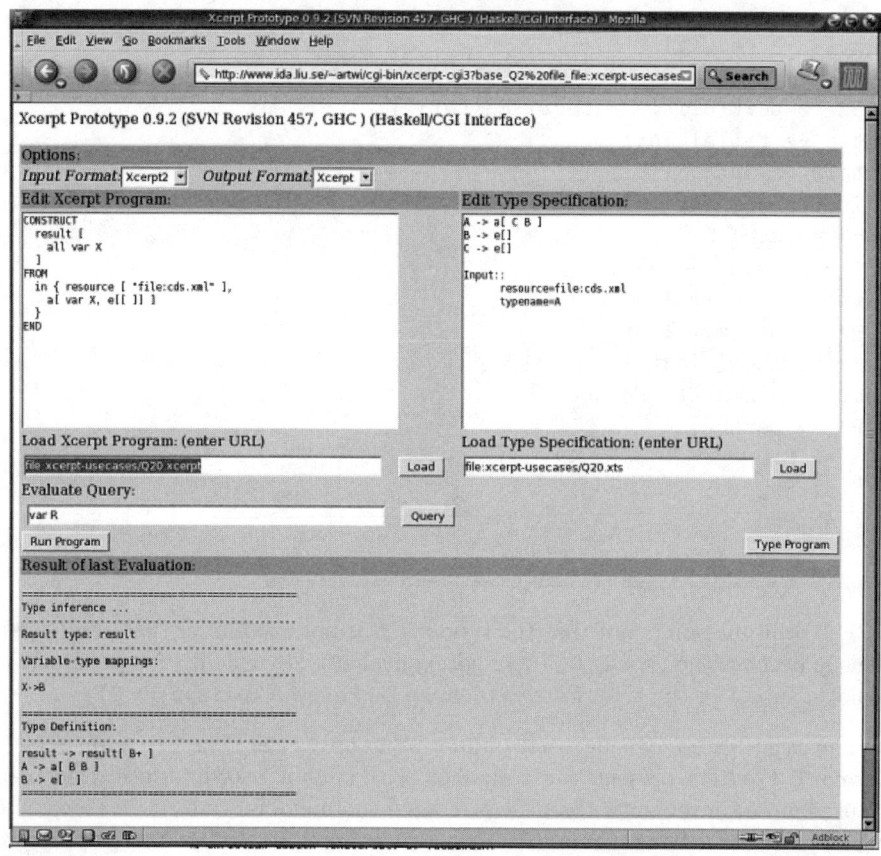

Fig. 1. Online user interface of the typechecker

- • The inferred program result type can be used for documentation of the program.
- – **Checking type correctness.** Given a specification of a result type for the program it can be checked whether the inferred result type is included in the specified one. A success of such inclusion check is a proof of type correctness of the program. In general, a typechecking failure suggests a possibility of a type error. However, such a failure is a proof of an unquestionable type error for a restricted class of Xcerpt programs and Type Definitions described in [7, Sect. 4.3.6].

3.1   Use Cases

Here we show simple scenarios illustrating the usage of the typechecker. The presented examples can be found and typechecked at http://www.ida.liu.se/~artwi/XcerptT.

Music store. Consider an Xcerpt program:

```
CONSTRUCT
  result [
    all entry [
      var ARTIST,
      all var TITLE
    ]
  ]
FROM
  in { resource [ "file:cds.xml" ],
    bib {{
      cd [[ var TITLE,  var ARTIST, "Pop" ]]
    }}
  }
END
```

The program queries the document *cds.xml*. It is intended to extract titles and artists of the CD's of the pop category. Then it should produce a result with entries containing an artist and a list of all his/her CD titles. We assume that a type of the document *cds.xml* and a type of intended query results are given by the following type specification:

```
Cds -> bib[ Cd* ]
Cd -> cd[ Title  Artist+  Category? ]
Title -> title[ Text ]
Artist -> artist[ Text ]
Category -> pop | rock | classic

Result -> result[ Entry* ]
Entry -> entry[ Artist Title+ ]

Input::
      resource=file:cds.xml
      typename=Cds

Output::
      typename=Result
```

As a result of typing the program we obtain the following printout:

```
================================================
Type checking ... FAILED: empty result type
------------------------------------------------
Result type: 0
------------------------------------------------
Variable-type mappings:
```

```
----------------------------------------------------
0
```

```
====================================================
Type Definition:
----------------------------------------------------
Cds -> bib[ Cd* ]
Cd -> cd[ Title Artist+ Category? ]
Title -> title[ Text ]
Artist -> artist[ Text ]
Category -> pop | rock | classic
Result -> result[ Entry* ]
Entry -> entry[ Artist Title+ ]
====================================================
```

The printout says that the typing of the program has failed. Formally, the program is not incorrect w.r.t. the result type specification (as the obtained result type is a subset of the specified type). However the obtained result type is empty. This indicates that the program will not give any results when applied to a document of type Cd. This clearly suggests an error. The error is a typo in the query term *cd*[[...]] as *Pop* is written with a capital letter while the type specification requires *pop*.

We correct the program changing *Pop* into *pop* and run the typechecker again. The result is:

```
====================================================
Type checking ... FAILED
----------------------------------------------------
Result type: result (not a subset of Result)


----------------------------------------------------
Variable-type mappings:
----------------------------------------------------
TITLE->Artist, ARTIST->Artist
TITLE->Title, ARTIST->Artist


====================================================
Type Definition:
----------------------------------------------------
result -> result[ entry+ ]
entry -> entry[ Artist (Artist|Title)+ ]
Cds -> bib[ Cd* ]
Cd -> cd[ Title Artist+ Category? ]
Title -> title[ Text ]
Artist -> artist[ Text ]
Category -> pop | rock | classic
```

```
Result -> result[ Entry* ]
Entry -> entry[ Artist Title+ ]
================================================
```

This time the inferred result type is not empty but type checking has failed again. This is because the inferred result type *result* is not a subset of the specified result type *Result*, due to type *entry* not being a subset of type *Entry*. To build data terms of type *entry* the program uses the variable *TITLE*; its values can be of type *Title* or *Artist* (see the "Variable-type mappings" section of the typechecker results). However, in order for the instances of *entry*[*all ARTIST*, *all var TITLE*] to be of type *Entry*, the variable *TITLE* has to be bound to data terms of type *Title*. To correct the query rule we restrict the variable *TITLE* in the rule body so that it is only bound to data terms with the main symbol *title*. (Thus it can be bound to any element of type *Title*, and to no element of type *Artist*). This is reflected by the following program:

```
CONSTRUCT
  result [
    all entry [
      var ARTIST,
      all var TITLE
    ]
  ]
FROM
  in { resource [ "file:cds.xml" ],
    bib {{
      cd [[ var TITLE -> title{{}},  var ARTIST, "pop" ]]
    }}
  }
END
```

Typechecking of this program shows that it is correct wrt. the type specification:

```
================================================
Type checking ... OK
------------------------------------------------
Result type: result
------------------------------------------------
Variable-type mappings:
------------------------------------------------
TITLE->Title, ARTIST->Artist


================================================
Type Definition:
------------------------------------------------
result -> result[ entry+ ]
Cds -> bib[ Cd* ]
```

```
Cd -> cd[ Title Artist+ Category? ]
Title -> title[ Text ]
Artist -> artist[ Text ]
Category -> pop | rock | classic
Result -> result[ entry* ]
entry -> entry[ Artist Title+ ]
================================================
```

Book store. Here we consider a program which queries a document representing a book store:

```
CONSTRUCT
  results [
      attr{},
      all result [ attr{}, var X, all var Y]
  ]
FROM
in {
  resource  {"file:bib.xml"},
  bib {{
    book {{var X -> author {{}},
          var Y -> title {{}}
    }}
  }}
}
END
```

This example of a query is similar to the one from the previous scenario. However, this time we specify types using DTD's instead of Type Definitions, and explicitly deal with XML attributes.[2]

This is a type specification for the program:

```
Input::
    resource=file:bib.xml
    typename=bib
    typedef=http://www.ida.liu.se/~artwi/xcerpt-schema/bib.dtd

Output::
    typename=results
    typedef=http://www.ida.liu.se/~artwi/xcerpt-schema/bibR.dtd
```

---

[2] A data term corresponding to an XML element with attributes $a1=v1,\ldots,an=vn$ ($n \geq 0$) contains $attr\{a1\{v1\},\ldots,an\{vn\}\}$ as the first argument between [ ]. In this section we change slightly the treatment of the empty attribute list; the previous sections allowed omitting the argument attr{}, while here this is not allowed. (The reason is simplifying the related Type Definitions.)

This is the content of the file *bib.dtd*:

```
<!ELEMENT bib   (book* )>
<!ELEMENT book   (title,  (author+ | editor+ ), publisher, price )>
<!ATTLIST book   year CDATA  #REQUIRED >
<!ELEMENT author  (last, first )>
<!ELEMENT editor  (last, first, affiliation )>
<!ELEMENT title  (#PCDATA )>
<!ELEMENT last   (#PCDATA )>
<!ELEMENT first   (#PCDATA )>
<!ELEMENT affiliation  (#PCDATA )>
<!ELEMENT publisher  (#PCDATA )>
<!ELEMENT price  (#PCDATA )>
```

This is the content of the file *bibR.dtd*:

```
<!ELEMENT results  (result* )>
<!ELEMENT result  (author, title* )>
<!ELEMENT author  (last, first )>
<!ELEMENT title  (#PCDATA )>
<!ELEMENT last   (#PCDATA )>
<!ELEMENT first   (#PCDATA )>
```

The printout from the typechecker for the program is:

```
==================================================
Type checking ... OK
--------------------------------------------------
Result type: results_1
--------------------------------------------------
Variable-type mappings:
--------------------------------------------------
X->author, Y->title


==================================================
Type Definition:
--------------------------------------------------
results_1 -> results[ &NoAttr result_1+ ]
result_1 -> result[ &NoAttr author title+ ]
bib -> bib[ &NoAttr book* ]
book -> book[ &book title (author+|editor+) publisher price ]
&book_year -> year{ Text }
&book -> attr{ &book_year }
editor -> editor[ &NoAttr last first affiliation ]
affiliation -> affiliation[ &NoAttr Text ]
publisher -> publisher[ &NoAttr Text ]
price -> price[ &NoAttr Text ]
results -> results[ &NoAttr result* ]
```

```
result -> result[ &NoAttr author title* ]
author -> author[ &NoAttr last first ]
title -> title[ &NoAttr Text ]
last -> last[ &NoAttr Text ]
first -> first[ &NoAttr Text ]
&NoAttr -> attr{ }
=================================================
```

It says that the program is correct w.r.t. the type specification. It also presents the Type Definition corresponding to DTD's used in the type specification.

The type system proved to be efficient for the presented examples. The time needed to perform type inference and type checking did not exceed 0.5 s and usually it was approximately 0.1 s (on a 1.2 GHz PC). However, one can devise Xcerpt programs for which type inference takes long time. The algorithm is inefficient if a program contains a query term $l\{q_1, \ldots, q_n\}$ or $l\{\{q_1, \ldots, q_n\}\}$, where many of query terms $q_1, \ldots, q_n$ are variables (or are of the form $\mathsf{desc}\, q$, or $\mathsf{var}\, X \rightsquigarrow \mathsf{desc}\, q$), and there are many type names in the content model of the corresponding type (from the given type specification) [7, p. 59]. For a simple example, where the content model is $(A|B|C)^*$ and the arguments between $\{\{\}\}$ are five or six variables, the computation times are, respectively, 4 s and 104 s.

4   Future Work

Further development of the type system prototype will address the following issues:

- Handling the full Xcerpt. Currently the prototype handles a fragment of Xcerpt. Assuming a most general type for constructs where no other type information can be inferred will make it possible to extend the presented techniques to full Xcerpt.
- Implementation of the techniques presented in [7] to handle multiple rule programs and to check type correctness of recursive programs.
- Locating type errors. The presented type system is able to check whether an error is possible, but it does not locate the error in the program. The programmer's role is to locate the actual error. An important issue is what additional information should be presented to the programmer to assist him/her in this task. The current prototype provides inferred types of variables. Another idea is to provide an example of a query rule result which is not intended by the user (i.e. a result which is not within the specified result type).
- The user should be given information whether the inferred result type is exact or it is an approximation. If the inferred type is exact then failure of type checking implies that the program is indeed incorrect.
- Some of the improvements outlined in [7,3], for instance those allowing computing more precise types, will be implemented.

Acknowledgements

This research has been partially funded by the European Commission and by the Swiss State Secretariat for Education and Research within the 6th Framework Programme project REWERSE number 506779 (cf. http://rewerse.net).

References

1. S. Berger, E. Coquery, W. Drabent, and A. Wilk. Descriptive typing rules for Xcerpt. In *International Workshop, PPSWR 2005, Dagstuhl Castle, Germany, September 2005, Proceedings*, number 3703 in LNCS, pages 85–100. Springer Verlag, 2005. http://www.springerlink.com/link.asp?id=8rejjqbwxbkydlwr. Errata available from http://www.ida.liu.se/~wlodr/errata.LNCS3703.pdf.
2. S. Berger, E. Coquery, W. Drabent, and A. Wilk. Descriptive typing rules for Xcerpt and their soundness. Technical Report REWERSE-TR-2005-01, REWERSE, 2005. http://rewerse.net/publications/#REWERSE-TR-2005-01.
3. W. Drabent. Towards more precise typing rules for Xcerpt. In J. J. Alferes, J. Bailey, W. May, and U. Schwertel, editors, *Principles and Practice of Semantic Web Reasoning 2006*, LNCS 4187, p. 120. Springer-Verlag, 2006.
4. J. E. Hopcroft and J. D. Ullmann. *Introduction to Automata Theory, Languages and Computation*. Addison-Wesley, 1979.
5. S. Schaffert. *Xcerpt: A Rule-Based Query and Transformation Language for the Web*. PhD thesis, University of Munich, Germany, 2004. http://www.wastl.net/download/dissertation/dissertation_schaffert.pdf.
6. S. Schaffert and F. Bry. Querying the Web Reconsidered: A Practical Introduction to Xcerpt. In *Proceedings of Extreme Markup Languages 2004, Montreal*, August 2004. http://rewerse.net/publications/#REWERSE-RP-2004-20.
7. A. Wilk. Descriptive Types for XML Query Language Xcerpt. Licentiate thesis, Linköping universitet, Sweden, 2006. http://www.ida.liu.se/~artwi/lic.pdf.
8. A. Wilk and W. Drabent. On types for XML query language Xcerpt. In *International Workshop, PPSWR 2003, Mumbai, India, December 8, 2003, Proceedings*, number 2901 in LNCS, pages 128–145. Springer Verlag, 2003.
9. Extensible Markup Language (XML) 1.1, February 2004. W3C Recommendation. http://www.w3.org/TR/REC-xml.

Author Index

Lecture Notes in Computer Science

For information about Vols. 1–4081

please contact your bookseller or Springer